BUILDING UP
THE WASTE PLACES

Building up the Waste Places

THE REVIVAL OF MONASTIC LIFE ON
MEDIEVAL LINES IN THE POST-REFORMATION
CHURCH OF ENGLAND

BY

PETER F. ANSON

Illustrations by the author

*"And thou shalt build the old waste places; thou shalt raise up the
foundations of many generations; and thou shalt be called, The
repairer of the breach, The restorer of paths to dwell in."*
Isaiah, 58:12 (Authorized Version)

THE FAITH PRESS
LEIGHTON BUZZARD, BEDFORDSHIRE, LU7 7NQ

First published in 1973

© *Caldey Abbey, Off Tenby, Pembs., S. Wales, 1973*

PRINTED IN GREAT BRITAIN
in 10pt. Times type
BY THE FAITH PRESS LTD.
LEIGHTON BUZZARD LU7 7NQ
SBN 7164 0255 6

TO ABBOT JAMES WICKSTEAD AND THE REFORMED CISTERCIAN
MONKS ON CALDEY ISLAND, SOUTH WALES

ACKNOWLEDGMENTS

The following people deserve thanks: Mr A. Calder-Marshall for permission to quote from *The Enthusiast;* Mr Douglas Lyne for photostats of material relating to Fr Ignatius of Jesus; and Dom Aidan Harker of Nashdom Abbey, who revised the epilogue. Then I am grateful to the Cistercians of Mount St Bernard Abbey who lent photographs from which some of the illustrations were copied, and the Archivist of Prinknash Abbey who allowed me to reproduce several of my own drawings.

CONTENTS

7

CONTENTS—*continued*

DRAWINGS

9

A

INTRODUCTION

" 'Tis strange—but true, for truth is always
stranger than fiction." Lord Byron, *Don Juan.*

IT is probable that this strange but true story would never have been written had I
not chanced, sixty-seven years ago at the age of fifteen, to pick up at Boots'
Library, Bournemouth, a copy of the recently published *The Life of Father Ignatius,
O.S.B., The Monk of Llanthony,* by the Baroness de Bertouch. Such was my intro-
duction to Anglican religious communities, and nothing could have been stranger,
for the biography reads like fiction. No matter, the flame lit by the authoress has
gone on burning ever since. It led to the writing of several books, e.g. *The
Benedictines of Caldey* (1940), *The Call of the Cloister* (1955), and *Abbot
Extraordinary* (1958). I have also mentioned Anglican monastic life in *A Roving
Recluse* (1946), and *The Hermit of Cat Island* (1957).

Having reached the age of eighty, I felt that a lot had been left unsaid, and that
the time had come for another book devoted especially to the building up of monastic
waste places on supposedly medieval lines. It began in 1863, with the foundation of
the first Benedictine community in communion with Canterbury since the Reformation. During the past hundred years many lovely legends have grown up and been
propagated by the devotees of the pioneers whose object was to revive a form of
monastic life which was reputed to have existed in the so-called "Ages of Faith".
Many of the legends are wishful thinking. With the best of intentions, imagination
has been allowed to run riot. Or to put it differently, where ignorance was bliss,
it was folly to be wise. I have no doubt that much of what I have recorded in these
pages will offend pious ears. Some readers may feel that it was uncharitable to have
dragged rotting corpses from their graves, and dirty linen out of cupboards.

Yet the whole conception of monasticism has changed since the 1965 Vatican II
Decree on the Appropriate Renewal of the Religious Life. It has affected to a greater
or lesser degree almost all existing Anglican Benedictine communities of men and
women. Today their observances have little or nothing in common with those described in this book, which has been written on Caldey Island, where in 1910 I
entered the novitiate of the Benedictine brotherhood founded by Dom Aelred
Carlyle.

But the way of Christian living led by those Anglo-Catholic monks has gone with
the wind, and none of those whom I met sixty-three years ago are now alive. Were
they able to return to Caldey Island I fear they would be shocked by the religion of
the Reformed Cistercians, and dismiss it as Papist Protestantism!

PETER F. ANSON

Caldey Island,
off Tenby,
Pembrokeshire,
South Wales

March 5, 1973

*Diamond Jubilee of
the "Caldey Conversions"*

11

PROLOGUE

First attempts to restore monastic waste places in the post-Reformation Church of England

Humanly speaking, there could hardly have been a worse period than the 'sixties of the last century in which to form communities of men and women observing the sixth-century Rule of St Benedict in "The Church of England by Law established under the King's Majesty".[1] As the inevitable result of the Gothic Revival in art and literature, monasticism could be conceived only in its later medieval development. The word "monastery" conjured up a picture of a ruined abbey with pointed arches. Most if not all the would-be restorers of monastic waste places looked back no further than the Middle Ages. If the monastic system could be revived in the Established Church, then its buildings would have to be replicas of those in the centuries in which Gothic architecture flourished. A few pioneers were prepared to accept Romanesque (or as they called it "Norman") religion and its outward expression, but they were not interested in anything of an earlier date. From the point of view of a High Church clergyman at the peak of the industrial revolution of the last century, it was regrettable that St Benedict had taken over a temple dedicated to Apollo on Monte Cassino and turned it into a monastery about A.D. 529. It was doubtful if a man could be a good monk if living in a pagan setting. It is a pity that none of the Tractarians tried to form religious communities like those founded by St Basil and St Martin in the fourth-century, or by St Pachomius and St Antony a hundred years before. Oddly enough almost the only Anglican author who showed any real interest in the so-called "Fathers of the Desert" was Charles Kingsley (1819-75), who was strongly opposed to all forms of asceticism, especially monasticism and clerical celibacy.

Persons who prided themselves on their "good taste", among whom were those who dreamed of founding monasteries, were convinced that nothing but Gothic (either Early English or Decorated) was permissible in churches. Heaven could be reached only by passing through a pointed arch, and this applied equally to monks and nuns as well as layfolk.

When it came to deciding on the outward observances of future Anglican monasteries, not much inspiration could be found in the Constitutions of Roman Catholic communities following the Rule of St Benedict—the basis of all monastic life in the Western Church. Most of them were overladen with accretions that were a far cry from the simplicity of early Christian monasticism. Again, it would have been difficult if not impossible to adapt contemporary Roman legislation to fit in with the Formularies of the post-Reformation Provinces of Canterbury and York.

The Act of Parliament (1 Elizabeth, c. 24), which suppressed the half-a-dozen monasteries of men and women restored by Queen Mary in 1555, asserted that the Religious State "is repugnant to the usage of the Holy Catholic Apostolic Church of Christ". All property belonging to religious communities was annexed to the Crown. A pension was granted to monks and nuns who renounced their vows and acknowledged the Royal Supremacy.[2] The result was that many religious fled overseas. By the middle of the seventeenth-century there were twelve male and more than

13

thirty female communities composed of self-exiled English citizens in France, Bavaria, the Spanish Netherlands, Portugal, Rome—even one in Poland.[3]

For nearly two hundred years there were no monastic communities in Britain, though usually a fair number of monks and friars living in disguise as Papist missionaries. Several attempts were made by individual Anglicans to establish what were known as "Protestant Monasteries" or "Colleges of Maids"—sometimes referred to as "Protestant Nunneries"—but none of them succeeded.[4]

In 1789 the property of the Church in France was confiscated by the National Assembly, which in August 1792 enacted that about 40,000 priests should be exiled. More than 100 were slain during a massacre at Paris. The following year "Reason" was decreed to be worshipped as a goddess. In the cathedral of Notre-Dame she was personified by an actress. By 1794 a vast number of bishops, priests, monks and nuns had found new homes in England. These "displaced persons" from overseas were treated like heroes by "John Bull". Their Popery was either ignored or forgotten. Loyal Protestants welcomed them with open arms.

So for the first time since the sixteenth century it dawned on English people that monks and nuns were human beings, not merely "reliques" of a remote past, like minstrelcy, and such like. The more romantic aspects of medieval "monkery", especially in the form of ruined abbeys and hermitages, had already been popularized by several "Gothick" novels, e.g. Horace Walpole's *The Castle of Otranto* (1764). Wealthy noblemen had erected sham hermitages on their estates, and in some cases even went so far as to pay wages to any man who was prepared to become an ornamental solitary.[5]

Within less than a year there were Benedictine nuns at Winchester, Hammersmith, Marnhull (Dorset), Preston (Lancs.); Canonesses of St Augustine at Hengrave (Suffolk); Canonesses of the Holy Sepulchre at Holme Hall (Yorkshire); Carmelite nuns at Lanherne (Cornwall), Bishop Auckland (Co. Durham), and Acton, near London. Dominican nuns had settled at Hartpury Court (Gloucestershire); Franciscan Third Order Regular Sisters at Winchester; Poor Clares at Haggerston Hall (Northumberland), and another community at Britwell (Oxfordshire). English Benedictine monks from Douai in France had found a home at Acton Burnell near Shrewsbury. Many more of them were scattered over England with no fixed abode. The Jesuits had re-established their Saint-Omer college at Stonyhurst in Lancashire.

There was great excitement in Dorset once it was revealed that there were half a dozen live Trappist monks secluded on Mr Thomas Weld's estates at Lulworth, not merely ornamental hermits, or plaster statues of anchorites.[6] These exiles came from Val-Sainte in Switzerland, and had intended to seek a new home in Canada, but the vessel on which they had arranged to sail weighed anchor before the appointed time. So the monks found themselves marooned on the shores of England. Their Superior, Fr John Baptist, gladly accepted Mr Weld's invitation of a temporary refuge in Dorset. The recently vacated chaplain's house became their monastery. After more than three-hundred years Cistercian life was revived in this country, but with the additional austerities of the Abbey of La Grande Trappe.

It is recorded that "no sooner was this new light set upon a candlestick (Matthew, 5:15) than it began to shine upon, and so attract the attention of the neighbourhood. Many surmises were afloat about what it could be; many strange conjectures were hazarded; and many impertinent questions were asked. The religious, dwelling in a foreign land, the language of which they could not speak, and with a faith hostile to their own, were naturally timid, and anxious to prevent any mispresentations of their intentions in this settlement upon English soil."[7] But after Mr Weld had arranged with local newspapers to publish articles explaining the monks' reasons for availing themselves of his hospitality, "rumour, with its hundred tongues,

14

was silenced. Many strangers were promoted by curiosity to visit their humble dwelling, and to examine the mode of life practised by these inhabitants of solitude and quietness."

It may seem irrelevant to devote so much space to a small Roman Catholic community of Trappist monks in a book dealing with the revival of monastic life in the Church of England, but there is no doubt that it was the "grain of mustard seed which a man took and sowed in his garden; and it grew and became a tree, and the birds of the air made nests in its branches". The "birds" were both Papist and Anglican.

In March 1796, the Trappists moved into a proper monastery which had been erected for them about half-a-mile from Lulworth Castle, which was dedicated to St Susan. We are told that, "though small in dimensions, yet it contained all the accommodation requisite for the perfection of a monastic life. Its style of architecture was plain early English.[8] The cloisters surrounded the quadrangle of the burial-ground, that the open grave, which is always renewed when one of the brotherhood is buried, might be constantly present to the contemplation of the religious whose chief object is to prepare themselves for a happy death. . . . The situation was admirably calculated for prayer, meditation, and heavenly stillness. It stood in the midst of a valley, shut in by gentle sloping hills, crowned by thriving plantations. Nothing broke the solemn silence which reigned through the lonely valley but the convent bell, and the whispering of the playful waves on the adjacent shore. Even the winds of heaven were restrained from visiting these sacred shades of retirement; for the Down stood up as a barrier against their fury."[9]

No wonder that St Susan's Monastery attracted visitors, for it was indeed a phenomenon. One wrote: "As we passed through the first court at Lulworth, we fancied ourselves in former days, when the Monastick orders flourished; so strange seemed the appearance of the Monks in the full habit of their order, gliding along intent on meditation, or employed in manual labour, but not a word spoken". Another visitor reported that "their faces were covered, so that only their eyes and noses were visible".[10]

It was also in 1796 that Mr Matthew Lewis published his "Gothick" novel entitled *The Monk*—a mixture of the supernatural, the horrible, and the indecent that surpassed the worst impressions formed of the Dorset recluses. Two years later Mr Samuel Coleridge's poem, *The Ancient Mariner* contained lines which could have been inspired by the Lulworth monks:

> "The Hermit good lives in that wood
> Which slopes down to the sea.
> How loudly his sweet voice he rears!
> He loves to talk with mariners
> That come from a far countree.
> He kneels at morn, and noon, and eve—
> He hath a cushion plump:
> It is the moss that wholly hides
> The rotten old oak-stump."

Neither could Mr William Wordsworth escape from the increasing fascination of ruined monasteries. In 1798 he wrote the poem entitled *Lines written above Tintern Abbey*. The Rev. Thomas Dudley Fosbroke, who was curate of Horsley, Gloucestershire, published some turgid verses with the title of *The Economy of Monastic Life* almost simultaneously with Mr Lewis' novel *The Monk*. He explained that it conveyed "only precise ideas of picturesque effect, chiefly founded upon the sense of vision".

Mr Fosbroke, elected R.S.A. in 1799, decided to devote himself to writing a serious treatise on the manners and customs of the Monks and Nuns of England, both ancient and modern. According to the memoir by his son, he was "determined to publish only records, MSS, or other matters new to the public, from the rich stores in the British Museum and the Bodleian Library".

In 1802 a community of Trappistine nuns, who since 1793 had been on the move between Switzerland, Austria, Russia, Poland, and Germany, found a permanent home in England. Mr Weld established them at Stapehill in Dorset, thus saving them a voyage to Canada. High walls were built around the convent to safeguard enclosure. At first they worshipped in the long, barn-like chapel of the mission dating from 1637, usually served by Jesuits, but the Lulworth Trappists helped them to make additions to the buildings. So great were the austerities of the nuns, and so many were the deaths, that Dr Collingridge, O.F.M., Vicar-Apostolic of the Western District after 1807, was forced to mitigate the observances, described as a "hothouse for Heaven". In 1813 Fr Antony was installed as first Abbot of St Susan's, Lulworth, the ceremony being performed by Dr Poynter, Vicar-Apostolic of the London District. History was made, because this was the first occasion of an abbot being blessed in England since the sixteenth century.

Protestants were still suspicious of this "pious brotherhood", which from time to time they "called hypocrites, concealing under the exterior garb of penance, the love of good cheer. Many visitors, on this account, became anxious to examine the kitchen, where they expected to find viands so delicious as to tempt the palate of a professed gournmand, hidden beneath the cabbages and the turnips, which were ready to be cast into the soup-pan. At another time, they were charged with harbouring a proud heart under a coarse vesture. Their strange dress was too much at variance with the present costume to be in any degree tolerable. Objections were made against their solemn vows, which were branded by the extremely ignorant as violations of God's Holy Word. Today the brethren were forbidden to receive any more novices; tomorrow they were allowed to do so, provided the vows were only for three years. Many thought they treated the brotherhood very mildly and very charitably when they simply called them fanatics. Others transformed them into French spies, occupied in subtracting the wealth of England, in order to carry it to France."[11] Eventually Abbot Antony was summoned to London, where the Prime Minister, Lord Sidmouth, interviewed him, with the result that the charges made against the community were declared to be entirely false.[12]

On July 10, 1817, the brotherhood, consisting of sixty-four persons in all, embarked at Weymouth for France. Louis XXVIII had granted permission for them to return to their native land, for the purpose of restoring the Cistercian Order. Their new home was the monastery of La Meilleraye in Brittany.[13] So after twenty-three years England was left without a monastic community for men with a medieval atmosphere, for the Benedictines at Downside and Ampleforth took the utmost care not to cause scandal by looking like what monks were supposed to be.

Mr Fosbroke's long awaited *British Monachism* was published in 1816, and proved a best-seller. As might be expected, this clergyman who was highly distinguished as a Freemason and the father of four sons and six daughters, had no use for clerical celibacy. He treated "Monkery" from the point of view of an antiquarian. Monks and nuns were interesting merely as "reliques" of the Dark Ages. His 419 pages book was illustrated by engravings of "Monastick Costume". One wonders what was the source of the Benedictine monk's costume which can only be described as bizarre, though there is not much wrong with either the "Franciscan Grey Frier" (*sic*) or the "Augustine Eremite", included on the same page. "The Habits of the Monks of La Trappe at Lulworth" based on sketches made by Mr Basire, who visited St Susan's Monastery in 1800, are certainly "very spirited", even if inaccurate in most details.

The author admitted that "those Lulworth Monks, though of course mere *automata*, are humble, inoffensive, and moral. Superstition, compatible with all religions and even with infidel principles, does not necessarily include vice; and these noble-minded Asceticks maintained 80 orphan children of the murdered French noblesse, and refused an asylum from the Emperor of Russia, because they would not rob a legitimate proprietor of his estate."[14]

Mr Walter Scott made "Friar Tuck" one of the characters in his novel *Ivanhoe* published in 1819. Both *The Monastery* and *The Abbot* appeared in 1820. The former centred round the monastery of Kennaquhair, of which the prototype was the Cistercian abbey of Melrose. The latter took its title from Father Ambrose, who was Abbot of Kennaquhair during the period of Mary Queen of Scots. Having been made a baronet, the popularizer of "olde worlde" monachism started to build a picturesque mansion with many quaint turrets beside the Tweed, to which he gave the name of "Abbotsford".

Another indication of the increasing interest taken in monks and nuns was the publication of an article in the December 1825 issue of *Blackwood's Magazine*. The writer, Dr Gooch, appealed to "all serious Christians to found an order of women like the Sisters of Charity in Catholic countries; let them be selected for good plain sense, kindness of disposition, indefatigable industry, and deep piety; let them receive not a technical and scientific, but a practical medical education; for this purpose, let them be placed both as nurses and pupils in the hospitals of Edinburgh and London, or in the county hospitals". Dr Gooch had visited some of the Béguinages at Bruges, and felt that conventual institutions of this sort would benefit the Established Church.

Things began to move in the direction of a revival of female "Monkery". The following year, the Rev. Alex. R. C. Dallas, then a curate at Woburn in Buckinghamshire, published a letter addressed to Dr Howley, Bishop of London, entitled *Protestant Sisters of Charity*. Mr Dallas, having lived in France, realized that the Church of England badly needed groups of dedicated women to give medical advice and visit the sick poor, like the Sisters of Charity of St Vincent de Paul.

In 1829, Robert Southey, the Poet Laureate, appealed even more strongly on behalf of Protestant Sisters of Charity, putting the question to his fellow Anglicans: "Why then have you no Béguines, no Sisters of Charity? Why in the most needful, the most merciful form that charity can take, have you not yet followed the example of the French and the Netherlanders? No Vincent de Paul has been heard in your pulpits; no Louise le Gras has appeared among the daughters of Great Britain! Piety has not found its way into your prisons; your hospitals are imploring it in vain; nothing is wanting in them but religious charity, and oh what a want is that!"[15]

The Poet Laureate may not have been aware that the nucleus of such a community existed in the quaint "Gothick" buildings overlooking Regent's Park, London, designed by Ambrose Poynter for the Royal Foundation of the St Katharine in Ratcliffe, whose members moved here from their hospital near the Tower of London in 1826. Established by Queen Matilda in 1148, and re-founded by Queen Eleanor in 1273, this venerable institution, consisting of a Master and three Brethren in holy orders, and three Sisters of equal rank, had managed to survive the storms of the Reformation. *The Book of Common Prayer* took the place of whatever offices were recited during the first four centuries of its existence. The Sisters had recently extended their activities to a school for poor children. Ten poor "bedeswomen" were also under their care. They were bound to attend divine service in their chapel, and to "behave themselves dutifully and reverently towards the Master".[16]

By 1830 Mr Ambrose Lisle Phillipps, the wealthy young squire of Garendon and Grace Dieu in Leicestershire, who had been received into the Roman Church at the age of fifteen, had begun to dream of founding a monastery on his estates. The chance came three years later when Fr Norbert Woolfrey was deputed by Fr Vincent, the superior of Mount Melleray in Ireland, to appeal to pious Papists in England on behalf of the new Trappist monastery in Co. Waterford. The result was that on March 25, 1835, Mr Phillipps wrote to Fr Norbert, saying that 227 acres of Charnwood Forest—most of it a "tract of wild desert land"—was ready to be handed over to the monks if they were prepared to make a foundation in England. Fr Norbert's first contact with Mr Phillipps was contemporary with the publication of the first three of the *Tracts for the Times*, written by Members of the University of Oxford on September 9, 1833. It was on July 14 that same year that Mr Keble preached his Assize Sermon in the University Church of St Mary, Oxford—a prophecy that the dry bones of *Ecclesia Anglicana* would live once more, and its waste places be rebuilt.

In 1836, at the same moment that Dr Newman, Dr Pusey, Mr Gladstone, and other High Church Anglicans were protesting against the appointment of Dr Hampden as Regius Professor of Divinity at Oxford, because they regarded him as a heretic, a small group of Trappist monks came over from Ireland and took up their abode in a half-ruined cottage in Charnwood Forest.

No time was lost in erecting the first part of a monastery, designed by Mr Railton in what was called the "Elizabethan style", and on October 11, 1837—four months after Queen Victoria had succeeded to the British throne—the chapel was dedicated. A visitor reported the function in the *Staffordshire Examiner*. Nothing like it had ever taken place in England since the Reformation, for "at an early hour, the bishop with his clergy, accompanied by Sir Charles Wolseley, Bt., in court dress, and Mr Ambrose Phillipps, who wore his uniform as deputy-lieutenant of the county, walked up by a beautiful private road from Grace Dieu to the entrance of the monastery land, a distance of about two miles".

If any of the Tractarian clergymen read the account of the imposing ceremonial, they may well have been envious. The long procession was headed by a crucifer vested in cassock and surplice. There were six acolytes similarly robed, and many banners held aloft. His Lordship the Bishop [Dr Baines, O.S.B. Vicar Apostolic of the Western District] was "vested in full pontificals, with his mitre and crozier, and his train borne by an acolyte in a white surplice. The choir monks were dressed in white habits and cowls, and the lay brothers in brown habits, according to the rule of the Cistercian Order." The Hon. and Rev. George Spencer, the youngest son of the first Earl Spencer, who had "gone over to Rome" in 1830, "pronounced a most eloquent eulogium on the nature of the monastic state". After the pontifical High Mass the ladies present were given luncheon in the guest room. The gentlemen, however, "partook of a monastic repast consisting of eggs and fruit, in the refectory of the monks; at the same time the monks took their own dinner, during which one of the brotherhood, according to custom, read a spiritual lecture". Later on Vespers were "solemnly chanted, and an admirable sermon was preached by the Very Rev. Dr Weedell, the president of Oscott College".

Fashions in what were supposed to be "correct" furnishings for a Catholic place of worship were fairly static in the middle of the last century. It is interesting to note how the *décor* provided for the oratory in the Anglican Priory of Our Ladye and St Dunstan at Norwich in 1864 were in keeping with those of the chapel at Mount St Bernard Monastery in 1837.[17] In the latter the monks' choir was "separated from the nave by a beautiful screen". There were three altars and a high altar, "ornamented with carving, adorned with a costly tabernacle, superbly gilded and covered in part with crimson velvet, richly embroidered with gold". Six gilt candlesticks were placed upon it, and between them were arranged "bunches of artificial flowers made of shells by Madame, the Baroness de la Tocnay", a noble lady who lived in a chateau beside the Loire, and who had been a great benefactress to the monastery.[18]

J. H. Newman was wishing to provide the Church of England with a monastery, though on a more modest scale than the one in Charnwood Forest, when he wrote to J. W. Bowden in January 1838: "Your offering towards the young monks was just like yourself . . . it will be most welcome. As you may suppose, we have nothing settled, but are feeling the way. We should begin next term; but since, however secret one may wish to keep it, things get out, we do not wish to commit young men to anything which may hurt their chances of success at any college in standing for a fellowship."[19]

That same year the first part of Hurrell Froude's *Remains* was published. It contained the statement: "It has lately come into my head that the present state of things in England makes an opening for reviving the monastic system. . . . Certainly colleges of unmarried priests (who might, of course, retire to a living when they could or liked) would be the cheapest possible way of providing effectively for the spiritual wants of a large population."

Things began to move, and in April 1838, J. B. Mozley wrote to his sister: "Newman has taken a house, to be formed into a reading and collating establishment, to help in editing the Fathers".[20] Such was Newman's subtle way of trying to revive the "monastic system" in the Church of England. The Abbé Guéranger had adopted more or less similar methods in France. He bought the priory of Solesmes in 1832, re-opened it the following year, and in 1837, having made a novitiate in Rome, was professed as a Benedictine monk. Gregory XVI then appointed him first Abbot of Solesmes. The original members of the little community were scholars, engaged in historical research, akin to Newman's projected "collating establishment".

On Ascension Day 1840, a month after the Abbé Lacordaire had been professed as a Dominican in Rome, Newman wrote to Mrs Mozley: "We have bought nine or ten acres of ground at Littlemore, the field between the Chapel and Barnes', and, so be it, shall erect a monastic house on it". Shortly before this he had informed Frederick Rogers: "Supposing a feeling arose in favour of monastic establishments, and my house at Littlemore was obliged to follow the fashion, and conform to a rule of discipline, would it not be desirable that such institutions should follow the Colleges of our two Universities, and be under their influence?" About the same time he confided to Dr Pusey: "An idea had revived in my mind, of which we have before now talked, viz., of building a Monastic House in the place and coming to live in it myself". Pusey encouraged the project, and wrote: "Certainly it would be a great relief to have a *moné* in our Church in many ways, and you seem just the person to form one".

So many young Roman Catholics were wanting to test their vocations at the Trappist *"moné"* in Charnwood Forest, that it became clear that the buildings would have to be enlarged. One Sunday afternoon in 1839 Mr Phillipps took the Earl of Shrewsbury to assist at Vespers. It is related that the latter was "profoundly edified and affected. The sound of that simple and solemn chant sung as of old in the blessed days of St Bernard; the sight of the monks in their antique monastic habits; their truly mortified and religious aspect; their humble and devotional demeanour; all contributed to produce the most powerful emotions in the pious

A. W. PUGIN'S DESIGN FOR MOUNT ST BERNARD MONASTERY, 1842

THE "UN-PUGINESQUE" MONASTERY AT LITTLEMORE, 1842

mind of the noble Earl."[21] The result was that he offered to give £2,000 towards building up the waste places in Leicestershire, but on condition that a new monastery was erected as part of the monastic estate, which had a more "romantic character". The Earl's architect, Mr Pugin, arrived shortly after this. He was ready to give his services gratis if allowed to design a Cistercian monastery on the lines of those in olden times.

There was nothing "romantic" about the site of Newman's monastery, which was in the centre of the village. It consisted of a T-shaped row of single-storied cottages —a far cry from what Mr Pugin visualised for his monastery. After the cottages had been adapted for monastic purposes, it was possible to receive a few "inmates". By August 1842 there were six, but with much coming and going. Few became permanent residents.

John Dobreé Dalgairns was the first postulant, having joined Newman in the autumn of 1841. In December he wrote to a friend: "You would smile if you saw the embryo monastery. It is nothing else but a sort of angular farmyard and offices with windows knocked into the granary wall, the stable being converted into a library . . . Bloxam has also called (the whole monastery) the *Union* workhouse; and it certainly does look vastly like its name. However, there have been more unpromising establishments to start with, and Newman's library beats most monkeries now-a-days to sticks. I believe it will be ready by next Lent."[22]

In May 1842 Dalgairns stated: "The place contains six sets of rooms, a library and a guest chamber. Each set of rooms was originally intended for a cottage for poor people to live in; but now what with bookcases, sundry (Roman) prints and so on, have really an air—what shall I call it, poor-gentleman-likeness about them; quite romantic. However, a truce to description; pray fancy nothing at all except a very cheap but not nasty place, very like almshouses, very anti-Puginian; after Oscott it will look quite low."[23]

The February 1842 issue of *The Dublin Review* had contained an article by Pugin describing the rising Monastery of Mount St Bernard, which must have filled the romantic medieval mind of Dalgairns with envy, for Pugin wrote: "The whole of the buildings are erected in the greatest severity of the lancet style, with massive walls and buttresses, long and narrow windows, high gables and roofs, with deeply arched doorways. Solemnity and simplicity are the characteristics of the monastery, and every portion of the architecture and fittings, corresponds to the austerity of the Order for whom it has been raised. The space enclosed by the cloisters is appointed for the cemetery; a stone cross, similar to those which were formerly erected in every churchyard, will be set up in the centre, and the memorials of the departed brethren will be inserted on plain wooden crosses at the head of the graves. The view from this enclosure is particularly striking. From the nature of the material used (a sort of rubble granite) and the massiveness of the architecture, the building already possesses the appearance of antiquity; and this being combined with the stillness of the place and the presence of the religious, clad in the venerable habits of their Order, the mind is most forcibly carried back to the days of England's faith."

Neither could the chapel in the Littlemore "monkery" compare with the great cruciform church at Mount St Bernard, with its "correct" rood-screen and loft separating the monks' choir from the nave. Pugin stated that "by the rules of the Cistercian Order", the rood-loft would be "used for all its ancient purposes", and "provided with the lecterns, standards for lights, and other necessary furniture". By June 1843 the Littlemore oratory had been "hung round with curtains as a mode of making it decent, yet without spending anything on the room itself". Newman asked Bloxam if it would be correct to "have a quasi-altar". No objection was made by this erudite ecclesiologist, so a small table was inserted. On it stood a pair of candlesticks and a realistic Spanish-American crucifix which came from Lima. The choir-stalls consisted of a "board" down the centre of the room. The "monks" stood on each side of this desk while reciting Matins and Lauds, Prime, Terce, Sext, None, Vespers and Compline. The daily offices of the *Book of Common Prayer* were said or sung in the Early English Gothic-Revival church, built by Newman, and consecrated in 1836. Jemima Newman and the Mozley sisters had already embroidered a rich altar frontal. Bloxam was "quite in ectasies about it". Here on Sundays and Red Letter Days the Lord's Supper or Holy Communion was celebrated. What was described as "the lack of sacramental services, compensating for the hardships, relieving the dreariness or monotony" was, in Newman's opinion, the reason why the community lacked stability.[24]

It is not surprising that the Littlemore "monkery" aroused curiosity. Newman recalled in his *Apologia* (chapter IV) how "Heads of Houses, as mounted patrols, walked their horses round those poor cottages. Doctors of Divinity dived into the hidden recesses of that private tenement uninvited, and drew domestic conclusions from what they saw there. I had thought that an Englishman's house was his castle, but the newspapers thought otherwise, and at last the matter came before my good Bishop."

At the same time even more people were finding their way to the Trappist monastery in Leicestershire. Mr Phillipps wrote to Lord Shrewsbury in 1842: "It is perfectly astonishing what crowds come to see the Monastery. The other day *again* more than 300 visitors were counted and no less than 50 carriages. The Church is generally crowded out at the hours of None and Vespers, by persons who come through curiosity. I believe that this Monastery will do more good than Missions."[25]

Alarmed by the spread of Papist conventual establishments, and also by the foundation of an Anglican "monkery", the Rev. Yate Fosbroke decided to publish a revised edition of his father's *British Monachism*, which appeared in 1843, at the price of one guinea. Dedicated to Dr Law, Bishop of Gloucester and Bristol, it contained the preface to the 1817 second edition, where the author stated: "Although many Monks were truly *good* Monks, men of high spiritual abstraction, yet their virtue was negative, except in acts of charity, although many things were only culpable, as deviations from the Order, still it ought not to be dogmatized that the austere Monastic System is possible, in a universal view, to be correctly exhibited, in union with riches. . . . The Monks were wealthy, consequently luxurious, and frequently debauched. . . . Popery, afraid of innovation, must of necessity be a consistent whole, although it manifestly implies tenacity of obsolete barbarism."[26]

To counteract the impression of the Middle Ages conveyed in such books as *British Monachism*, Mr James Toovey issued a prospectus in 1843 for *The Lives of the English Saints*, edited by the Rev. John Henry Newman, B.D., Fellow of Oriel College. The object of this series was virtually the same as A. W. Pugin's *Contrasts*, published in 1836, of which a second edition had appeared in 1841—"a parallel between the noble edifices of the fourteenth and fifteenth centuries and similar buildings of the present day; showing the present decay of taste". More or less everything was good in special and religious life between 1300 and 1500, and thoroughly bad after 1800. The rottenness of Protestantism was proved by, e.g., Joseph Smith authorizing polygamy among the Mormons and the Disruption of the Presbyterian Church of Scotland, both occurring in the year 1843. A team of Tractarians was roped in to write the books.[27] Two were permanent members of the Littlemore "monkery": John Dobreé Dalgairns, and William Lockhart.

As A. W. Hutton pointed out in his Introduction to the six-volumes reprint of the *Lives*, published in 1900: "It was unfortunate that the Series seemed to suggest that Saints were chiefly, if not exclusively, to be looked for in the hermitage or in the cloister, and especially under the severest of all rules, that of the Cistercians. Presumably it was the recent foundation by Mr Ambrose Phillipps de Lisle, of Mount St Bernard's Monastery, in Leicestershire, that turned the writer's thoughts in this direction."[28]

The frontispiece to Dalgairns' *Life of St Aelred* conveyed the medieval atmosphere needed for a revival of the monastic system—an engraving by Pugin, depicting the twelfth-century Cistercian abbot vested in a late Gothic form of chasuble, apparelled alb and amice, and standing in a much-crocketted niche. In the *Life of St Waltheof*, he wrote nostalgically: "If Melrose could be roofed afresh, and the vaulted ceiling restored, the painted glass replaced in each oriel, and the niches filled again, it would certainly not be a facsimile of the Melrose of six hundred years ago. But the building would not be so unlike its predecessor as the new members would differ from their brethren of old, though they wore the same habit and kept the same rule. But it is wrong to mourn over what must be; and perhaps the new brethren would in some respects surpass the old."[29] So far, however, there was little or no sign of the dry bones of the Scottish Episcopal Church having breath put into them, or of Sir Walter Scott's Monastery of "Kennaquhair" being restored and filled with monks.[30] Dalgairns revised the *Life of St Gilbert of Sempringham* written by Lockhart, which is brimful of yearnings towards the monastic life. It ends with the words: "Very few of us can be monks and nuns; but all are called upon to live above the world, and by daily self-sacrifice to train themselves to give up at a moment's notice whatever is most dear. And they especially who have apparently least duties, unmarried persons, should wait calmly on the Providence of God, ready to accept whatever lot in life He may prepare for them, wishing for nothing but what He wills. Meanwhile, they have more time than others for frequent prayer and for long and steady contemplation of our blessed Lord, in the great mysteries of the faith. Then, as the wonders of heaven, by God's grace, grow upon them, they will see the excellence of the good part of Mary, to sit at the Lord's feet and to hear the words He speaks to the soul."[31] Readers were reminded that "Monks and nuns are not commodities to be found everywhere, and to be moulded for the nonce wherever they are wanted. Funds may be found, and buildings raised, and vestments manufactured, but it requires a special vocation from God to make men or women renounce the world."[32]

Frederick W. Faber, the young bachelor Rector of Elton, Huntingdonshire, pointed out in his *Life of St Paulinus* that it was "the monastic character of the early Saxon Church" that managed to subdue "the England of the ancient times to the Cross". This in itself intimated to *Ecclesia Anglicana* of the nineteenth century that, "however lawful it may be in itself, and, if so be, of primitive warrant, yet a sturdier weapon than a married clergy can alone hope to convert (for we may not use a milder word) the crowded multitudes of modern England".[33]

Faber shocked Protestants even more by his *Life of St Wilfrid*, in which he never ceased to draw attention to what could be achieved by celibate monks and priests. On the other hand he deprecated "the architectural pedantry displayed here and there, and the grotesque earnestness about petty trivialities, and the stupid reverence for the *formal* past. Altars are the playthings of the nineteenth-century societies, and we are taught that the Church cannot change, modify, or amplify her worship; she is, so we learn, a thing of a past century, not a life of all centuries; and there is abusive wrangling and peevish sarcasm, while men are striving to force some favourite antiquated clothing of their own over the majestic figure of true, solid, abiding Catholicism. It is downright wickedness to be going thus *a-mumming*

23

(a buffoonery, doubtless correct enough out of some medieval costume-book), when we should be doing plain work for our age, and our neighbours."[34]

The future Superior of the London Oratory had no use for Mr Pugin's mock medievalism, or for what his ecclesiologically-minded contemporaries called "the thousand and one vestiges of better times in England, lingering relics of Catholicism". He ended a long tirade against the relics of a past age with the query: "A broken choir in a woody dell—if it be sweet to the eyes, and not bitter in the thoughts—if it soothes, but humbles not, what is it but a mischievous thing over which it were well to invoke a railroad, or any other devastating change. Let us be men, and not dreamers; one cannot dream in religion without profaning it".[35] In the long run "the pursuit of Holy Virginity" was far more important.

This lack of respect for medievalism, in any shape or form, was not shared by other writers of the *Lives of the English Saints,* who hoped and prayed that sooner or later a miracle would be performed by *Ecclesia Anglicana's* transformation into what it looked like in the fourteenth and fifteenth centuries. They agreed with Mr Ambrose Phillipps that the first thing was to restore monastic life in England, secondly to restore Gregorian chant; and thirdly—to quote his own words—"to restore the Anglican Church to Catholic Unity, and thus to reunite England to the See of St Peter, as St Edward the Confessor foretold".[36]

A Church without monasteries is a body with its right arm paralysed, so before all else the waste places of England must be rebuilt and filled with Anglican monks. Dalgairns summed up this point of view in the first chapter of his *Life of St Stephen Harding:* "We must find our cross in sitting still, to watch in patience the struggle which is going on about us. Yet while we wait for better days, we may comfort ourselves with the contemplation of what [the Church's] sons once were, and admire their virtues, though we have not the power, even though we had the will to imitate them."[37]

Still it was already possible to imitate the English Saints by reciting portions of the Divine Office. As early as 1838 Newman had ventured to write in Tract 75, entitled *On the Roman Breviary as embodying the substance of the devotional services of the Church Catholic:* "There is so much of excellence and beauty in the services of the Breviary, that were it skilfully set before the Protestant by Roman controversialists as the book of devotion received in their communion, it would undoubtedly raise a prejudice in their favour, if he were ignorant of the circumstances of the case, and but ordinarily candid and unprejudiced".

In 1841 Mr A. H. D. Acland-Troyte compiled a vernacular diurnal entitled *The Hours: being prayers for the third, sixth, and ninth hours, etc.* This little book was followed in 1844 by *The Day Hours of the Church with the Gregorian Tones,* edited by the Rev. Albany J. Christie. While the *Lives of the English Saints* were appearing at intervals, Mr Samuel Wood, Dr Pusey and others published *The Order of the Psalter for the Week with the Ordinary of the Office of the Season.*[38] The only details which suggest that this is an Anglican publication are the wording of the Creed, and the omission of the prayers for the Pope and the bishops from the Ferial Preces at Lauds and Vespers. The antiphons of Our Lady are translated in prose, not in verse. This book was used in the Littlemore chapel, so, if only by corporate prayer, the quasi-monks felt that they had taken the first step in "setting forth the deeds of the old missionary monks and holy founders of those glorious abbeys to provoke (their) own generation to a godly jealousy".[39]

But it was not only at Oxford that men were dreaming of a revival of the monastic system. In 1843, the Rev. John Mason Neale, then a lecturer at Downing College, Cambridge, published a novel entitled *Ayton Priory, or the Restored Monastery.* He pointed out that "there is perhaps hardly any subject which has recently

24

occupied a larger share of the attention of Churchmen, than the possibility and expediency of a revival of the Monastick System. Hints have been dropped, and papers circulated, recommending a return to it; but the former have entirely confined themselves to generalities. The following tale is intended, as well as to set forth the advantages, and all but necessity, of the re-introduction of monasteries, as to suggest certain practical details connected with their establishment and subsequent working." Mr Neale added, however, that "the recommendation of a re-adaptation of the system must, of course, proceed from our spiritual fathers, before it is seriously taken up by the inferior clergy and laity."[40] On the other hand, it was doubtful if Dr Allen, then Bishop of Ely, in spite of his diligence in promoting religion and morality, would favour monks working under him. There was no chance of Mr Neale becoming a monk himself, for he had taken a wife in 1842, and between 1843 and 1846 lived chiefly on the island of Madeira.[41]

He appears to have been convinced that "The Good Old Times of England" would return by a providential putting-back of the clock four hundred years. Already he had raised the clarion cry: "England's Church is Catholick, though England's self be not". In God's good time there would be long processions again in aisles dim with incense, priests in copes, chanting Gregorians, banners borne aloft, and the veneration of holy relics.

The Rev. John Mason Neale and the Rev. Benjamin Webb, the joint founders of the Cambridge Camden Society—still leading the Ecclesiological Movement— provided useful advice on how the places of worship of Anglican monasteries ought to be designed and decorated in *The Symbolism of Churches and Church Ornaments*, published in 1843. This was a translation of the *Rationale divinorum officiorum*, written by William Durandus, a legal official of the Roman Curia, who was Bishop of Mende, between 1285 and 1296. These two clergymen were "not prepared to say that none but monks should design churches, or that it is impossible for professional architects to build with the devotion and faith of an earlier time", but they did "protest against the merely business-like spirit of the modern profession", and demanded "from them a more elevated and directly religious habit of mind". What was needed first was "the deeply religious habit of the builders of old", before architects had been perverted by "worldliness, vanity and dissipation". Moreover, no tiny detail of a church must be inserted that was not symbolic of something, setting forth the allegorical meaning of numbers. Added to this encyclopedia of symbolic ceremonial was a translation of the first and second chapters of *De Sacramentis Christianae Fidei* by Hugh of St Victor, a Canon Regular of St Augustine at Paris from 1115 until his death in 1141; an erudite treatise in which he worked out his symbolist conception of the universe as the sensible expression of a Divine thought.

The Rev. William Gresley, Prebendary of Lichfield—a prolific writer of Tractarian fiction—was another clergyman who shared Neale's opinion that the moment had come for a revival of monasticism. In 1842 he published the first part of *Bernard Leslie*. He put the question: "Why should we not also have un-married clergy, who shall devote themselves to God's service . . . unmarried priests and deacons, who shall dedicate themselves to reclaiming the waste places of the heathen? Nay, why should we not also have unmarried laymen, who shall 'Spurn delights, and live laborious days'; not amassing wealth, or winning renown before men, but labouring for God's glory and the salvation of their souls." A start towards building up the monastic waste places could be made by "the establish-ment of colleges of priests or laymen, not bound by the compulsory vows of celibacy, though generally proposing to themselves an unmarried state, and as long as they maintain it, living together under the control of the parochial priest, whom they shall aid in his ministrations. The time seems almost ripe for an attempt of the sort."[42] If nothing else, this would be the thin end of the wedge.

No doubt there were other clergymen besides Mr Robert Aitken, even some who were married, who had heard a clear call to become monks. In November 1843, the Rev. Walter Hook, Vicar of Leeds, wrote that he was "uneasy" about this Yorkshire incumbent, saying: "He has fitted up the schoolhouse adjoining his church with cells, each containing a bed and a cross; he has some young men with him who have forsaken all; his rule is very strict; he has daily Communion; they fast till 4 every Wednesday, when he allows himself and themselves meat. On Friday they fast till 4, and then have fish. In the meantime he, having a family residing five miles away, sleeps in his cell four times a week. . . . His wife complains of his neglecting his six or more children."[43]

The Rev. Samuel Fox, Rector of Morley, Derbyshire, published a book in 1845, entitled *Monks and Monasteries*, which was a reasonable apologia for the revival of the late medieval monastic system in the mid-nineteenth century Church of England. He pointed out in the Preface that "the fallacy seems to be at length giving way, which identifies the name of monastery with the worst errors and corruptions of the Church of Rome, and fills the mind with reminiscences of nothing but vice and profligacy, at the very mention of the monastic system". Most of the *Lives of the English Saints* had already made it clear enough that the majority of monks of olden times were saintly ascetics, far from being profligates. Mr Fox continued: "We are, therefore, beginning to regard the venerable ruins which are scattered throughout the length and breadth of this land with feelings of shame and sorrow".[44] But his attitude towards these ruins was nothing if not realistic. Were they to be rebuilt and filled with monks, they would help to relieve social distress, resulting from liberal utilitarianism. He mentioned one reason that could be assigned for the "universal failure" of schemes to improve conditions in the industrial areas was that the rulers of the nation had "hitherto appeared to be afraid of standing in the old way, and asking for the old paths, where is the good way and walking therein, lest they should give offence to that utilitarian spirit, which has unhappily so long prevailed in the counsels of the nation".[45] In fact, were "monasteries once more established and adapted, not merely to the altered condition of the Anglican Church, but to the present state of the country, the people who now feel themselves despised and neglected, would at the gate of the monastery, learn that their sufferings were not unheeded. There they might, perhaps, be induced to forget the exasperating influence of the Poor Laws."[46]

Just when everything seemed opportune for a nation-wide crusade to restore the monastic waste places, by diverting mainly Irish navvies from building railways, most of whom, being Roman Catholics, would have felt they were gaining merit in digging the foundations of monasteries, the visions melted into thin air by the closing down of the only Anglican "monkery" in Britain on October 9, 1845. On that day Newman, Bowles, and Stanton were reconciled with the Roman Church by Fr Dominic, the Passionist. Dalgairns and Lockhart had taken the same step earlier in the year. On November 17 Faber and seven of his Society of Joseph at Elton entered into full communion with that Church, whose more exotic forms of spirituality and worship they had already embraced so wholeheartedly.

Yet both young and old Tractarians went on dreaming dreams and seeing visions of what were usually called "Brotherhoods".[47] Already in 1844, Alexander Penrose Forbes, then a curate at St Thomas-the-Martyr's, Oxford, and subsequently Bishop of Brechin, had founded a Guild of St Mary the Virgin. Its chief object was to foster ecclesiastical art, but its members were bound by a simple rule of life. On January 28, 1847, Mr Keble, the Vicar of Hursley, wrote to Mr Butler, the Vicar of Wantage, reminding him that St Saviour's Leeds, built by Dr Pusey in memory of his wife, and opened in 1845, was "meant to be a sort of College of Curates, and in a humble way an effort at Anglican asceticism".[48]

There was much to turn the minds of cultured people back to the Middle Ages after they had recovered from the "Railway Mania", the repeal of the Corn Laws, and Chartist demonstrations in London. In 1849 Mr Ruskin published *The Seven Lamps of Architecture*. His verdict that Gothic was the noblest style of architecture was regarded as almost infallible. The "Seven Lamps" symbolized Sacrifice, Truth, Power, Beauty, Life, Memory, and Obedience. Before long the Irvingites, who preferred to be called "The Catholic Apostolic Church", decided that seven lamps must be suspended in front of the altars of their richly furnished places of worship, in which eucharistic vestments were worn and incense burned.

Four months after Miss Priscilla Lydia Sellon had founded the Anglican Sisters of Mercy at Devonport, Fr Bernard Palmer was blessed as the first Abbot of Mount St Bernard's. He was the first mitred abbot in England since the suppression of the monasteries by Henry VIII. Both John, sixteenth Earl of Shrewsbury, and Ambrose Lisle Phillipps, Esq., the two founders of this Trappist monastery, took care that the ritual and ceremonial conformed to Pugin's principles of medieval Catholic worship. The stately function was carried out by Dr Ullathorne, O.S.B., Vicar-Apostolic of the Central District, who was assisted by the Cistercian Abbots of La Meilleraye and Bellefontaine in France, and Mount Melleray in Ireland. Dr Wareing, Vicar-Apostolic of the Eastern District, added glamour by appearing in *pontificalibus*", so it was reported. Seven lamps hung before what was supposed to be the correctly furnished high altar in the still unfinished cruciform church. February 17, 1849, is an important date in the history of the building up of monastic waste places in Britain.

An indication that Anglican sisterhoods, even if there were very few of them, with a total membership of not more than fifty, were arousing curiosity in 1850, is an article in *Punch*, entitled "Convent of the Belgravians".[49] The woodcut depicts a young lady in a crinoline, gazing at a mirror. Another damsel, similarly costumed, looks on demurely. The walls of the room are decorated with mock-medieval heraldic emblems, including a goose-rampant. We are informed that "everybody who has a proper veneration for the reredos, without holding extreme opinions on the subject of the dalmatic, feels correctly on that of the alb, who has a soul that can appreciate medieval art, particularly the beautiful fore-shortening of our ancestors, and who would revive their ecclesiastical practices and institutions to an extent just tastefully Romanesque, will be 'Rhyghte gladde' to hear that it is proposed to found a Convent on Anglican principles, under the above title. The Vulgar, who think that a minority is necessarily a sect, will, of course, call it a Puseyite Nunnery; that cannot be helped."

Mr Punch explained that "The Convent will be under the superintendence of a Lady Abbess, who will be a real Countess at the least".[50] Every novice would have to pay "at least £10 a week, that sum being the minimum at which it will be possible to defray the expense of the establishment, and keep it select. She will be also expected to bring two silver forks, and all the usual requisites of the toilet." Not much was said about the furnishings of this Belgravian nunnery, apart from a brief reference to "the chairs and piano beautifully and grotesquely carved". The nuns would observe fast-days by "religiously eating red mullet and raspberry jam tart. If there is no red mullet to be had, John Dory, salmon, or any fish in season may be substituted." The cynical attitude towards the quasi-medieval uniforms adopted by Anglican communities is apparent in the statement: "The costume of this sisterhood will consist in a judicious admixture of the conventual style with the fashion

27

of the day. The Nun will not be obliged to sacrifice her hair, but only to wear it plain *à la Madonna,* and it will be permitted to be partially visible." Moreover the members of the Belgravian community would have to "appear in society, in order to display the beauty of sanctity". Their chief occupations would be "devoted to practising the charities of life by making morning calls, and occasionally visiting soup-kitchens and model lodging houses in a properly appointed carriage, or if they walk, attended by a footman.[51] Otherwise their leisure will be employed in illuminating books of devotion, practising ecclesiastical tones, and working slippers for the younger clergy.[52] The inordinate indulgence in maceration, encouraged by Rome, will be disallowed; and the only means sanctioned for the restraint of the flesh, will be the gentle and moderate compression of stays.[53] That the Anglican Convent thus constituted, will lead to 'perversions' there is no fear. Alas! The hard multitude will rather say that the Puseyite sisters are only playing at Roman Catholics, and the vile monster will remark that their Convent is more a Monkey House than a Nunnery."

Miss Priscilla Lydia Sellon, otherwise the Lady Superior of the Devonport Sisters of Mercy, had already expended most of her patrimony in the purchase of ground overlooking the Mere at Plymouth on which to build a permanent home for her growing community, whose Rule was based on that of St Benedict. She had assumed the title of Abbess soon after the Sisterhood had been founded on October 27, 1848, when they opened a "Home for the Orphan Daughters of British Sailors and Soldiers". Not long after *Punch* had publicized the imaginary "Convent of the Belgravians", Abbess Lydia decided to use the remainder of her dowry, supplemented by sums raised by public subscriptions, to the erection of an Anglican conventual establishment which would be able to hold its own with the Roman Catholic Abbey of Mount St Bernard. She visualized it as the Mother House of all Religious Communities beginning to flourish in the Church of England, with herself as Superior General.[54]

Mr William Butterfield was engaged to prepare designs for St Dunstan's Abbey— the first post-Reformation "abbey". Just as in the case of Mr Pugin, when employed by the Trappist monks, he refused to accept a fee for his services. Abbess Lydia had grandiose ideas, and insisted on an extensive range of buildings in the Early English style of Gothic "of about 190 feet long, fronting the south, with two wings extending about 75 feet to the north . . . calculated to accommodate a large number of inmates, having extensive kitchen, bakehouse, pantry, dining-room, dormitories, and every other requisite". There would also be a stately conventual church, evocative of Dr Neale's *Good Old Times of England,* "ere, in her evil day, from their Holy Faith and their ancient rites her people fell away".[55]

October 5, 1850, was the date of "a momentous event—the first instance since the dissolution of the monasteries in the sixteenth century, of a Bishop of the Church of England blessing the foundation of a Religious House".[56] It was indeed courageous on the part of "Henry Exon" (Dr Phillpotts) to show that he approved of the revival of "monkery", but this independent Tory and High Churchman of the old school was no coward. Having celebrated the Holy Communion in St Peter's Church, vested in a balloon-sleeved rochet, chimere, and black scarf, he took his position behind the choristers, and the clergy in their black gowns. Following them in the procession were "nearly one thousand poor people, men, women and children, all of them wearing the badge of the Sisters of Mercy, a blue rosette on the left breast". A journalist reported that "on arriving at the site, a group composed of the clergy [to the number of fifty, including Dr Pusey and Archdeacon Denison], the scholars, and the Sisters of Mercy, was formed round the stone . . . and the Bishop proceeded with the ceremony". Prayer was offered up, and foundation-stone blessed,

28

but without incense or holy water. After this many of the faithful "fell down on their knees on the green grass to receive his blessing".[57]

Abbess Lydia had arranged for a dinner to be served for over a thousand persons, who "were regaled in a most plentiful manner". Mr Dingle of Stonehouse supplied eleven hundred weight of roast beef. The "No Place Inn" provided 105 gallons of ale, and "a vast amount of good sized, pleasant looking plum puddings".

The festivities ended, however, with the Protestant mob breaking in, "pelting the Sisters and clergy with potatoes and plates", and drinking "up the ale with lamentable results". Eventually "a large force of police had to be sent for to clear the field and escort the Sisters and their guests back to Wyndham Square. . . . At a later hour, when the crowd had left the ground" the Lady Abbess, assisted by Dr Pusey, "stood on the commencement of the wall of her future home, and surveyed the fine prospect that it commands".[58] Such was the real start of building up the monastic waste places in the post-Reformation *Ecclesia Anglicana,* a week after Pius IX restored the Roman Catholic Hierarchy in England and Wales, with the Metropolitan See fixed at Westminster.

On April 6, 1851, Archdeacon Manning made his submission to the Church of Rome, the Gorham Judgement having destroyed his faith in Anglicanism. On May 1 Queen Victoria opened the Great Exhibition in Hyde Park, London. Its Medieval Court showed how the churches and chapels of restored monasteries ought to be furnished. There was a surfeit of Gothic altars, pulpits, fonts, lecterns, screens, church-plate, vestments, etc. Protestant visitors were shocked by the replicas of medieval chalices, candlesticks, flower-vases, cruets, croziers, thuribles—even monstrances—but "Puseyite" clergymen found them inspiring. Some longed to buy the sanctuary lamps and statutes of the Virgin Mary and other saints; or to create a dim religious light in their churches by the beautiful stained-glass exhibited.

Six months before the royal opening of the Great Exhibition, whose Medieval Court made the general public familiar with what the Prime Minister, Lord Ashley, had already denounced as "mummeries of superstition", *Punch* felt it worthwhile to publish an article entitled "A Monastery in Pimlico". It stated that "the monks will be young Anglican clergymen of a class not now uncommon, whose state of mind needs a temporary seclusion; and who, if they had not an Abbey to go to, would be sent to some other asylum". This Pimlico fraternity would be employed mainly in "rubbing brasses", but a soup-kitchen would be conducted, with its chief viand "mock-turtle"; concocted to "suit the taste of those who affect, but cannot quite swallow, the original". The monks would enjoy recreation by "occasionally riding in the Park, rather than shun observation. The Father Superior will use a mule, and as many donkeys will be kept in the monastery as there are Friars to ride them."[59]

An ideal "asylum" for young Anglican clergymen needing permanent or temporary seclusion was available after Whitsunday 1851, when the Collegiate Church of the Holy Spirit on the island of Greater Cumbrae was dedicated. This neo-monastic foundation resulted from the generosity of the Hon. George Frederick Boyle, fourth son of the fourth Earl of Glasgow, who had provided the Scottish Episcopal Church with a Collegiate Church, served by a body of secular canons under a provost.

The College stood above "a pleasantly sheltered small bay" round which stretched the "neat modern village and much frequented bathing place" of Millport. Mr Punch's Belgravian monastery could not offer its inmates "magnificent views of nearly the whole Firth of Clyde, the highly cultivated and richly wooded slopes of the Ayrshire sea-board, thickly embellished with villas and with the body and wings of Fairley and Largs, the spiry and bold mountains of Arran, the gentle and charming coasts of the Isle of Bute, the rugged outlines of the Argyleshire alps—a *tout ensemble* of grand and beautiful and picturesquely varied sea and land scenery, always refreshing, and, in certain tintings of the oft-rich drapery above, absolutely thrilling".[60] It almost looked as if this small island might evolve into a modern Iona.

Mr Butterfield had designed a picturesque range of Early English Gothic buildings, not only for the modern Culdees, but also for other clergy seeking retreat, or as guests. Provision was made for young men reading for holy orders. The little cells in the dormitory, with their lancet windows filled with diamond-shaped leaded lights, helped to create an old world atmosphere. Indeed, the whole establishment was evocative of the Trappist monastery of Mount St Bernard, and really much more romantic. Far away to the south could be seen the lofty islet of Ailsa Craig. Nearer lay the Lesser Cumbrae, where there were ruins of an ancient chapel dedicated to St Vey, a ninth-century virgin, said to have lived in solitude surrounded by birds and beasts. According to a legend, there had once been a Celtic monastery on this adjacent island, dependent on St Colum Cille's community.

The church, though of small dimensions, was richly furnished and decorated. The lofty stone screen between the nave and chancel created a sense of mystery. The ceiling above the sanctuary, with polygonal rafters, was painted with dog-roses and ferns. The twelve stalls of either side of the choir looked quite monastic. On the south side of the sanctuary the niched sedilia awaited the celebration of High Mass, according to the Scottish Episcopalian Liturgy. The windows were filled with Hardman's stained glass. The altar furnishings, specially designed by Mr Butterfield, were absolutely "correct" according to the standards imposed by the Ecclesiological Society. The church was illuminated by gas. A row of several hundred jets at the string-course line of the nave produced a most devotional effect, even if the smoke was already darkening the wall behind.

The daily services were fully choral. Six boy-choristers were boarded with the organist in a separate Gothic Revival building and taught by him. Not only were Mattins and Evensong chanted, but the Canons also recited the Day Hours of the Breviary. Mr Boyle had supplied them with a two-volume office book, entitled *The Hours of Prayer*, published at Glasgow in 1851. Part II included the Nocturn Office and Lauds. The first Provost, the Rev. G. Cosby White, was an advanced Tractarian, who after his resignation in 1853, was appointed first Vicar of St Barnabas', Pimlico in 1866.[61]

Unfortunately the ceremonial of the Collegiate Church had to remain what was described as "modest" because of the regulations drawn up by Dr Ewing, the far from High Church Bishop of Argyll and the Isles, who was proud to call himself a loyal Protestant. For this reason "the frequent Celebration of Divine Service by a Collegiate Body under circumstances favourable to religious learning", which was the Founder's intention, lost all its glamour after 1854, when Bishop Ewing appointed himself as Provost. Only the setting remained.[62]

What was visualized as a nucleus of a "Puseyite" monastery came into being at Birmingham in 1851, with a brotherhood known as the Guild of St Alban the Martyr. There was every inspiration at hand, because Hardman & Co. had their headquarters here. No other firm in England was producing so much medieval church furnishings, most of it designed by Mr Pugin, including brass-work and stained glass. This lay-brotherhood looked suspiciously like Mr Punch's Pimlico monastery, although its founders stated that there would be "no affectation of medievalism, even if the 'principles' were 'those of the ancient religious bodies' ". The Guild's chief object was "to assist the Clergy in maintaining and extending the Catholic Faith, and to spread a knowledge of the True Doctrines of the Church of England as fundamentally a reformed branch of the Catholic Church, though lethargic in practice, and also as that part of the Catholic Church with justification and authority in this country".[63]

While the walls of St Dunstan's Abbey, Plymouth, were rising, the Guild of St Alban the Martyr increased in membership. Foundations were made in London and other places. The "Fellows" and "Brothers" used to assemble in private oratories, correctly furnished according to the rules drawn up by the Ecclesiological Society, which was awarded nearly the same authority as that of the Roman Congregation of Rites.[64]

When time could be spared from their secular avocations, these "lay-monks" found spiritual uplift by reciting Prime, Terce, Sext, None and Compline. An office book was compiled, though it was not published (in two volumes) until 1866.[65]

The picturesque costume worn by the brethren consisted of a black habit and girdle, together with a collar of deep blue corded silk, a bronze medallion and a plain cross. Thus garbed they added to the glamour when they walked in processions before the "High Celebration" or after Evensong, carrying candlesticks or banners. They did not begin to wave thuribles until the eighteen-sixties, and even then only in a few churches. So the services, especially in the new Gothic Revival places of worship designed by Brooks, Butterfield, Carpenter, Pearson, Scott and Street, began to be enriched with mild Catholic ceremonial, which loyal Protestants denounced as "Popish".[66]

Interest in medieval "monkeries" increased. In 1852, the same year that Mrs Harriet Beecher Stowe published her anti-slavery novel *Uncle Tom's Cabin* in serial form, an anonymous monk of Mount St Bernard's put his *Concise History of the Cistercian Order* on the market, shortly after the Anglican sisterhoods of the Holy and Undivided Trinity, St Thomas the Martyr, All Saints, and St Michael and All Angels had been founded. The title-page of this bulky volume was adorned by a quaint heraldic device with the words: *"Sancte Bernarde, ora pro nobis"*. Nothing could have been more romantic than the steel engraving provided as the frontispiece. In the foreground was a group of hooded monks garbed in the picturesque habit of their Order. Behind them arose Pugin's Abbey of Mount St Bernard's as he hoped it would look like when completed; the great church with its central tower and broach spire being the central feature. On the left of these buildings, surrounded by an enclosure wall, the rugged landscape was dominated by a pile of jagged rocks, surmounted by a tall calvary. The whole picture was enough to make young Tractarians eager to make a pilgrimage to Leicestershire.

Even after seven years since the foundation of the first of the ten Anglican sisterhoods, only two of their conventual establishments could boast of pointed arches and lancet windows—St Dunstan's abbey, Plymouth, and St Saviour's Home, Osnaburgh Street, London.

The Introduction to this 382 pages book started off with a highly imaginative account of "the ruins of the magnificent monasteries which, previously to the destructive era of the Reformation, adorned this island". For "bold, bad men, who reviled and cast dirt upon the spotless spouse of Christ, fell, like a volcanic eruption, on monks and monastic institutions". Yet it was a consolation that in these more enlightened times an elite were taking an interest in "the delicate proportions of fairy-like tracery, peculiarly rich and pleasing by moonlight". Gentlefolk with a conservative outlook were admiring many a "green and retired spot, on which the mighty fragments of all that is grand and sublime in architecture is scattered—varied and beautiful"—usually beside "murmuring rivulets, and all the charms requisite for scenery, where contemplation and piety love to dwell".

The Trappist author stated: "the circumstances of the time imperatively demand the restoration of similar institutions to those which flourished in 'The Good Olde

THE CHURCH, MOUNT ST BERNARD ABBEY

Designed by A. W. Pugin in 1842, and only half completed, it became the inspiration for all Anglican rebuilders of monastic waste places.

Times of England' ''. (1) "Religious Houses did not confine their deed of benevolence to the relief of mendicants; they were not the mere ancient prototypes of the present workhouse. No; they were the dispensaries of charity in all its various branches—pouring out upon needy and suffering humanity its sweet waters through many channels and pleasant rivulets." (2) Monasteries "were inns for the way-faring, who heard from afar the sound of the vesper bell, at once inviting to repose and devotion, and who might sing his matins with the morning star, and go on his way rejoicing". (3) "The virtues of the monks assumed a still higher character, when they stood forward as protectors of the oppressed—Monasteries possessed the right of sanctuary, in which innocence was shielded, and the hot pursuit of revenge excluded." Even more important for utilitarian reasons was that (4) "Monasteries were central points whence agriculture was to be spread over bleak hills and barren downs, and marshy places". They were also (5) "the depositories of learning which then existed, and well-springs of future literature; the preservers of learning, both divine and human, by their learned works and laborious manuscripts". They were likewise (6) "nurseries of art and science, giving the stimulus, the means, and the reward to invention, and aggregating around them every head that could devise, and every hand that could execute". It should be remembered that they were (7) "hallowed enclosures, happy gardens—not as the Eden of old, exposed to the wily and infernal serpent's ingress—but carefully watched and guarded by many sentinels, into which the child of innocence was transplanted from the infectious air of this corrupted world, ere wickedness had altered his understanding, or deceit beguiled his soul". Previous to their destruction by Protestants, religious houses were (8) "the abodes of meek-eyed peace, founded by the piety of our ancestors, with the charitable design to give a retreat to such persons as had a wish to detach themselves from the affairs of the world, and dedicate their lives to the service of God, in a state of quiet and devotion". Monasteries were (9) "sacred asylums of penance, to which many, whose lamp of virtue had gone out, came to rekindle it, and to spend its later and brighter flame in the employment of their Maker, in effacing, by its eminent lustre, the darker shades of past life, the frailties and the ignorances of their youth". Those abodes of peace were likewise (10) "prominent and well-discerned beacons, throwing afar upon the adjacent country, the light of good example". Finally they were (11) "houses of prayer", as described by the Rev. Edward Young in his blank-verse poem *Night Thoughts on Life, Death, and Immortality* published in 1742-5.

> "Prayer ardent opens heav'n, lets down a stream
> Of glory on the consecrated hour
> Of man, in audience with the Deity,
> Who worships the great God, that instant joins
> The first in heav'n, and sets his foot on hell."

Yes! Medieval monasteries were indeed "houses of prayer, the gates of which were never closed, from midnight hour till after the set of sun. For is there an hour, asks the poet, in all nature, when the heart should be weary of prayer—when man should have no incense to offer before God's altar—no tear to confide to the bosom of his mercy? Hence the devout inhabitants of religious houses sought by their untiring assiduity to repair the coldness and contempt thrown upon this sacred duty by a vain and giddy world. They broke off the midnight slumber, and anticipated the loud clarion of the wakeful bird, so early with his matins—and the swift chariot of the rising sun—and seven times in the day, in imitation of Sion's royal bard, they poured forth their souls in praises to their Maker."

For the above eleven reasons "the restoration in England, wherefore, of one of the most illustrious branches of the great Benedictine family, in all its primitive

33

c

discipline and fervour of purpose", was in the year 1852 "highly gratifying to every Catholic anxious to see his country regain the long forfeited appellation of the Island of Saints". More and more Tractarian clergy and laymen began to cast wistful eyes on Mount St Bernard Abbey, as the only place in Britain where the medieval monastic system had been revived. Many were dreaming of founding brotherhoods, more religious in character than the Pre-Raphaelite one formed by Holman Hunt, Rossetti and Millais in 1848, who merely wanted to revert to the primitive outlook of the early Italian painters.

Anything "Gothic" was popular in art, literature and music, after Mr Tennyson had included the "Morte d'Arthur" in the two volume edition of his poems published in 1842. Richard Wagner sought inspiration for his opera *Lohengrin* (one of the Knights of the Holy Grail) in a thirteenth-century poem. Matthew Arnold also made use of Malory's *Morte d'Arthur* for his poem "Tristram and Iseult" published in 1852. Robert Schumann had chosen the thirteenth century as the period for his opera *Manfred*, composed three years before. Even Charles Kingsley, who had a holy horror of Romanism, had written a poem about St Elizabeth of Hungary, entitled "The Saint's Tragedy", for this thirteenth-century Franciscan Tertiary had been torn between her natural affections and her religious duties as enforced by a domineering monk.

Among the many young Tractarians—or "Puseyites" as people called them in derision—who made a pilgrimage to Mount St Bernard as being the only real monastery in England, was Edward Burne-Jones, then aged eighteen. After his death in 1898 his widow wrote: "Though it is doubtful whether he ever saw the place again with his bodily eyes, the thought of it accompanied him through his whole life. Friends, wife, and children all knew the undercurrent of longing for the rest and peace which he thought he had seen there that day; he did not disguise it from them, and in his later years often spoke of the dream which had walked step by step with him ever since, of some day leaving every one and everything and entering its doors and closing them behind him."[67]

He entered Exeter College, Oxford, in 1853, where he soon developed a close friendship with William Morris. They used to worship at St Thomas's, where the services were conducted by Mr Chamberlain on what were then regarded as very "advanced" lines.

Morris and Burne-Jones would not have found anything archaic or Pre-Raphaelite had they been curious enough to attend Sunday Mass in Oxford's only Roman Catholic place of worship at that date—St Clement's Chapel, hidden away just over Magdalen Bridge. It stood back from the road, next to an inn, and was "a plain rectangular building of yellow local stone, with a classical front, and an alcove for the altar, flanked by Corinthian pillars. There were probably no statues."[68] Again, there was the risk of their being fined by the University authorities for frequenting this schismatic chapel, were they discovered by the "bulldogs".[69] Moreover St Clement's was a place of unhappy memories for "Puseyites", reminding them of how Mr Newman and his fellow perverts had heard Mass there the first Sunday after "going over to Rome".[70]

Gothic-shaped chasubles were worn at St Thomas-the-Martyr's. Gregorian chants provided medieval music. Dark stained glass helped to create a dim religious light. The brass gas corona with glass balls increased the devotional atmosphere. A few black-robed nuns—members of the Sisterhood of St Thomas the Martyr—added to the old worlde ethos. Miss Blencowe's recently published handbook on church embroidery, supplied them with designs for decorating vestments, pulpit-falls, alms-bags, and hassocks. Every detail had to be symbolical, according to the rules laid down by the Ecclesiological Society.

Burne-Jones wrote on May 1, 1855: "I have set my heart on our founding a Brotherhood. Learn 'Sir Galahad' by heart; he is to be the patron of our Order. I have enlisted one in the project up here, heart and soul." Later on he wrote again about "this Crusade and Holy Warfare against the age", which would involve both celibacy and a quasi-monastic life. On October 16 the following year he said: "The Monastery stands a fairer chance than ever of being founded. I know that it will be some day".[71] Morris was prepared to devote the whole of his fortune to this "monkery" dedicated to Sir Galahad of the Holy Grail.[72]

All these twilight dreams had little in common with the spirit of the Trappist community at Mount St Bernard's. The monks would have advised Burne-Jones to seek inspiration from the lives of their founders SS. Robert, Alberic, and Stephen, or from the writings of Abbot de Rancé, and to steer clear of any version of the *Morte d'Arthur*, ancient or modern. But as time went on "the old ideals melted away before larger enthusiasms, the mistress art of architecture, with all else—music, painting, the whole range of forms and colours and sounds—swept up into its trains, took a continually deeper and more dominating hold".[73]

Would-be founders of Anglican monasteries, who had visions of emulating the Knights of the Holy Grail, feared that it would not be possible to have public oratories furnished in a Catholic manner unless they conformed to the judgment given by the Court of Arches in 1856, that an altar cross was illegal, since it could be regarded only as one of those "images" which the injunctions of Edward VI ordered to be destroyed, having been used for superstitious purposes. It was a great relief, however, when they were told that the Privy Council had decided that a cross could be used symbolically, also that altar-lights, a chancel-screen, frontals (of various colours), and a credence-table were permissible.

Contemporary with the Burne-Jones and Morris dream of a monastery dedicated to Sir Galahad was the brotherhood of St Mary, founded by a young layman, Edward Steere, on September 1, 1853. It was badly needed if only to counteract the influence of Roman Catholic communities. By that year the Oratorians had houses in London and Birmingham. The Rosminians had been working mainly in the Midlands for eighteen years. There had been Passionists since 1841 and Redemptorists since 1843. Italian Capuchins settled in Peckham, London, in 1850, and Belgian ones at Pantasaph, North Wales, in 1852. The Dominicans took over a new Gothic Revival priory at Woodchester in 1850, which had been built for the Passionists. The Jesuits, with colleges at Stonyhurst and Mount St Mary's, also in charge of a fair number of missions, had invaded London, where they opened a church in the heart of Mayfair in 1849. The Marists also appeared on the scene in 1850, and so did the Vincentians. More accommodation was needed at the Benedictine priories of Ampleforth and Downside, owing to the increase in the number of monks and the boys educated by them.

Mr Steere's part-time monks worshipped in St Matthew's, City Road, London, where the services were conducted on advanced Tractarian lines, on a par with those at St Barnabas', Pimlico; St Mary Magdalene's, Munster Square; St Mary's, Crown Street, Soho; and Margaret Chapel. Before long the little Brotherhood was affiliated with the Guild of St Alban the Martyr. In May 1855 he gave up his chambers in the Inner Temple, having decided to retire to the country in order to lead a real monastic life, with a few companions who called themselves the Brotherhood of St James. Several properties were inspected, and eventually a medieval chapel near Tamworth, dedicated to St Edward, was bought. They took possession of it at the same time that five of the Devonport Sisters of Mercy and three of the London Sisterhood of the Holy Cross were helping Miss Nightingale to nurse soldiers wounded in the Crimean War at the barracks-hospital at Scutari.

Most of the novices at St Edward's Spital, so it is recorded, were more attracted by the picturesque externals of monasticism than by its penitential character. They "dreamed with delight of singing out of illuminated breviaries", and "admired midnight matins", but "got up with difficulty between seven and eight". The founder realised that neither Dr Lonsdale, Bishop of Lichfield, nor any other bishop would be prepared to ordain either himself or any of his "monks" until after serving a diaconate in a parish, so the Brotherhood of St James was disbanded. Mr Steere soon managed to get ordained deacon and priest, and in 1858 became curate-in-charge of Skegness, where he was much loved by the Lincolnshire fishermen as "a downright shirt-sleeve man and a real Bible parson".[74]

The publication of several more vernacular office books encouraged Anglican clergy and layfolk to adopt medieval forms of worship. Mr John David Chambers had been studying them since he was appointed Recorder of Salisbury in 1842, for this post enabled him to work in the Cathedral library, where he browsed among ancient liturgical and ceremonial books and manuscripts. In 1852 he issued *The Psalter or Seven Ordinary Hours of Prayer according to the Church of Sarum*. It contained plainsong melodies for his translations of the office hymns. Two years later the Rev. H. P. Liddon, the first Vice-Principal of Cuddesdon Theological College, compiled *Occasional Offices for the Hours of Prayer*. He was assisted by Frederick G. Lee, one of the first students at the College, opened in 1854. A vernacular version of *Compline, according to the Use of the Church of England* appeared about the same time. The first edition of *Day Hours of the Church of England, newly translated and arranged according to the Prayer Book and the Authorized translation of the Bible* was published by John Masters in 1858, and proved a best-seller, for most sisterhoods soon adopted it. The editor, the Hon Frederick Lygon, who became 6th Earl Beauchamp in 1866, took care that this diurnal contained nothing which could be regarded as "Romish". No direct invocation of saints was admitted, only imprecation. The Society of the Holy Trinity, however, continued to use manuscript translations of the Sarum Breviary, some elaborately illuminated. In 1854 Abbess Lydia Sellon ordered "Deane" Amelia Warren to retire to a remote cottage near Windsor, so that she could spend most of the time translating the whole Sarum Breviary. Her companion was Sister Margaret, then a novice, who joined the Church of Rome in 1858. With the pseudonym of "The Nun of Kenmare" she published in 1869 a scurrilous autobiography entitled *Five Years in a Protestant Sisterhood and Ten Years in a Catholic Convent*.[75]

Frederick George Lee (1832-1902) deserves special mention, because he never ceased trying to convince his fellow Anglicans that they must revert to the Middle Ages in their beliefs and forms of worship for nearly half a century. He will be mentioned frequently in subsequent chapters since he was closely connected with almost every effort to build up monastic waste places, even as late as 1898.[76]

Between 1854 and 1858 he and the Rev. John Purchas, then a curate at St Paul's, Brighton, kept busy with launching a crusade to revive the glories of medieval ritual and ceremonial. Both dreamed of the days—not very far off it was hoped—when the full splendour of Sarum worship would be restored to most parish churches—even some cathedrals. They pictured three, five or seven deacons vested in dalmatics, and as many subdeacons in tunicles; two or more thurifers waving censers, and three cross bearers during processions. There would be copes galore, and gorgeous Gothic chasubles, likewise an intricate colour-sequence. The ritual-fan must be restored, and waved over the celebrating priest. All this sort of thing would indicate that *Ecclesia Anglicana* had not been truly described by Anthony Trollope in his Barchester novels, or by George Eliot in *Scenes from Clerical Life*.

So Mr Lee and Mr Purchas pursued their liturgical labours. In 1858 the latter published the first edition of *The Directorium Anglicanum*, which was "humbly dedicated to the Archbishops and Bishops in Visible Communion with the See of Canterbury . . . with every feeling of profound respect". It is doubtful, however, if many of them approved of the not always "Sarum" birettas, buskins, chalices, copes, chasubles, croziers, sandals, and much more "medieval mummery" illustrated by engravings. They were hardly in tune with the billowing crinolines then being worn by ladies of fashion, or even the tall top-hats, overcoats and cloaks favoured by "men about town".

A sequel to the *Directorium* was an unofficial missal, entitled *The Priest to the Altar, or Aids to the Devout Celebration of the Holy Communion, Chiefly after the Ancient English Use of Sarum*. The compiler was P. G. Medd, Fellow of University College, Oxford, and it was published privately in 1861. This modest missal did not stir up nearly so much strife as *Essays and Reviews* by seven Anglican authors, who advocated free inquiry into religious matter—completely contrary to the Medieval Mind.

Mr Lee strove to combat these heretics by a novel entitled *Clinton Maynard: A Tale of the World, the Flesh and the Devil;* editing *Sermons on the Reunion of Christendom*, and Dr Boileau's *Reformed Monastery;* also many sermons which were printed. He rallied round support for Mr Bryan King at St George's-in-the-East during the "Ritual Riots".[77] The *Daily Telegraph* stated that "his personal conduct is literally offensive. . . . We abandon Mr Frederick George Lee to the judgment of his conscience, whenever it is convalescent, and of the public, who may now decide whether or not he is fit to wear a surplice, with or without a green stole, or a chasuble, plain and decent, or bordered with gold, in imitation of Roman religious harlotry."[78]

Three attempts were made to established brotherhoods in the Protestant Episcopal Church in the United States of America between 1842 and 1847, but not exactly on monastic lines, and all of them soon faded out.[79] It was not until 1884 that the Order of the Holy Cross was founded with a quasi-monastic character, and it managed to survive.

In England, the collapse of Newman's quasi-monastery at Littlemore, Faber's Society of St Joseph at Elton, and Steere's Brotherhood of St James near Tamworth, indicated that it was a waste of time and money trying to establish any more male communities in *Ecclesia Anglicana*, granted that there were practical reasons in favour of active sisterhoods. Yet even these were alarming Protestants as early as 1851 when a bill was introduced in the House of Commons for the inspection of convents. The object was "to make provision for preventing the forcible detention of females in houses wherein are resident persons bound by monastic vows". Practically all Anglican bishops were strongly opposed to women binding themselves by the three vows of religion, some maintaining that they were illegal; others that such vows tended to encourage Romish abuses and superstitions, especially among young ladies.

Sisterhoods were regarded as hotbeds of so-called "Ritualism" against which open war began to be waged in 1855. Their chapels were private places of worship, in which all sorts of strange rites and ceremonies could be conducted behind locked doors, without danger of interference.[80] Ritualism was also encouraged by the Ladies' Embroidery Society founded in 1854, whose members gave their services gratuitously. Feminine frippery in churches tended to get out of hand. Mr Wigley's English version of *St Charles Borromeo's Instructions on Ecclesiastical Buildings* published in 1857 encouraged the more advanced "Puseyite" clergy to adopt Roman fashions in church furnishings and vestments, to the horror of conservative-minded Ecclesiologists.

Between August 1859 and July 1860, the majestic Classical church of St George-in-the-East, Stepney, London, was the scene of wild ritual riots, which *The Times* described as "devilish". At the close of an evening service, during which the Gregorian chants were disturbed by cat-calls and shouting by the mob, a rush was made towards the altar. The cross and two candlesticks were hurled down, hassocks were thrown at the gas chandelier suspended over the apsidal chancel—all this because the rector, the Rev. Bryan King had introduced a surpliced choir, lighted candles, and worn a chasuble in the celebration of the Holy Communion.

Punch, having a good idea of what would amuse most of its readers, attacked Puseyite parsons as typified by Mr King, who was reported to have said that he "could never again put on those beautiful robes". "Oh, my handsome stole! Oh, my splendid cope! Oh, my pretty alb! Oh, my love of a chasuble! Oh, my duck of a dalmatic! Boohoo!" *Punch* readers were asked to send "Poor Mr King a pair of ear-rings to match his beautiful robes, and to set them off in proper style a variety of Crinoline".[81]

It would have been foolish for anybody to think of building up the monastic waste places of England on medieval lines at such a moment, but as William Cowper wrote in 1779, when threatened with insanity:

> "God moves in a mysterious way
> His wonders to perform;
> He plants his footsteps in the sea,
> And rides upon the storm."

This is what happened at Plymouth in the year 1861, when a recently ordained Anglican deacon was sure he heard a clear call from God to revive the medieval monastic system in his beloved National Church, though as yet he had not even glanced at the *Rule of St Benedict,* or crossed the threshold of any monastery. From every point of view no worse rebuilder of the waste places could have appeared on the scene, except that he had an intense belief in what he regarded as a divine vocation.

NOTES

[1] *Constitutions and Canons Ecclesiastical* (1604), III.

[2] This Act of Parliament was not repealed until 1929, although it had been a dead-letter since the passing of the Roman Catholic Relief Act in 1829.

[3] Cf. Peter Guilday, *The English Recusants on the Continent 1558-1795* (1914), Vol. I.

[4] Cf. A. M. Allchin, *The Silent Rebellion* (1958), pp. 15-35; P. F. Anson, *The Call of the Cloister* (2nd revised edition 1964), pp. 1-25.

[5] Cf. Edith Sitwell, *English Eccentrics* (1933); P. F. Anson, *The Call of the Desert* (1964), pp. 193-6.

[6] There had been a succession of Papist chaplains at Lulworth Castle since 1641. An elegant chapel in the Classical style was erected in 1786. George III, together with Queen Charlotte Sophia and the three elder princesses, came by sea from Weymouth in 1789, to enjoy Mr Weld's hospitality for a few weeks. In 1794 he handed over Stonyhurst Hall to the exiled English Jesuits from Saint-Omer.

[7] A Cistercian Monk, *A Concise History of the Cistercian Order* (1852), p. 182.

[8] As will be noticed further on, most of the earlier conventual establishments built for both Anglican and Roman Catholic communities were designed in what was regarded as the purest style of Gothic. Narrow lancet windows were supposed to be helpful to leading the monastic life.

[9] ibid, p. 184.

[10] T. D. Fosbroke, *British Monachism* (1816), p. 301.

[11] *Concise History of the Cistercian Order*, p. 201.

[12] As early as 1796 Mr Weld had appealed to Dr Courtney, Bishop of Bristol, whose diocese then embraced Dorset, on behalf of what more rigid Protestants denounced as a "gloomy abode of ignorance and nastiness". The Bishop was sympathetic, referred the matter to Dr Moore, Archbishop of Canterbury and the Governors of Queen Anne's Bounty, with the result that they expressed their regret that the squire of Lulworth "should have suffered any

causeless uneasiness on this subject", which had been described as an "Establishment for un-fortunate objects". (Cf. John Hutchins, *History of Dorset*, Vol. IV, ed. Gough, p. 351, quoting *Monthly Magazine*, October 1800.)

[13] St Susan's, Lulworth, was also the parent-house of Mount Melleray in Ireland (1815); Gethsemani (1848) and New Melleray (1849) in the United States; and Mount St Bernard (1835) in England.

[14] op. cit. (3rd edition, 1843), p. 301.

[15] *Sir Thomas More, or Colloquies on the Progress and Prospects of Society*, Vol. II, p. 318. It was not until 1839 that the Roman Catholic Sisters of Mercy made their first foundation in England, and not until 1857 that the Sisters of Charity of St Vincent de Paul appeared on the scene.

[16] Cf. Catherine Jamison, *The History of the Royal Foundation of St Katharine* (1952). In 1948 the Patron, Queen Mary, approved the re-establishment of this "Royal Peculiar" on a religious basis as nearly as possible on the original lines in East London. The Chapter now consists of members of the Community of the Resurrection and the Deaconess Community of St Andrew. The headquarters are in Butcher Row, Ratcliffe, E.14.

[17] See p. 32.

[18] *A Concise History of the Cistercian Order*, etc, by a Cistercian Monk (1852), p. 276.

[19] *Letters and Correspondence of J. H. Newman*, ed. by Anne Mozley (1891), Vol. II, p. 249.

[20] *Letters of Rev. J. B. Mozley*, edited by his sister (1884), p. 78.

[21] *A Concise History of the Cistercian Order*, p. 280.

[22] Cf. R. D. Middleton, *Newman and Bloxam* (Oxford, 1947) p. 86. John Rouse Bloxam (1807-91) was an Anglican ceremonialist and historian. From 1837 to 1840 he was Newman's curate at Littlemore, where he introduced two gilded candlesticks, wooden alms-dish, black silk stole, credence table, litany-desk, etc. He kept up close relations with Roman Catholics until 1841.

[23] ibid, pp. 25-6.

[24] Cf. *Correspondence*, p. 311.

[25] E. S. Purcell, *Life and Letters of Ambrose Phillipps de Lisle* (1900), Vol. I, p. 81.

[26] op. cit., pp. vii-viii.

[27] James Barrow, R. W. Church, R. A. Coffin, J. B. Dalgairns, F. W. Faber, J. A. Froude, William Lockhart, Thomas Mozley, Frederick Oakeley, Thomas Meyrick, Robert Ornsby, Mark Pattison, and John Walker.

[28] Vol. I, p. xxix. Dalgairns undertook the Cistercian saints: Stephen Harding, Aelred, Robert of Newminster, and Waltheof.

[29] op. cit. (1900 edition), Vol. 5, p. 396.

[30] Nevertheless, Anna Jemima and Sarah Anne, the younger and elder daughters of Dr Terrot, who was Bishop of Edinburgh from 1841 to 1872, embraced the religious life as members of Abbess Lydia Sellon's Devonport Sisters of Mercy. In 1897 Sister Sarah Anne (later Eldress) was decorated with the Royal Red Cross by Queen Victoria, for her efficient nursing services in the hospitals at Scutari.

[31] op. cit. (1900 edition), Vol. 4, pp. 154-5.

[32] ibid, pp. 52-3.

[33] op. cit. (1900 edition), Vol. 4, p. 160.

[34] op. cit. (1900 edition), Vol. I, p. 445.

[35] ibid.

[36] E. S. Purcell, *Life and Letters of Ambrose Phillipps de Lisle* (1900), Vol. I, p. 349.

[37] op. cit. (1900 edition), p. 3.

[38] Another instalment of this translation of the Roman Breviary, containing the Night Office, seems to have been published in 1845.

[39] F. W. Faber, *Life of St Paulinus*, p. 160.

[40] op. cit.

[41] op. cit., p. iv. It was not until 1855 that he founded the Society of St Margaret, nine years from his appointment as Warden of Sackville College, East Grinstead.

[42] op. cit., p. 169.

[43] C. P. S. Clarke, *The Oxford Movement and After* (1932), p. 251.

[44] op. cit., p. ix.

[45] ibid, p. viii.

[46] ibid, pp. xiv-xv. Mr Fox was thinking of the Poor Law Amendment Act (1834) which forbade outdoor relief in Britain and established workhouses. He would have been gratified, had he been told, that about 45 years later his book would inspire a teenager, then living in South America, to revive the Benedictine Order in the Church of England.

[47] The Pre-Raphaelite Brotherhood, founded in 1848 by Holman Hunt, Rossetti and Millais, with the object of returning to the outlook of the early Italian painters, had nothing monastic about it. On the other hand it had a certain influence on the background of Anglican religious communities founded in the 1850s when the three artists and other members were exhibiting their pictures.

[48] *Life and Letters of W. J. Butler* (1897), p. 38.

[49] Vol. XIX, p. 162.

[50] Miss Sellon, the foundress of the Devonport Sisters of Mercy, had assumed the title of abbess already.

51 In 1851 common lodging-houses were placed under the watch of the police. The first "model lodging-houses" were built in London in 1845.

52 By 1850 there were several books on sale devoted to the art of illumination. Some of the Devonport Sisters of Mercy had already illuminated Psalters, Profession Services, etc. The "ecclesiastical tones" could be studied in Mr Helmore's manuals on Gregorian chant. Miss Monica Thurgood had published her helpful little guide to *Church Embroidery* with full directions how to make altar-kneelers, alms-bags, antepedia, banners, bannerettes, chalice-veils, chancel-carpets, cushions, sachets, sermon-cases, stoles—even slippers and smoking-caps for clergymen.

53 Dr Pusey encouraged, or at least tolerated, much more "maceration" in his Sisterhood of the Holy Cross (1845), including the use of the discipline. During the Lent of 1850, Sister Katherine Ogilvie, in spite of frail health, took no food, other than a dish of thick oatmeal. She prolonged her daily fast until 9 p.m. From Maundy Thursday until Easter Day, not even a drop of water passed her lips. The result was that she retired to bed with "symptoms of gastric fever", and died the following June. (Cf. T. J. Williams and A. W. Campbell, *The Park Village Sisterhood* (1965), pp. 67-8.)

54 Cf. T. J. Williams, *Priscilla Lydia Sellon* (1965), p. 77.

55 See p. 137.

56 ibid, p. 78.

57 ibid, p. 79.

58 ibid, p. 80.

59 November 1850, Vol. XIX, p. 189.

60 *The Topographical, Statistical and Historical Gazetteer of Scotland* (Glasgow, 1842), Vol. II, p. 357.

61 His predecessors had been curates of St Paul's, Knightsbridge.

62 For more than one reason it proved impossible to maintain the College of the Holy Spirit on its original lines. In 1875, the Founder, who became 6th Earl of Glasgow in 1869, made over the property to the Scottish Episcopal Church. The following year the church became the Cathedral of the Argyll and Isles Diocese.

63 Most High Church Anglicans regarded the restored English and Welsh Hierarchy set up by Pius IX on September 29, 1850, as schismatic, having neither authority nor jurisdiction.

64 A schism took place in the Cambridge Camden Society in 1845, when the more progressive members formed themselves into the Ecclesiological Society, with its headquarters in London.

65 *The Canonical Hours according to the Use of the Guild of St Alban the Martyr*. A second edition appeared in 1874, and a third in 1912.

66 Cf. George H. Smith, *Story of the Guild of St Alban the Martyr 1851-1951* (1951).

67 *Memorials of Edward Burne-Jones* (1904), Vol. I, p. 53.

68 Meriol Trevor, *Newman, The Pillar of Cloud* (1962), p. 362.

69 This happened to Gerard Manley Hopkins, the future Jesuit poet, and a companion in 1868. (Cf. Alfred Thomas, *Hopkins the Jesuit* (1969), p. 15.)

70 Ecclesiologists at Cambridge had greater temptation to participate in Papist worship. The Church of St Andrew, designed by A. W. Pugin, opened on St George's Day, 1843, was pronounced by the Camden Society to be "a hidden gem".

71 J. W. Mackail, *Life of William Morris* (1899), Vol. I, p. 61.

72 Sir Galahad, in Malory's *Morte d'Arthur*, is (by enchantment) the son of Launcelot and Elaine, daughter of King Pelles. He is predestined by his immaculate purity to achieve the quest of the Holy Grail.

73 ibid, Vol. I, p. 66.

74 Cf. F. M. Heanley, *Memoir of Edward Steere* (1888), pp. 36, 43. The founder of the Brotherhood of St James became third Anglican Bishop in Central Africa. He died at Zanzibar in 1882.

75 Deane Amelia's translation was not completed until shortly before her death in 1869. It was finally published in 1889 with the title of *The Breviary of the Renowned Church of Salisbury, Rendered into English According to the Use of the Society of the Most Holy Trinity, Devonport*.

76 See p. 83.

77 See p. 45.

78 Cf. H. R. T. Brandreth, *Dr Lee of Lambeth* (1951), p. 21.

79 Nashotah Community, Wisconsin (1842); Community in Essex County, New York (1845); Society of the Holy Cross, Valle Crucis, North Carolina (1847).

80 The Society of St Margaret at East Grinstead became familiar with the extra-liturgical Roman rites of Exposition and Benediction after Dr Neale had acquired a monstrance in 1858.

81 op. cit., November 19, 1859.

CHAPTER I

How the nineteen year-old Joseph Leycester Lyne heard a call in Glenalmond to embrace the Rule of St Benedict, and build up the monastic waste places of Britain on medieval lines (1856-1862)

TRINITY COLLEGE, Glenalmond, Perthshire, can claim to be the place where the seed was planted that grew eventually into the tree composed of numerous communities of men and women in the Anglican Communion observing the Rule of St Benedict today.[1]

In 1856 a nineteen year-old youth named Joseph Leycester Lyne became a theological student there. He was born on November 23, 1837, five months after Queen Victoria ascended the throne. His origins were nothing if not aristocratic, and he was the second of seven children. His father, Francis Lyne, claimed descent from an old Welsh family which had settled in Cornwall. He and his brother had inherited a vast fortune from John James Stephens, a Portuguese merchant who adopted them. Joseph's mother, Lousia Genevieve Leycester, belonged to the illustrious Cheshire family of De Tabley. She could count among her cousins more than one member of the peerage and baronetage.[2]

The future Benedictine monk was brought up in a typical early-Victorian upper-class environment. His parents took care about the moral and religious training of their children. Joseph was educated at St Paul's School, London, until the age of fourteen, but on account of his delicate health had to be put under the care of private tutors for the next five years. He was a serious little boy, and related long afterwards: "I recollect that the Quakers elicited my warmest sympathy and interest as a child, because of the stand they seemed to make against the world for religion's sake".[3]

He appears to have been extremely pious, but to quote his own words: "My religion gave me a great deal of trouble and anxiety, but no peace. . . . At the age of nineteen I was very anxious to prepare for Holy Orders in the Church of England, but I had imbibed very strong High Church ideas, and my father was most strongly opposed to them, and refused to help me in any way. My dear mother, who had a special fondness for me on account of my delicate health, took to my cause, and arranged with Dr Eden, the Bishop of Moray and Ross, a connection of hers, to have me placed at the Scotch Theological College of Glenalmond in Perthshire. There under Dr Hannah and Prof. Bright, the present Regius Professor of Ecclesiastical History at Christ Church, Oxford, I received my education for the ministry."[4]

This picturesque and romantic Highland glen, watered by the river Almond, with mountains on its north side rising to 2,044 feet above sea-level, made an instant appeal. Mr Butterfield's Gothic Revival buildings were in tune with young Lyne's Tractarian yearnings. One evening he heard, very faintly, his first call to the cloister. As dictated to his biographer more than half-a-century later:

"When the great bell of the monastic vocation sounded its solemn Angelus in the soul of Leycester Lyne, he was engaged in the very perfunctory act of crossing the Quad of Glenalmond Seminary in company with sundry of his fellow students. It was the hour of Evensong, and they were all *en route* for the Collegiate chapel.

Somehow, by the way, a touch of hyperbolical illusion crossed one of the number. 'I say', he exclaimed suddenly, turning to his comrades, 'we look just like ye monks of ye nineteenth century processing to ye Vespers'. . . . The allusion, which to the others fell as the chaff before the wind, came upon him as the good seed comes upon the fallow furrows, and it took root and flourished accordingly. That short, commonplace little walk was the first step into the cloisters of the Monk's life. It gave realism to his dreams, absolute foothold in the current where he had often found himself eddying and drifting to no defined end. . . . But his secret was too precious for expression even to his mother, and his own intelligence taught him the utter madness of breathing so much as a monkish whisper into the ear of his country's Church."[5]

Mrs Lyne confirmed this in after years; when writing to a friend: "He then felt that he had found the very thing he wanted, and he made up his mind to give his whole life and soul to God by becoming a monk; but he did not mention his feelings to me until after he was ordained, when he became a curate at Plymouth".[6]

Looking back more than thirty years, Lyne recorded that he was well taught at Glenalmond "so far as head knowledge was concerned", but as yet he "knew nothing of Jesus Christ". He maintained: "I left college as ignorant of Jesus as my personal Saviour as when I entered it. Neither Dr Hannah nor Prof. Bright would give me 'the knowledge of salvation for the remission of sins'. The Holy Ghost could alone do this, by 'taking of the things of Jesus and showing them to me'."[7]

The strain of life at Glenalmond proved too much for the highly sensitive and emotional would-be monk, and he begged Dr Hannah to give him the Last Sacraments which he refused to do, "not thinking it prudent to encourage what he deemed to be his pupil's 'extreme tendencies'."[8] After what appeared to be a miracle, Mr Lyne managed to pass his final examinations.

Bishop Eden decided that although this neurotic student could not be ordained for the next two years, there was nothing to prevent his becoming a Catechist, so he summoned him to Inverness. At that date there was only a small Episcopalian chapel and school.[9] The Baroness related that "the arrival of the delicate and gentlemanly-looking young stranger was a social event. He was a novelty, and a charming addition to the select role of the local set; moreover the inevitable 'little bird' having whispered that the newcomer was one of the rich Lynes, all the hunting mammas for miles around put on their 'pink' and mustered for a run."[10] With good reason too, for the Catechist (from the social point of view) was quite eligible as the son-in-law of any Episcopalian laird, even if a bit too "High Church" for most of them.

It was not long before Mr Lyne caused scandal by what was regarded as "Romanism" in his instructions. Bishop Eden felt it safer to move him to Glen Urquhart, where in 1853 Mr and Mrs Cameron of Lakefield had erected a small Episcopalian church near Drumnadrochit. The latter—referred to as "Mamsie"— soon became a second mother to the Catechist. But after about eighteen months he had stirred up so much opposition from the local Free Kirk minister and his flock, that the Bishop was obliged to withdraw Mr Lyne's licence, and even closed St Ninian's until further notice.

This episcopal action resulted in what was then known as "brain fever", together with "inflammation of the heart and often alarming symptoms". So "Mamsie" took her protégé to convalesce at Nairn, but the bracing sea breezes of the Moray Firth did not effect a cure. Mrs Lyne had to be summoned, and she transported her son to London by easy stages in 1859.

Thanks to negotiations by his father, it was arranged for him to proceed to holy orders. But the future clergyman and would-be monk got scruples about the validity of his baptism. He was re-christened conditionally by the Rev. G. R. Prynne, who had agreed to take him on as a curate. The ordination to the diaconate was performed in Wells Cathedral on December 23, 1860, with letters dismissory from Dr Phillpotts, Bishop of Exeter, and at the hands of Lord Auckland, Bishop of Bath and Wells. Mr Lyne was appointed to an honorary curacy at St Peter's, Plymouth. Thanks to two legacies he found himself with a capital sum of £300. Still mindful of a call to the cloister, he took a private vow of celibacy. Not being a graduate of a University, he had to remain a deacon for three years. Bishop Phillpotts laid down that he must not preach in the Exeter diocese until he had received priest's orders.

These restrictions, however, did not prevent the embryo monk from performing the first of his many alleged miracles. He claimed to have cured a fourteen year-old girl of abject idiocy, after cursing her mother Mrs Egg (or Hatch). Dr Pusey, who happened to be staying at Plymouth, urged that this paranormal business should be kept secret, and remarked: "You are too young for the notoriety, whether favourable or the reverse, to be anything but a spiritual temptation and hindrance".[11] A bit later the deacon exorcized in a melodramatic manner a raving maniac.

Meanwhile he had formed a guild of men and boys with a medieval monastic flavour about it, which was called The Society of the Love of Jesus. This Plymouth brotherhood soon had forty members. It was in tune with the backwash of the Pre-Raphaelite Brotherhood as depicted on the paintings of Dante Gabriel Rossetti and his disciple, Edward Burne-Jones.

"Brother Joseph", as Mr Lyne now preferred to be addressed, felt that his community ought to be put on a more secure footing. For some reason he had not called at St Dunstan's Abbey, the mysterious range of Early English Gothic buildings, with narrow lancet windows, designed by William Butterfield, only part of which had been completed. The Abbey was quite near St Peter's Church, but the vicar and his wife had told him that Mother Lydia Sellon was an invalid, who seldom received anyone, least of all a stranger, discouraging the curate from trying to meet her.[12]

One day he summoned up his courage and, as he recalled nearly fifty years later, stood outside the high enclosure walls before giving a pull at the medieval door-bell. Then the iron grille was gently opened by a "demure old nun", who asked his business. She went off, and in a few moments a "sweet-faced nun" ushered him "into the presence he so longed and yet feared to penetrate".

"The Lady Abbess was reclining on a *chaise-longue*, being afflicted with a spinal weakness. 'Come and sit down, Brother Joseph', was her kindly greeting, 'I have heard so much about you already'; and, to her amusement, Mr Lyne sat himself on a stool at her feet—'just like one of my nuns', as she herself remarked, when she observed the very lowly position he had chosen to assume."[13]

Br Joseph opened his heart to the Lady Abbess, "as to a spiritual mother", while she on her part cheered and encouraged his monastic leanings. After this first interview, she consulted Dr Pusey. He urged the foundation of a "monkery" as soon as possible, no matter on how modest a basis.

The Baroness biographer commented: "It was a strange combination, this trefoil of force, blending into one prolific leaf. Dr Pusey, the sublime torch-bearer of the Tractarian Reformation; and hand in hand with him the saintly Abbess Priscilla, that strong yet gentle incarnation of vertebrate spirituality, whose single arm had raised the corpse of consecrated womanhood in her Mother Church. Then, last of all, their supplement, the delicate, almost boyish figure of the one whose voice was to go crying through the wilderness of an entire world."[14]

This phraseology may strike the modern reader as turgid, but how perfectly it conveys the world in which the would-be monastic-founder was living—absolutely in tune with the thrills thousands of readers were deriving from the recently published novels *East Lynne, The Woman in White*, and *The Cloister and the Hearth*, by Mrs Henry Wood, Wilkie Collins, and Charles Reade respectively.

If Br Joseph was shown some of the treasures at St Dunstan's Abbey, they would have stimulated his romantic approach to the monastic life. Among them were the "Seven Great Rules" engrossed on parchment, signed by the Abbess and sealed with her seal of office; a parchment-bound copy, with an illuminated cover, of "The Chapter Service" (the "Washing of the Sisters' Feet by the Lady Superior"); and two hand-printed Office Books; not forgetting two silver *bénetiers* of elaborate Spanish workmanship.[15]

The Lady Abbess offered a house at Stoke Damerel on an indefinite loan. Furniture was collected for this monastery, and one of its rooms transformed into an oratory. There was a little altar with a crucifix and some candlesticks on either side of it. Only two members of the Society of the Love of Jesus had the courage to test their vocations. They went on before the Founder. That night the whole house "seemed full of supernatural light". The two postulants were alarmed, and on entering the oratory found that a candle had been lit by unseen hands after they had retired to bed.

Dr Pusey, on being informed, "interpreted the manifestation as a Heaven-sent sign of Divine approval, and the lighted taper as an emblem of the illuminating influence which monasticism was to shed upon the Church. At the same time, he urged the Brothers and their Superior to treasure these marks of favour in the silence of their own spirits, and as things too sacred to be desecrated by the touch of public curiosity."[16]

Community-life, however, lasted only forty-eight hours. Br Joseph was laid low with typhoid fever, and nearly died. When he was in delirium, imagining that he was being roasted alive in hell-fires, Dr Pusey sent him a message, which seemed to effect a miraculous recovery. The patient had no doubt that God meant him to be a monk.

Mr and Mrs Lyne decided to take their son to Belgium for convalescence. Abbess Lydia, determined that he shoud not forget that she was sure of his divine vocation, got her sister Caroline to make a nondescript habit, which was posted to London. Mr Lyne Snr. opened the parcel and disposed of the contents. It was only after Br Joseph reached Belgium that he discovered the trick played on him, and informed the Abbess. So she forwarded "a second edition of the habit". The deacon donned it for the first time during solemn Benediction in the Redemptorist church at Brussels. It is recorded that "the Sellon-Pusey garment was a simple monastic dress consisting of a rough serge cassock and hood belonging to no special monkish denomination". As the Rev. Mr Lyne had no idea what species of monk God intended him to be, the costume which he assumed that afternoon was quite suitable. What the congregation thought about this English clergyman robing himself in a monastic motley during Benediction is not recorded.

He stated many years later: "My aim was to discover a Rule which, by its antiquity and conservatism, should render its observance consistent with fidelity to the English Church".[17] We are told that while he was in Belgium "he had every opportunity of studying a diversity of Rules and their sources", because monasteries and convents were "planted almost as thickly as plums in a cake". It is not surprising, however, that he failed to discover the Rule of St Benedict, for at that date the only Benedictine monastery in the country was Termonde in the diocese of Ghent, canonically restored in 1841, and united with the Congregation of Subiaco in 1858. Still, what he supposed was a "monastic vocation" deepened every day. To quote his own words: "I longed to be, to our beloved Church of England, what Père

Lacordaire and other religious men were in the Churches of France and Belgium".[18] For Mr Lyne knew that "he was already a monk in the eyes of God and His Church, having sealed an irrevocable promise with the Supreme Superior of All Things, to live the life of prayer and sacrifice which alone constitutes the essence and glory of the Monastic Intention".[19]

Six months' spiritual diversion in Belgium, restored Br Joseph's health, and he returned to England with his parents. The Rev. Charles Fuge Lowder, who had met the would-be monk in Brussels, invited him to become one of his curates at St Saviour's Mission, in the parish of St George's-in-the-East. This church had obtained nation-wide notoriety during the riots over Ritualism, which started in 1859. Mr Lyne (otherwise Br Joseph) hurled himself into a hectic apostolate in the slums off Ratcliff Highway, then the heart of London's Sailortown, brimful of brothels, dance-halls and gin palaces. His preaching attracted crowds, and he performed a few more alleged miracles, including raising a dead girl to life by touching her breast with a relic of the Holy Cross.

On December 17, 1861, three days after the death of the Prince Consort at Windsor Castle, Mr Lyne called at St Michael's Priory, while staying with the vicar of Clehonger, near Hereford.[20] One of the community, Dom Alphonus Morrell, wrote in his diary: "A young Puseyite came to the church and remained for about half-an-hour at prayer—some portion of the time *prostrate*. At the end he went to Father Prior who happened to go into the Cathedral, and asked for a *hair-shirt!* This led to a little conversation in the guest-rooms—he saw through the monastery, but did not give his name—he was a visitor to this part of the counry."[21]

Never having visited any Benedictine monastery, the group of buildings at Belmont made a deep impression on him. Designed in a simple Gothic style by young Edward Pugin, they were dominated by the still unfinished cruciform church. The interior was devotional, thanks to the varied "Decorated" tracery of the windows, already being filled with stained glass, and the clustered piers and rich arches of the crossing. Moreover there was a proper monastic choir with stalls.

Br Joseph came away with a copy of *The Rule of St Benedict* in Latin, but without the requested hair-shirt. Then he made a pilgrimage to Llanthony Priory in the Black Mountains, founded by Canons Regular of St Augustine in 1103. His biographer related that "a kind of Vision Beautiful dawned upon the enthusiast . . . to restore that Priory, and people it with devout Monks. The train of thought was an enthralling one, all the more because it teemed with impossibilities."[22]

"I read the Rule of St Benedict carefully", so Mr Lyne recorded more than thirty years later. "There was nothing in it inconsistent with fidelity to the English Church. Instead of drawing up a Rule for myself, which would have no authority, I determined to embrace that of St Benedict, which had received the approval of the Western Church in general, and of the Church of England in particular, since the tenth century."[23]

"So I became a Benedictine"—all quite simple. No need to bother about the fifty-eighth chapter of the Rule, entitled "Of the Discipline of receiving Brethren into Religion". Joseph Leycester Lyne was quite sure that *he* did not require "a senior one who is skilled in gaining souls . . . to watch over him with the utmost care, and to see whether he is truly seeking God, and is fervent in the Work of God, in obedience and in humiliations". Already he was fully aware of "all the hard and rugged paths" by which he would "walk towards God". St Benedict was not visualising anybody like this young Anglican deacon when he laid down: "Let not an easy entrance be granted, but, as the Apostle saith, 'Try the spirits if they be of God'."

To continue in the words of this embryo monk: "Two other people were willing to join me now. My father was very angry, and refused to give me any further help. I must also leave my curacy and its stipend and make a beginning. I realised that I should be penniless. I had already drawn a very crowded congregation at Father Lowder's Mission Church, but I had made up my mind to break away from every tie. Relatives, except my mother, would have nothing to say to me. My bright prospects in the Church would be for ever ruined; the world would say I was mad; the Church would regard me as most dangerous, a kind of ecclesiastical Ishmael. I should have to face persecution of every kind—want, suffering, poverty. Yet I firmly believed God was calling me, and I must obey. Also at this time I received many signs from God that I was specially called to this difficult work.[24] Yet I felt how utterly unfitted for it I was. I was very young, not yet in priest's orders, wholly ignorant of the world, and a ready prey for any who care to take advantage of me, as I soon found out."[25]

Having embraced the *Rule of St Benedict*, he determined to act on the Gospel precept: "No man, when he hath lighted a candle, putteth it in a secret place, neither under a bushel, but on a candlestick, that they which come in may see the light. Take heed therefore that the light which is in thee be not darkness".[26] It was an obvious duty to make himself as conspicuous as possible, and to do his utmost not to lead a hidden life. The revived Benedictine Order needed boosting. So there could be no question of taking literally the injunction in the fifty-fifth chapter of the Rule: "Let clothing be given to the brethren suitable to the nature and the climate of the place where they live. . . . And let not the monks complain of the colour or coarseness of these things, but let them be such as can be got in the country where they live, or can be bought most cheaply." So Mr Lyne invented a monastic motley which was utterly unsuitable to the social background of the eighteen sixties, or the climate of England; definitely not the cheapest obtainable.

A striking photograph of him "at the beginning of his campaign against World and Church", taken about the same time that the mortal remains of the Prince Consort were enshrined in the neo-Byzantine-Romanesque mausoleum at Frogmore, shows the deacon posed against a spindly-legged "occasional table", with his left hand gripping the base of a large crucifix, beside which is draped a Rococo-shaped white stole. His hood resembles those he had seen worn by monks of the Anglo-Benedictine Congregation at Belmont Priory, and falls over the back and front of the long scapular. The Franciscan triple-knotted white cord, which he adopted instead of the traditional Benedictine leather belt or cloth cincture, hangs down beside a rosary of black beads, with a large metal crucifix at the bottom. His right hand holds a book, which might be either a Bible or a breviary. There is a haunting beauty about his features. His dome-shaped brow is framed by a wavy tonsure, with his shaven head protected by a *pileolus* or *zucchetto*. It is easy to understand that the pale young curate created a sensation when he first displayed himself on the streets of Shadwell and Wapping in this fantastic ensemble.

Mother Elizabeth Neale and her Sisters of the Holy Cross, who had been founded by Fr Lowder in 1857, attracted far less attention. They shared in the work of this suddenly self-clothed so-called Benedictine monk, and lived in the former Mission House in Calvert Street, providing a home for a few girls rescued from the numerous brothels on and around Ratcliff Highway. Jostling on the pavements with the cosmopolitan crowds of seamen, whose sailing-ships were berthed in the London Docks, their simple black costume was hardly noticed as they ministered to the desperately poor families, housed usually in the squalid streets and alleys. The Monk would have been surprised, had he been told, that this small Sisterhood would develop into a flourishing enclosed Benedictine community, out-living his own foundation.[27]

Framley Parsonage—the fourth of Anthony Trollope's Barsetshire novels—was published in the same year that Mr Lyne decided to become a Benedictine. It is a pity that he did not introduce a young clergyman who yearned for the monastic life, for the opinions of Mrs Proudie, the wife of the Bishop of Barset, on Anglican Benedictinism would have been worth reading.

The Monk's next step was to write a stirring pamphlet on the revival of the Order of St Benedict in the Church of England. It was distributed far and wide among clergy and layfolk likely to give financial help. "The first fruits of this labour were showers of letters from all corners of the kingdom, and, as might be expected, an epistolary hurricane from his own father."[28] On the other hand, Dr Forbes, Bishop of Brechin, wrote: "I thank God for putting into the heart of a Deacon of our Church to restore the Rule of St Benedict of Nursia in our midst".[29]

Sensational Saturday night raids on the notorious "Old Mahogany Bar", "The Prussian Eagle", "The White Swan" (known as "Paddy's Goose"), "The Blue Anchor", "The Brown Bear", and other gin palaces or dance halls around "Tiger Bay" were regarded as helpful towards the restoration of the Benedictine Rule, for the Deacon "felt *called* to come before the world as a Monk", although he knew he would "be exposed to the chaff and ridicule of a world opposed to Monks". He was ready to "suffer every indignity, and perhaps martyrdom".

His bizarre costume caused consternation among some of the patrons of St Saviour's Mission, who threatened to withdraw their subscriptions if the curate persisted in making himself a buffoon. Fr Lowder was worried, and one day he suggested that the Deacon ought to revert to ordinary clerical garb. "Do let me beg of you to do so, Mr Lyne", he said earnestly. "Here are all these people saying they will never give a penny to the Mission unless you respect their objections. What answer am I to give them?"

Mr Lyne silently took up his scapular, and with both hands, measured the space of less than an inch upon its hem. "Tell your patrons", he said slowly, "that I will not yield *that* much of *this*", and he reverently pointed to the sombre black serge and the measured modicum that lay between his thumbs. "But I will do something else", he added, suddenly cheering up, "something that will help you out of your difficulty quite as well, and even better—I will leave!"

Looking back long afterwards he wrote: "I have been pelted with mud and rotten eggs, hooted and jeered by a yelling mob, spit upon, and often in fear of my life; yet, for all that, I wear my Monk's dress still".[30]

The next thing was to choose a religious name for himself. The Monk decided that no better patron could be found than St Ignatius of Loyola, the founder of the Society of Jesus. The militant spirit of this sixteenth-century Papist "Salvation Army" would be the ideal aimed at by the nineteenth-century Anglican Order of St Benedict.

An offer of a monastery came from the Rev. George Drury, Rector of Claydon, Suffolk, who suggested Ipswich as a suitable place for the foundation. The Fish Market was up for sale. So Br Ignatius of Jesus, O.S.B., spent a weekend at Claydon in November 1862, and preached in the church. Mr Drury took him to Ipswich, where they met two lawyers, one of whom, Mr Jackaman, agreed to act as treasurer for the Order. The Deacon returned to London without anything definite having been arranged.

On January 19, 1863, he wrote to Mr Drury: that if the Order were to come to Ipswich "*all* business matters would have to be left in the hands of those who had invited the monks". He felt unable to sign any agreement with the solicitors, explaining: "If we come down *without* the promised aid to start with, we should positively not have food to eat. . . . So you see I must place our Ipswich Mission *entirely* in

47

the hands of the Church there. If I HAD money and was going to take the house myself, I should sign myself only as Brother Ignatius on behalf of the brothers in general. I suppose the Fish Market would be the place for our Chapel and School. The Church Institute I suppose would not interfere with the Cloistered privacy of the Monastery?" This rambling letter was inscribed: "✠ IGNATIUS, O.S.B. Supr."[31]

Feeling sorry for the Monk, Mr and Mrs Drury finally decided to offer temporary hospitality in an unused wing of their large rectory. This would enable the Benedictines to gain the support of Tractarian-minded clergy and layfolk in Suffolk, and perhaps enable them to rent or buy the former Fish Market at Ipswich as the first monastery of "The English Order of St Benedict". Its nature was as shadowy as that of the medieval world depicted in the latest volume of Mr Tennyson's *Idylls of the King,* which people had been reading since 1859. They contained the poems entitled "Enid", "Vivien", "Elaine", and "Guinevere".

NOTES

[1] The College had been founded in 1846 on High Church lines, the scheme having been planned five years earlier. The first part of the buildings, designed by William Butterfield in the Gothic Revival style, were ready for occupation in 1847. Dr Charles Wordsworth, Bishop of St Andrew, Dunkeld and Dunblane from 1853 to 1892, was the first Warden.

[2] The 2nd Baron de Tabley was treasurer of Queen Victoria's household from 1868 to 1872. The lineage of the Leycesters of Toft, Cheshire, went back to the 14th century.

[3] *Autobiography of Father Ignatius, O.S.B.* (1896), p. 4.

[4] ibid.

[5] The Baroness de Bertouch, *The Life of Father Ignatius O.S.B., The Monk of Llanthony* (1904) p. 65. All subsequent quotations, unless otherwise stated, are taken from this biography. It is really an autobiography, for the Monk often dictated whole sections to the authoress, thus revealing how he wanted people to picture himself and his career.

The Baroness, born Miss Elmslie (related to the Salvation Army family of Booth), had married a Danish nobleman whose family claimed descent from the 6th century Lords of Malines and Charlemagne. She became a Roman Catholic, but separated from her husband, having published a book of poems entitled *Passion Flowers.* After her conversion by Fr Ignatius at the Portman Rooms, London, she offered to write his Life. For the greater part of two years she and her son, the future Baron Rudolph, stayed at Plas Genevieve, Llanthony, where this unique biography was written according to the wishes of the subject. The style may be flamboyant, but there are few facts that are not correct.

[6] ibid, p. 66.

[7] *Autobiography,* p. 4.

[8] De Bertouch, op. cit., pp. 66-7.

[9] St Andrew's Cathedral was opened in 1869. The vast diocese of Moray, Ross and Caithness was very poor when Dr Eden was appointed bishop in 1851, with only eight parishes and two rectories.

[10] p. 70.

[11] p. 87.

[12] Priscilla Lydia Sellon (c. 1821-1876) was the daughter of Commander W. R. B. Sellon, R.N. In 1848, when about to leave England for health reasons, she changed her plans at the last moment as the result of a public appeal by Bishop Phillpotts, for workers among the destitute poor in Plymouth, Devonport and Stonehouse. This led to her founding (with Dr Pusey's help) what was first known as the "Church of England Sisterhood of Mercy of Devonport and Plymouth". It grew rapidly, and in 1856, Mother Lydia united her own community with the Sisterhood of the Holy Cross, founded by Dr Pusey in 1845. Having assumed the title of Lady Abbess, she gave the amalgamated body the name of the "Society of the Most Holy Trinity". (Cf. T. J. Williams, *Priscilla Lydia Sellon* (revised edition 1965).)

[13] p. 93.

[14] pp. 94-5.

[15] Cf. T. J. Williams, *Priscilla Lydia Sellon* (revised edition, 1965), pp. 341-43 (contents of the Iron-bound Coffer).

[16] p. 97.

[17] p. 105.

[18] p. 103.

[19] p. 105.

[20] In 1859 Mr F. R. Wegg-Prosser handed over to the English Benedictine Congregation the church which he had started to build while still an Anglican, together with the adjacent land situated on his estates. A monastery was erected and was turned into a general novitiate for the Congregation, also a house of studies. Belmont was raised to the status of Pro-Cathedral of the diocese of Newport and Menevia, whose first bishop was the Benedictine monk, Thomas Joseph Brown, who died in 1880.

[21] A. Calder-Marshall, *The Enthusiast* (1962), p. 77.

[22] p. 129.

[23] *Autobiography*, p. 6.

[24] The alleged miracles.

[25] ibid, pp. 6-7.

[26] Luke 11 : 33 (Authorized Version).

[27] See p. 268.

[28] p. 135.

[29] p. 107.

[30] p. 133.

[31] Cf. Calder-Marshall, op. cit., pp. 80-1.

CHAPTER II

Nine months of monastic life at Claydon Rectory: the Suffolk
"Subiaco" of the Anglican "Order of St Benedict" (1863)

SHROVE TUESDAY, 1863, deserves to be remembered as the birthday of the first attempt to build up the Benedictine waste places of *Ecclesia Anglicana*. That morning Br Ignatius of Jesus and two young men left London on the Eastern Counties Railway, bound for Ipswich, whence they were driven to Claydon, a distance of three and a half miles. Its parish church, dedicated to St Peter, restored by Mrs Drury, who had designed the new chancel, stood on high ground commanding an extensive prospect. The grounds of the rectory and its gardens were neatly arranged and ornamented with fine timber. The services were conducted on quite advanced "Puseyite" lines. This monastic migration attracted little or no attention, for the general public was far more interested in the arrival of Princess Alexandra of Denmark in London, who married the Prince of Wales on March 10.

The large rectory, with its staff of servants, afforded more comfortable accommodation than the cave in the mountains near Subiaco, which became the home of Benedict of Nursia after he had heard the call of the cloister about A.D. 500. Unlike his patron Ignatius of Loyola, Ignatius of Jesus saw no reason to spend a year in solitude before founding his Order. Throughout his life he was always terrified of being left alone, even at night.

Having embraced the sixth-century Rule of St Benedict the Anglican deacon did not think it worth while for him to acquire an idea of how it was being observed by monks in the nineteenth-century. He could have done so at Ampleforth, Downside and Belmont Priories belonging to the venerable English Benedictine Congregation, re-founded by Pope Urban VIII in 1633. Yet it can be believed that he would have been shocked by the somewhat mitigated presentation of monastic life in each of the three establishments. Ampleforth and Downside had colleges for boys attached to them. Ignatius of Jesus would have been disgusted by the sight of the monks disguised as ordinary clergymen outside the immediate precincts. Perhaps he would have found St Augustine's Monastery, Ramsgate, more congenial. It had been established in 1856 from the Proto-Abbey of St Scholastica, Subiaco, when Dr Grant, the Roman Catholic Bishop of Southwark, handed over the missions of Ramsgate, Margate and Deal to the monks. But, unlike Ignatius of Jesus, Abbot Casaretto had no intention of encouraging the young Benedictines in exhibitionism. In fact, he took every precaution not to stir up Protestant antagonism on the Isle of Thanet, though permitting strict rules of fasting and abstinence, also rising during the night to recite Matins and Lauds. Neither did Ignatius bother to pay even a flying visit to Mount St Bernard's Abbey, where he would have been impressed by the austere life of the Trappist community.

The revival of the Benedictine Order in the Established Church of England by a freelance deacon was merely a pebble on the beach or a drop of water in the ocean compared with the state of the now world-wide Benedictine family in 1863. Since 1852 Bavarian and Swiss monks had founded five monasteries in the United States of America. English Benedictines began missionary work in New South Wales in 1832, and Spanish ones in Western Australia in 1846. Monastic life was growing steadily in France. In 1850 Père Muard had formed a community of Benedictine missionaries at Pierre-qui-Vire, and in 1853 Abbot Guéranger of Solesmes had founded a priory at Ligugé. The establishment of the provisional monastery at Claydon Rectory was contemporary with the re-founding of Beuron Abbey in Germany by Dom Maurus Wolter.[1]

On arriving at Claydon the two young postulants were given the religious names of Anselm and Martin. The former was an ardent "Ritualist", known in the world as Charles Walker. The Superior had very vague ideas as to how his Order was to be run, and accepted Mr Drury's offer to deal with all mundane business, with Br Anselm as Prior. The rector, however, did not regard it necessary to consult the Hon. John T. Pelham, fourth son of the second Earl of Clarendon, who had been Bishop of Norwich and titular Abbot of St Benet's, Hulme, since 1857, about the foundation of a Benedictine brotherhood in his diocese. Neither did he bother to ask his Local Ordinary to license the deacon as curate of Claydon.

Thanks to Charles Walker's *Three Months in an English Monastery*, published in 1864, after its author had returned to the world, having found it impossible to keep the Ignatian interpretation of the Benedictine Rule, we have a vivid and detailed knowledge of what life was like during the nine months spent by the monks at Claydon Rectory.

Two hours after midnight the Superior went round the bedrooms, holding a large candle, arousing the sleepers with the injunction *Benedicamus Domino*. If the monk—before long there were about half-a-dozen—failed to wake up, he had to recite the whole psalter between Sext and Nones as a penance. "Nocturns" and all the other offices were recited in the parish church. The only liturgical book available was a folio seventeenth-century *Breviarium Monasticum*. Charles Walker recalled that "it involved the translation, often extempore, of the antiphon, lessons, collects, etc., as well as the expurgation of anything 'Roman' that might occur in the former or latter portions". Br Ignatius and Br Anselm were the only two members of the little community who had any knowledge of Latin. The hymns were taken from Helmore's *Hymnal Noted* (1851) which provided Gregorian chants—not nearly tuneful enough to satisfy the Superior's taste. The *Psalter Noted*, published by Helmore in 1849, gave the "correct" tones for the Prayer Books psalms.

Br Anselm also recorded that "it was no easy matter to find the places in the large folio resting on the lectern and the smaller book of Common Prayer that supplied the psalms, collects, etc., nor to give out the antiphon in a voice sufficiently audible to reach the Superior at the organ. It not infrequently happened that on a feast day, when the antiphon was of unusual length, and had to be broken up into short pieces in order to be remembered, the Superior would conclude that a portion was the whole and the remainder would be omitted."

Most mornings Mr Drury celebrated the Holy Communion, wearing eucharistic vestments. The rectory cook had to prepare special *maigre* menus for the monks, for they did not take their meals with the family. On the other hand, it was not regarded as incompatible with their Rule to play with the Drury children during times of recreation, occasionally wheeling the younger ones round the garden in "an old four-wheeled chaise of a date anterior to perambulators". The brethren also made themselves useful by teaching in the church schools.

Ignatius of Jesus, O.S.B. had no scruples about his monks being treated as objects of charity. He soon ceased to worry about finding a permanent monastery. One day he got a shock when Mr Drury asked him to contribute £40 a year towards the board and lodging which had been provided gratis since Shrove Tuesday. There was no cash in hand, but the Superior was sure that there would be another miracle sooner or later.

This untraditional, not to say unconventional, presentation of monastic life would have puzzled the pre-Reformation Benedictines of Bury St Edmunds (1020), Colchester (1095) and Walden (1136) had they returned to East Anglia. What the Cistercians of Coggeshall (1140) and Tiltey (1153) would have thought about it is difficult to imagine. Nevertheless some people were greatly impressed by what they found at Claydon Rectory. One visitor stated that it was "a living panorama of the times of St Benedict and St Basil, or the ages when those far Egyptian deserts were peopled with Antonys and Pachomiuses".

The Suffolk "monkery" never lacked publicity. A writer in *The Union Review* (probably Dr F. G. Lee) wrote enthusiastically about "this quiet spot, with its careful ritual, the constant round of the Brothers' Offices, its waking the dead of night with its call for Nocturns, and the deeper booming of the Angelus at early morning, noon and again at even; the Brothers seen here and there in their sombre and picturesque habits". Indeed, he could almost "fancy that the Re-Union of Christendom, which is the object of our prayers, had already taken place at Claydon".[2]

The privacy of the rectory gardens and grounds was often disturbed by the crowds who wanted to get a peep of the monks. Within three months Claydon village became a veritable Mecca for pilgrims, pious and otherwise. The main attraction, however, was "the strange young Ascetic, whose fiery eloquence, peculiar dress and fragile appearance made him a target for a volley of gossip and idle speculation".[3]

Loyal Protestants all over Suffolk were aroused by the reports of Romanism in disguise, and mummeries of superstition indulged at the Claydon "monkery". It was hardly credible that a banner embroidered with a figure of the Virgin Mary had been borne aloft during a procession on Ascension Day, so that all could bow down and worship it. Even more sinister were the reports of the goings on at the patronal festival, held on St Peter's day, June 29. The Superior, garbed in his monkish motley, had presided at what was called the "High Celebration", leading the village lads and lassies while they sang a *Kyrie* adapted from bits of Mendelssohn's *Elijah;* a *Sanctus* and *Benedictus* taken from Mozart's second and twelfth Masses, with the *Agnus Dei* and *O Salutaris,* said to be by various composers. But this was not all the idolatry: after choral Evensong black-robed Benedictines carried banners during an outdoor procession. Acolytes in scarlet cassocks and lace-trimmed surplices held crucifixes and candles, while one boy even waved a smoking censer. The chief attraction, so it was said, had been the Monk's sermon. The church was packed to suffocation. Men and boys squatted on the floor. People had driven over to Claydon from miles around for the chance of listening to Br Ignatius of Jesus.

So optimistic was he of the success of his building up the monastic waste places, even if he had not yet found a proper monastery, that he suddenly decided to establish a Third Order for the benefit of layfolk of both sexes. What he either forgot or ignored was that there never had been Benedictine Tertiaries since the Rule had been drawn up on Monte Cassino early in the sixth-century.[4]

Most of the local farmers were staunch Protestants, and they encouraged their tenants and servants to harass the monks. One wealthy landowner promised to give £1000 to anybody able to destroy this hornets' nest. A rat-catcher employed by him boasted that he would "do" for that Ignatius before very long. The Tertiaries were mobbed on their way to church, which was desecrated, and a stained-glass window smashed. Gentlemen had to conduct ladies home at night. One day it was reported that Mr Drury had been killed. The rectory servants fainted or indulged in hysterics, but the Rector had only been hit by a stone. Br Ignatius fully expected that he would be martyred by the rat-catcher some evening. So wide-spread became the notoriety of Claydon that even *The Times* felt it worth while to publish an article on the riots aroused by the Benedictines.

No such scenes of violence had occurred in 1857 when a community of Roman Catholic Benedictine nuns had moved from Winchester to East Bergholt, ten miles south of Claydon, where a new convent had been built for them.[5] There appears to be no record of Ignatius visiting St Mary's Abbey. Had he done so, he could have learned much from these enclosed nuns, with an unbroken history of more than 250 years.

By this time, Dr Pelham, Bishop of Norwich, was very worried by the disturbances at Claydon. He summoned Ignatius to Norwich, and begged him to give up his eccentricities and absurd dress, but to no purpose. The result was that the Monk was inhibited from preaching in any church of the diocese. Mr Drury was told that nobody but himself could occupy the Claydon pulpit. So "Father Blazer" (as the Protestant agitators called Ignatius) went on giving "lectures" in the rectory barn. More riots took place. A huge bonfire was lighted one evening on which the Superior would be cast and roasted alive. This nearly happened, but just as Ignatius was being hauled off an old woman hit his capturer with "a mighty pewter teapot . . . fair and square on the top of his head".[6] The Monk was led back to the rectory. Its doors were locked and windows barred for fear of a mass attack by the infuriated mob.

When the Rev. Joseph Leycester Lyne decided to become a Benedictine, he visualised his life as a holy war, with himself as a general or sergeant-major ruling his subjects with a rod of iron, and military discipline. He saw no reason to try to emulate St Benedict, who stated in the Prologue of the Rule: "Our task, therefore, is to establish a school of the Lord's service, in the setting forth of which we hope we shall not make rules that are harsh or burdensome". He had no vision of Benedictine peace in the traditional sense, but of a constant battle against the world, the flesh and the devil.

After six months at Claydon, Ignatius of Jesus was so exhausted with fighting the good fight with all his might that friends feared that another attack of "brain fever" was imminent. Mr and Mrs Drury—probably craving for a brief spell of peace—managed to persuade him to take a brief holiday in the Scottish Highlands, and agreed to look after his monks, lest they got up to mischief. This journey appeared to be justified because Ignatius had heard of talk of establishing a sisterhood in the Scottish Episcopal Church, with himself as founder. His old friend, Mrs Cameron of Lakefield, Glenurquhart, offered to cover the cost of the trip to "North Britain". The Benedictine travelled in his picturesque black uniform, mindful of the Gospel precept: "Let your light shine before men, that they may see your good works, and glorify your Father which is in heaven".

He appears to have met with no opposition, except at Carrbridge, Inverness-shire, where the Free Kirk minister denounced him as a Jesuit in disguise. The Monk and "Mamsie" (Mrs Cameron) felt it wiser to move on to Kingussie, where they found lodgings with "some excellent Roman Catholic people". Here "the religious climate was warm with spiritual sympathy and suggestion, and its genial influence, added to the magic of the bracing Highland air, achieved wonders in building up the weary nerves and energies of the overworked young Monk."[7]

There was no Episcopalian place of worship within access, but on Holy Cross Day, September 14, the Rev. George Akers, then assisting the Rev. F. G. Lee at St Mary's, Carden Place, Aberdeen, came over and celebrated the Scottish Liturgy in the "best parlour" of the cottage, with the table adorned with lights and flowers. Ignatius recalled forty years later that after this "House Mass", "the chalice containing the Sacred Elements was borne slowly round the garden, Mr Macdonald heading the procession with a standard Cross of mountain heather". We are told that the

Benedictine returned to Claydon "as a giant refreshed—a giant of energy, if not of strength". But the Anglican sisterhood he had hoped to found got no further than his imagination.

On arriving at the rectory he was informed by Mr and Mrs Drury that he must find new quarters for the community. By this time they realised that it was quite impossible for them to go on dispensing hospitality to half-a-dozen able-bodied young men who maintained that they lacked the means to contribute a penny towards board and lodging. Ignatius was in a quandary, and feared he might be forced to disband his Order of St Benedict. This is what Mr Lyne Snr. hoped would happen, and he offered to pay for his deacon-son to spend the winter in Italy. A prolonged rest and change of scene was obviously needed. If Joseph would give up all further idea of leading the life of a monk, his father was willing to help him to find a congenial curacy.

The Benedictine was in such a state of mental and physical prostration when he received this letter that he was tempted to submit, but he resorted to prayer for several days before giving an answer. One morning when Mr Drury was celebrating the Holy Communion and had elevated the Host, Ignatius had a vision—"in that breathless space the Monk saw a single ray of glory leap out of the resplendent orb, flash like a mirror across the silent sanctuary, and bury itself finally in his own troubled heart".[8]

He knew for certain that this meant he was to pursue his self-chosen path, and that God had chosen him to revive the Order of St Benedict, even if he was penniless. He started to look around for a property that would serve as a monastery, but all were quite beyond his means. One day a gentleman arrived from Norwich, inviting him to inspect a rambling old house there with about forty rooms, which stood on part of the site of the Dominican Priory founded in 1226. After Ignatius had gone over Elm House he felt sure it would make an ideal monastery, even if the adjacent medieval chapel of the Black Friars now served as a dance-hall.

The news of the probable migration of the monks to Norfolk was received with mixed sentiments. Even now the more militant Protestants plotted to murder "Father Blazer". One day when walking through Ipswich he was attacked by a mob, and hit by a brick. A miracle occurred in the shape of a certain Miss Mayhew, opening her door, and dragging the monk inside. He was revived by a glass of wine, and after an hour's rest returned to Claydon. "Strange to say, not so much as a child looked at him askance as he wended his way home that day."[9]

So hated was Ignatius of Jesus that a Suffolk Rural Dean gave orders that a brick some workmen had asked the Monk to bless must be taken out of the wall of the house, although several courses of brickwork had to be removed for the purpose. This clergyman feared that it would contaminate his parish.

Money had to be raised somehow, and Mr Drury suggested a preaching tour. It started at Ipswich where the profits came to £13. Then the Monk travelled from town to town in the south and west of England, as far as Portleven in Cornwall. He returned to London, where St Mary Magdalene's, Munster Square, was packed to the doors, so great was the curiosity to see a real live Benedictine. The collection amounted to £30—just what he needed to make up £300. The service over he boarded a bus, and on dismounting found his purse was missing. The recital of ten "Our Fathers" worked yet another miracle by the purse being given back to its owner.

Soon after rejoining his brethren at Claydon Ignatius was visited by three gentlemen from Norwich, who said a deposit of £50 would give the Benedictines right of entry. The remainder of the purchase price of Elm House—£500—could be paid by small instalments. On January 20, 1864, the Monk wrote to a friend: "Today I received the intelligence from Norwich that the old Dominican premises are ours. *Deo gratias!"*

NOTES

[1] Br Ignatius and his two novices were not the first Anglican religious to appear in Suffolk. In 1861 Dr Neale sent a few members of the Society of St Margaret from East Grinstead to Ipswich, where they worked for some years.

[2] op. cit. 1963, p. 544.

[3] p. 139.

[4] A short-lived Cistercian Third Order had been founded by Dom Augustine de Lestrange, appointed Abbot of La Grande Trappe in 1794, while its monks were exiled in Switzerland. Its purpose was the instruction of youth, but it was suppressed after the death of the Abbot in 1827.

[5] This community had been founded at Brussels in 1598 by Lady Mary Percy, for English women obliged to seek the religious life overseas. The nuns managed to escape during the French Revolution and were given a house at Winchester, where they conducted a small girls' school. They remained at East Bergholt from 1857 until the beginning of World War Two, when they were evacuated to their present home—St Mary's Abbey, Haslemere, Surrey.

[6] p. 148.

[7] p. 152.

[8] p. 159.

ELM HILL PRIORY, NORWICH, 1864–1866

"A weird and rambling old mansion, containing about forty rooms, some in a half-ruined condition. . . Since those good old days, it had lain long unused, its last tenant having been a rag merchant. . . There was the ghost of Monachism to be met at every turn." (Baroness de Bertouch.)

CHAPTER III

*How the Benedictines returned to Norwich after three centuries
and of the life led by them at the Priory of Our Ladye and
St Dunstan for eighteen months (1864-1865)*

IT was about 1096 that Bishop Herbert Losinga, formerly a monk of Fécamp,
introduced the Benedictines to Norwich and placed them in charge of his new
cathedral, which continued to be staffed by monks until 1538, when the prior became
the first dean, and six prebendal stores were created. January 30, 1864—the feast of
St Charles King and Martyr, abolished by Royal and Parliamentary authority in
1859, without consent of the Church as represented in Convocation—was indeed a
historic occasion with the return of the Benedictines to this city after an interval of
326 years. But there were no public rejoicings. The whole business had to be kept
secret lest the Bishop, Dean and Chapter tried to prevent the foundation.

It was a bitterly cold day with snow on the ground. The brethren shivered in their
sombre uniforms, and one hopes they managed to get iron foot-warmers to prevent
their bare feet getting chilblains in the unheated third-class carriage on the train.
Their new home had served partly as a rag-warehouse for several years. Many of
its windows and doors were broken. The wind soughed through the empty rooms.
There was only one small bed. Two of the monks had to sleep on the bare boards that
first night, with a dog to keep them warm. The community, consisting of three men,
were not yet the legal owners of the property, which had been purchased in the
name of Mr Stephen Balls, a member of the Third Order.[1]

The Baroness de Bertouch felt it worth while to devote about 150 pages of her
monumental biography to the two years spent by the Benedictines at Norwich, but
which can only be dealt with briefly in this book. If Ignatius has been asked why
they were so troubled, he could have quoted the words of our Lord: "Suppose ye
that I am come to give peace on earth? I tell you, Nay; but rather division: For
henceforth there shall be five in one house divided, three against two, and two against
three. The father shall be divided against the son, and the son against the father."[2]

Within a fortnight half-a-dozen young men turned up to test their vocations to
the monastic life. Some seem to have chosen the monastery as the alternative to the
workhouse, or as a temporary refuge from the streets. Br Ignatius was ready to give
a home to anybody. He never bothered to obtain testimonial letters from aspirants,
or to fulfil the conditions imposed by Roman Canon Law for valid admission to a
novitiate.

Although the now twenty-seven year-old Superior had never fallen into line with
the procedure for admitting brethren as laid down in chapter fifty-eight of the Rule
of St Benedict, yet he felt justified in taking life-vows of Stability, Conversion of
Manners and Obedience soon after he arrived at Norwich. It is not certain who
received these vows, but both Dr Pusey and Mr Drury are possible. After this
Ignatius assumed the style of "Father".

Fortunately the miscellaneous group of monks was soon regarded as a deserving
object of charity. Offerings were made—sacks of coal or coke, baskets of fish, pots
of jam, pats of butter, small portions of meat, loaves of bread, packets of tea,
coffee, cough-lozenges, and soap, likewise bags of potatoes. One woman brought

THE CHAPEL, PRIORY OF OUR LADYE & ST DUNSTAN, NORWICH, 1865

"In the Tabernacle dwelt the Eucharistic Presence, and before it hung the sentinel lamp which never sleeps. . . This Catholic resurrection, executed under the artistic eye of the Superior, can only be compared with an awakening from an unbroken sleep of nigh three hundred years." (Baroness de Bertouch.)

two fenders, having nothing else to give. Another presented her own frilled flannel dressing-gown to the Father Superior. A doctor offered his services gratis. The first of many alleged miracles at the Priory was the tolling of a bell on its own volition.

One of the upper rooms were turned into an oratory, and opened to the public on Ash Wednesday. We are told that "the place was literally crammed to suffocation, many who could not elbow their way further contenting themselves with being squeezed into a few cubic inches in the passage". From then onwards the oratory was "systematically thronged with Dissenters, Roman Catholics, and Anglicans alike, and indeed by all denominations except that of the Protestant party, to whom this new outrage on the part of the 'terrible Monk' was the challenge it was impotent to avenge". Looking back on the past, Fr Ignatius told his biographer that in less than two months of his arrival at Norwich, it was "no exaggeration to assert that the largest city in all eastern England, and the hotbed of Protestantism, might have been mistaken for a Clairvaux or Assisi, so utterly had it passed under the dominion of the young stranger Monk. The name of Ignatius was now in every mouth. It rushed into print, furnished the theme for drawing-room gossip, and found its way into the more serious circles of clerical conclaves."[3]

The Monk took the line that the Priory was exempt from the jurisdiction of the local ordinary, thus it was unnecessary to ask for the oratory to be licensed, like a proprietary chapel, so that the Holy Communion could be celebrated therein. Ignatius was also convinced that, although merely a deacon, he had the right to reserve the Consecrated Elements. He said that he had read somewhere that this was "sanctioned by the Early Church". He was still under a ban, and forbidden to officiate in any church of the Norwich diocese.

The Rev. Gerard Moultrie, then a curate of a parish near Bristol, was appointed by Ignatius as non-resident chaplain. After his first brief visit of only three days he wrote a letter which was published in the *Church Times,* stating: "The movement may be fanatical, and it may be irregular in its working at first, but it is assuredly not a thing to be laughed at. . . . Give that young Monk standing-room, and he will shake English Protestantism to its centre. I could not have believed that in two months, or in two years, such a work could have been done for souls as I saw before me at Norwich. It was marvellous."[4]

A sensation was caused by what seemed the miraculous conversion of the hitherto "Low Church" Mr E. A. Hillyard, rector of St Lawrence's. The community started to attend his church on Sunday mornings. This resulted in riots. Membership of the Third Order increased rapidly. Men and boys were "ready to stand by the Reverend Father like faithful bulldogs when danger signals were along the line".[5] Before long there was said to be nearly five-hundred lads attending Bible Classes at the Priory. Great indignation was aroused throughout the Norwich Diocese after Ignatius had ordered his bulldogs to rip up the pews in St Lawrence's, because he disapproved of pew-rents.

The monastic finances remained in a state of chaos, for the Superior insisted on keeping all money in a baize bag. When there was nothing left, he went off and gave a Mission, being sure that he would return home with it bulging again.

Such vast crowds were now attending the unlicensed oratory that the Monk turned two rooms on the ground floor into a more spacious chapel, which was furnished in the most ornate manner. There was a magnificent tabernacle on the high altar. The walls were cluttered up with banners, statuettes, and pious pictures. Not only was there a Lady Altar, but also shrines dedicated to St Benedict, St Dunstan and St William, the twelfth-century boy-martyr of Norwich, alleged to have been murdered by two Jews. The services were enriched by ceremonial supposed to be either Anglo-Saxon or medieval English.

The great attraction throughout Lent were two large pictures indicative of Eternity and Punishment hung on either side of the altar; the former represented by a life-size skeleton, and the latter by a human figure writhing in the flames of hell-fires. "So graphic and realistic are these pictures said to have been, that on first seeing them several of the congregation are reported to have shrieked aloud."[6]

By this time a certain Br Augustine had been appointed private secretary to the Superior, also choirmaster because he was good with men and boys. Shortly after Easter 1864 he published a leaflet entitled *The Benedictine Brothers at Norwich*, stating that there were ten men in residence at the Priory of Our Ladye and St Dunstan, living under the strictest form of the Benedictine Rule. He continued: "It is indeed a marvel to the nineteenth-century people of Norwich to find revived in their midst the real Monastic Life in its fullness, to see the sandalled and tonsured Monk again pleading with sinners in burning language to turn to a pardoning God. Nightly over the sleeping city, soon after midnight, the sweet sound of the Convent bell is heard calling the monks to their solemn Nocturn service; and now and then, returning from some nightly debauch, the man of the world may stroll into the Convent Chapel invited by the strange and mysterious note of the Matin bell, as it strikes the still night air, chasing away possibly many an evil spirit from its old abode, unable to linger lest perchance the adoring hymn or the plaintive chant should steal upon its unhallowed ear."

The monks were desperately poor, dependent entirely on alms. They "could not even afford to have the roof of their ruinous abode repaired, and other positively necessary things done in the Monastery". Also urgently needed was the sum of £600 to pay off the remainder of the purchase money for the property. Both bedding and furniture were wanted. If only kind friends would donate "trinkets, jewellery and lace", for conversion into money to beautify God's House.

Br Augustine related that "A Boys' School is already commenced in the Monastery, and a working Confraternity for young men living in the world, which already consists of several members in Norwich—and many more are applying for admission to its ranks. Throughout the length and breadth of the land young men are applying to the Superior respecting the Order, and the qualifications for entering the novitiate. . . . The Brothers are most anxious to fit up a wing of their house for the reception of twelve boarders, whose education would be carefully superintended by those Brothers who have been accustomed to the tuition of youth. A good classical and general education would be imparted. It would require about £100 or more to prepare a portion of the Convent for the reception of pupils. Earnestly do the Brothers crave the assistance of Churchmen for this special object."

This vision of the Anglican Benedictine Priory at Norwich (banned by the Bishop) becoming a rival to the colleges conducted by the Roman Catholic monks of Ampleforth and Downside never took shape. Neither did the new chapel able to hold 4,000 persons ever materialise. Br Augustine's leaflet ended with the words: "Oh! If the Monks could raise the funds to repurchase the magnificent Priory Church of the old Blackfriars which adjoins the Monastery—a glorious shrine for God! They long to do so, and would do so, if Christians would enable them."

Still there was enough money in the baize bag during Paschal-tide for the Reverend Father to tighten up the material enclosure of his monastery. Although only obligatory in post-Tridentine Roman Canon Law for female communities with Papal Enclosure, a wooden grille was erected, also a "turning-box" through which objects could be passed between the monks and layfolk. This helped to create a sense of monastic mystery, even if the brethren were still able to mix freely with females in the chapel. Its furnishings grew more and more gorgeous, as can be seen in an old painted photograph. The *tout-ensemble* must have been stupendous, for no Anglo-

Catholic church in Britain had reached such a stratospheric height by the spring of 1864.

The constantly changing members of the community were able to enjoy both festive and penitential functions. On one occasion, to drive home the horrors of sin and hell-fire to his flock, Ignatius of Jesus ordered a converted prostitute to make reparation for her evil life. She stood bare-foot before the congregation, clad in a white sheet, and holding "a sordid tallow candle". Part of the ritual involved drinking a glass of water mingled with ashes. It is recorded that "the brave composure with which she supported this humiliating ordeal, could have been nothing less than an echo of the joy which the angels of God were surely experiencing at that moment over the one sinner who repenteth".[7]

Having added the reclamation of fallen women to their works of mercy and charity, the half-dozen or so young monks, none of whom were as yet professed even in simple vows, must have found it difficult to lead a normal sort of monastic life. They were already trying to run a boarding-school for boys, directing a confraternity for youths, as well as an increasing Third Order.

Although Ignatius of Jesus when he was ordained deacon had given his assent to the twenty-eighth Article of Religion stating that "The Sacrament of the Lord's Supper was not by Christ's ordinance reserved, carried about, lifted up or worshipped", yet within three months of arriving in Norwich he decided that the extra-liturgical rite of Benediction was essential for the spiritual uplift of his Benedictines. Strange to say, the monks who had served the Cathedral from 1096 to 1538 had managed to get on without it.[8] It was not enough that that consecrated Bread should be reserved lifted up, and worshipped in the Priory chapel, the more it was carried about the streets of Norwich, so much the better.

First of all it was necessary to find out how Benediction, Exposition, and processions of the Blessed Sacrament must be carried out correctly. The first edition of Mr Purchas' *Directorium Anglicanum*, published in 1859, was no help because it only gave directions how the services in the *Book of Common Prayer* could be enriched "According to the Ancient Uses of the *Church* of England". No matter: the fullest possible instructions were forthcoming in the second edition of *The Sacristan's Manual* by the Rev. J. D. Hilarius Dale, issued in 1860, where every detail "harmonized with the most approved commentaries on the Roman Ceremonial and the latest Decrees of the Sacred Congregation of Rites".

So the Anglican deacon took care to acquire a *Remonstrance* "of material as costly as can be well afforded", with a *lunette* of gold or silver gilt "placed in the centre of rays resembling a sun". Even if not mentioned in the "Things appertaining to Churches" of the *Constitutions and Canons Ecclesiastical* (1604), or ornaments of the Church of England in use "by the authority of Parliament, in the second year of the reign of King Edward the Sixth", the Reverend Father felt it his duty to buy many more devotional articles. He had no intention of falling into line with the "rubrick" of the Prayer Book: "The chancels shall remain as they have done in times past".

Fr Ignatius did his best to obey the orders of Fr Hilarius by purchasing a couple of censers, boats (with spoons), humeral veil, a Throne of Exposition, and a white veil to cover the monstrance when not in use. At least a dozen candlesticks had to stand on the gradines of the high altar, also plenty of flower-vases. Chasubles, copes, cottas, dalmatics and tunicles were required. A procession of the Most Holy Sacrament would not be correct without a canopy or *baldacchino* of white costly materials, supported by six or eight poles, with small bells hanging from its deep-fringed borders. Four processional lanterns, containing candles, were obligatory.

The first outdoor eucharistic procession took place on Ascension Day, 1864, without permission from Bishop Pelham. The Benedictine related to his biographer that "for the first time since the prohibitive knell of the Reformation was heard in the British Church, the Blessed Sacrament was carried in pious jubilee through the streets of Norwich, with bell, lights, and incense, and accompanied by a huge concourse of people (townsfolk of all denominations), besides Monks, Acolytes, and Third Order Brothers and Sisters. The Brothers bore an image of the Blessed Virgin in their midst, while the Sisters carried Her banner. One of the most beautiful features of the proceedings was the group of young girls dressed in white and blue, who scattered flowers in front of the glittering monstrance. It is stated by contemporary journalists that the blaze of light emanating from this historical cortège could be seen at a distance of four miles off."[9] Ignatius himself took no active part in the function beyond walking beside the canopy and keeping a close watch on the crowd with his hypnotic eyes.[10]

A second and even more magnificent procession of the Blessed Sacrament took place on the feast of Corpus Christi, but the Father Superior was prevented by illness from accompanying it. A furious mob charged on the crowds within a few moments of leaving the Priory, and the priest carrying the Host had to make a hasty retreat. Order having been restored by the police, the procession wended its way through the streets. An imposing *reposoir* had been erected on St Andrew's Plain. We are told that "it was a glorious and incredible sight to see the shining monstrance raised to the four quarters of the compass before breathless masses of the many denominations of Christianity in which the provincial heart of England so plentifully abounds."[11]

Newspapers throughout England found good copy in this spectacular function. A local journalist reported that "at the instigation of the notorious Superior of Elm Hill Priory, 'the Host' had been actually carried in broad daylight through the streets of Protestant Norwich". No wonder that the Church Association was founded shortly afterwards to maintain the Protestant ideals of faith and worship in the Church of England.

Determined to demonstrate that he was an Anglican Loyalist by defying his local Ordinary still further, the suspended Deacon organised the first of several public pilgrimages to St Wulstan's Well, about four miles from the city. Parties of over four hundred set out, led by the Monks and the Third Order Brothers and Sisters. The wealthier pilgrims followed in cabs and carriages, the poorer ones on foot.

Throughout the year 1864 life in this East Anglian school of the Lord's service was marked by a series of thrilling paranormal experiences. Among them was the "Fantastical Fire" in the chapel, which Ignatius believed to be of satanic origin, but which he managed to quench by making the sign of the cross over the flames—"pale-coloured and bluish, like those produced by the igniting of some spirituous substance". Even more extraordinary was the God-raised thunderstorm which dispersed the vast mob waiting to attack the monastery. Some of the Third Order members, notably Sisters Faith, Hope and Charity, arrived with pistols and rifles. It is related that they "distinguished themselves by characteristic and truly beautiful displays of individual courage and strategy". Sister Charity even went so far as to fill a kettle with vitriol to pour on the heads of the hooligans. The chapel was packed to the doors at Compline. The Father-Superior presided at the harmonium trying to sooth his monks and tertiaries with soft music while the murmur of the angry multitude grew nearer and louder and louder. Then with a crash "the warfare of Heaven was hurled on Norwich". The mob bolted in a few moments, but it was long after midnight before the male and female tertiaries wended their way home. A policeman remarked: "Any one could see that the Almighty had taken up them Monks".[12]

There are several references in the *Rule of St Benedict* to the excommunication of contumacious, discontented, disobedient or proud brethren, who show opposition and contemptuous disregard for the orders of the Abbot. It is laid down in chapter twenty-three that if a monk is "thoroughly bad, let him undergo corporal punishment". Ignatius of Jesus, even if only a freelance deacon, believed he had the authority to inflict such punishments on members of his Third Order.

Having given orders that none of the Tertiaries could attend a charity ball advertised to take place in St Andrew's Hall, formerly the Dominican church, he sent along a monk after the dance had got under way, to find out if any of the ladies and gentlemen had dared to disobey him; if so, they were to be told to leave at once. Mr Hillyard, the vicar of St Lawrence's, was discovered among the revellers. He replied that he had no intention of kotowing to this dictatorial young deacon. Ignatius was furious and read the riot act.

Sunday came and the masterful Monk gave out the names of the contumacious tertiaries of both sexes. Unless they made public penance, they would be excommunicated with bell, book and candle. Ladies would have to lie prostrate in their crinolines in ashes during the whole of Vespers. Gentlemen would carry brown "tallow dips". Youths would be caned on the altar steps by the Father Superior himself. It is easy to believe that "the scene was unique. . . . Not all the incense in the swinging censer would quell the horrible flare and perfume from those tallow candles, nor even the most ascetic mind remain impervious to the incongruous but salutary contrast afforded by the flutter of silken skirts and furbelows and the ominous scrunching of ashes during that most strange solemn prostration." The Monk recalled that "long before his wielding of the rod was over his arm was tired out".[13]

Mr Hillyard was solemnly excommunicated, and the Benedictines never darkened the door of his church again. They started to attend the Order of the Administration of the Lord's Supper or Holy Communion at the nearby church of St Saviour's. Mr Cooke, the Evangelical incumbent, was told by Bishop Pelham: "If these Monks present themselves for Communion in their ridiculous dress, you have my permission to pass them over".

Ignatius of Jesus, O.S.B. would have done better to remain at home and try to keep order in his monastery, but the community, as usual, was on the rocks financially, so he rushed off to Newcastle-upon-Tyne to make money by preaching. On the morning of September 9, he received a cutting from the *Norwich News,* entitled "IGNATIUS AND HIS SINGING BOYS". A certain Mrs Hase reported that her fifteen year old stepson had received letters from Br Augustine, one of which was printed verbatim, leaving little doubt that amical relations between the monastic choirmaster and the boy chorister had exceeded what is permitted by St Benedict's injunction that the juniors are to be loved.[14] The Superior hurried back to Norfolk, expelled Br Augustine and replied to the allegations stating: "I can only account for the absurd and ridiculous letter by really believing that it was penned during a fit of insanity". The Baroness-biographer commented: "Himself *sans peur et sans reproche,* he could afford to face the scathe of public scrutiny, and look it straight in the eyes".[15]

Anybody but Fr Ignatius would have hesitated to admit any more boys into the monastery after the exposure of Br Augustine in several newspapers, but he was naïve enough to emulate Mr and Mrs Boffin in Charles Dickens' novel *Our Mutual Friend* (then appearing in serial parts), who had adopted a blue-eyed baby from the slums of Brentford. The Benedictine made an equally generous offer to the mother of a blue-eyed boy aged two years and nine months. She had been left penniless after being abandoned by her husband. "The Monk was strangely susceptible to the winning ways of childhood, and towards this poor little fellow in especial, he felt himself irresistibly drawn. One thought led to another. He knew it would be pleasing to the Lord that a baby Samuel should be given to His Temple, and wholly in accordance with the monastic code that the Community should adopt an oblate in its midst.[16] . . . He felt it would be a pleasure and solace to have the patter of tiny feet about him, and a spotless soul which from the very dawn of its infant perceptions he might train and fashion from bud to blossom, as an oblate indeed of unsullied purity, and worthy to number among such as are of the Kingdom of Heaven."[17]

On the Octave of the Nativity of Our Lady, September 15, 1864 (six days after the *Norwich News* had suggested that the morals of the monastery needed attention), the baby boy was handed over by his mother to Ignatius, and a deed of gift was duly signed. After this he was wrapped in a fair linen cloth, and baptized with the name of Ignatius of Mary. At 9 o'clock the Holy Communion was celebrated by the Rev. Gideon J. Ouseley, then acting as resident chaplain.[18] The mother got a last peep of her son as he was carried into the enclosure where, behind the grille, he was vested in a white habit (symbolic of baptismal innocence), and miniature sandals.[19] For the next ten years the boy-oblate was the object of the Superior's incessant care, and they shared a bedroom. Whenever possible he accompanied his foster-father on journeys.[20] Monastic life radiated round Ignatius of Mary, until the patter of his feet—no longer tiny—ceased to be a pleasure and solace.

The Order of St Benedict was not growing as fast as its restorer wanted, so he went off to Bristol, where he delivered an impassioned oration on the revival of the monastic life at the Church Congress. One gratifying result was the conversion of a wealthy young man named Charles Amesbury Whitley Deans Dundas, great-grandson of the first and last Baron Amesbury, who had inherited large estates in Berkshire and Flintshire. Having been enrolled in the Third Order and given the religious name of Cyprian, Mr Dundas collected a handful of ritualistic youths. It was not long before they were installed in a species of monastery in Trinity Street, under the shadow of Bristol Cathedral.[21] These amateur monks recited the offices in a richly furnished oratory. On Sunday afternoons they chanted Vespers in the Broadmead Rooms. Br Cyprian installed himself as Prior, and his "monkery" became notorious.

The financial affairs of the Priory of Our Ladye and St Dunstan remained in a muddle, just as the monastic observances were huggermugger. The Father Superior refused to bother about anything so sordid as money, or to listen to advice from anybody. The sum of £500 had still to be raised to complete the purchase of the property. On December 10 Br Dunstan wrote to Mr Cundall: "We cannot get the money. Will you please write to Mr Gross and say so. If we cannot get it by Xmas what shall we do? We shall have to spend the day in the cold."[22] Within the next fortnight, however, a friend who wished to remain anonymous offered to lend the £500, after which Ignatius of Jesus felt he need not worry any more. So confident was he in Divine Providence that early in 1865 he gave orders for the foundations of a red-brick church (estimated to cost about £2,000) to be laid in the Priory garden.[23]

Feeling that his community could do with further stimulus, their life being a bit monotonous for the moment, the Father Superior decided to wage war against crinolines. Some ladies needed three chairs in the chapel so billowing were their skirts. A retiring room was provided, and a notice pinned up that no female wearing the fashionable crinoline would be admitted, but if she wished to divest herself of the steel framework of petticoats before service, this could be done modestly with the aid of a Third Order Sister. One of the Brothers recalled that "it was a queer sight. The pegs were full of crinolines of all sizes, colours and descriptions, and in the church itself every woman looked as if she had just had the steam-roller over her."[24]

Shortly before his death on February 18, 1865, Cardinal Wiseman invited Fr Ignatius to call on him in London. He was curious to hear more about the attempt to form a Benedictine brotherhood in the Established Church. The interview (at which the "Infant Samuel" was not present) ended with His Eminence blessing the Anglican monk, having expressed his regret that "so brilliant a labourer in the great vineyard, elected to make his heavenward journey via Canterbury instead of Rome".[25]

Having returned to Norwich, the Benedictine prepared to welcome Dr Pusey and Abbess Lydia. They had heard glowing reports of the growth of the Third Order, and how more and more young men were wanting to test their vocations to the strictest form of the monastic life. The Lady Abbess decided to rent a mansion known as Samson and Hercules House, facing the Cathedral Close, with the intention of sending a few Sisters of her Society of the Most Holy Trinity to occupy it. By this time Ignatius felt that his Benedictine Order ought to emulate the trinitarian structure of Mother Lydia's sisterhood. There were already enough young women at his disposal to form a Second Order. They took up their quarters in Samson and Hercules House, and were given the name of the Oblate Congregation of Mount Calvary. Although in frail health, the Lady Abbess gave much help to the foundation, while Dr Pusey heard confessions and acted as general arbitrator.

The *John Bull* magazine reported that on her forty-fourth birthday, March 21, the feast of St Benedict, the Lady Superior of Devonport took part in "a celebration with much pomp". She was vested "in the full robes of an Abbess", with "an acolyte bearing her pastoral staff"; making a striking figure in her "Benedictine scapular and head-dress". It was indeed a historic occasion for no Abbess had officiated in Norfolk since the sixteenth century when the Benedictine nunneries of Blackenborough, Carroe and Thetford were suppressed, as well as the Cistercian abbey at Marham, and the convent of Augustinian Canonesses at Crabhouse.

Early in June, a month before William Booth and his wife Catherine had come to the conclusion that the Churches had failed the people and that a new form of Christianity was needed to save the down-trodden masses, Fr Ignatius conducted his first London Mission in St Martin's Hall, Long Acre, while Booth was preaching among the swings and coconut-shies on Mile End Waste. Mrs Lyne came to London to keep a motherly eye on her son, who with the Infant Samuel lodged at St Saviour's Hospital, Osnaburgh Street, where the Sisters of the Most Holy Trinity acted as nannies to the little boy. Unfortunately he caught scarlet fever. The Monk was right in his element denouncing the Sins of Society. Many ladies were so roused by his oratory that they tore off their jewellery to drop into the collection plate as it was passed round for the benefit of the Order of St Benedict. It was a painful shock one morning when a letter arrived from Dr Wilberforce, Bishop of Oxford (dated June 9)—a reply to a request for advice on the revival of monastic life. "Soapy Sam" (as this prelate was often called) stated:

"Watching your career, so far as I have been able to do it from a distance, I have come to such conclusions as the following:

1. That God has given you great energy, great powers of usefulness, and a noble spirit of self-devotion to His Service. That the present day specially needs such gifts, and that had you also the wisdom that is profitable to direct them, there is hardly any limit to the service you might render to Him, and to your brethren in the Church.

2. But that the greater part of this usefulness you are flinging hopelessly away.

65

(a) Your adoption of a dress never suited to English habits—and now pre-eminently unsuitable—is a sacrifice of the kernel to the shell such as I have never seen equalled. *(b)* That in adopting this startling exterior you are acting in direct opposition to the principle on which the Order you have assumed did act. For they took the dress to help the work. You mar the work to have the dress. In this merely outward thing I am bound to say that I see the key to all your real hindrances. You are sacrificing everywhere the great reality for which you have sacrificed to a puerile imitation of that phase of service which it is just as impossible for you to revive in England as it would be for you to resuscitate an Egyptian mummy and set it upon the throne of the Pharoahs.

Now, my dear sir, all this I fear, unless you can be persuaded to review your whole position will make your life useless."[26]

Bishop Wilberforce ended his letter with the remark: "I believe that colleges of clergymen, living and acting under the parochial clergy, might meet many of our great spiritual wants; further, I believe that brotherhoods of unordained men not in Holy Orders might be of most excellent use; but if you persist in your present line you will indeed make it practically impossible that for another generation such efforts should succeed."

A sure proof that the "present line" was more or less a farce came a few mornings later while the Benedictine was shaving his Franciscan-shaped tonsure. He was informed that Br Stanislaus wanted to see him on urgent business. We are told that "a single glance at the newcomer's face must have convinced the Reverend Father that he was in the presence of an execrable villain".[27] This novice reported that the monastery was in a state of mutiny. Ignatius of Jesus had been unanimously deposed as superior, and another elected by Chapter. Stanislaus produced a formal deed of deposition, which waited the signature of "the ex-Abbot". This obtained, a copy would be sent for approval to the Archbishop of Canterbury (Dr Longley). Would the Reverend Father kindly affix his name without delay? The bearer wanted to catch the next train back to Norwich, and forward the document to Lambeth Palace.

Ignatius felt inclined to treat the whole business as a joke, and told Stanislaus to complete the shaving of his Celtic tonsure, meanwhile asking for further details of what had happened during his absence. He heard that most of the brethren had deposed him, and that the chaplain, Fr Ouseley, had gone over to the rebels. Br Philip, the extern-porter was one of the few who remained loyal. He had refused to hand over his keys, so a legal summons was taken out against him. Locks were broken open, private papers ransacked, and all money found pocketed by Br Stanislaus and Br Marcus—the newly elected Abbot—who had only been admitted to the community as a postulant a few days before Ignatius had left for London.

Apparently the latter received a tremendous welcome from his Tertiaries on the arrival of the train at Norwich station. It is recorded that "the whole town seemed seized with a glad delirium".[28] The postern gate had been left ajar, so the deposed Superior crept in unnoticed, while Marcus, Stanislaus and Philip were fighting it out before the magistrates. "Dirt and disorder reigned everywhere." Even worse, the villains "had robbed the tabernacle of its Divine Occupant. . . . The consecrated Hosts had been buried in the garden, and the contents of the Chalice poured over them into the ground." Reparation had to be made for this sacrilege. Candles were "lighted round the small enclosure, a crimson chalice veil spread over the place, and flowers—every sweet and fragrant bloom that could be obtained strewn profusely around."[29]

The summons against Br Philip was dismissed. On the return of "Abbot" Marcus and Br Stanislaus to the Priory the deposed Superior wasted no time in excommunicating them as the ringleaders of the rebellion, having managed to get back his own pectoral cross from the former, who was still wearing it. Stanislaus cleared off with a boy from the Guild of St William as his companion. Marcus—unknown to Ignatius at the moment—had stolen his letters of ordination. Mr Drury wrote that the mutiny was what might have been expected, because most of the young monks "had become very disorderly and grossly misconducted themselves, and great scandals were occasioned to the Order, and considerable injury done to the buildings".[30] The Benedictine storm in a tea-cup was reported fully in several newspapers. It inspired *Punch* with a cynical paragraph on July 15, entitled "Ignatius and his Monkeys".

Taking for granted that peace had been restored at the Priory, the Father Superior went off to Sheffield. There was no money left in the baize bag. The only way to raise it was to conduct another Mission. On July 4 he informed Mr Drury that during his previous absence the conduct of the community had been shameful. "The brothers were more like devils than men while under the terrible influence of that dreadful man Br Marcus", who had been admitted two days before he and the infant Oblate left Norwich for London. To make matters worse, "Br Brannock was quite mad". But as the brethren had been put under penance, all was "right and quiet, thank God". There could be "no reform in the monastery except by the brothers returning to their obedience again as they have done".

On July 14 the Elm Hill property was purchased in the name of Mr Drury, to whom the title-deeds were conveyed. A mortgage of £500 was granted to a Miss Stone who wished to remain anonymous. Ignatius did not realise that the rector of Claydon had made himself the landlord. The result was a costly and futile litigation which dragged on for eleven years.

Meanwhile Ambrose Phillipps de Lisle, who in 1857 had been mainly responsible for the formation of the Association for the Promotion of the Unity of Christendom, with the blessing of Cardinal Wiseman, had been taking an interest in the Anglican Benedictine brotherhood. On September 16, 1864, the English Roman Catholic hierarchy, mainly at the instigation of the future Cardinal Manning, had condemned the organisation, forbidding the faithful to have any further part in its activities.

On his way back from Sheffield Ignatius accepted an invitation from de Lisle to spend a few days at Mount St Bernard Abbey, of which he was the founder.[31] An old guest-book contains the entry: "1865, July 31. The so-called Br Ignatius and Br Aloysius—left on the 2nd of August". So far as is known, this was the first monastery at which the Anglican Benedictine had stayed. Its narrow lancet windows, gables, cloister-garth, half-completed church, and newly-opened chapter-house would provide the inspiration for the sort of abbey he hoped to build for his monks before very long. Whether the Trappists were eager to offer hospitality to this eccentric "Protestant" monk and his companion is doubtful, but they had to defer to the wishes of their founder.

About forty years later the Baroness de Bertouch recorded: "Nothing could have exceeded the kind and unqualified welcome to the Anglican Benedictine by his Roman *confrère*.[32] Far from being received as an outsider or interloper, every deference was conferred on him, which befitted an honoured guest. He was placed beside the Abbot at the High Altar, given the stall next to him in choir, and censed immediately after Him—three marks of distinction which in monastic etiquette mean much."[33]

Having attended 2nd Vespers of his Jesuit patron and Compline, Ignatius retired to rest in the Gothic Guest House. Shortly before 2 a.m. a novice who was not ecumenically-minded towards schismatics conducted him to the tribune at the back of the church so that he could assist at Vigils. The Baroness tells us that "the Cistercian Abbot, missing his guest in choir, naturally inquired why he was not present, whereupon the Novice had to own that he had taken him, together with several Roman priests, who happened to be staying there, to the Visitors' Gallery—a piece of information which was met with a severe reprimand. The next moment our Reverend Father was translated from banishment to the stall beside the courteous Abbot, who lost no time in apologising for his Brother's unpardonable mistake. 'He is a convert, you know', he said, laughing 'and they are often a little peculiar'."[34]

Later on the distinguished "heretic" sat in choir at the conventual Mass of St Peter's Chains. After this, amid pouring rain, he was driven to Grace Dieu Park, accompanied by Abbot Bartholomew and Fr Augustine.[35]

De Lisle and his then eighteen year-old son, Osmund, had already left for the Abbey, but missed the expected guests, so when they arrived at Grace Dieu his wife entertained them. She was the eldest daughter and co-heir of the Hon. Thomas Clifford, fourth son of Hugh, Lord Clifford of Chudleigh, and Henrietta, Baroness Von Lutzow. As a cousin of the second Baron de Tabley, P.C., treasurer of Queen Victoria's household from 1868 to 1872, the Anglican Benedictine was quite at home in this aristocratic environment. De Lisle's hospitality was always on a lavish scale, so it may be presumed that the luncheon left nothing to be desired. During the afternoon Ignatius inspected the private chapel, with its carved oak rood screen, and Gothic ciborium over the Blesed Sacrament altar, designed by A. W. Pugin.

Although de Lisle was disappointed that the Association for the Promotion of the Unity had been condemned by a papal rescript, he still dreamed of a Uniate Church being formed in England sooner or later. His visions found expression in the chapter he contributed to *Essays on the Re-Union of Christendom,* published two years after Ignatius' visit to Mount St Bernard. So it is probable that he painted to his guest a glowing picture of Catholic worship already found in more and more Anglican churches—"restored in all their ancient grandeur. The sweet perfume of holy incense is again inhaled in our ancient temples, the names of Mary and the Saints are again honoured and invoked, and men are once more called to the practice of sanctity, and the imitation of the saints".[36] He had no doubt that "such additions would be made as would validate [Anglican] ordination services of bishops, priests, and deacons; and make orthodox and perfect the celebration of the Holy Eucharist". We can be sure that, unlike Bishop Wilberforce of Oxford, he did not feel that the Anglican Benedictine was flinging away his usefulness by adopting a mock-medieval costume for building up monastic waste places. Heavy showers of rain prevented Abbot Bartholomew, Fr Augustine and their schismatic guest from returning to Mount St Bernard before a quarter past four.

According to the Baroness, Ignatius and de Lisle kept up a "fragmentary correspondence" until the latter's death in 1878; the year after the foundation of the Order of Corporate Reunion.[37] She wrote: "It must have been a matter of weird comparison, in the Reverend Father's mind, to have reviewed the calm, unmolested routine of monastic life at Charnwood Abbey, side by side with the limb-from-limb jeopardy in which his own efforts in an analogous direction were constantly placing his individual existence. Nevertheless, he went on his way undismayed, and inasmuch as to move the wheels of his Revival at all meant the expenditure of a great deal of money, these funds had to be raised by preaching and pleading his cause broadcast throughout the English provinces. So the odds had to be taken and the mobs faced, even though the result should mean death. . . . This visit to Mount St Bernard was one of distinct refreshment to soul and body, although of such brief duration. The Monk went back to his own strenuous labours with a pleasant sense of fellowship hitherto unfelt. He had participated in the daily life of an Order, which, like his own, retained the primitive rigour of Rule and Enclosure, and the experience had been full of instruction and encouragement."[38]

In spite of the apparently cordial welcome by Abbot Bartholomew and most of his monks, Ignatius never revisited Mount St Bernard's. So far as is known, he never stayed at any other Roman Catholic monasteries before his death forty-three years later.

On his return to Norwich the Father Superior had more than enough to keep him busy. Reports from Bristol showed that the Catholic Movement was making great progress. Early in 1865 Prior Cyprian had moved the Benedictine Tertiaries from Trinity Street to a former workshop in Trenchard Street, where a chapel was opened. The congregation consisted mainly of teenagers who often behaved in an irreverent manner. One day a mob of between 400 and 500 persons assembled outside. When the black-habited brethren emerged they were attacked, and had to run for their lives. Some were injured in the scuffle.

A journalist wrote: "Last night I heard a great noise in Trenchard Street, caused by a small crowd following a procession of what appeared to be monks, bearing several crucifixes of different sizes and a statue of the Madonna. They all had on long black dresses and cowls over their heads, a few wearing foreign-looking four-cornered hats, with what seemed like wings on them. They went into a house there which I believe they have fitted up as a chapel."

Mr Dundas (otherwise Prior Cyprian) found it quite as difficult to control his quasi-monks as did Fr Ignatius. Troubles occurred during a service, and he ordered two of the brethren to depart. They refused to budge, with the result that the police were summoned. On hearing of this disobedience Ignatius advised Cyprian, although he was merely a layman, to make the rebels don white sheets and do public penance in the oratory, according to the "Norwich Use". They remained obdurate, so they were solemnly excommunicated amid scenes of uproar.

The feast of the Assumption 1865 was celebrated by the Bristol Tertiaries with probably far more external solemnity than by the Papist Jesuits at St Mary's-on-the-Quay, or even by Canon Bonomi and the clergy at the Clifton Pro-Cathedral. The Downside Benedictines were put to shame, for Prior Cyprian's brethren set them an example by rising at midnight to recite Matins and Lauds. After these nocturnal devotions there was an outdoor procession. The pseudo-monks carried crosses, banners and lighted candles. Leaving Trenchard Street, they moved up St Michael's Hill, chanting the Litany. Having reached St Michael's Church, they knelt outside the door, reciting prayers. A large crowd followed; at intervals joining lustily in the chorus of the then popular song: "Slap, bang, here we are again!".

The Prior rebuked the mob for its levity, but the jeering grew louder. The procession turned back, and made its way along Park Row about 2.30 a.m. A policeman ordered the brethren to stop singing, otherwise they would be locked up for committing a breach of the peace. Cyprian tried to argue with him, but with no effect. So the banners and crosses were lowered, the candles extinguished, and the community returned quietly to their monastery after this night out.

Not long after these ritualistic orgies at Bristol, Fr Ignatius felt obliged to depose Prior Cyprian, who, emulating his Major Superior, then proceeded to excommunicate a few more of his male and female Tertiaries. After this he transformed the loyal remnant into an Augustinian fraternity, which appears to have survived until 1873.[39]

Such were but a few of the worries that faced the Father Superior following his return to the Priory of Our Ladye and St Dunstan after his brief visit to Mount St Bernard. There was now no resident chaplain, for Fr Gideon Ouseley had departed, and resigned from the Third Order on April 27, while Ignatius was giving his first London Mission. Shortly after the publication of the broadsheet *"The Monastery in an Uproar"*, a newspaper printed a letter in which the former chaplain stated: "I have frequently but vainly remonstrated with him against abuses and extravagances directly opposed to the Benedictine Rule and to the spirit of the English Church, to which he professes to adhere. My priestly counsels and monitions (as well as those of other friends) were always met with contempt. I felt that I could not as a Catholic priest of the English Church tolerate the un-Catholic and un-English innovations and extravagances which he has from time to time introduced."

Three weeks after enjoying Trappist hospitality and the luncheon party at Grace Dieu, Ignatius of Jesus broke down. On the feast of St Bartholomew, August 24, he had what was described as "a slight stroke of paralysis", while celebrating the Ante-Communion service in the Priory chapel. This was followed by visions of angels, and of a demon four feet high, with a face like a turnip. For the next two weeks he was nursed by Brothers Edmund and Philip, aided by Sister Mary Magdalene of the Congregation of Mount Calvary. So desperate was the poverty of the little community that the nun sold a petticoat to buy a bottle of champagne to stimulate the Reverend Father. The monastic practitioner advised that a change of air would be beneficial; recommending "the magical sea breezes of Margate". He was sure that ozone would bring back "some degree of strength and recuperative vitality to the emaciated and almost discouraged convalescent Monk".[40] Too weak to walk Ignatius was carried to the railway station, and lifted onto the train.

NOTES

[1] The O.S.B. was not the first Anglican religious community to appear in the Norwich diocese. In 1854 Miss Lavinia Crosse founded the Sisterhood of All Hallows, with the approval of Bishop Hinds. Its object was the reclamation of fallen women. The Sisters moved to Ditchingham in 1859, and in 1864 the first part of a new convent was dedicated by Dr Samuel Wilberforce, Bishop of Oxford.

[2] Luke 12: 51-53 (Authorized Version).

[3] p. 173.

[4] p. 177. Mr Moultrie had no doubt that when celebrating the Holy Communion one morning he saw the figure on the cross turn its eyes with "a smile of ineffable sweetness" towards Ignatius who was playing the harmonium.

[5] p. 188.

[6] p. 217.

[7] p. 221.

[8] So far as is known, the only other Anglican places of worship where Benediction and Exposition had been started by 1864, were the chapels of Dr Neale's Society of St Margaret. Within a year of its foundation in 1855, the Sisters were enjoying these eucharistic devotions.

[9] p. 217. It is improbable that the Jesuits, who had served the only Papist church at Norwich since it was opened in 1827, would have dared to put on an outdoor procession of the Blessed Sacrament at that date, even if ordered by Dr Amherst, second Bishop of Northampton. It appears that it was not until 1899 that the first Roman Catholic procession with the monstrance took place through the streets of a town—from the Italian Church of St Peter, Clerkenwell, London.

[10] One of the pole bearers of the canopy was the Rev. Charles Grafton, a young American Protestant Episcopalian clergyman, who in 1865 became one of the first novices of Mr Benson's Society of St John the Evangelist at Oxford. Elected second Bishop of Fond du Lac, Wisconsin, in 1889, he was closely associated with several attempts to revive Benedictine monasticism in the Anglican Communion until his death in 1912. (See pp. 181, 186.)

[11] p. 218.

[12] pp. 234-8.

[13] p. 252. For his belief in the spiritual benefit of flagellation, see p. 89. An indication of the hypnotic influence exercised by him on persons of all classes of society is that the wife, daughter, and son of Mr Utton-Browne (a well-known Norwich magistrate) were ready to lie publicly on cinders and be flogged.

[14] Chapter 4, "What are the tools of Good Works", No. 69.

[15] p. 265.

[16] Chapter 59 of the *Rule of St Benedict* is entitled "Sons of the Nobility or of the Poor who are offered". Poor parents who have nothing to offer may simply draw up a document and offer their son with the oblation in the presence of witnesses.

[17] pp. 231-2. The boys' school appears to have closed down after a brief existence.

[18] Fr Gideon, the son of a general, was baptized in the Roman Catholic Church. Educated as a Protestant at Trinity College, Dublin, he was ordained in the Church of Ireland, but soon

crossed over to England and became a rabid Ritualist. After a brief spell with the Benedictines, he acted as curate to Provost Fortescue at St Ninian's Cathedral, Perth. His next step was to join the Greek Orthodox Church. Then he decided to be received into the Catholic Apostolic (Irvingite) Church, and was re-ordained, his Anglican orders being regarded as invalid. Having been suspended for heresy by the surviving Apostles, he made his submission to the Roman Church. Eventually he founded at Brighton what was called "The One Holy Catholic Divine-Human Apostolic Church of Israel". In his earlier years this clerical rolling-stone published eight books on ritual and ceremonial. Among his later works are *The Order of Cremation by Fire* (1890), *How to Keep a Cat in Health,* and *The Gospel of the Holy Twelve,* both issued in 1901. He died in 1906, two years before Fr Ignatius.

[19] Later on this footgear was venerated as holy relics.

[20] See pp. 68, 72, 73-7.

[21] Another aristocratic Tertiary about this time was Digby Mackworth Dolben (1848-67), who was clothed as a novice, with the name of "Brother Dominic" when he was still at Eton. His religious and devotional poems were edited with a memoir by Robert Bridges in 1915. There are references to Fr Ignatius in the latter's *Three Friends* (Oxford, 1932).

[22] Cf. Calder-Marshall, op. cit., p. 116.

[23] Today it has become a training establishment for shoe-makers, evoking memories of the tiny sandals made to fit the baby Ignatius of Mary before he was clothed in a Carthusian habit after his baptism by Fr Gideon Ouseley on the Octave of the Nativity of our Lady, 1864 (see p. 63).

[24] De Bertouch, op. cit., p. 223.

[25] p. 209.

[26] A. R. Ashwell and R. G. Wilberforce, *Life of Samuel Wilberforce* (1880-88), Vol. III, p. 166. This letter was written shortly before the Bishop received a request from the Rev. R. M. Benson for the approval of the community which was given the name of "The Society of St John the Evangelist", founded in August 1865.

[27] p. 272.

[28] p. 278.

[29] p. 283.

[30] Cf. Calder-Marshall, op. cit., p. 121.

[31] See p. 18.

[32] John Bartholomew Anderson (1820-1890). He entered the novitiate in 1843, was elected abbot in 1862, and blessed the following year. He ruled over the community for 28 years.

[33] p. 210.

[34] p. 211.

[35] Fr Augustine (Henry Collins) was a convert clergyman who took the road to Rome in 1857, and was one of the first four Papist members of the Association for the Promotion of the Unity of Christendom. He was soon re-ordained as a secular priest. Having served as chaplain to de Lisle at Grace Dieu, he entered the community in 1861, and is best remembered as the author of several well-known hymns.

[36] op. cit., p. 262.

[37] See pp. 106-7.

[38] pp. 211-12.

[39] Dundas seceded to the Roman Church that year, and in July 1874 he stood (unsuccessfully) as Conservative candidate in the Bedminster area of Bristol. Aged 28, he died at Clifton on September 9.

[40] p. 292.

CHAPTER IV

Two years spent by Fr Ignatius of Jesus, O.S.B., as a gyrovag
(September 1865—June 1867)

For the greater part of the next two years the Superior-General of the triune Order of St Benedict was a rolling stone gathering no moss. He survived the whole-day journey from Norfolk to the Isle of Thanet. We are told that "a general 'scraping up' of stray pennies" raised enough money to pay, not only his own fare, but also tickets for Br Edmund, and Sisters Ambrosia, Louisa, and Veronica. Br Ignatius of Mary (no longer an infant in arms) needed a half-fare ticket. The monastic sextette stayed in furnished apartments at Margate.

The ozone off the mud at low tide soon worked what seemed to be a miracle. At the end of a fortnight the Monk felt able to move eastwards with his entourage to the more genteel village of Kingsgate. Before long he was fit enough to accept an invitation to preach to the Plymouth Brethren at Ramsgate. There is no record of his calling on either the Benedictine community at St Augustine's Monastery, or the enclosed nuns at St Mildred's Priory.

"After awhile, the desire to move on further seemed to move him, and in his endeavour to select a sympathetic spot as the climax of his proposed travels, the remembrance of the far-away ruins in the valley of the Black Mountains came back upon him like a flash of inspiration, and in a moment his thoughts centered on one cherished ambition—a pilgrimage to Old Llanthony Priory, and if God saw fit to give him strength, a Mission to the dwellers amongst the distant Welsh Hills".[1]

Still accompanied by Br Edmund, Sister Louisa, Sister Veronica, Sister Ambrosia, and "Baby", the Roving Recluse made the long journey from Margate to Bristol. On October 31 (Halloween), the party, together with eleven still loyal *confratres* of the Third Order, set off for the Black Mountains. They stayed at the inn built into the ruins of the Priory. The Monk preached an impassioned sermon in the coach-house.

It is related that his eventual return to Norwich in Advent "was celebrated by the faithful as a triumphant jubilee, and fervent hopes were entertained far and near that the wheels of Elm Hill Priory routine might once more resume their busy whirr".[2] But this monastic momentum came to a sudden stop just before Christmas, when the Reverend Father had another breakdown. Sister Ambrosia, who was watching at his bedside, believed him to be dead. Suddenly the Monk rose up, whispering that he heard angels singing, with the refrain: "Make us love Thee more and more". Towards midnight on New Year's Eve the celestial melodies faded out softly until there was silence. Sister Ambrosia was bidden to close the window. Her patient immortalized what he knew was yet another supernatural intervention in a poem which starts:

> "A Guardian sent us
> From Thy sweet Land of Love,
> To tell us peaceful stories
> Of Things above."[3]

Dr Allen told the community that if their Father Superior "was ever to resume work, he must rest body and mind for an indefinite time, otherwise he would not answer for the consequences". "A prolonged tour or a sea voyage" were recommended, but the triune Order of St Benedict lacked the money to pay for either method of convalescence. The only alternative was another dose of ozone, and the nearest place where it could be obtained was Lowestoft. Lodgings having been found, a party composed of the Superior, Sister Ambrosia, the boy-oblate, Ignatius of Mary, and young Br Edmund, to whom the Father was much attached, set out for this health resort. Its winter climate was reputed to be far above the average of seaside places for dryness, sunniness, and moderate temperature.

But poor Ignatius of Jesus found no peace of mind. One morning a letter arrived with the news that the excommunicated Brothers Marcus and Stanislaus, each of whom had been presented with a five-pound note to enable them to reach their respective families, had blown the money on a trip to Paris. Finding themselves down and out, the two unfrocked Benedictines had borrowed money from the chaplain to the British Embassy. Even worse, Marcus had stolen and altered "by means of some chemical application" the Reverend Father's Letters of Orders. By these documents he managed to obtain a curacy at St Martin's, Worcester, where he joined no less than thirty-three couples in unholy matrimony during the period he posed as a bona-fide clergyman.[4]

The monastic quartette was so poor that they hardly knew how to pay their landlady's account for board and lodging. Neither did their funds permit mock-turtle soup and port-wine which had been prescribed by Dr Allen for his patient. Just when the situation was becoming desperate another miracle occurred. Sister Ambrosia, the widow of a Sheffield merchant, heard that she had been left a considerable legacy. Her first thought, naturally, was to devote it solely to her beloved spiritual father. His biographer related: "With all the power of persuasion she could command, this excellent soul urged him to leave England without delay, and thus escape the trying winds of a cruel British winter. Not only for his own sake, said Sister Ambrosia, should he make this summary decision, but as a duty which he owed to his Community, and even to the entire enterprise of Anglican Monasticism, then actually dependent on his life."[5]

Ignatius of Jesus himself never had a moment's doubt that God had chosen him to comfort all the monastic waste places of Britain, to make her wilderness like Eden, her desert like the garden of the Lord, where gladness, thanksgiving, and song would be found sooner or later.[6] There was no other clergyman in the Church of England capable of performing this herculean labour, but his immediate reaction to Sister Ambrosia's suggestion was to exclaim: "I will go to Jerusalem, and I will start tomorrow, please God".[7]

A proof of the state of his mind at that moment can be detected in his apparent indifference to the triune-Order of St Benedict of which he was the self-appointed Superior-General. All he did was to write two letters: the one to Abbess Lydia, telling her that he was off to the Holy Land; the other to the handful of Brothers left at Norwich, placing them in "solemn charge of the Priory, its chapel, and St William's Guild, etc.", stating that Br Edmund would act as his *socius* on the pilgrimage. Back came a telegram from Br Philip, the Keeper-of-the-keys: "If you don't take me with you, I shall be damned". Such being the case, the Reverend Father felt he must dispense with the companionship of his beloved Edmund and make do with the far less sympathetic Philip, described as "a rough but faithful son of St Benedict".[8]

Having informed the Lowestoft landlady that he would be vacating her lodgings the following day, Ignatius departed for Dover, accompanied by Br Philip, Sister

Ambrosia, and the Infant Oblate. There was no question of the two monks going into mufti. They travelled in their black habits, that of the Superior covered by his voluminous cowl. Sister Ambrosia appears to have worn a nondescript nun's habit, while little Ignatius of Mary looked very pretty all in white.

The pantomime-like pilgrims spent a week in a hotel at Dover, where a letter was received from Abbess Lydia stating that she and Dr Pusey were about to leave for "the Land of Promise", suggesting that the Benedictine might like to meet them at Malta and go on to Jerusalem. Recalling how St Benedict wrote in the sixth chapter of his Rule: "But as for coarse jokes or frivolous talk or making people laugh, these we condemn to be for ever barred in all places, and for such conversation we do not allow a disciple to open his mouth", it might be wiser to pass over the grand tour. For there is also the advice in the first chaper referring to the Sarabites and Gyrovags—"of the most wretched life of these it is better to say nothing than to speak". On the other hand, it is impossible to understand the rest of the story of this would-be restorer of monastic waste places without a brief reference to his wanderings around Europe.

Having crossed the Channel, and spent a night at Calais, the travellers reached Paris, where "the reverend Father became so exhausted that a stay of some days had to be endured, before he was sufficiently recovered to be moved". His biographer told the truth when she wrote: "There must have been a pathetic as well as picturesque aspect about this unusually garbed quartet, which even in France, where the religious dress was in those days to be seen every hour in the open street, seems to have excited a good deal of public attention. The central figure of attraction was without doubt the delicate-looking Superior robed in the sombre canonicals of his Order, but the baby Ignatius was likewise the object of much restrained mobbing. The spectacle of a three-year-old Monk in full feather is not to be seen every day, and the little child in his white serge habit and tiny sandals was a novelty with which the passers-by seemed to be hugely mystified and pleased."[9]

With stops at Dijon and Arles the four pilgrims arrived at Marseilles. Here they boarded a small steamer, coasting along the French and Italian Rivieras, calling at Genoa and Leghorn. On landing at Città Vecchia the papal *doganieri* and *caribinieri* took them for a troupe of mountebanks. Duty had to be paid on many bits of their luggage, including the Superior's brass crucifix. Eventually they reached Rome and found furnished apartments in the Via Condotti, near the Piazza di Spagna. Ignatius of Jesus immediately retired to bed. The mental and physical strain of the long journey by land and sea had utterly prostrated him.

Gossip soon started amid the British Colony. Among them was one of the Monk's many aristocratic kinsmen, Augustus Hare—who was a Hare of Hurstmonceaux.[10] He persuaded a lady friend to call on Ignatius, who even allowed her to chat with the Infant Samuel, although he was usually forbidden to speak to strange women. The story went round Rome that on being asked who were his parents "Baby" replied: "I'm the child of Jesus Christ, of the Virgin Mary, and of the holy St Benedict".

The Vatican grew alarmed on hearing of the presence of these extraordinary pilgrims. It may have been Cardinal Antonelli, who for nearly twenty-seven years had been the virtual temporal ruler of Rome, who ordered the Rev. W. R. Brownlow, a priest at the English College "to act as an interpreter and cicerone to his fellow countrymen". Moreover, "a very charming Roman Sister was dispensed from Enclosure and lodged *pro tem* in rooms opposite those occupied by the Reverend Father and his party. Thus Sister Ambrosia was relieved from the sense of loneliness and isolation which, but for the friendly ministrations of Sister Ignatia, must inevitably have been the portion of any woman similarly placed."[11] It is easy to believe that "the Holy Office literally bristled with excitement" when told that two English Benedictine monks were co-habiting with a nun and a baby boy.

Fr Brownlow managed to arrange for Ignatius to have a private audience with the seventy-four year-old *Pio nono*.[12] The Pope must have got a shock at the sight of a *"monaco Protestante"* arrayed in all his war-paint, and his head gashed in a dozen places—the result of nervousness while shaving his tonsure that morning. The Baroness devoted four-and-a-half pages of her biography to that unique audience. It is not surprising that Pius IX said: "Remember above all things"—handling the Monk's hood emphatically as he underlined each syllable—"remember that it is not the *cowl* which makes the Monk". Ignatius—who firmly believes that he could not be a real Benedictine unless he wore his cowl all the time—answered instantly but reverently: "No, Holy Father; it is the *life*".[13]

Cardinal Antonelli tried to prevent the aged pontiff from presenting the Protestant monk with a medal of the Immaculate Conception, but the Holy Father waved him aside with the words: "Wear this in memory of a visit to an old man".

Yet the Monk's health failed to improve as the result of all this spiritual excitement. "Every project that spelt exertion had to be abandoned, even the refusal of two pressing invitations from the Superiors of Subiaco and Monte Cassino." One sunny morning, however, he felt able to face the drive in a *carozza* to S. Paolo-fuori-le-Mura, where he paid his respects to the Abbot-nullius. Another morning he called at what is described as "a Benedictine Institution within the walls of the capital"—probably the Monastery of S. Ambrogio, the headquarters of the Subiaco Province of the Cassinese Congregation. If so, then it may have been Abbot Casaretto who "refused to allow his guest to kiss his ring of office".[14]

On Ash Wednesday, 1866, the party drove to S. Sabina on the Aventine, where the observances of the French Dominicans were said to be very strict. Ignatius was shocked to find that Vespers had been anticipated to 11.30 a.m. to enable the Friars to dine at midday. He was "suddenly seized with one of the fainting fits, to which, from heart-weakness, he was still frequently subject". The novice master, who spoke English, carried the monk up to his own cell and laid him on the bed.

Ignatius did make a brave effort to visit Monte Cassino on the way to Naples, but had a complete black-out on the platform of its railway station. When the next train from Rome stopped, the porters lifted the monk's prostrate body into a compartment.

The day after the Palestine pilgrims had arrived at Naples, Br Philip vanished from the hotel, leaving his Superior alone with the nun and the boy-oblate. "The shock of this sudden desertion was so great that it brought on a serious relapse." Sister Ambrosia managed to get hold of an English doctor, who pronounced that the Monk was at death's door, bidding her telegraph to his relatives. "Nonsense", she replied boldly, on grasping the sense of his diagnosis: "he is no more dying than you are. Only get him into the fresh air, and he will soon be all right again."[15]

Br Philip soon returned like a prodigal son. He had tried to make his way back to Rome on foot, with the intention of seeking admission to the Dominican community at Santa Sabina. Suddenly he heard an inward voice telling him that God wanted him to remain a Benedictine. By this time he was very tired and hungry, having no money. The truth was that having seen what the real religious life was like he realised the difference between it and what he had sampled at Norwich. Br Philip was no fool.

It was still a long, long way to Jerusalem. Ignatius was desperate to hurry on to Malta, where he hoped to join up with Dr Pusey and Abbess Lydia. The voyage from Naples to Messina was stormy. "Baby" was very sea-sick. Having rested a few days in this city, the party boarded a paddle steamer, which pitched and rolled after leaving the coast of Sicily. The Monk was an utter wreck by the time that Malta was sighted, and had to be carried down the gangway in Valetta harbour by two sailors.

The pilgrims found lodgings with an English lady at Sliema. The monk had the joy of meeting his youngest brother, Augustus Adolphus, then serving in the Royal Navy. They were photographed together, each in his own uniform. The tonsured Benedictine held a crucifix in one hand, and laid the other on the curly head of the kneeling midshipman, who grasped his sword. Another day the Archbishop of Rhodes, Metropolitan of the Cyclides, invited the Anglican monk to call on him. There was also the consolation of meeting Dr Trower, Bishop of Gibraltar, who heard his Confession before administering Holy Communion.[16] The Benedictine's spirit was even "more refreshed by the spontaneous enthusiasm displayed by the Maltese people in their insular churches".[17] Unfortunately Dr Pusey and Abbess Lydia had already left Malta. Ignatius felt that his health would not permit him to follow them to Palestine. The weather grew hot, and he decided to start on the homeward journey to his East Anglian cloister.

A succession of fierce squalls between Malta and Marseilles caused the Monk to endure long hours of physical suffering. His presence on board ship invariably caused meteorological disturbances. He stepped ashore, more of a shadow than a man, on the morning of Palm Sunday. Still he had the satisfaction of knowing he had prevented a fellow passenger from committing suicide with a razor.

There were more than enough churches in Marseilles offering Holy Week functions besides the ancient Cathedral, and the recently consecrated Basilica of Notre-Dame de la Garde. The obvious thing for the two Anglican Benedictines to have done was to seek hospitality from the monks at the Priory established from Solesmes in 1865, and to leave Sister Ambrosia and "Baby" in a convent or pension. Ignatius, however, decided that more sightseeing would soothe his overstrung nerves, so the quartette travelled on to Montreux which was reached on Maundy Thursday after stops at Grenoble, Chambéry, Geneva, and Lausanne. The "Gyrovags" spent Easter at the Hotel Glwn, overlooking the Lake of Geneva. An excursion was made to the Castle of Chillon, where an eagle nearly grabbed hold of the Infant Samuel, probably mistaking him for a white rabbit. Another day while driving through mountains, the party just escaped being precipitated "headlong over an unfathomable precipice", when the horses stumbled. The Reverend Father seized his adopted son, and hurled him on to the safe side of the road. The boy asked with tears in his eyes: "What for my Fa' throw away his ba' like that?"[18]

Judging from the wording of a letter written to Mr Drury on April 5, Ignatius was in no hurry to return to his cloister. He explained that, were he to be "pestered with troubles about money", he would only get ill again; still, he was "very anxious to know how things are at the Monastery", if any funds had been collected in the past three months, and if the annual subscriptions had been collected. If not, "then it was Mr Cundall's fault as he kindly undertook to see to them". He asked if "the poor Monks had any priests at the Monastery this Easter", saying that he was glad to hear that Mr Drury had visited them in Lent. The letter ended with the words: "You are the only priest we have really been able to trust thro' all our troubles. Next to God, our gratitude is to you."[19]

The truth was that the pilgrims were running short of money. Since leaving Lowestoft Sister Ambrosia's legacy had covered not only Ignatius' own expenses, but also those of Br Philip and "Baby". The grand tour of the continent, otherwise the pilgrimage to Jerusalem, had enabled him to escape from realism into romance.

His biographer stated: "He was now destined to tread the uninterrupted platitude of the beaten track, and to face as best he might the bitter disappointments and disillusions that were to greet his home-coming".[20] Leaving Montreux the weary pilgrims stayed in hotels at Basle, Strasbourg, Luxembourg, and Brussels before reaching Ostende. Here another halt of several days was made owing to the Monk's exhausted condition.

He appears to have received a letter from Mr Drury at Brussels, intimating brutally that the Norwich Priory's debts now amounted to about £1,000, and that everything there was in a state of chaos. On April 23, S George's Day, "Ignatius O.S.B. Spr" wrote to his "dearest friend", starting off: *"Will you* see Mr Cundall and Mr Balls as soon as possible and tell them that my health is such that I cannot return to Norwich, or have anything to do with the Mission there until the business and money part of the matter is quietly and properly settled. I can no longer attend to everything. Directly they tell me that those things are settled and proper provision made for the future that we may honestly go on with the work with God's help, I will go on with the Spiritual part of the work. Since I have been ill, no one has made any appeal or any attempt to raise funds—everything has been neglected."

The absentee Superior-General of the First, Second, and Third Orders of St Benedict hinted vaguely that he had been offered "a house in a distant County as a refuge for the Brothers". He hoped that Mr Drury would feel that he was justified in moving them from Norwich. The letter continued: "The four brothers at Norwich and six others will be ready to go into residence with me. I feel that I have been most cruelly neglected and treated during my absence, and that the *pretended* friends of the Order ought to be made to do something. The Third Order alone (500 in number) could easily raise £1,000 if they chose."

Demanding an immediate reply from the rector of Claydon, giving his opinion on the various matters mentioned, the Monk ended with the words: "I wish you could run over and see me here. Harwich to Rotterdam, Rotterdam to Ostende."[21]

The reference to a "Mission" at Norwich suggests that—for the moment—Ignatius had given up the idea of restoring the Benedictine Order in England, and was prepared to be merely a freelance monk-missionary. On the other hand, he seemed willing enough to retire to the depths of the country with the ten young men mentioned in this letter, so long as he had no more financial or business worries.

Mr Drury, however, did not feel in the mood to leave his family and parish to oblige Ignatius O.S.B. Why should he "run over" to Belgium at his own expense? What he did do was to go to Norwich on May 6. He found only three monks left at the Priory. They were reduced to abject poverty, almost starving, and badly in need of clothes. The buildings were in such a dangerous condition that he had to call in an architect. He discovered that Mr Balls had not been paid the £60 lent for buying more property, and that the purchase had not yet been completed. Neither had Miss Stone received a penny towards the lease, although she had written to Ignatius on April 30 that she would not exert pressure. Mr Drury recommended that she ought to get friends to take over the whole monastic property on mortgage. Having completed his investigations, he resolved to close down the establishment at once. Br Alban was the only member of the now moribund fraternity who wished to persevere in the monastic life. Abbess Lydia invited him to stay with her in the Isle of Wight.

Distance often lends enchantment, and in 1896 Igatius could only picture himself as an innocent victim, having no responsibility for the *débâcle* of thirty years previously, for he wrote: "I found myself broken down entirely, and in shattered health—from the worldly standpoint a ruined young man. The Monastery at Norwich and the Church I had built were not mine, but Mr Drury's, the Rector of Claydon. It is a long story of a cruel fraud practised on me. When the Archbishop of Canterbury heard of it, he said it was my duty to try to recover the property. My father

77

took the matter up, and began a lawsuit extending over ten years. A property worth £10,000 which was to come to me, was entirely sacrificed in law expenses."

Having survived the voyage from Ostende to Dover, the Monk had really no alternative but to accept an invitation from his parents to stay with them at Hambleden in Surrey. Sister Ambrosia took the Infant Samuel to Scarborough, and Br Philip joined Br Alban in the Isle of Wight.[22]

To all intents and purposes the Order of St Benedict had collapsed. Its only monastery had been closed. The Oblates of Mount Calvary had been disbanded. The Tertiaries in Norwich, Bristol, London, Leeds, and elsewhere were left to their own devices. Mr Lyne Snr. advertised in more than one newspaper that his son had dispersed his monks, and given up all idea of reviving the Benedictine Order in the Church of England, but this canard was instantly contradicted. Both Dr Pusey and Abbess Lydia were informed. Mr Lyne also consulted Dr Longley, Archbishop of Canterbury since 1862, who agreed to meet the deacon at Lambeth Palace on condition that he discarded his ridiculous costume. Ignatius felt that the end might justify the means, and compromised with a cassock. The interview took place. The Primate of All England appears to have been sympathetic, but doubted whether his visitor showed the requisite qualifications for a cure of souls. Yet if Mr Lyne would consent to dress as an ordinary clergyman and work quietly in some parish as a deacon, perhaps it might be possible to confer the priesthood on him eventually.

The Archbishop said he would write to Canon Benham, the rector of Margate, who replied that he was prepared to consider taking on the ex-monk as his curate. So, accompanied by one of his brothers, Clavering Mordaunt, Ignatius went down to Margate for the weekend. The Canon soon discovered that he had no intention of leading a curate's life. His intention was to found a monastery on the Isle of Thanet, where the monks would be controlled by a rigid rule. They would be strictly enclosed, but should they need exercise would be permitted to go walks in procession, two by two. The Canon recalled later on in his *Clerical Reminiscences:* "I spoke kindly and warned him that all his former troubles would recur, and his would be a wasted life; and I entreated him to dismiss past fancies and follies, and serve his Mother Church with simplicity and godly sincerity. But I was compelled to stop, for he turned pale and faint, and I had to lead him into the open air. He was unfit for evening service; and spent the time writing to the Archbishop. We met at breakfast; and without further discussion, he left by an early train; and I saw him no more."

Canon Benham had no intention of allowing an Anglican monastery to be established at Margate. For the past eight years a monk from Ramsgate had been celebrating Mass in his parish every Sunday and holyday of obligation. In June 1866 the Papist church of SS. Austin and Gregory had been reopened by Dr Grant, Bishop of Southwark, after extensive repairs. The Canon also realised that "Ignatius and his Monkeys" would not only be a nuisance to himself, but also an embarrassment to the flourishing Benedictine community at St Augustine's, Ramsgate, who were already planning to make foundations at Tenterden in Kent, and in Ireland.

Bitterly disappointed, Ignatius returned to Hambleden. His father was furious that his well-meant efforts had led to nothing. The situation became strained to breaking point. On hearing this, Abbess Lydia offered the Monk a temporary home at Southlands, near Blackgang Chine, in the Isle of Wight, where Brothers Alban and Philip were already among its miscellaneous lodgers.[23]

Meanwhile Ignatius had summoned some of the scattered members of the Third Order to meet him in London. Then he rushed off to Norwich. His father had arranged for him to state his own version of the "cruel fraud" perpetrated by Mr Drury. It is difficult to understand the point of view of Mr Lyne Snr. In spite of his detestation of "monkery", he was quite prepared to expose the Anglo-Catholic swindlers who had stolen what he believed was his son's lawful property. Nothing resulted from this meeting.

On returning to the Isle of Wight Ignatius found that Southlands had been left in charge of a caretaker. Abbess Lydia, Dr Pusey, and the two Brothers Alban and Philip had made a hasty departure for London, for the Abbess had decided to open an emergency hospital for cholera patients in Bethnal Green. The Monk, to his horror, for he was always terrified of being left alone, had no choice but to lead the life of a hermit. On the tenth Sunday after Trinity 1866, took place what he regarded as the most momentous event in his life, which fills up fourteen pages in the Baroness's biography. As this "Conversion" hardly affects the history of the revival of Benedictine monasticism in the Church of England, it need only be dealt with briefly in this book.

The setting was the beach of Chale Bay, at the foot of Blackgang Chine, and in tune with the state of his mind, for "to the early Victorians it represented the pitch of terror and grandeur, and was a place of 'savage sublimity', much engraved with a wreck in the foreground and the wrath of God striking black above the towering crags".[24] It was about seven o'clock in the evening and the sun was setting beyond the Needles. "No sound to be heard except the soft monotone of the waves drifting farther and farther with the ebb-tide." In sheer desperation the Monk had dashed out of the private oratory, "where Dr Pusey (when in residence) said daily Mass" believing that he was damned. Then came a vision of Mary, Joseph and the Babe of Bethlehem. "Give him to *me*, even to me also!" the Benedictine cried aloud. Mary turned to the agonised monk and replied: "Jesus is for *you* as much as for Simon". Coming forward on the wet sands she laid the Infant on Ignatius' breast. "I dare not dwell upon the rapture of that Divine contact. It seemed as if the Priceless Treasure rested upon my heart, a Voice—whether His Own or some listening angel's I know not—whispered the comfort to my wounded spirit which it had thirsted for so long, so passionately and hitherto in vain, *'None shall pluck thee out of My Hand'*." So it was in that "awful moment" that the black robed, tonsured, sandalled Benedictine "Found Salvation". Still holding the shabby red-bound Methodist hymnbook which he had carried with him from the oratory, he climbed up the Chine reciting the final words of the Salve Regina—"*O clemens, O pia, O dulcis Virgo Maria*".

The crowds of summer trippers who haunt Blackgang Chine today have nothing to remind them of the miraculous Conversion of the Anglican Benedictine monk as they roam through the Hall of Mirrors, Smugglers' Cave, floodlit Water Garden, Maze, and Gnomes' Garden. Ignatius of Jesus deserves a statue, or at least a plaque, among the attractions of this Fun Fair. He is of greater historic interest than the entire skeleton of a Greenland whale, wrecked on the Island in 1845, which is exhibited in the Museum.[25]

Having already agreed to take duty at Streatham the following Sunday, the converted Monk returned to London. Quite by chance he was invited to preach at St Bartholomew's, Moor Lane. Its rector, the Rev. William Denton, persuaded him to accept the post of Sunday lecturer, with a salary of £120 per annum. The duties also included a Bible Class every Friday evening. A few weeks later the Benedictine rented a modest little house in Milton Road, Stoke Newington, as a provisional monastery. The community consisted of himself, Brothers Alban and Philip, the Infant Samuel and Sister Ambrosia. For the next six months the Superior spent the weekends with Mr and Mrs Denton in Finsbury Circus, and the rest of the time at Stoke Newington.

It was not long before Ignatius of Jesus became the "talk of the town", his name appearing in the newspapers frequently. On August 31 *The Times* reported "an enormous congregation" at that hot-bed of Romanism in disguise—St Michael's, Shoreditch. The preacher was "The Rev. James Leicester (*sic*) Lyne, formerly known as Fr Ignatius of the Norwich monastery". The real "star turn", however, was Mr Julius, Bishop of Iona, who looked every inch an oriental-occidental prelate in his gorgeous garments.[26] He had already offered a "validate" the orders of any deacon or priest of the Church of England. Had he been asked, this freelance bishop would have been quite willing to raise Ignatius of Jesus to the priesthood.

On September 19, a letter from Archbishop Longley was printed in *The Times*, who stated that he had washed his hands of Mr Lyne and his "monkery", also that he had never promised to make him a priest.

To keep his infantile purity unsullied, it was decided that Ignatius of Mary ought to receive his first Communion, for he was now three years old. Dr Littledale saw no reasons against falling into line with Eastern Orthodox custom and agreed to perform the ceremony on Christmas Day. It appears to have taken place in the chapel of the Society of St Margaret (East Grinstead) which then had a small convent in Ash Grove, Hackney.[27]

The ten and a half months spent by the Benedictine at St Bartholomew's, Moor Lane, proved most profitable, thanks to his preaching. In March 1867 he moved his mixed-community from Stoke Newington to a Mission House in the city of London, where they remained three months. A Holy Week Mission at St Ethelburga's, Bishopsgate, nearly resulted in riots. Many conversions took place. Two wealthy ladies begged to be admitted to the Third Order, and became known as Sister Frances and Sister Winifred.

Among others who "Found Salvation" was the Rev. Douglas Boutflower, a naval chaplain, whose first meeting with Ignatius was at the Bristol Church Congress of 1864. He had paid more than one visit to the Norwich priory, and was shocked to hear of the "disgraceful fraud" by which the good monks had been robbed of their lawful property. Having been clothed as a Tertiary, with the name of Fr Bernard, he offered to pay the rent of any house to serve as a temporary monastery until the brethren could regain possession of their home at Norwich. So at long last there was the prospect of the Benedictines ceasing to be Gyrovags.

NOTES

[1] p. 293.

[2] p. 295.

[3] A few years later when Ignatius had founded another monastery these verses were sung as a gradual at Mass on the greater festivals.

[4] It was not until 1876 that this former member of the Ignatian Order of St Benedict was arrested and sentenced to a long term of imprisonment. His accomplice, so it was said, finally ended up in a Trappist monastery in South America.

[5] p. 308.

[6] Cf. Isaiah 51: 3.

[7] p. 309.

[8] p. 10.

[9] p. 311. Benedictine monks were then an uncommon sight in France for the only monasteries in 1866 were the abebys of Solesmes and Ligugé, and the priories of Marseilles and Pierre-qui-Vire. The latter belonged to the Cassinese Congregation of the Primitive Observance, the three others to the Solesmes Congregation.

[10] Born in 1834, he was the author of *Walks in Rome, Memorials of a Quiet Life*, and many other artistic, antiquarian and biographical works. He died in 1903.

[11] p. 317.

[12] In 1884 Fr Brownlow was appointed 4th Bishop of Clifton.

[13] pp. 320-1.

[14] p. 324.

[15] p. 326.

[16] Trower was Bishop of Glasgow and Galloway from 1848 to 1859, so he may have met Lyne when he was a student at Trinity College, Glenalmond.

[17] p. 332.

[18] p. 339.

[19] Cf. Calder-Marshall, op. cit., p. 154.

[20] p. 339.

[21] ibid, pp. 135-6. Ignatius' punctuation was so erratic, that full stops and commas have been added to the printed version of this letter.

[22] Another refuge for these two Benedictine Brothers might have been found in a little house off the Iffley Road, Oxford, where since August 1865 the Rev. R. M. Benson, the Rev. Charles Grafton, the Rev. Oliver Prescott, and a few other men were testing their vocations as the first members of the Society of St John the Evangelist. The rules of this "college of clergymen" had already been approved by Dr Wilberforce, Bishop of Oxford. Brothers Alban and Philip also had the chance of staying with the Rev. R. Tuke in Hackney who was planning a small religious community to which he gave the name of the Society of St Joseph in the summer of 1866. In Lincolnshire the Rev. T. R. Mossman had begun to draw up rules for the Brotherhood of the Holy Redeemer for poor ordinands. In Hampshire the Rev. George Nugée, "in the absence of higher authority and sanction", was dreaming of reviving the Order of St Augustine, "in the hope of the reunion of Christendom, and especially that of the Anglican and Western branches of the Western Church".

[23] The property had been bought by Dr Pusey in 1865, after her medical adviser had decided that "weakness of the lungs" necessitated "change and rest in a retired watering place" (T. J. Williams, op. cit. p. 237).

[24] Pennethorne Hughes, *The Isle of Wight* (Shell Guide, 1967), p. 25.

[25] Cf. Pennethorne Hughes, op. cit., p. 25.

[26] Jules Ferrette, a lapsed French Dominican who, having cast off the yoke of Rome in 1856, worked for some years with the Irish Presbyterian Mission at Damascus. Having been raised to the episcopate by Mar Bedros, Bishop of Emesa (Homes) of the Syrian Jacobite Church—so it was said—he turned up in England claiming to be its Patriarchal Legate for Western Europe. After about four months most of the ritualistic clergymen who had befriended him, decided that he was bogus, and he disappeared to North America. (Cf. H. R. T. Brandreth, *Episcopi Vagantes and the Anglican Church* (2nd ed. 1961, pp. 70-89); P. F. Anson, *Bishops at Large* (1964), pp. 31-47.)

[27] Richard Littledale (1833-1890) is best remembered by his *Plain Reasons against joining the Church of Rome,* first published in 1880.

F

CHAPTER V

"The Second Spring": the First Order of St Benedict revived at
Laleham-on-Thames, and the foundation of its enclosed nunnery
at Feltham, Middlesex (1867-1870)

IGNATIUS first thought of moving his few monks to the Black Mountains of Wales, but without reflecting how they were to be housed. That could be left to the ever-helpful angels. He got in touch with the agents of Mr Walter Savage Landor, who told him that there was no chance of Benedictines being allowed to rebuild the ruined Priory at Llanthony.

Eventually he decided to rent for three years what was described as "a small but uncomely red brick house" at Laleham-on-Thames, two miles south of Staines. Workmen were engaged to transform it into a monastery. The first essential feature was a grille through which conversation between the monks and seculars of both sexes could be carried on without violating enclosure. Doors were pierced in what was called the "Cloister". The outer lodge was adapted to serve as "a shelter for waifs and wayfarers", who as Ignatius' biographer explained, "are never slow to avail themselves of the hospitality traditional to a residence of Monks". The coach-house was turned into a chapel, which at certain hours would be open to the public. We are told that this was "a step keenly appreciated by the somewhat mystified but at all times kindly disposed natives".[1] The Superior could now feel that in a modest manner he was rebuilding the waste places of the Benedictine abbey at Chertsey, two miles down the river, founded by Erkenwald, afterwards Bishop of London, in 666, and refounded by King Edgar in 964. The brethren, including the Infant Samuel, migrated from London to Laleham in June 1867.

The Reverend Father, however, had so many irons in the fire that it was necessary to him to maintain a "Metropolitan Mission House" as well as a monastery at the far end of Middlesex. The former was situated at 51 Hunter Street, Bloomsbury; under the charge and financed by Sister Gertrude of the Third Order. Weekly sermons had to be preached at St Edmund's, Lombard Street, and St Paul's, Bunhill Row. By this time Ignatius had broken off relations with Mr Denton at Bartholomew's, Moor Lane, who protested that the "lecturer" wasted gas by holding Sunday evening "levées" in the vestry. So the Benedictine still remained more or less of a Gyrovag in the sense that much of his time was spent in trains between London and Staines.

One Sunday evening in September the Monk led a large number of his Third Order Brothers and Sisters, as well as members of his Bible Class, to St Michael's, Shoreditch. He wanted to demonstrate his approval of the strong line taken by Bishop Grey of Cape Town, who had solemnly excommunicated Dr Colenso, Bishop of Natal, for heresy the previous year. It was an obvious duty to rally round this faithful soldier of Christ. He was one of the seventy-six bishops attending the first Lambeth Conference, and had agreed to preach at this ritualistic stronghold. A sensation was caused when the procession of men and women, headed by the black-cowled and tonsured Benedictine, entered the church, which was already filled. All they could do was to kneel down in the aisles and empty corners. Bishop Grey noticed them, stopped in the middle of his sermon and imparted a special benediction.

Punch, in its issue of September 21, described this magnificent function as "Ritualistic Theatricals in Shoreditch". Quite correct, for the high altar was illuminated by no less than fifty-six wax candles, besides two large candelabra. There was a long row of tapers on the chancel-screen, and a profusion of gas jets in addition. The floral decorations equalled in brilliance anything witnessed at the Horticultural Gardens. The many acolytes were vested in scarlet cassocks and cambric cottas. Such was the sort of Catholic worship that appealed to Ignatius of Jesus.[2]

The problem of finding a resident chaplain for the Laleham "monkery" was solved by the arrival of a Bavarian priest named Fr Lohrum. He had no scruples about saying a Latin Mass in this schismatic place of worship. It is recorded that "the affection which he conceived for his surroundings was quite touching". Archbishop Manning, in whose diocese the Anglican monastery was located, heard of these goings-on, and caused a visitation to be made by one of his clergy. "The sturdy Bavarian elected nevertheless to stand his ground. He was not, he argued, saying Mass in a parish church, but in a monastic chapel, which was extra-diocesan, and therefore beyond the pale of jurisdiction. And upon the strength of this precedent, he quietly ignored the admonition, and persevered."[3] Yet he compromised up to a point by leaving the chalice on the altar to be administered by the deacon Superior, when he happened to be in residence.[4]

It may well be that Fr Lohrum was a disciple of his fellow-Bavarian, Dr Döllinger, who as early as 1861 had published two lectures in which he attacked the temporal power of the Papacy. The promulgation of the Syllabus of Errors by Pius IX in 1864, attacking Liberalism in a set of eighty theses, helped to fan the flames of a fairly wide-spread detestation of Ultramontanism. It was not easy for Ignatius to find another chaplain. None of the Anglican clergymen in the neighbourhood of Laleham were prepared to administer the Lord's Supper or Holy Communion in this unlicensed monastic chapel. Neither would any of the Jesuits at Beaumont College have dared to say Mass at the Priory of Our Ladye and St Dunstan, even if they were sympathetic towards the Benedictines. There were no other Roman Catholic priests within easy access to whom the Superior could appeal.

Still there was one Anglican incumbent who was quite prepared to minister to the monks occasionally—Dr F. G. Lee, who had been presented with the living of All Saints', Lambeth, early in 1867.[5] It was easy for him to board a train for Staines, his church being under the shadow of Waterloo station. One morning when he was celebrating the Holy Eucharist with the intention of renewing the Consecrated Elements in the tabernacle, there were only two of the Brethren present, one of them Ignatius. Just as he was about to deliver the chalice, a third monk materialized. Suddenly he drew his hood over his head and vanished without communicating. As this priest claimed to have had countless paranormal experiences since boyhood, having been brought up in a house near Aberdeen said to be haunted, and as his first poem, written at the age of seventeen, was entitled "The Vampyre", it is not surprising that he was the first to encounter this phantom monk.[6] He made his presence felt on several occasions at Laleham, and later on after the community moved to the Black Mountains of Wales in 1870. The spectre was seen by many in broad daylight as well as during the night, when he was alleged to carry "a covered lamp of old-world fashion". Otherwise his hands were hidden beneath his black scapular, the hood being "drawn closely over his bowed head". Those who had a glimpse of his face described it as "pale and handsome, its expression denoting deep but not ungentle melancholy".[7] For the next forty years the Ignatian revival of Benedictine monasticism was made more melodramatic by ghosts manifesting themselves.

83

The Reverend Father spent little time with his monks, all of whom were postulants or novices, for he had to make money to feed and clothe them by preaching at St Edmund's, Lombard Street.[8]

Feeling sure that Dr Tait must be impressed by the soul-saving campaigns in his diocese, the Benedictine implored the Bishop to give him to the priesthood. The only result was a letter in which the Bishop begged the deacon "to give up the attempt to engraft on the Church of England parts of the Roman sysem which are disapproved of by the whole of our Church governors". The otherwise kindly letter ended: "I am greatly interested in what I hear of your zeal and of the earnestness of your preaching, but you must suffer me to remind you as set over you in the Lord, that the course which you pursued in Norwich, and which I fear you are anxious to pursue again, seems to have so much self-will in it that it cannot be expected to be followed by God's blessing."[9]

This was just what Ignatius of Jesus intended to do, and he lost no time. First of all he professed Br Philip of the Holy Cross and Br Dunstan of the Crown of Thorns; then he resolved to found a community of enclosed nuns.[10] The Oblate Sisters of Mount Calvary at Norwich had been disbanded, but some of them wanted to resume the religious life, so Abbess Lydia was consulted.[11]

The foundation was visualized as "a twin community, according to the precedent of the Old Saxon Abbeys".[12] What the would-be Founder forgot or ignored was that their Major Superior was invariably a woman, just as was the case with all later double-monasteries, with the exception of the Gilbertines.[13]

One member of Abbess Lydia's Third Order, Sister Ella, on hearing of the project of establishing a twin-community, was already "determined to become a Benedictine Nun—an ambition which she had hitherto been unable to realise, owing to the non-existence of an Anglican enclosed Order."[14]

This lady, as Miss Emily Harriet Stewart, had been associated with the Devonport Sisters of Mercy since 1849, when she helped to nurse patients during a cholera epidemic. Her first meeting with the future Fr Ignatius was when he was Mr Prynne's honorary curate at St Peter's, Plymouth, in 1861. On September 4, the following year, she entered the novitiate of the Society of St Margaret at East Grinstead. Her profession took place in the chapel of the temporary convent on September 8, 1863.[15] It is recorded that Dr Neale himself preached on "the day she took the habit" (with the religious name of Ella), and when she was professed with two other Sisters, "Dr Littledale came, bringing his cope". There was "Benediction at 7, and Dr Little-dale preached."[16]

Sister Ella spent only four years with this community, and left East Grinstead about the time of Dr Neale's death in August 1866, i.e. shortly after Fr Ignatius' conversion in the Isle of Wight. Her next step was to join Abbess Lydia's Sisters of Charity in London. She was one of the many women who ministered to the patients in the temporary cholera hospitals erected by the Abbess. It was while she was working in Bethnal Green that she met Br Philip, Br Alban, and the Hon. Charles Wood (the future Viscount Halifax), all of whom were employed in the men's wards, unpacking blankets or doling out food and medicines.

It is improbable that any of the founders of then existing Anglican sisterhoods would have agreed with Ignatius that the moment had come for the establishment of an enclosed community of women. The point of view of the average High Church clergyman or layman had been expressed in 1866 by the Rev. Sabine Baring-Gould, who wrote: "One thing is very evident throughout Europe, even under the most favourable circumstances, the contemplative orders are fading away, and the active societies are stepping into their places. We would not suggest any reproduction of a purely contemplative and ascetic order in England. There seems to be no demand for it, no field for it to occupy."[17]

So far as is known, Ignatius had never visited any Roman Catholic Benedictine nunneries. Neither had Sister Ella nor Abbess Lydia.[18] Their knowledge of the enclosed and contemplative life for women was based on what they had read or heard. It is fairly certain that Dr Tait, Bishop of London, would have refused to give his blessing on a strictly enclosed nunnery in his diocese, for he had already urged Ignatius to stop trying to "engraft on the Church of England parts of the Roman system which were disapproved of by the whole of our Church governors".[19] Again, most Anglo-Catholics otherwise sympathetic towards the religious life, were unlikely to support the proposed foundation if they heard it was being sponsored by Dr Pusey and Abbess Lydia. By this time churchpeople had begun to gossip about their platonic relations, in much the same way that the general public joked about Queen Victoria's infatuation for John Brown. In 1865 he had been appointed "The Queen's Highland Servant", and was her inseparable companion and confidant.

After April 3, 1868, there was an even stronger reason to be suspicious about a twin-community on Anglo-Saxon lines, in which men and women would live together in close proximity. The *Morning Post* printed a letter from an ultra-Protestant clergyman with the caption "STARTLING DISCLOSURES ABOUT FATHER IGNATIUS". Thanks to a wealthy lady, the Hanover Square Rooms, London, had been hired. The ex-Br Stanislaus was going to make a personal appearance and reveal many a secret of the cloister. He hinted that they would include "the grossest and most indecent" stories, "listened to with avidity by the monks" at Norwich, who had also "sold and purchased the most improper books". Ignatius bade his biographer to write: "The aim was to brand the Norwich Community as a hotbed of unnameable iniquity, presided over by a Superior unworthy of the title, who had been either too callous or too idle to root out an evil which was daily ripening and rotting under his very nose. There was no mincing up so foul a matter. Such a man must be a fool or a devil, and to this obvious conclusion the clerical liar had no difficulty in leading his hearers, with a result that may be easily imagined."[20]

One Sunday evening after Ignatius had ended his sermon at St Edmund's, Lombard Street, a boy had the courage to reveal that he and others had been brought to London, and lodged with a clergyman, who was coaching them in what they must say at the Hanover Rooms meetings. These lads were being well supplied with money and drink. "The prodigal son besought the forgiveness of his deeply injured Superior." But "at the height of the crisis, and when every door seemed closely shut, the Hand of God intervened, and turned the tables of the 'disclosures' on the guilty parties. Two remarkable things happened almost in the same breath."[21]

The editor of a newspaper placed his columns at the disposal of the Monk. Stanislaus repented of his sins, went to confession, and cast himself at the Reverend Father's feet, begging final forgiveness, and imploring re-admission to the community, but with no success.

When the Rev. J. L. Lyne decided to become a Benedictine in 1862, he was absolutely certain that he would have to face persecution of every kind, perhaps martyrdom, and things had worked out much as he expected. Smarting under defeat, and the failure of their machinations, militant Protestants lost no time, so determined were they to prevent the building up of the monastic waste places in Middlesex. On Sundays and festivals gangs of hooligans arrived at Laleham from London. They roared and ranted outside the coach-house chapel, disturbing the Work of God. Not content with brawling outside the enclosure these ruffians tried to force an entry by breaking open doors. They adorned their hats and caps with "No Popery" badges. It is recorded that "The Reverend Father remembers with lively gratitude, the plucky way in which the local police and neighbours charged on the band of rowdies, and drove them pell-mell into the high road in full retreat. But even in spite of this gallant defence, a considerable amount of damage was done by the mob; and amongst other aggressions, they seized and literally smashed to pieces a large image of the Madonna, which happened to be enshrined in the garden, and therefore was within reach of their insane fury."[22]

Yet this was not the end of the troubles. Once again the kind-hearted Superior admitted a young man who turned out to be a wolf in sheep's clothing. Aged twenty-six, Br John had served in the 67th Regiment, and after a wild life in the Army asked to join the community as a penitent. He soon became violent and deceitful—even worse, he was "troubled with a mania for murder", so it was recorded in the Register. Then he disappeared, and it was said that he submitted to the Church of Rome.

Lurid reports of idolatry at Laleham were published in *The Rock*, so Ignatius O.S.B. replied: "The Host was not carried; no prayer, or anything like one, was made to the Virgin. No woman draped in black, or anything else, walked barefoot; nor was a doll carried representing the Infant Saviour. We did not 'scrupulously conceal any of our proceedings from the public eye', as we are proud of our religion, and have nothing to conceal. We were compelled to send for a carpenter to nail up hangings round the house and chapel, as Mr ——— and his companions were so violent and abusive that we required this protection."[23]

Fearing that the Reverend Father was on the verge of another breakdown, the community and some of the Third Order persuaded him to accept an invitation from his old friend Mrs Cameron ("Mamsie") to stay with her in Glen Urquhart. He travelled to Scotland with the Consecrated Elements among his luggage. This meant that every Sunday he was able "to communicate his friends from the Contents of this mysterious casket", but without permission from Dr Eden, Bishop of Moray, Ross, and Caithness.[24] We are told that "this short holiday was indeed a blessed respite from the weary tension of mind and body", yet "it was a wild sky that broke over the close of the year 1868, and a darker one still which shadowed the commencement of its successor, 1869. Flashes of sun, rushes of clouds, and the final domination of the latter. Clouds everywhere and on all sides! Clouds that held thunder, hail and tempest; clouds that very nearly broke and blotted out the sun."[25]

On his reurn to Laleham, Ignatius decided to go ahead with the foundation of a double-community of monks and nuns, determined that the latter must be under his immediate supervision. Hence the necessity for their convent to be as near as possible to his monastery. The only suitable property at the moment was a picturesque seventeenth-century farmhouse at Feltham, four miles north-east of Laleham. It stood in a large neglected garden, secluded by high hedges. The village—as it was a hundred years ago—lay off the London-Southampton road, between Hounslow and Staines. The level countryside consisted of fields and market gardens. There were about 1,000 inhabitants, some flax-mills, but nothing of special interest.

What may well have decided the Monk to rent this property on a twenty-one years' lease was that the parish church, rebuilt in a neo-Norman style in 1802, was dedicated to St Dunstan. He was quite capable of believing that his footsteps had been directed to this farmhouse, about a mile from the railway station, by this Anglo-Saxon Benedictine, successively Abbot of Glastonbury, Bishop of Worcester, then of London, and finally Archbishop of Canterbury.

The first thing that Ignatius did was to ensure that his nuns—like his monks—should never forget that they were walled up from the wicked world for the rest of their lives, unless, which God forbid, they had to be excommunicated, or even worse, leapt over the walls and ran away. Their home must be a living tomb, and their slogan *"memento mori"*. So at Feltham, as at Laleham, he had to take care that the inmates of the conventual establishment were correctly "enclosed". No doubt, if money had been forthcoming the Superior-General of the twin-community would have tried to obey most of the rules laid down by St Charles Borromeo in his legislation for convents, found in the *Instructions on Ecclesiastical Building*.[26] Considering the attacks made on the Laleham monastery by gangs of ruffians, Ignatius would have been justified in conforming to the Borromean regulation that the garden walls of a convent must be twenty-two feet in height. The high hedges surrounding the property were hardly enough protection from intruders. Just as in the Archdiocese of Milan, so in the Diocese of London, so many precautions had to be taken to prevent violation of chastity. For the moment all that could be done was to erect a wooden grille in the midst of the room which would serve as the chapel. This would prevent the nuns from being seen by seculars. Another ground-floor room was chosen as the parlour. A grille was inserted between the door and the fireplace; covered with red flannel curtains. Behind them members of the community would be able to converse with visitors while remaining invisible. Illuminated texts from the Bible and engravings of saints on the walls helped to create a conventual atmosphere. The poverty of the establishment was expressed by a ragged carpet and an old couch. The Superior-General furnished a bed-sitter for his own use, believing that his status allowed him to enter the enclosure whenever it suited him.

One day—the actual date has not been discovered—Sister Ella travelled from Waterloo to Staines, whence she either walked or was driven to Laleham. Having cast off the blue habit of Abbess Lydia's Sisters of Charity, she was clothed by Fr Ignatius with the black Benedictine tunic, veil, scapular, knotted cord girdle, rosary and sandals. He gave her the religious name of Hilda, because she was to be the superioress of the female section of the first Benedictine double-community established in Britain since Anglo-Saxon times.

As soon as the old farmhouse was ready for occupation Mother Hilda was installed as Prioress.[27] Miss Agnes Huthwaite, who had been an Oblate of Mount Calvary at Norwich, was made Sub-Prioress, with the name of Sister Mary Etheldreda.[28] Before long some novices were clothed, among whom were Sisters Cecilia, Werburgh, and Mary Agnes.

It is a pity that we have no first-hand memories of the life led by this little community, and what were their observances, but it may be presumed that Fr Ignatius took the utmost care that, so far as was possible, his nuns kept the same *horarium* as his monks, and that he imposed the same penances upon them.

Still, his biographer painted what is probably a fairly true picture of his own life after the nunnery was founded: "Needless to say, these new developments gave the Reverend Father a ceaseless protraction of labour and anxiety which he was physically unequal to meet, but he had no thought except to the manipulation of the mighty ball that his individual efforts had unearthed and set rolling through the land. Every day that passed had now become a fresh and crowded page of life. The weekly programme was indeed an arduous one. From Monday to Thursday inclusive, the Superior divided his time between his two Communities of Monks and Nuns, and every Friday he resumed his duties at the Hunter Street Mission House, and fulfilling engagements at the different churches to which he was at that time attached."[29] The sermons continued to attract vast congregations.

Neither the monks nor the nuns were allowed to use any of the already available Anglican office-books, which would have made what St Benedict calls "The Work of God" so much easier and less distracting. This meant that the Divine Office was mainly bits of the *Breviarium Monasticum* translated into English and handwritten, but certain portions, e.g. the Antiphons of Our Lady, the *Benedictus* at Lauds, and the *Magnificat* at Vespers remained in Latin. The Book of Common Prayer provided a vernacular version of the psalms. "Devotions" of this or that nature were tacked on to some of the offices.[30]

In more ways than one the life of these enclosed nuns in Middlesex must have been somewhat exotic, for they wore long red veils at Mass and Benediction, and white ones for Exposition of the Blessed Sacrament.[31] These 'Romish' additions to the traditional Benedictine habit would have astonished St Hilda, and other Anglo-Saxon nuns, who had never even heard of the rites of Benediction and Exposition.

It was not often that a clergyman could be found to administer the Lord's Supper or Holy Communion at the Feltham convent, and there was no resident chaplain. Should the Superior-General happen to be staying with the nuns, he adopted the same ceremonial as with his monks, by celebrating a sort of "Dry Mass", known as "The Offering of the Blessed Sacrament". Vested in alb, deacon's stole and cope, he recited the Common and Proper of the Holy Communion service for the day, omitting the prayers at the offertory, also the Prayer of Consecration. Then he took the ciborium and the chalice from the tabernacle, elevated them for adoration, after which the *Agnus Dei* was sung. Communion was given under both species.[32]

After his miraculous "Conversion" in the summer of 1866, the restorer of the Benedictine Order ceased to attach much importance to the sacrament of Penance. All that counted was the inward sense of having "Found Salvation". So it did not matter much that his monks and nuns had few opportunities to go to Confession. On the other hand, he demanded frequent "manifestations of conscience" being made to himself.

It is doubtful if any Benedictine monasteries at any period of history ever had such a rigid system of penances as in those ruled over by Ignatius of Jesus. By 1868 there were forty-nine so called "Observances", which had to be read daily, each with its own special penance. If a monk or nun broke some domestic utensil, it had to be held aloft during Vespers. If a bit of a newspaper, a book, or a letter lying about was read without permission, it was tied round the neck of the offender for several days. To look at a secular involved being blindfolded and sitting in choir facing the grille at each office throughout the day. The usual penalty for speaking to layfolk was to wear a piece of lay-clothing over the habit for a day or two. A monk or nun late for an office was made to kneel in the midst of the choir till the end of the service. Religious of both sexes had to genuflect before speaking to the Superior-General, and kiss the hem of his cowl. Because he firmly believed that he held the place of Christ in his double-community, Ignatius of Jesus took for granted that he himself was dispensed from keeping any of the forty-nine "Observances", as well as the rigid rules of abstinence and fasting he imposed on his subjects.

Monks and nuns were forbidden to converse with each other outside times of recreation. If anybody had to speak, it could be done only in a whisper—hands beneath the scapular, and in the case of a monk, with the hood drawn over the head. The penance for breaking Solemn Silence between Compline and after Prime was to recite the entire Psalter in church, either before going to bed, or at some other time. This took up nearly three hours. Serious breaches of silence—even in the early Norwich days—involved reparation by tracing a cross with the tongue on the ground. Even in the hottest weather, not a sip of water could be drunk outside meal-times. The monks were strictly forbidden to eat anything left over from the ample repasts provided for the Reverend Father. They had to be respected as consecrated elements. There was no rubric permitting chosen members of the community to "reverently eat and drink of the same" as provided in the *Book of Common Prayer* for "any remaining Bread of that which was consecrated". Unconsumed bits of food had to be disposed of reverently. Neither were the brethren allowed to spread their bread with the dripping from the beef or mutton roasted exclusively for him who held the place of Christ in the monastery.

Like Dr Pusey, Ignatius believed that flagellation was most beneficial to the spiritual life of those who had been called to the cloister, though it is nowhere recorded that he ever used a whip on himself, or got anybody else to scourge him. On the other hand he seldom lost an opportunity to inflict corporal punishment as recommended in the Rule of St Benedict for those who will not amend after frequent correction.[33]

Blind obedience was demanded. Ignatius of Jesus agreed with Abbess Lydia, his spiritual mother, that it must be given "without sign of hesitation or repugnance", otherwise a Sister had "failed to resist a temptation of the Evil One". The Superior-General of the Order of St Benedict regarded himself as virtually infallible, not only when he made pronouncements *ex cathedra* at Chapter. He discouraged serious reading among his subjects, and never tried to make Mother Hilda and her community emulate some of the erudite medieval Benedictine nuns, in fact he did everything possible to prevent what he called "worldly studies" among his own religious of both sexes.[34] Mr Donald Attwater pointed out: "Yet his reading on the religious life was deplorably limited: his basic ideas were derived from Cassian and Dalgairns' Tractarian account of St Stephen Harding and the foundations of Citeaux; but his daily guides in monastic and spiritual life was Montalembert's *Monks of the West*, and Butler's *Lives of the Saints*, and there could hardly be worse ones for a man of his temperament and upbringing."[35]

Having founded his so-called "twin community according to the precedent of the old Anglo-Saxon Abbeys", he proclaimed that his monks and nuns were the only *true* religious in the Church of England, explaining that he had "the sanction of the *whole* Church for monasticism and the Benedictine Rule" upon which the double-community was supposed to be revived. There was only one Anglican community that he recognised apart from his own—Abbess Lydia's Society of the Most Holy Trinity. By 1868 there were twenty sisterhoods, large and small, scattered over England, but Ignatius used to say that they merely pretended to be conventual when they were not, because they were directed by clergymen, some of whom were married.[36]

The Superior-General continued to be a sort of monastic-Martha, "distracted with much serving, anxious and troubled about many things". These included the groups of Tertiaries in London, Bristol, Birmingham, Brighton, Leeds and elsewhere which had to be visited at intervals.

Sister Gertrude, the Prioress of the London Third Order, began to be troublesome. One day she asked Ignatius to allow her to take life-vows. A wedding ring was produced for him to bless as symbolic of the consecration of a virgin. "It was in vain that he reminded her of the great 'gulf stream' lying between the cloistered nun and the Christian lay-helper, and demonstrated the hopeless incongruity of straining to bridge over the unbridgeable—she was not to be convinced, and the germ of friction arose from that moment."[37] It is possible that Sister Gertrude was jealous of the Prioress of Feltham, because she was a *Mother*, not a mere *Sister*.

The situation became strained. Finally the Reverend Father delivered an ultimatum: either Sister Gertrude must recognise his authority over her, or pack up and clear out. Having sunk all her money in this Bloomsbury boarding-house she sat tight and refused to budge. Finally Ignatius decided to unsheathe "the sword of separation" or amputating knife as ordered in the twenty-eighth chapter of the Benedictine Rule, and to expel this wicked woman. So she was solemnly excommunicated.

The deposed Prioress then called on Dr Tait, Bishop of London, at Fulham Palace, informing him that she had been excommunicated from *the Church of England*, not merely the Third Order. With good reason the Bishop was shocked, and sent a letter to *The Times*, denouncing this uncanonical action by the deacon-monk; inhibiting him from further preaching in the London Diocese.

Following this, Ignatius had an interview with Dr Tait, who offered to release him from his monastic vows. The Benedictine replied: "My Lord, what you ask of me is tantamount to asking me to go to Hell!" The Bishop's comment was "Then really, Mr Lyne, I don't see what more I can say upon the subject".[38] This did not stop the inhibited Monk from preaching. He hired the Shore Street Music Hall, off Tottenham Court Road, and for the next few months, it was a case of "House Full. Standing Room Only" every Sunday evening.

Soul-saving was far more important than keeping an eye on his monks and nuns. Ignatius, accompanied by his mother, went off to Margate for another Mission. On the morning of February 18, 1869, a newspaper informed them that the ex-Br Stanislaus, and his youthful companion, Br Osmund, had appeared before the magistrates at the Marylebone Police Court on a charge of drunkenness and disorderly behaviour on the streets. The latter had stated that the Superior of the Norwich monastery had condoned and even encouraged their relationship "by performing on their behalf, and in his church, a ceremony which in itself was blasphemous and sacrilege of the most revolting kind".[39]

These sordid revelations led to the publication of a leaflet entitled *The Results of Monasticism*. It was more than enough to convince the man in the street that conventual establishments were now worse hotbeds of vice than when *The Awful Disclosures of Maria Monk* was first issued at Montreal in 1835—a booklet which was still being distributed and sold by Protestant organisations.

Yet the Monk did not return to his monastery at Laleham. He moved on from Margate to Folkestone, where he had been booked to give a Lenten Mission. Other members of the Lyne family joined him. It is possible that the audiences were larger than usual because the President of the Evangelical Mission had plastered the hoardings with defamatory posters, not only at Folkestone, but also at Dover. Mr Lyne Snr. instituted a prosecution for libel, which led to an apology in *The Times*. The Order of St Benedict got more than enough boosting in the spring of that year. *The Results of Monasticism* proved a best-seller.[40]

Meanwhile the case of Lyne v. Drury dragged on. In March 1869 a Bill of Complaint of over 6,000 words was filed in Chancery by the Rev. Joseph Leycester Lyne against the Rev. George Drury. Mr Lyne Snr. had taken up the matter, and was supporting his "young and unsuspecting son", but the solicitors realised that the case was hopeless—merely throwing money down the drain. On May 31 Miss Louisa Stone, who had give about £550 towards the foundation, informed Mr Drury that the charges which Mr Lyne was making against him appeared to her to be totally unfounded. On July 29, 1870, the Lynes finally agreed that it would be too risky to take the case to open courts. They accepted the Vice-Chancellor's decision to pay the defendant's costs, amounting to £165 16s. 0d. The accusations made by the Benedictine against his former generous benefactor and spiritual director were so widely inaccurate and brimful of inconsistencies that the Lyne family was well advised to let the matter drop.[41]

Neither Lyne Snr. nor Lyne Jnr. were ever logical. As to the latter, if he had really taken Solemn Vows early in 1864, which he claimed to have done, then from the point of view of Western Canon Law, he was incapable of holding property in his own name. Right from the start of his effort to revive the Benedictine Order he had stated again and again that he could not be bothered with business matters, insisting that others must relieve him of them. Actually it was not until April 1866 that he first put forward that he was the legal owner of Elm Hill Priory, yet everything pointed to the fact that this was far from being the case. The Monk's mind was always in a muddle.

Such was the stormy background against which the Benedictine twin-community came into being. For the greater part of eighteen months the ubiquitous Founder, who was always on the move, seldom had time to pay more than flying visits to his monks at Laleham and his nuns at Feltham. Still, there was a rift in the dark clouds and a gleam of sunshine in the autumn of 1869 when Sister Winifred Early of the Third Order presented Ignatius of Jesus with £1,000, which was followed soon afterwards with the lump sum of £1,300 from Fr Bernard Boutflower (the naval chaplain Tertiary). This wealth roused him to take immediate steps to buy the ruins of Llanthony Priory. Once again the Landor family refused to sell the property. So determined was Ignatius to make a Benedictine foundation in this valley of the Black Mountains, formerly the home of Austin Canons, that he was quixotic enough to jump at the offer of thirty-three acres of arable and pasture land, together with the right of a sheep-walk, four miles beyond the Priory, just over the border of the County of Brecknock.

Throughout his life, Joseph Leycester Lyne was a romantic rather than a realist. It probably never struck him how difficult and costly it would be to build a monastery in this remote spot at the back of beyond. Quite likely he believed that it would be erected by angelic hands. Having found that Laleham was too isolated as a base for his multiform activities, and made London the usual base of operations, he was now prepared to cut himself off from the metropolis one hundred and eighty miles instead of eighteen. The site chosen was eleven miles from the nearest railway station, whence a cart track led to Llanthony Priory. After this there was merely a rough path, so indistinct that strangers often got lost in what was a virtual desert. The only signs of human habitation at Capel-y-Ffin were an old farmhouse, a derelict cottage, and a tumble-down barn.

If Ignatius of Jesus had decided to preach a sermon on this monastic migration to the mountains of South Wales, the prophet Jeremiah could have provided a text:

"Oh, that I had in the wilderness a lodging place of wayfaring men;
that I might leave my people and go down from them! For they are
all adulterers, an assembly of treacherous men."[42]

NOTES

[1] p. 382.
[2] *Punch* had already drawn attention to "the *Ignatius chaussure*", recommending that clergymen should adopt sandals as an "embellishment for the foot and ankle in association with the crinoline, and of making an edifying exhibition of Balmoral boots" (June 10, 1865).
[3] p. 387.
[4] Ignatius always maintained that the suppression of the chalice to the laity was in itself enough to prevent him ever becoming a Roman Catholic. He had a horror of what he called a "mutilated Sacrament".
[5] At that date it was in the Winchester Diocese, whereas Laleham was in that of London.
[6] Among Lee's books were *The Other World, or Glimpses of the Supernatural* (2 vols. 1875), *More Glimpses of the World Unseen* (1878), *Glimpses of the Twilight* (1885), and *Sights and Shadows* (1894).
[7] p. 389.
[8] On one occasion, so it is said, a crowd of 60,000 persons tried to get into the church. On leaving it Ignatius was attacked by hooligans, one of whom hurled a stone at his face, but yet another miracle was performed for unseen hands deposited the missile very gently at his feet as he sat in the cab. (See Bertouch, p. 419.)
[9] R. T. Davidson and W. Benham, *Life of Archbishop Tait* (2nd ed. 1891), Vol. I, pp. 503-4.
[10] Fr Ignatius invented his own system of monastic probation. After three years a brother was called a "professed novice", with the title of "father". Unlike Abbot Aelred, he never

adopted the modern Roman Catholic system of admitting a monk to Solemn Vows after three years in Simple Vows. (See p. 192.)

[11] Since her return from the Hawaian Islands in 1867, she had either been resting at "The Foreign Mission House" in the Isle of Wight, or directing the multiform activities of her tripartite Sisterhood at St Saviour's Hospital, Osnaburgh Street, London.

[12] p. 393.

[13] The first double-monastery in England was founded by St Hilda at Whitby in 659, with herself as abbess. Other similar communities were established at Bardney, Much Wenlock, Repton, Ely, Barking and Wimborne. They fell into decay after two hundred years, and finally disappeared. Double-monasteries were revived in France by St Robert of Arbrissel, the first at Fontrevault (1100). Women always outnumbered men, and the abbesses had supreme jurisdiction over the monks. The Gilbertines were founded at Sempringham, Lincolnshire, about 1130. The last attempt to form double-monasteries was made by St Bridget of Sweden in 1346. Her Order of the Most Holy Saviour had one house in England—Syon Abbey, Middlesex, founded in 1415. Its female section still survives at South Brent, Devonshire.

[14] ibid. Between 1856 and 1861 Abbess Lydia's "Englishe Nuns—denominated of the Sacred Heart"—had led a purely contemplative life in a stately mansion of the Elizabethan and Queen Anne periods at Bradford-on-Avon. The Constitutions of this Second Order of the Society of the Most Holy Trinity were based on those of St Colette, who in 1430 began a reform of the Poor Clares. The Bradford-on-Avon Rule forbade the nuns ever to come out of enclosure save for attendance at the parish church, or on the direct orders of their absentee Major Superioress. Their chief object was the offering "day and night throughout the four and twenty hours . . . the voice of mourning for sin, of interceding for grace, of adoration of the Majesty of the Divine Trinity and of the Love of Jesus". The original habit was white, and the "Englishe Nuns" wore neither stockings nor shoes in the house, but donned sandals over their bare feet out of doors. Their observances could hardly have been more austere and penitential. There was one nun who led the life of an anchoress, keeping perpetual silence, with Dr Pusey as her spiritual director. A watch was kept in turn by the nuns in the chapel between Compline and Matins at 3 a.m. A Holy Hour of Reparation to the Sacred Heart was observed on the eve of every Friday, starting at midnight. Eventually a few mitigations were allowed, for Abbess Lydia realised that not many women could endure this more than Trappist existence.

[15] The foundation stone of the present convent was laid on August 7, 1865.

[16] T. J. Williams, op. cit., p. 235, note 1.

[17] "On the Revival of Religious Confraternities", in *The Church and the World*, edited by Rev. Orby Shipley (1866), p. 109.
Baring-Gould (1834-1924) was a "Mission Priest" at Horbury Bridge, Yorkshire, in 1866. Later he became rector of Lew Trenchard, Devonshire, and was the author of several religious novels, as well as of *Lives of the British Saints* (16 vols., 1897).

[18] At that date there were eight Papist Benedictine convents in England: Stanbrook Abbey, Worcestershire (1525); East Bergholt Abbey, Suffolk (1598); Oulton Abbey, Staffordshire (1652); Teignmouth Abbey, Devonshire (1662), and Atherstone Priory, Warwickshire (1859). Attached to the Cassinese Congregation (Province of Supiaco) was a priory at Ramsgate, founded from Rosano, near Florence, in 1865. The Trappistine convent at Stapehill, Dorset, had been established by exiled French nuns in 1802.

[19] See p. 65.

[20] p. 398.

[21] p. 399.

[22] p. 407.

[23] p. 406.

[24] This was giving the rubric in the Scottish Liturgy a broad interpretation. It states that "according to long existing custom . . . the Presbyter may reserve so much of the Consecrated Gifts as may be required for the Communion of the Sick and others who could not be present at the celebration in church". It is somewhat doubtful if the Deacon was justified in transporting the "Gifts" over 600 miles, even presuming that his Middlesex monastery was exempt.

[25] pp. 408-9.

[26] As stated already, an English translation was published in 1857.

[27] It appears that the vows she had taken as a member of the Society of Margaret were regarded as adequate, so she was dispensed from another novitiate.

[28] After her death in 1886 it was recorded that she was "a tall and ladylike figure, always cheerful, yet rigid in her adherence to rule or the slightest whim of Fr Ignatius." (See p. 121 for account of her funeral.)

[29] p. 393.

[30] It would have saved a lot of bother had Fr Ignatius followed the example of the Sisters of the Poor in Shoreditch, who from their foundation in 1865 had used the Monastic Breviary in Latin for the Day Hours. (See p. 268.)

[31] The red veils may have been inspired by the red scapulars which had been adopted by the Canonesses Regular of St Augustine at Newton Abbot when they started Perpetual Adoration between 1860 and 1870. Or they may have been taken from the red veils worn by the Congregation of the Sacred Hearts of Jesus and Mary (usually known as "The Picpus Sisters"), who don them while engaged in adoration before the Blessed Sacrament. It could be that Ignatius found inspiration for the long white veils from the white cloaks worn by the Picpus

Sisters in choir. On the other hand, he may have borrowed them from the Institute of Marie Réparatrice, whose members wear a long white veil and cloak over their blue habits and scapulars in choir.

[32] This rite is vaguely evocative of the Catholic Apostolic (Irvingite) *"Order for the Administration of the Communion on the Lord's Day to those not present at the Consecration"*. Ignatius may well have attended Irvingite services. A new Liturgy, based on Roman and Eastern models, was first used in 1842. Incense and reservation were started about 1850.

[33] There is a story that Ignatius made one of his monks do penance for some trivial breach of the rule by lying under the refectory table for the whole day until Vespers. After this he had to give himself fifteen stripes on his bare back in the presence of the community. Then he was bidden to cover his lacerated body with the upper part of his serge tunic. About twenty years after the foundation of the Feltham convent, Ignatius confirmed that he encouraged the use of the discipline, or "cat o'nine-tails" among his nuns. Sister Mary Agnes revealed that it was the Prioress who sometimes wielded the scourge and whipped the naked backs of individual Sisters. (Cf. *Nunnery Life in the Church of England* (1891), pp. 97-9.)

[34] See p. 125. Still one of the nuns at Feltham, Sister Mary Etheldreda, was said to have been "a very highly educated woman. Were German or French people among her visitors, she would hold conversation with them as easily as with her English guests". After she migrated to Llanthony with the "loyal remnant" in 1881, she studied Welsh, "read her Welsh Bible and Prayer Book, and illustrated Welsh scrolls for the Church".

[35] *Father Ignatius of Llanthony* (1931), p. 73.

[36] Cf. *Leonard Morris or the Benedictine Novice* (1871), pp. 89-91).

[37] p. 423.

[38] Cf. p. 425.

[39] p. 430.

[40] Thirty years later Ignatius assured his biographer that had not the Rev. John C. Chambers (incumbent of St Mary's, Crown Street, Soho, from 1856 until his death in 1874) "recommended the man Br Stanislaus as an excellent and deserving person", he would not have been admitted to the Norwich monastery. Being the author of *The Priest in Absolution*. Mr Chambers ought to have been a better judge of character. Neither could Ignatius see that he was in any way responsible for the morals of Br Osmund, formerly a member of St William's Guild.

[41] In 1876 Ignatius made a final attempt to regain possession of the Norwich priory by forcing an entry, but without success. (See p. 106.)

[42] Authorized Version, 9: 2.

CHAPTER VI

Monastic life at New Llanthony Abbey, and how its Abbot
excommunicated Mother Hilda and her degenerate daughters
(1870-1878)

WORN out by the perpetual strain of building up the Benedictine waste places of Britain on supposedly Anglo-Saxon lines, Ignatius of Jesus resolved in November 1869 "to serve the Lord God apart from this most wicked age, in solitude, self-denial, labour and prayer".[1] Feeling that he deserved another holiday, he left Laleham for the windswept, treeless Lleyn peninsula in the extreme north-west of Wales. His object was to make a pilgrimage to Bardsey, once known as "The Island of 20,000 Saints", or "The Rome of Wales". Incessant gales, however, prevented him from attempting the five miles voyage from the mainland.[2] The Monk's travelling companion was the Rev. Edmund Husband, who was described as "a worthy, but withal secular priest, who has just returned to the communion of our ancient English Church from the Schismatic Sect established in our country twenty years ago by the Bishop of Rome". But Ignatius added: "Yet our Church and bishops be not without blame in this matter; having most woefully corrupted the Old Faith, Discipline and Ceremonies of our National Church". Having cast off the yoke of Rome, Fr Husband joined the Benedictine Third Order.

Refreshed after a week or two at Aberdaron, Ignatius made the long journey across Wales. On March 17, 1870, St Patrick's Day, Fr Husband celebrated the Holy Communion on a table in the old farmhouse at Capel-y-Ffin, after which the Monk laid the foundation stone of the future monastery.[3] Mr William Buckeridge agreed to design the first abbey to be built for Benedictine monks in communion with Canterbury since the sixteenth-century. He was told that the church must be an exact replica of the one four miles down the valley, erected by the Canons Regular of St Augustine after 1103. This involved a length of 212 feet, with western towers, aisled nave of eight bays, central tower, transepts, and a choir of three bays without aisles. The Founder was indifferent to the domestic arrangements. All he insisted on, so it appears, was that none of the narrow lancet windows admitted a ray of sunlight, for which reason they must face north. Views over the mountains might tempt his monks to return to the world. No doors or windows were allowed in the outer walls, so the brethren ultimately would only be able to gaze at the lofty nave across the cloister garth.[4]

Individual cells were regarded as too luxurious. All that Ignatius permitted were tiny matchboarded cubicles in an open dormitory, with no form of heating. On the other hand, he saw no reason why his cosy little sitting-room should not be given a quaint oriel window looking across the valley. The abbatial quarters would be separate from those of the monks.

It is recorded in his biography that after "the consecrated stone was laid, and the preliminaries of the building contract fully completed, the Founder of the new Abbey in embryo returned to Laleham to resume Community-life, and fulfil the numerous Mission engagements which awaited him in all parts of England".[5]

A week or two later the property in the Vale of Ewyas was legally acquired. A proof that Mother Hilda had the confidence of her Superior-General is found in the Llanthony Register where he recorded: "Owing to the persecution of Monastic Orders in England, which forbiddeth them to hold any property in land, our new Abbey lands were purchased in the Name of Mrs Emily Stewart, who in the religion of our Order is styled The Reverend Dame Mary Hilda of Jesus, a fully professed Nun of the Order of St Benedict, the Prioress of the Nuns of Feltham Priory in the County of Middlesex. There is only the name of Emily Stewart then named in the title deeds of this Property."

If Ignatius believed that as a monk it was illegal for him to buy land in South Wales, it is hard to understand why he had moved heaven and earth to prove that he was the legal owner of property in Norfolk. In regard to the "new Abbey lands" he had put himself into the hands of Mrs Emily Stewart in the same way as he had done with Mr Drury over the Norwich priory.

He was far too busy to give personal supervision to the building operations so he sent Fr Philip and Br Serene to keep an eye on them. As the lease of the farmhouse had still a year to run, it could not be used as a temporary monastery. A small shed with a flagstone floor was rushed up. The desolation of the site, its remoteness from any town or village, the lack of comfort, and the hard labour of dragging stone over mountain tracks aroused many a protest among the workmen.

On April 5, 1870, the Rev. Francis Kilvert paid his first visit to the now much talked of monastery.[6] He recorded that he noticed:

"two black figures working in a sloping patch of ground laid out as a garden, one digging and the other wheeling earth to him in a barrow. They were dressed in long black habits girt around the waist with scourge cords knotted at the end and dangling almost to the ground. The black hoods or cowls were drawn over their heads leaving their faces bare, and their naked feet were thrust into sandals with which they went slip slop along as with slippers down at heel . . . They both seemed studiously unconscious of our presence, but I saw Brother Serene glancing furtively at us from under his cowl when he thought he was under cover of a heap of earth."[7]

Kilvert added that the two masons working on the foundations of the monastery "spoke with great respect and some awe of the monks and did not seem the least inclined to laugh at them". He gathered that Fr Philip and Br Serene lodged at a nearby farmhouse, and that their diet consisted mainly of milk. No woman was allowed to come near them. They did their own washing. However, there was little of that to do, for they wore nothing beneath their black habits, and "looked very much like old women at work in the garden". The diarist commented:

"It does seem very far off at this age of the world in the latter part of the 19th century to see monks gravely wearing such dresses and to work in them in broad day. One could not help thinking how much more sensible and really religious was the dress and occupation of the masons and of the hearty healthy girl washing at the Chapel House, living naturally in the world and taking their share of its work, cares and pleasures, than the morbid unnatural life of these monks going back into the errors of the dark ages and shutting themselves up from the world to pray for the world. *'Laborare est Orare.'* "[8]

Kilvert gathered that the monks had bought 32 acres of land, and were "said to have collected £50,000, which may probably be divided by 10". Very few people had attended the foundation stone laying on St Patrick's Day.

On July 4 he jotted down in his diary that Mr and Mrs Lyne, together with their son and daughter, were staying at the Swan Inn at Hay, because Fr Ignatius was "soon expected down to look after his monastery in the Black Mountains". From what he had heard, they seemed "to be very odd people".[9] A fortnight later, on

95

St Swithin's Day, Kilvert met Miss Lyne for the first time, played croquet with her, and "longed to kiss her beautiful white little hand" as she bade him "Good night and Good bye".[10]

Towards the end of June the Father Superior decided that the moment had come to move the rest of the community to the Black Mountains. The Laleham Priory was evacuated, and on July 21, the feast of St Mary Magdalene, the exodus took place. It consisted of Ignatius himself, Fr Dunstan, two novices, Maurus and Placidus, also the Infant Samuel now aged eight-and-a-half. Both the South Western and Great Western Railways ought to have provided a Guard of Honour. The Monk recorded: "Above all the King of Kings himself did vouch to be with us on this our first arrival to inhabit this Place. For the Most Sacred Tabernacle containing the Divine Mysteries was brought by us from the Chapel at Laleham. It was of strong oak, curiously wrought and finely ornamented with gold and painting."

The Benedictine Superior-General and his entourage got off the train at Llanfihangel-Crucorney station after a long journey from Paddington. He and "Baby" started on the eleven-miles drive in an old dog-cart. The horse broke down en route, but was revived miraculously following fervent prayers before the Sacred Tabernacle, while the boy-Oblate sheltered in the cottage of a reputed witch. The rest of the party, which included "Frederick, an acolyte, and Henry Bower, a Christian man, who doth greatly assist our Order", had no alternative but to walk. They did not reach their destination until about 4 a.m., having lost their way among the mountains.

"Baby" and his foster-father were housed in a shed. The monks and hangers-on had to make the best of a larger hut. The following day "the Divine Mysteries were . . . removed with the altar from the barn in which the Brothers were dwelling, into a small roofed room, leading off the unfinished cloister, at the south end. This room was nicely hung with crimson curtains over the stone walls, and the Altar was decently vested in a cloth of blue velvet and silver." Several days elapsed before the furniture arrived because the vans got stuck four miles down the valley. Their contents had to be brought along piece-meal in country carts. The barn had to serve as refectory, dormitory and storeroom; the shed as the Abbot's cell, choir and chapel.

Ignatius felt justified in assuming the status of an Abbot, and adopted pontifical insignia, although no Anglo-Saxon abbot had ever worn a mitre or wielded a crozier. Having put himself on a par with the Trappist Abbot of Mount St Bernard, he remained the only ruling Benedictine abbot in England and Wales for the next twenty-nine years. Other Roman Catholic abbots were merely titular until 1899, when Dom Ansgar Höckelmann was blessed as Abbot of Erdington.[11]

It was not until August 15, the feast of the Assumption, that a clergyman turned up for the first administration of Holy Communion, and renewed the Consecrated Elements in the tabernacle. As might have been expected, the "Monkery" in the Black Mountains aroused wide-spread curiosity and gossip. Tourists and trippers felt it worth while to face the perils of the long drive up the Vale of Ewyas, in the hope of getting a peep of these mysterious hermits. On August 29, John Patrick, third Marquess of Bute, arrived from Belmont Cathedral Priory, accompanied by the Prior, Lady Herbert of Lea, and another gentleman whom Ignatius took to be Charles George, second Earl of Gainsborough. These distinguished Roman Catholics are said to have been "deeply interested in all they heard and saw, especially Lord Bute, who, before leaving, accompanied the Father to the shed, and joined with him in a prayer before the Blessed Sacrament. The ladies of the party were, of course, excluded from crossing the cloistered precincts, but from a distance they were enabled to get a very comprehensive view of the estate and the progress which the workmen were making with the erection of the new monastery."[12]

Mr and Mrs Lyne, accompanied by young Clavering and his flirtatious sister, were still staying in the neighbourhood. Being anxious to meet the young lady again, Kilvert went over to Capel-y-Ffin on September 2, and found the quartette had just arrived from Prontrilas; "sitting out on a garden seat under a tree in a pretty little dingle". Mrs. Lyne introduced Fr Ignatius to the curate of Clyro. Here are his impressions of the Abbot:

"He struck me as being a man of gentle simple kind manners, excitable, and entirely possessed by one idea. He always spoke to his father and mother as "Papa" and "Mamma" and called me "Father". I could not persuade him that my name was not Venables. His head and brow are very fine, the forehead beautifully rounded and highly imaginative. The face is a very saintly one and the eyes extremely beautiful, earnest and expressive, a dark soft brown. When excited they seem absolutely to flame. He wears the Greek or early British tonsure all round the temples, leaving the hair of the crown untouched. His manner gives you the impression of great earnestness and single mindedness. The voice and manner are very like Clavering's, and it was with difficulty that I could tell which of the two was speaking if I did not see them. Father Ignatius wore the black Benedictine habit with two loose wings or pieces falling in front and behind, two violet tassels behind, the knotted scourge girdle, a silver cross on the breast, and a brazen or golden cross hanging from the rosary on black beads under the left arm."[13]

Kilvert was shown round the foundations of the monastery, and noticed the little community "issuing from a barn where they had engaged for an hour or so in an 'examination of conscience' ". It happened to be a Friday, and "Mrs Lyne, not having much faith in the larder", especially on a day of fasting, "had wisely taken the precaution of bringing with her an honest leg of mutton and two bottles of wine" which the curate was invited to share. We are told that "the monasterial garden provided potatoes and French beans, very good, and luncheon was under the trees in the dingle, waited on by the novices cowled and robed like the monks. They addressed Father Ignatius as 'dear Father' whenever they spoke to him, and bent the knee whenever they approached or passed him."[14]

One of the novices "was a fine noble looking boy, a gentleman's son with a sweet open face and fair clustering curly hair. He had been sent to the new monastery by his parents to learn to be a monk." The observant diarist notices that

"the boy seemed to be devoted to Fr Ignatius and came running up with a basket of mushrooms he had just bought to show them to the Father. His cowl was thrown back and his fair young head, bright face and sunny hair made a striking contrast to his black robe. 'Yes, dear Father, No, dear Father.' And off he went in high delight with the mushrooms and the approval of the Father, as happy as a king and much happier. Poor child. I wonder if he will ever become a monk. I hope he is reserved for a better fate. He shook hands with us all before he went off to the barn. His hand was small, soft and white as a girl's. They call him 'Manny'. Another of the novices, of lower rank in life, one who waited on us at luncheon, had a peculiarly sweet and beautiful face. He is called Brother Placidus."

Towards the end of the picnic in the dingle voices were heard close up. No sooner did the Abbot hear them, and saw a strange face peering over the hedge, than "he dashed the cowl over his head and face and bolted up the bank among the shrubs like a rabbit". The Lynes explained that their monk-son had been "much intruded

97

on and persecuted, and dreaded seeing strangers about the place". The previous night some men had come up the valley, and "rung the monastery bells violently, and were very rude and insolent". But they had been treated very kindly, and "they apologized for their conduct and went away conquered".

Before returning to Clyro its curate laid a stone "at the particular request of Fr Ignatius. Then he was taken into the Oratory

"a tiny square room in the Cloister, fitted with a lace and silk-covered altar upon which stands a super altar or Tabernacle in which he informed us in a low awestruck voice was 'the Blessed Sacrament'. There was a couch in the room on which he sleeps. The altar lace came from France and was very expensive. There was a crucifix above the altar. It came from Spain and had been broken, but it was a beautiful figure. Fr Ignatius said that once when he was praying Gerald Moultrie who was present saw the crucifix roll its eyes, then turn its head and look at Fr Ignatius . . . He did not know what to think about it, but he could not help believing that Moultrie saw what he declared he saw.[15] As he was talking about this in a low eager whisper, he looked strange and wild, and his eyes were staring and blazing. He apologized for Mr Lyne's not kneeling at the altar by saying that his father did not believe in the Real Presence."[16]

Kilvert was told that "the Order of St Benedict was now worth about £60", and that the monks were supported entirely by Ignatius' preaching. The sermons made about "£1,000 a year". They were appreciated far more by "Low Church" than "High Church" Anglicans. The "Dissenters considered [the Benedictine] to be a second Wesley". Yet Ignatius admitted that

"a man must be of a very rare and peculiar temperament to become and remain a monk. A monk he says must either be a philosopher or a 'holy fool'. He also allows that monkery has a strong tendency to drive people mad. Out of 50 novices he could only reckon on making three monks. The rest would be failures. One in seven was a large percentage."

The clergyman-visitor, then aged thirty (three years younger than the Abbot), formed the opinion that the whole project was crazy, even if interesting, and wrote:

"Fr Ignatius thinks every one is as good as himself and is perfectly unworldly, innocent and utterly unsuspicious. He gave the contractor £500 at first, and took no receipt from him. And so on. The consequence is that he has been imposed upon, cheated and robbed right and left. This work was begun in March and ought to have been finished long ago. But there was no one to look after the workmen and they did as much or as little as they pleased."

Kilvert and Ignatius talked for some time in the lane beside the little non-conformist chapel of Capel-y-Ffin in the lane where a bridge crosses the Honddu. The Abbot was asked "if he would not find an ordinary dress more convenient and practical and less open to insult and objection". But he scouted the idea of abandoning what he believed was the only uniform for a monk and going into mufti. He admitted that "he had once given it up for a few days, but felt like a deserter and traitor till he took to the habit again". His last words to this Anglican priest were: "Father! Will you remember us next time you celebrate the Holy Communion?". Fr Kilvert replied: "Yes. I will."[17]

On the same September afternoon as the Llanthony conversations on the revival of monastic life on supposedly medieval lines in the Church of England the Emperor Napoleon III had surrendered himself in person and given up his sword to the King of Prussia after the Battle of Sedan. Two days later there was a revolution in Paris. A provisional government of national defence was set up, and a Republic claimed. Nine days after Ignatius had told Kilvert that "monkery has a strong tendency to drive people mad", Pope Pius XI refused the sovereignty of the Leonine city offered by King Victor Emmanuel, saying that he preferred to be a voluntary prisoner in the Vatican.

To secure privacy, the Abbot diverted the workmen to building a tiny hermitage on a lovely spot overlooking a deep ravine—"an ideal fine weather sanctum, where he was wont to pass many a quiet hour with no companion but the birds and the wild flowers, and in a silence broken only by the soft obligato of warble, wind and water-fall".[18] It was in this retreat that he wrote a sentimental novel entitled *Brother Placidus and Why he became a Monk,* published in the late autumn of 1870.[19]

The Benedictine author split himself into three persons: Father Theodore, the magnetic mission-preacher, Father Cuthbert, the Superior, living in his cell with a boy-oblate; and Father Dunstan, the organist and choirmaster. Brother Placidus was a rich young man, who, disgusted with the pomps and vanities of the world, found peace in the cloister after a model novitiate. So glamorous was this novel, that many a ritualistic youth heard a call to lead the monastic life amid the back-of-beyond mountains. Nearly all, however, were soon disillusioned when confronted by the sordidness and squalor of the Abbey of Our Ladye and St Dunstan. There was little in common between it and the romantic, twilight, early medieval world conjured up by Mr Tennyson in his poems *The Coming of Arthur* and *The Holy Grail,* published in 1869.

Ignatius inspired his biographer to write that "with the close of September the air of the mountains grew keen, and by the commencement of the autumn fall, the sufferings of the Community increased to the verge of the unbearable. One Brother became so ill that the Reverend Father decided to send him back to his friends; and two others, who were not sick, but only faint-hearted, ran away. There were, however, six who remained faithful, and with this small handful, the daily round of the monastic Hours was cheerfully fulfilled. Every spare moment was occupied with raids up the mountains in search of sticks, for 'fire' had become a necessity of life long before the leaves were off the trees, and coals were out of the question in so remote a corner of the earth. By Advent-tide, the prayed-for Cloister was at length under cover—that is to say, its roof was completed, and sundry panes of glass were gradually filling the upstairs window frames."[20] Taken all round, life was more than Trappist in its austerity. "Baby" must have been a tough little boy to have endured the cold and damp.

On paper, the trivial round and common task of the monks remained the same as it had been at Laleham, Norwich and Claydon. Remembering that the ever-changing personnel seldom mustered even a dozen, usually less, it is difficult to believe that the elaborate *horarium* could have been followed without frequent modifications. Young men arrived frequently, but few of them stayed for long. The majority soon found that the Llanthony road did not bring them daily nearer God, or furnished all they ought to ask—to paraphrase the verse of Mr Keble's well-known hymn.

The Brethren rose for Matins and Lauds at 2 a.m., and spent about two hours in the recitation of these two offices. Throughout Lent they remained on in choir monotoning the Lamentations of Jeremiah until about 5.30, otherwise they retired to their cubicles for a second sleep. Prime was said at 6 a.m., followed by the reading of the Martyrology, a commemoration of the dead, and the singing of the Angelus. This took up nearly an hour. Should a clergyman happen to be staying at the monastery, he celebrated the Holy Communion, with ceremonial believed to be based on the Sarum Rite; if not, then a half-hour was devoted to spiritual reading. Terce was recited before the monks partook of "Pittance"—a frugal breakfast of dry bread and coffee. The *Veni Creator* was chanted at 9 o'clock before manual labour started, which took up the rest of the morning. Should the Abbot be in residence he often decided that a Bible Class would be beneficial, and curtailed manual work. This involved each monk reading a verse, and if he possessed the gift of exposition it could be used to advantage, while another offered extempore prayer.

The Angelus and Sext was sung at midday. Then followed the Chapter of Faults when the Abbot was at home. Each religious was told that espionage was a virtue, and encouraged to accuse others of breaches of the Rule. As stated already, he often imposed most brutal penances. During the first years at New Llanthony Abbey manual labour was resumed until 3 p.m. when Nones was chanted. By the time that the community sat down for dinner—the only full meal of the day—they must have been hungry.[21] In theory it consisted of three courses —soup, vegetables (with eggs or fish) and a pudding; but as the monastery was sixteen miles from the nearest shops, with farm-carts for transport, there was no certainty what the amateur cooks would be able to provide. The flesh of four-footed animals was allowed only at Christmas and Easter.

The Abbot, however, needed a special diet because of his poor health. It included roast beef, mutton or game. Apparently his "pittance" often consisted of ham, eggs, and fish—if procurable. A one-time novice recalled that at dinner Ignatius drank four or five glasses of wine or stout, which may well be true. He wrote that the Reverend Father's strength "required no little keeping up, and he had to take a good deal of stimulant, and every luxury in food: fast days never affected him". Because of his frequent fainting fits he took care that a flask of brandy was hidden beneath his cowl before he delivered a sermon or oration.

Vespers and the Angelus were sung at 5 p.m., followed by adoration before the tabernacle. Then came recreation, but only for those who had not broken rules of silence. Supper was a simple meal, seldom consisting of more than bread and butter washed down with tea, though jam was an extra on feastdays. At 7.55 a long series of "devotions" preceded Compline—the Latin collect *"Sacrosancte Pater Benedicte"*, the Lord's Prayer, Creed, *Ave Maria,* Office for the Dead, Litany of Our Lady, the invocation "Blessed and Praised be Jesus in the Most Holy Sacrament", one or two hymns, a brief meditation, and a reading from Butler's *Lives of the Saints*. It was not until about 9 o'clock that the brethren retired to their draughty cubicles for their first sleep.[22] Their final act of devotion was singing another *Ave Maria.*[23]

Christmas Eve 1870 was marked by yet another miracle. Fr Cyril, a curate at one of the City churches in London, who had been appointed non-resident chaplain to the community, broke his journey at Hereford, having a great devotion to its thirteenth-century bishop, St Thomas Cantalupe (the last Englishman canonized at Rome before the Reformation). On arrival at Llanfihangel-Crucorney station late in the afternoon, he set out to walk the eleven miles to the monastery. The ground was soon covered with deep snow and he lost sight of the path. Suddenly he beheld the figure of a man radiating light, who beckoned to him to turn round, and he was certain that this apparition must be St Thomas. His devotee realised that he had overstepped his goal in the darkness. Following the figure he reached the monastery just in time to celebrate Midnight Mass.

The only Abbot in the Anglican Communion spent the greater part of the year 1871 as a Gyrovag, having so many irons in the fire. First of all he had to rush off to London to confer with his father who had been summoned to attend a meeting in connection with Mr Newdigate's proposed bill for the supervision of conventual institutions by a system of Government inspection. As New Llanthony Abbey and Feltham Priory were then the only *enclosed* Anglican communities, it was feared that some very awkward questions would be asked if the bill was passed by Parliament. The Order of St Benedict got into the headlines again after the Abbot Ignatius was bold enough to walk arm-in-arm with the notorious atheist, Charles Bradlaugh, to the platform of the Hall of Science in London, where they took part in a two hours' debate on "Is Jesus Christ an Historical Reality?" More publicity was obtained in the summer of that year. Newspapers splashed headlines such as *"Startling Revelations of Llanthony Abbey"—Kidnapping a Monk"— "Father Ignatius and Ward of Chancery"*. The accusations were true enough. A seventeen year-old Richard Todd (known in religion as Br Aelred) had been lured to Llanthony and clothed as a novice without his parents' knowledge or consent. Ignatius got off lightly, but he was attacked by a rowdy mob when leaving the Court of Chancery on July 24. Yet he could not resist being in the limelight, and felt he must accept an invitation from his cousin Mrs Vaughan, wife of the Master of the Temple, to take part in a monster "At Home". This gave him a unique opportunity to preach "JESUS ONLY", not only to Christians of many denominations, but also to a Mahomedan and a Hindoo, whose eyes were said to be "moist with tears" after the Anglican monk had asked everyone present to kneel down while he offered prayer" for the increase of their faith in Supreme Salvation through the Precious Blood of Jesus".[24]

Encouraged by the sales of *Brother Placidus and Why he became a Monk*, the Abbot dashed off another novel, entitled *Leonard Morris or the Benedictine Novice*, which was published in 1871. This sensational story has a historical importance as it reveals what were Ignatius' visions of his twin-community within three years of its foundation. When Mother Hilda read it, she realized that the Superior-General intended to move the nuns to Llanthony as soon as possible. She gathered that "the Perpetual Adoration makes the absolute and entire communion with Heaven; the grand work of the religious". It was easy for the nuns to see and smell the "white cloud of incense slowly rising before the altar". On and around it "glittered a hundred wax tapers, shining star-like in the dimness of the sanctuary".

Whether Mr Helmore, the recognized authority on Gregorian chanting, would have accepted the music as being in the Anglo-Saxon tradition is somewhat doubtful; no matter, it "well-nigh brought tears to the worshippers, especially when Sister Mary Lydia sang alone in a soft clear voice", varied by "the sweet-wailing harmonies of the nuns; three of them singing a plaintive trio . . . answered in a soft duet by two of the novice boys in the monks' choir".

The Feltham community was warned that "the sacred mountain shrine" to which it would migrate was "unmistakably awful". Here the nuns would find "the monks 'relieving guard' before the Glorious Sacrament . . . carrying on the *one* work to which they have dedicated their lives". In imagination Mother Hilda could picture "the Most Holy Sacrament exposed in a magnificent *ostensorium*, standing in a throne over the tabernacle; a rich canopy of velvet and lace hung over it". Some of the nuns may have yearned for "the deep silence, the mystic light, the gorgeous altar, glistening amongst the shadows, which thirty or forty crimson lamps flung over it; a soft glow of holy fire seemed to wrap the choir, falling from the ruby glasses of the lamps, swinging in the air, high up before the Exalted Presence".

Another means of edification once the Feltham community moved to "the sacred mountain shrine" would be the daily spectacle of a monk, each in his turn, stripped of scapular, girdle and sandals, kneeling on the altar steps. From their choir in a tribune they would be able to gaze at him with a rope round his neck being led into the church, as if he were a criminal about to be strangled or guillotined. Part of this macabre ceremonial involved the victim being given no food for the rest of the day, but he was allowed to beg a small portion from each of his brethren.

The nuns read that the monks had as their companion a boy-oblate called "Sunbeam" because of "his bright face and fair curly tonsure". He made "quite a picture of pure joyous happiness". Little "Sunbeam", so it was stated, was supposed to keep perpetual silence. He never came to recreation with the community, but was allowed to climb on the Reverend Father's knees, and to be cuddled by him.

"I'm the monastery baby", he used to whisper. By the age of nine he was "quite a theologian and a wonderful Latin scholar". There was nothing he enjoyed more than a good caning by the Abbot, and always asked for more "for dear Jesus' sake".[25] The author continued that "the little darling was beaten well too. He received the Sacrament with almost a rapture. His fair, bright face and sweet blue eyes were upturned to the Host with such rapture, but his little face suffused crimson from pain".[26]

It seems to have been the sanctity of "Sunbeam", and his precocious enjoyment of flagellation, that finally decided "Leonard Morris" to become a Benedictine, for the long account of the beating of the "little darling" ends with the remark: "Well, upon my word, I never could have believed such a thing possible. It is a wonderful thing this religious life."[27]

The only reason for quoting from this novel is that, with its predecessor *Brother Placidus,* it was intended as official propaganda for the twin-community of the Order of St Benedict, and put forth with absolute sincerity.[28] Ignatius of Jesus O.S.B. wrote these romances with the same seriousness as that of the members of the second Vatican Council who were responsible for the *Decree on the Appropriate Renewal of the Religious Life.* The Abbot of Llanthony's conception of how the twin-form of Benedictine monastic life ought to be "renewed" in the Church of England a hundred years ago could not have been expressed more clearly and with such detail. The two novels were, in fact, his *Apologia pro vita sua.*[29] It could be that their sensationalism roused Dr Pusey to write about the same time to the Hon. Charles Wood (later Lord Halifax): "Fr Ignatius is a most impracticable man . . . He is a good revivalist preacher wasted; very amiable, vain, and ignorant of human nature in the concrete".[30]

There appears to be no evidence as to how and where Abbot Ignatius was inspired to found an Anglican double-monastery in which the chief work would be Perpetual Adoration of the Blessed Sacrament. Evidently it was a matter of indifference to him that it was not until after the devotion of the Forty Hours, begun in 1534, and established in 1592, that Perpetual Adoration became popular. Later on religious communities started to be founded for this object, and a few older ones adopted it. In 1871 (the year in which *Leonard Morris* was published) the only Roman Catholic communities in England engaged in Perpetual Adoration were the Benedictine nuns at Colwich and Teignmouth, the Canonesses of St Augustine at Newton Abbot, and the Sisters of Marie Réparatrice in London. Quite likely the inspiration first came during his travels in Belgium, France, Italy and Switzerland before the "Conversion" in 1866. The décor of the high altar described in *Leonard Morris* could have been derived from memories of the chapels of Père Eymard's Congregation of the Most Blessed Sacrament (1811), Institute of Adoration Réparatrice (1848), Institute of Perpetual Adoration (1856), or the Congregation of Perpetual Adoration of the Most Holy Sacrament of the Altar ("Picpus Sisters") (1794-1817). Joseph Leycester Lyne—never consistent at any period of his career—was not satisfied with adoration before the tabernacle: his

Anglican monks and nuns must go further and enjoy the frequent exposition of the Blessed Sacrament in a monstrance.[31]

The Ignatian ceremonial for a monk being led to the altar with a rope round his neck, as if going to the scaffold, may have been based on the observances of the Benedictines of the Blessed Sacrament, founded by Mère Mechtilde in 1655. She ordered that during the Conventual Mass one of the nuns should kneel in the middle of the choir with a rope round her neck, and holding a lighted candle by way of reparation to the Holy Eucharist, so frequently insulted. But the other nuns did not have to walk over her body and spit on it, as was the Llanthony "Use".

For the time being the visions of exotic functions recorded in the two abbatial novels had to remain the shape of things to come, for lack of enough monks and nuns, as well as of money.

Looking back three decades, Fr Ignatius told his biographer that "the year of grace 1872 was a busy one in mind and body" so far as he was concerned. As a Missioner-Evangelist, or "the Moody of the Upper Classes", as a playful journalist was pleased to style him, the Father was obliged to keep his eye on the world's game of chess, and make special notes of the moves not only of the Bishops, but of its Royalties also".[32]

The first of the many Royalties whose moves the only Abbot in the Anglican Communion had to watch was the widowed Queen Victoria, Defender of the Faith, who at her coronation had promised to maintain "the laws of God, the true profession of the Gospel, and the Protestant reformed religion as it is established by law". From early in December 1871, heaven had been stormed by the monks and nuns for the recovery of the Prince of Wales from a severe attack of typhoid fever, but unfortunately their Superior was not invited to join the bishops at the national service of thanksgiving held in St Paul's Cathedral on February 27 the following year, so both he and "Sunbeam" missed the chance of seeing the Queen, or enjoying the decorated streets and the illuminations at night.

It was also Ignatius' duty to keep up to date with the movements of the monarchists and republicans in France, as well as those of King Victor Emmanuel, who had transferred his court to Rome, now the capital of Italy. The power of the papacy was waning. An Old Catholic congregation had already been formed at Paris. There were rumours that the famous Carmelite preacher, Père Hyacinthe Loyson, was about to cast off the yoke of Rome. Over in Germany Dr Döllinger had advocated union between the Old Catholics and the Church of England.

"The Moody of the Upper Classes" heard a clear call to leave his monastery for the whole of Lent so that he could conduct mission services, and thus add to the income of his community. On the feast of St Benedict, March 21, Kilvert jotted down in his Diary:

"Dora writes, 'Fr Ignatius and his monk caused a great sensation at Bath last week. They were staying at rather a grand house where there were some pretty fashionable girls, and the unfortunate monk was bound by his vow, not to look at a woman. They live on vegetables and dates entirely in Lent and look very ill. On Sunday they came into Bathwick Church for the Communion and Thersie said they looked so odd coming very fast up the aisle against the stream of people coming out [from Mattins]. All the young ladies' eyes were on them but the monk's eyes were never raised from the ground."[33]

On April 26, a proclamation of Don Carlos as Charles VII of Spain led to civil war, which, so we are told, was to the Abbot "an event of great interest".[34]

Ignatius wrote to the Spanish "pretender" promising the prayers of his monks and nuns for this "righteous cause". The would-be King is said to have ordered his military chaplains to make a memento of Llanthony Abbey in their masses. It is recorded that Queen Margherita also corresponded with the Anglican Abbot. A committee in London supplied arms and money. Among its most active members was Colonel Charles Edward Stuart, who claimed direct descent from "Bonnie Prince Charlie", and to be the *de jure* King of Great Britain and Ireland. He seems to have been on friendly relations with the Abbey of Our Ladye and St Dunstan. So although it was hidden away at the far end of a valley in the Black Mountains, the monks behind grilles kept their eyes on political and ecclesiastical "games of chess" all over Europe.

On Ascension Day the first Llanthony "Pilgrimage" was inaugurated with flamboyant ceremonial. On August 22, the Octave of the Assumption, the Abbot laid the foundation stone of the great church, and recorded in the Chronicle: "The Ceremony was exceeding solemn, and took place after Nones". Six days later he wrote: "We do bless Thee oh! Lord Jesus, because Thou hast sent hither, Thy Servant, this Noble Person, the good Lord Hereford, who owneth the mountains about us, and hast inclined his heart towards us Thine unworthy servants". Hereford allowed the monks to quarry land, but ten years elapsed before the three bays of the choir were completed. The long nave and transepts were never started.

More publicity was needed, so in 1872 Ignatius published a leaflet in which he stated that New Llanthony Abbey was being built "for Benedictine monks of the Church of England, i.e. for persons in her pale who desire to devote themselves, in seclusion and under a sanctioned rule, to a life of prayer and praise and self-denial; to serve God altogether for Himself, and not to the praise of men; for persons who believe with all the greatest Doctors of the Church that by a life of praise they can best glorify God and benefit men, and cause their 'light to shine' with the purest and most unalloyed flame. No such House exists in the Church of England, and many leave her pale to find one. There are persons in our Church wholly unsuited by disposition and talent for an active, bustling life, and yet long to dedicate their peculiar talents to God . . .

"Secondly, in connection with this house of praise and sacrifice we desire (and not inconsistently with this cloistered life) to open a home for poor and aged clergymen who have no home in their old age in which to pass peacefully from time into eternity, for poor and sick curates, who, unable to work, have nothing to depend upon . . . Also we desire to provide a retreat for all desperate cases of every kind of human sorrow, which have no such refuge of religious love at present offered them in our Church. Many a suicide would be prevented, many a despairing soul saved, were such Houses restored in our English Church."

So the Abbey of Our Ladye and St Dunstan would become not only an eventide-home for retired clergymen (presumably without wives) and a clerical rest-house, but also a refuge for bums, hobos, tramps, vagrants and vagabonds, waifs and strays of every species.

The Abbot explained that his "nuns would similarly offer such a retreat, and are already doing so at Feltham, to such cases as far as their very slender means afford. Poor sick governesses, ladies by birth, taste and education, who in sickness are often cast out from their situations to almost starvation; and poor seamstresses, who through illness and virtue have become homeless for a time; for ladies and others who crave a temporary but entire separation from the world's din and unrest, which our 'active' Sisterhoods do not afford."

The Superior-General spent very little time with his monks during the year 1872, but wrote frequent long letters to some of them of which this is a typical specimen.

My dearest child,

You must not let Satan let you feel lonely—You are a child of God, one of Jesus' own beloved ones, and you are dwelling with your beloved. I am sadly grieved with poor Br Placidus' letters—I can see the world will be his destiny in August next. Poor child, his letters make my heart ache—Do you pray for him regularly? I should like almost to have our monastery changed into a hermitage. *No* one, *no* one shall dwell with us but those whose hearts are given to our precious dearest Lord. Oh! my dear child, *do* try to hide in His dear heart, *do* wrestle in prayer with Him that you may rest in the sweet *assurance* of being *only* and wholly His. There are several young men wanting to take Br Ethelred's and Br Charles' place, but I simply *dread* having any *more* just now. Br Thomas is very much improved, the nuns are very pleased with him. He keeps the rule, especially silence, beautifully. He is so loving and good too. I hope he will make a good monk. Our sweet Jesus bless you.

Your loving Father in His love,

Ignatius of Jesus, O.S.B., Superior.

In another letter from Feltham Priory, the Abbot urged this novice to spy upon Fr Philip—even if he were in life vows—and note down every breach of the forty-nine rules he had committed. Such espionage would be beneficial for his own spiritual life. The novice must summon up his courage and accuse this professed monk at Chapter—"boldly for the love of Jesus' glory, for love of the Monastery, and for his soul's sake and the souls of others". If he was too timid, then he would be guilty of "the sins of cowardice, dishonesty, self-indulgence, sloth, insincerity and uncharitableness". Of course Fr Philip would be roused, but the accusations must appear to be spontaneous, without a hint that they were ordered by the absent Abbot.

Next came instructions that the abbatial bed must be examined, and the blankets well-aired, to make sure that there were no fleas. Ignatius continued: "I shall require sleep very badly after my hard brain work here, which people say is enough to *kill* me".[35] He added: "I am very happy in my sleepless nights, but I have no business to encourage them, they weaken me so. *Fleas* would certainly keep me sleepless.[36] Baby must sleep in the visitors' dormitory for the future and have his bath there, so that *my* room may now be kept quite unused and my bed cleaned.

"I shall D.V. come home at an hour when you are not aware, in order that I may see whether you are *watching*. Is the Superior's room lovingly kept in order, I wonder, clean and scrupulously tidy? Or is it otherwise? Our Lord sees—perhaps I shall too. No cats are to be allowed upstairs this hot weather. You must be careful of this, or the fleas will of course multiply . . . If any kittens come when I am away, they are to be drowned by Jenkins at once."

It was only "the want of money" that kept the Abbot from returning to his dearest children, so he explained. He found it more and more of a struggle "to make the two ends meet". His "dear enclosure" called him, yet he knew it to be God's will for him to be a Gyrovag, for "Jesus doeth all things *well* for his *own* people".[37]

It may strike some readers as uncharitable to print the above quotations, yet they help to convey an idea of the exotic atmosphere of the Abbey of Our Ladye and St Dunstan in the early eighteen-seventies. At the same moment Charles Taize Russell, a former Congregationalist and Alleghany haberdasher, was equally sure that Jesus had called him to found Jehovah's Witnesses at Pittsburgh, Pennsylvania. At Munich, the Old Catholics were just as certain that they would be able to provide a spiritual home for those who had been excommunicated for refusing to submit to the rulings of the Vatican Council.

The Superior-General of the triune-Anglican Order of St Benedict continued to spend the greater part of the time roaming around England giving Missions, attending Church Congresses, and fulfilling other non-monastic engagements. One can picture him at the Missions, pedalling away at a portable harmonium, robed in his black Benedictine cowl, his rosary jangling against the large crucifix as he roused the audience with *"The Bugle Call of the Mission"*, or soothed them with the hymn *"Let me come closer to Thee, JESUS, Oh! closer day by day"*. Yet when he did return to the Black Mountains he made every effort to see that white clouds of incense still went on rising before the altar, on and around which glittered a hundred wax-tapers shining star-like in the dimness of the sanctuary. For the great and grand work of the Perpetual Adoration must not cease. On all the greater festivals the Host was exposed in a jewelled monstrance, standing in a throne above the tabernacle, draped with velvet and lace. This theatrical ceremonial made reparation for the Public Worship Regulation Act, which received royal assent on August 7, 1874.

Having denounced his cousin Dr Stanley, Dean of Westminster, as an infidel at Scarborough in September 1876, when the old Theatre Royal was packed from stalls to gallery, so great was the attraction of a real live Benedictine monk on the gas-lit stage, the Abbot of Llanthony decided to try to regain possession of what he still regarded as his lawful property at Norwich. It had been sub-let to a female Baptist minister, and he felt he must try to prevent further sacrilege. Accompanied by two or three monks, also the Divine Mysteries in a tabernacle, he forced an entry into the Priory, which some Tertiaries soon tidied up and made reasonably habitable. The long disused chapel was refurnished, with blue draperies hung round the wall. A few mornings later the Sheriff's officers knocked at the door when the brethren were in choir. They agreed to wait until the service was ended. Then a writ of expulsion was handed to the Abbot, but he refused to leave the chapel unless expelled by force. Giving him time "to secure the Blessed Sacrament, which he held folded in the corporals, and reverently clasped to his breast, the officers made summary disposal of his person by seizing him between them, and depositing him outside the monastic precincts".[38]

The Abbot and his monks retired to the house of a Tertiary, where, so we are told, "they were speedily joined by a continuous influx of enthusiastic and indignant sympathisers". Before leaving Norwich Ignatius held mission services in St. Andrew's Hall, also from the balcony of a public house. The monastic invasion ended with a defeat, for "the fraudulent usurper", i.e., Mr Drury, remainder the legal owner of the property.[39]

Little has been recorded of life at Llanthony at this period, but its Abbot seldom lacked press publicity. In June 1876 he jotted down in the Chronicle: "I have apprenticed him [Ignatius of Mary] to sea". Sad to say, in spite of having been trained and educated as a future Carthusian, almost certain to end up a Prior, the Infant Samuel, having reached the age of fourteen, showed clearly that he had no vocation to the religious state.

In the early autumn of 1877 there were rumours that Ignatius of Jesus was the Order of Corporate Reunion "Provincial of Caerleon in the Principality of Wales", and that a Dutch bishop had raised him to the episcopate on board ship in the English Channel. Another version of the story (reported in *The Star*) was that the consecration had been performed on the Venetian lagoons by "a Coptic prelate, an Armenian Patriarch, a Greek Archimandrite, and an Irvingite Archangel". For nearly two years the general opinion was that the Abbot of Llanthony had been made a bishop, especially as he never felt it worth while to deny this in print.

The fact that he was a close friend of Dr Lee of Lambeth, i.e. "Thomas, Pro-Provincial of Canterbury", was more than enough to make people suspicious. Again the Monk appeared to be mixed up with most of the leaders of the Anglican underworld, including Provost Nugee of the Order of St Augustine. On August 30, 1878 *The Times* reported that Fr Ignatius of Llanthony had been sub-deacon at the "High Celebration" on the feast of St Augustine, when the chapel in the New Kent Road, near the Elephant and Castle, was ablaze with lights and filled with the fumes of incense.

The death of Mrs Louisa Genevieve Lyne on July 21, 1877 merely led to a quarrel affecting the whole Lyne family, between whom relations became very strained the following year, after Mr Lyne Snr. published *A Memorial of a Mother*. The monks and nuns were bidden to pray for the repose of her soul, as "Benefactress and Promoter of our Holy Order, and the Devoted Mother of the First Superior, Ignatius of Jesus".

Life became more and more difficult, what with one thing after another, and there was little Benedictine *"Pax"* for the Superior-General of the Order of St Benedict. His nuns were showing signs of contumaceousness, indifferent to his God-given authority. Here is his own version of the story:

"Towards the end of 1878, a spirit of unrest manifested itself among the Benedictine Nuns at Feltham. For some time past, a little cloud of insubordination had been gathering over this Home of religious womanhood, but now this cloud was about to take definite shape and develop into a storm. Not possessing the gift of ubiquity, it was impossible for the Superior of two distant Settlements, and a busy Missioner besides, to be in more than one place at once. At Feltham, the secondary reins of authority were delegated, in the Abbot's absence, to the Prioress in residence—an inevitable arrangement not altogther guaranteed from complica-tion.[40] The time had come when the Prioress had learned not only to steer the government of her Community, but to handle the ropes with an independent touch, somewhat too pronounced in one who had vowed unquestioned obedience to the Founder of her Order."[41]

One cause of this "spirit of unrest" among the nuns was their resentment towards Sister Mary Agnes. It is recorded that "she was one of the Father's pets, and he wanted her to be professed". Mother Hilda, however, doubted this novice's vocation to the Benedictine life. Neither would she agree to the Abbot's demand that this vivacious young lady should be raised above six or seven already professed nuns, merely because he chose to trust her as his confidante, over revealing matters which concerned the Prioress alone.[42] The trouble was that Ignatius saw nothing irregular in demanding manifestations of conscience from his nuns outside the confessional. Since he was only a deacon he could not give them absolution, only ghostly counsel and advice. So he enjoyed gossiping and interrogating Subprioress Etheldreda, Mother Werburgh, Mother Cecilia, and Sister Mary Agnes, who were his favourites. To continue the story in the words of the Baroness biographer:

"For many months, Fr Ignatius had noted with surprise and pain the gradual growth of this self-assertive spirit, and it became his duty to check the evil—as he hoped—in the bud. I have seen a copy of the letter which in this intention he wrote to the Reverend Mother, reminding her very kindly of her obligations towards himself, and exhorting her in the future (together with her Nuns) to cultivate a more ideal standard of loyalty to the holy Rule. The result of this letter was a division in the camp. When the Abbot next visited his Nunnery, he found it in open revolt. The Prioress was full of grievances—one of which was

THE DREAM-ABBEY OF OUR LADYE AND ST DUNSTAN IN THE BLACK MOUNTAINS, 1870

The church would have been the same size as that of Llanthony Priory, built for Austin Canons after 1103. This involved a central tower, transepts, and two western towers. Only the three bays of the choir were built.

ABBEY OF OUR LADYE AND ST DUNSTAN, LLANTHONY, *c.* 1885
Unfinished Church (left), Abbot's Lodging (right).

"Consider in your beautiful Cloister Home, you have the grand business of serving 'Jesus only', with nothing to hinder you. . . You have the Monastery boys to lead in the highest steps of holiness and self-denial for Jesus' sake. . . The Monk is as far above the rest of Christians, as the Sun is above the Moon in brightness, and fructifying power. . . Your Monastery in the House of Spiritual Multiplication by the figure 1,000. '*One day* in Thy Courts is *better* than 1,000'." (From *22 Teachings of Ignatius, the Monk*, 1881.)

the Superior's reluctance to make her Abbess of the Order—and she openly expressed her disinclination to be considered a religious Vice-Reine. More than half the Nuns had gone over to the Rebel Banner, only four remaining faithful to their Rule and their Abbot. Expostulation was useless, and Father Ignatius saw the necessity for prompt action before the whole of his Community should be demoralised."[43]

Yet he tried to be patient, and gave the rebels three weeks in which to meditate on their sins of disobedience to himself as their self-appointed Major Superior. It was ridiculous to allow Mother Hilda to be given the rank of abbess, for this would mean a delegation of authority.

Finding no signs of repentance, the Abbot suddenly descended on Feltham like a hurricane off the Black Mountains. Realising that only four nuns were prepared to lick the ground and grovel at his feet, he told the sacristan to vest the altar with a black frontal. The Prioress and the whole community were ordered to gather in the choir. Robed in a black cope, the Deacon pronounced a sentence of anathema on the rebels.[44]

When he reached the last words of this solemn service "Unless they repent of their sin, may they be blotted out of the book of life, Amen, Amen", the bell tolled as if for a Requiem, or as when a newly-professed nun was borne into her "Living Tomb".[45]

We are told that "the Abbot then removed his four spiritual children from the company of their degenerate Sisters, and lodged them *pro tem* in an outer portion of the Convent, under the care of an Extern Sister, in whom he could place confidence. This done, he set about seeking them a new residence, it being his purpose to shake off the dust of Feltham from his sandals, and leave the excommunicated Prioress with her flock in possession."[46]

Within five days this extraordinary Abbot had worked what was a virtual miracle. He dashed off to Devonshire, signed the lease of a "picturesque old Chantry" at Slapton, six miles south-west of Dartmouth; furnished it, and was waiting on the platform at Kingwear when the loyal remnant arrived after their long journey. We are told that when the nuns reached their new convent "every detail was in apple-pie order. Tea spread ready on the table, floors and stairs warmly covered with coco-nut matting, and a well-aired bed awaiting each tired traveller—the work, from beginning to end, of *five* short days".[47]

What Ignatius of Jesus seems to have forgotten is that his obligations towards Mother Hilda were just as binding as those which he claimed she owed him. For "Mrs Emily Stewart" was still the legal owner of "New Llanthony Abbey of Our Ladye and St Dunstan". Had she chosen to go to law, she might have been able to evict the Abbot and his monks. It could be, however, that she felt no urge to migrate from Middlesex to the Black Mountains, where she knew that life would be infinitely more difficult than it was at Feltham. It was enough to have gained freedom from such an impossible Superior-General, and to be able to lead a normal religious life on the lines of those with which she had been trained by Dr Neale at East Grinstead—far better than being the nominal head of the female section of a Benedictine twin-community.

The whole story reminds one of what the Rev. Harris Barham wrote in *The Jackdaw of Rheims:*

> "Never was heard such a terrible curse!
> But what gave rise to no little surprise,
> Nobody seem'd one penny the worse!"

NOTES

[1] This quotation is taken from the vellum-bound chronicle he started to keep soon after the move to Llanthony.

[2] It seems that this trip to Caernarvonshire was responsible for arousing his interest in Celtic monasticism, which found expression in a long poem, dedicated to the 3rd Baron Newborough, whose ancestors had owned Bardsey Island for centuries.

[3] It was not regarded as necessary to seek permission from Dr Connop Thirwall for this monastic foundation within the Diocese of St Davids, for of course it would be exempt from episcopal jurisdiction.

[4] Buckeridge had already designed a gloomy Gothic Revival convent at Oxford for Mother Marian Hughes and her Sisterhood of the Holy and Undivided Trinity, the first part of which had been opened in 1868. All its windows were filled with thick bottle glass, creating a dim religious light. The cells encouraged self-mortification, for they were brick-walled, with bare scrubbed floors.

[5] p. 440. The first of these was at the proprietary chapel of St James's, Brighton, where the former Br Anselm (Charles Walker) ensured that Mr Purchas carried out his own version of the Sarum Rite correctly. This included hanging a stuffed dove over the Communion Table on Whitsunday.

[6] At that date he was curate of Clyro near Hay. A selection of his Diary covering the years 1870-9, made by William Plomer, was first published in 1938.

[7] *Kilvert's Diary*, paperback edition 1971, p. 21.

[8] ibid, p. 22.

[9] ibid, p. 49.

[10] ibid, pp. 54-55.

[11] That same year Dom Edmund Ford was elected first Abbot of Downside, and in 1900 Dom Oswald Smith became first Abbot of Ampleforth. Fort Augustus in Scotland got a ruling abbot in 1888. Others followed in England: Buckfast (1902), Farnborough (1903), and Ramsgate (1909).

[12] p. 449. Abbot Ignatius hoped that Bute would become a generous benefactor, but he preferred to donate his money to the English Benedictine Congregation. He helped to defray the cost of Fort Augustus Abbey, which was opened in 1878.

[13] *Diary*, p. 70.

[14] ibid, p. 71.

[15] See p. 59.

[16] ibid, p. 72.

[17] ibid, p. 73. Judging from entries in the Diary, he seldom "said Mass" more often than once a month.

[18] De Bertouch, op. cit., p. 357.

[19] He also found time to write several pamphlets, the titles of which indicate what were his chief interests about this time: *Nineteenth-century Devils, Haunted Houses, The Attacks of Modern Science on Jesus Christ, The Death of God, The Infidelity at Oxford and its Consequences in England.* The errors of Romanism were exposed in the pamphlet entitled *Popery.*

[20] p. 450.

[21] Later on, dinner was put back to midday, immediately after Sext, at which Ignatius often preached a sermon, should any layfolk be present.

[22] It appears that the Feltham nuns kept the same time-table as the monks.

[23] Ignatius did not start direct invocation of Our Lady and the saints until after his "Conversion" in 1866. Previously he had obeyed Dr Pusey, who did not permit his penitents to go further than comprecation.

[24] p. 490.

[25] It is laid down in the 30th chapter of the *Rule of St Benedict* that "whenever boys or youths, or any who cannot appreciate how great a penalty excommunication is, commit an offence, they are either to be punished by severe fasting, or else corrected by sharp stripes, for their own good". In chapter 45 it is stated that children who make mistakes in the oratory "are to be beaten".

[26] op. cit., pp. 146-7. "Sunbeam", i.e. Ignatius of Mary, at the age of ten was described by a former monk in his memoirs as "a beautiful little boy, with a sweet voice, barefoot, dressed in a short white serge frock, scapular and cord. He had light, bright short hair, large blue eyes, full red lips, which promised to grow coarse. He was much beloved by the Reverend Father, always with him, and destined in future to be the head of a Carthusian monastery. The Reverend Father believed him to be an angelic child, but there was, in truth, much evil in him—cunning, treacherous, and the most accomplished liar I have ever met—always cheating."

[27] op. cit., pp. 146-7.

[28] *Brother Placidus* was published in the same year as Disraeli's *Lothair,* and Dickens' (unfinished) *Mystery of Edwin Drood. Leonard Morris* came out along with Lewis Carroll's *Alice through the Looking Glass,* and Ruskin's *Fors Clavigera.*

[29] It is worth comparing them with *Religious Communities in the World of Today* (A Paper presented to the Advisory Council on Anglican Religious Communities, with a commentary by A. M. Allchin), published in 1970. The whole idea of the nature of the monastic life has changed in the past hundred years.

[30] Cf. Calder-Marshall, op. cit., p. 104, note 1. Both Dr Pusey and Abbess Lydia appear to have broken off relations with their former protégé after 1866. The latter died in 1876, the former in 1882.

[31] Yet this involved what Ignatius called "mutilating the Sacrament", since only the consecrated wafer was exposed. To be in keeping with his eucharistic theology he ought to have instituted Perpetual Adoration of the Precious Blood.

[32] p. 463. Dwight L. Moody (1837-99), the American evangelist, first visited England in 1867, returning with Ira D. Sankey in 1872, who accompanied him with singing and organ-playing. Their joint hymn-book appeared in 1873, and soon became popular at Llanthony. It was also used at Fr Ignatius' mission services.

[33] op. cit., p. 167.

[34] p. 463. "Carlist" was the name given to those who fought to make Don Carlos, later his son and grandson, King of Spain. A series of civil wars went on between 1837 and 1876.

[35] It is related that about this the Abbot usually slept in "a nice woollen undergarment", and had "a blue dressing gown lined with silk"

[36] Ignatius refused to allow life to be taken, except for some special reason, so fleas found in the abbatial bed had to be put out of the window, one by one.

[37] The letters quoted are taken from some unpublished memoirs of life at New Llanthony Abbey, written by one of the many novices who found they could not endure the Ignatian presentation of the Rule of St Benedict.

[38] p. 500.

[39] A plaque on the wall of the house in Elm Hill records that Fr Ignatius spent two years there in an independent monastery established by him. The street, now named "The Monastery", serves as the drive into a car-park.

[40] This statement shows that Ignatius had no intention of allowing his nuns—or his monks—to be ruled over by a woman, as was the case in the double-monasteries of the Benedictine congregation of Fontrevault, the Brigdettine Order, or those Anglo-Saxon twin-communities of which he was so fond of talking.

[41] p. 539.

[42] In 1891, Sister Mary Agnes, having returned to the world, published *Nunnery Life in the Church of England, or Seventeen Years with Father Ignatius*. It is a poignant account of life led in convents under his rule, even if some of the details may have been exaggerated in retrospect.

[43] ibid.

[44] This was not altogether incompatible with the letter of the Rule of St Benedict, for it is laid down in chapter 28 that if corporal punishment has had no effect, neither the application of "fomentations and dressing by his exhortations", and "as a last resort he has applied the cauterizing of excommunication and the strokes of the rod", then he "must at last use the amputating knife in accord with the sentence of the apostle: 'Expel the wicked man from your midst. If the unbeliever departs, let him depart' (1 Cord. 5, 1 Cor. 7), lest one diseased sheep should infect the whole flock."

[45] See p. 117. The Ignatian ceremonial may have been derived from the *Ordo excommunicandi et absolvendi* printed in the 1596 *Pontificale Romanum* of Clement VIII. Here the bishop, vested in a violet cope, is surrounded by twelve priests, each bearing a lighted candle. These are thrown to the ground when the sentence has been pronounced, after which all other bishops of the province must be notified.

[46] p. 540.

[47] p. 451.

CHAPTER VII

How Fr Ignatius of Jesus moved his loyal remnant of nuns from Slapton to Llanthony, and established a Benedictine double-monastery on Anglo-Saxon lines in the Black Mountains, where more apparitions, miracles and visions took place, while Mother Hilda and her rebel nuns continued to lead a hidden life at Feltham and Twickenham (1879-1893)

MOTHER Hilda Stewart assumed sole charge of the enclosed Benedictine convent at Feltham, Middlesex, almost at the same moment that Mrs Mary Baker Eddy became first pastor of the First Church of Christ Scientist at Boston, Massachusetts, having published *Science and Health, with a Key to the Scriptures* in 1875. The nuns were reduced to dire poverty, able to benefit no longer from the profits made by their Founder's Missions. It is recorded that their faith never wavered, and that "Almighty God always sent them unexpected help in their extremity".[1] Except that they were enclosed, the Feltham community reverted to much the same position in the Church of England as the ten sisterhoods which had been established since its own foundation in 1868. Most of these were small groups of dedicated women, usually under the direction of parochial clergy, and all engaged in active works of charity and mercy. With few exceptions, the bishops left them alone, and they were allowed to develop on their respective lines. Anglo-Catholics ceased to be persecuted after 1879, following the imprisonment in Lancaster Gaol for twelve months of the Rev. Sydney H. Green.[2] The Feltham Benedictine nuns had no resident chaplain, and were dependent on the ministrations of sympathetic clergymen. Neither were they recognised by Dr Jackson, a pious and tolerant Evangelical, who remained Bishop of London until his death in 1885, when he was succeeded by Dr Temple, translated from Exeter.

The story is told how "one day two wealthy ladies came to visit the convent, and were entertained to lunch by Mother Hilda with true Benedictine hospitality. When they left the convent, she sent one of the little orphans who lived with the nuns to take them to the station. On arriving there, they gave the child some coppers, and one said to the other: 'They call themselves a poor community, and they could provide a lunch like that!' The ladies did not realise that, in order to do so, the nuns had dined in the refectory on bread and cheese".[3]

Monastic life at Llanthony was far less peaceful. In January 1879 one of the monks became a Roman Catholic and got married. Abbot Ignatius broke down in health, and was unable to undertake any outside engagements for the whole of February, but he was consoled by the gift of £80 from a lady—an offering for her much-loved brother lately departed "to join the Choirs of Paradise". Three novices were clothed in March. It is recorded that one of them, a priest, "turned out a terrible scandal, and a severe trial to our Superior, for whom to the very last moment before leaving the Abbey he professed such love and reverence. He remained in the Valley circulating evil reports respecting us all, until he suddenly disappeared, and was heard of no more, leaving a companion in mischief to follow up the wrong he had begun. Truly the sorrows and bitter trials of God's Saints have been our lot. The weak health of the Superior became weaker. But prayer unceasing was made to God for him by his many loving children in the Lord in different places. This month he was enabled to preach a Mission in Sheffield."[4]

After this wicked priest left Llanthony "many bright services and holy meditations helped to make the faithful Monks realise that the Cloister was, indeed, to the true lover of the Heavenly Spouse, a very paradise on earth". The Ascension festival was attended by "great numbers of pilgrims, and liberal offerings were made". These included "a gorgeous pair of large jewelled candlesticks . . . The Benediction Service after Vespers was the crowning glory of the day; the many devout pilgrims knelt in the outer Church gazing in wonder upon the magnificence of the scene at the gloriously illuminated Shrine of the Divine Presence which was elevated on the great Throne in the large blazing Monstrance, used only on State occasions. Br Dunstan and the Rev. Father both played the organ at the services of the day." On July 22 the bells of the Abbey tolled very solemnly for the repose of the soul of the Founder's mother, and Requiem services took place. The feasts of the Holy Name of Jesus and the Assumption of the Blessed Virgin were celebrated with "Exposition on the High Throne from early morning till Compline".

Abbot Ignatius and his monks devoured stories of apparitions of Our Lady and the saints, both in ancient and modern times.[5] They were keenly interested in occultism. It is reasonably certain that they devoured the two volumes of Dr F. G. Lee's *The Other World, or Glimpses of the Supernatural*, published in 1875, also *More Glimpses of the World Unseen*, which appeared three years later. The Llanthony community probably read that one evening in August 1879 two women had sworn that they had seen the Holy Mother of God in a sort of transparency against the gable of the Roman Catholic chapel in the remote village of Knock, Co. Mayo. One of them, Mary Beirne, the priest's housekeeper, related that on either side of the Blessed Virgin were St Joseph and a bishop, wearing Mass vestments, and holding a book. She thought he must be St John the Evangelist. Even more marvellous was the sight of a fully adorned altar on which stood a live lamb. The vision lasted for two hours, and was witnessed by about fifteen persons. Three more apparitions were reported on January 6, February 10, and 12, 1880. The Bishop of Tuam, having investigated the phenomena, declared that "the testimony of all, taken as a whole, was trustworthy and satisfactory".

Six months after the last of these apparitions beside a Roman Catholic chapel in the far west of Ireland, similar phantasmagoria took place at the Anglican Benedictine monastery in South Wales. On the morning of July 30, 1880, while Br Dunstan was at watch before the altar, the Monstrance began to manifest itself outside the massive doors of the tabernacle, very shadowy at first, but gradually becoming perfectly distinct. The vision lasted for about an hour. On the evening of August 30 four boys swore that they had seen "a bright dazzling figure gliding across the meadow" towards them, and that "a halo of glory shone out from the Figure all round in an oval form". They said that it reminded them of the pictures of the Immaculate Conception, and one of them was very frightened. He cried out: "If it comes near me, I'll hit it". A week later, a bush in the meadow was "all aglow with light". The monks and the boys began to sing hymns and say prayers, after which the feminine Figure re-appeared, followed by "the Form of a man unclothed, save for a cloth round his loins". On September 15, the Abbot having returned from his nuns at Slapton, he was one of those who beheld what was "concluded to be a cohort of Angels, assembling to welcome Blessed Mary". Directly the monks, boys and laymen began to sing, they "observed outlines of bright light Forms flashing about in all directions". Then the Reverend Father bade them to chant an *Ave Maria*. No sooner had they begun it "than the whole

113

heavens and mountains broke forth in bulging circles of light, circles pushing out of circles". The light poured on their faces and the buildings, "and in the central circle stood a most Majestic Heavenly Form, robed in flowing drapery. The Form was gigantic, but seemed to be reduced to human size as it approached. The Figure stood sideways, facing the Holy Bush. The Vision was most distinct, and the details were very clear; but it was in the twinkling of an eye." This was the last of the Visions, which the community was sure had been vouchsafed by God's mercy to them. They praised "His Holy Name for this Confirmation of the Christian Faith in this age of unbelief".[6]

Ignatius of Jesus had no shadow of doubt that these visions were the final proof of God's blessing on his revival of the Benedictine Order in the Church of England, especially as the year 1880 was being kept as the fourteen-hundredth anniversary of the birth of St Benedict. Considering that there were 107 Roman Catholic Benedictine monasteries, and an estimated total of 2,800 monks scattered over the world, it was remarkable that in none of them, so far as could be ascertained, had a monstrance moved out of a tabernacle on its own volition, or the Mother of God manifested herself four times in a fortnight, as was alleged to have happened in the only Anglican Benedictine monastery at that moment.[7]

Professor William Crookes and other scientists of that date would have been amused by the official narrative of the Llanthony phantasmagoria. They would have assured Fr Ignatius that the movement of the monstrance probably resulted from mechanical action controlled by an intelligence of "ectoplasmic rods", proceeding from a medium, as in the levitation of tables. They could recall similar cases at séances of solid objects being carried through the walls or ceiling of a room, which had every opening sealed and fastened. Then they would have found no difficulty in producing evidence that a remarkable medium, Miss Florence Cook (controlled by a spirit known as "Katie King"), had managed to materialise bodies much more often and effectively than the materialization of the Form of a Woman and a Man in South Wales. As to the lights which flashed in all directions against the dark mountains, similar luminous appearances had often taken place in the late eighteen-seventies during the séances held by Stainton Moses, Henry Slade, and others.

Professor Crookes, whose *Researches on the Phenomena of Spiritualism* had been published in 1874, might have formed the opinion that Fr Ignatius, Br Dunstan, Sister Janet, and the boys were unconscious mediums. The phenomenon of the grass being both dry and warm where "The Woman" had stood that damp evening could have explained that it had precedents among spiritualists. Indeed, the Professor and his colleagues would have been prepared to accept the stories about the materialization of the Forms of a Woman and a Man. It would not have surprised them that, considering their background, the recipients of the visions took the "forms" to be Mary and Jesus. The teenagers in France who claimed similar visions, being simple-minded Roman Catholics, naturally presumed that the lovely lady they beheld was "La Sainte Vierge".[8]

Fr Ignatius did not bother to send wild rhubarb leaves from the "Holy Bush" to his degenerate daughters at Feltham, as he did to his devoted ones at Slapton. It is said that they cured the novice-mistress, Mother Cecilia, who had been crippled for thirty-eight years, seldom without pain.

The year 1881 deserves to be remembered for the erection of the first definitely planned Anglican Benedictine convent . . . "one of the golden rifts in the thunder clouds at a time of many storms".[9] Ignatius's biographer related that "the translation of the Nuns from Slapton to Llanthony, furnished a bright light to the year 1881, likewise the entry into the Extern Sisterhood of one of the most familiar figures of the Reverend Father's latter-day *entourage*—Sister Annie, the faithful friend and benefactress of Llanthony, who until a week before her death [which occurred in 1903] was an unfailing pillar of the Monk's Missions".[10] During the translation, which involved a long railway journey from Kingswear to Llanfihangel-Crucorney, the nuns were put under strict obedience to keep their black veils down, lest their faces should be seen by men.

Having reached their destination after the eleven miles drive up the Vale of Ewyas, the Abbot conducted them into the "Living Tomb" in which they would be walled up alive. This was a ramshackle convent of corrugated iron and matchboard, built on level ground adjoining the east side of the monastery. A small garth was the only space for fresh air and exercise. The narrow lancet windows, filled with diamond-shaped leaded lights, helped to create the correct medieval atmosphere. The walls and ceilings of every room and cell were of dark-stained pitch-pine. Once the nuns were re-enclosed in the Priory of St Scholastica, their Abbot imposed on them far more rigid confinement than had been possible at either Feltham or Slapton. These women were forbidden to set eyes on persons of the opposite sex. Conversation with them, if necessary, had to be carried on behind a curtained grille. A "turning-box" on the Borromean model, enabled objects to be passed from the convent into the monastery, or vice versa. Otherwise there must be no contact between the monks and nuns. The Abbot, however, had no scruples about entering the nuns' enclosure whenever he felt inclined to do so.[11]

It took nearly ten years to complete the three bays of the choir—all that materialized of the replica of the great church of the Austin Canons. On September 30, 1882, Ignatius recorded in his Chronicle: "On this day also the Choir was closed to the Divine Office and Mass was said in the East Cloister of the Abbey, forasmuch as the great Altar is to be completed, a large new organ built, and the new oaken stalls to be erected. The working men are expected next week. On September 28: I did after Vespers remove the Most Holy Sacrament into the Oratory in the adjoining Priory of St Scholastica."

There had been a magnificent function on Ascension Day that year. A newspaper reported that "at 8 o'clock the ancient Latin Benedictine service was used with all its attendant Romish ceremonies. . . . It was a gorgeous service. Stout curtains drawn over the windows completely kept out the daylight, to give effect to the hundreds of tall and short wax tapers lighting up the shrine, and the enthroned statues and images presenting a most fairy-like appearance through the thick films of incense which filled the lofty edifice . . . The oriental appearance of the whole was very similar to the sight presented at a Latin-Greek church on the Continent." The procession must have been awe-inspiring as the sacred ministers and monks entered "with a tremendous clash of cymbals". Before long they were lost in a fog produced by a "white-robed youth swaying a censer" (sic). The music was sugary, for it started with the *Kyrie* sung as a duet by the Roman Catholic priest from Tenby and an Anglican incumbent—an instance of ecumenical co-operation far more surprising in 1882 than it would be today. The liturgy was interrupted later by the *Gloria, Nicene Creed, Agnus Dei, Qui tollis,* and *Dona nobis,* no doubt accompanied by soft modulations on the harmonium. We are told that "a voluptuous swell of music swept through the building", thanks to "the solemn voices of the chanters". Just as spectacular was the annual pilgrimage of Our Ladye of Llanthony, instituted in commemoration of the apparitions in 1880. Vast crowds came along, mainly for the sake of hearing a sermon by Ignatius.

The Benedictine Calendar ("compiled from Ancient uses of the English Church") enables one to picture the liturgical life at this Anglican double-monastery during the eighteen-eighties. On January 30 "Charles, King and Martyr" was kept as a Greater Double, with "Solemn Exposition of the Blessed Sacrament, in Expiation for the National Sin" committed in 1649. The Sarum colour sequence was followed, also its Holy Week ritual and ceremonial—with Ignatian variants.[12] St Augustine, being "Apostle of the English"—not of the Welsh—was reduced to an "Inferior Double" on May 30. Corpus Christi was celebrated with "Solemn Exposition of the Most Holy Sacrament all day at the Abbey Church at Llanthony". Special offerings were requested "for the Solemn Feast of Reparation, which are considerable". July 21 was the "Requiem Anniversary for Louisa Genevieve, Mother of our Founder", St Ignatius Loyola was a Greater Double, being "the Patronal Feast of our Founder", and according to the Sarum Use he got yellow vestments. On August 30 the Feast of the Apparition of Our Lady of Llanthony was kept as a Greater Double, and on September 15 another feast commemorating the "Vision of her Descent from Heaven in glory upon Llanthony Abbey". Ignatius did not accept the dogma of the Immaculate Conception, so December 8 was merely an Inferior Double. On the other hand the Apparition of the B.V.M. of Llanthony was given an Octave, also the "Reappearance of the Vision".

None of the two or three other Anglican male communities could offer anything approaching the Catholic Privileges that were available at Llanthony, nor could any of the more numerous sisterhoods. Believing that the Benedictine Order needed further publicity a pamphlet was published in 1881, entitled *Twenty-two Teachings of Ignatius the Monk, to the Monks and Nuns of his Monasteries*. Here are some of the attractions worth quoting, for they reveal his whole outlook on the monastic life, which was nothing if not romantic.

"(1) Consider in your beautiful Cloister Home, you have the grand business of serving 'JESUS *only*', with nothing to hinder you; (3) You have your whole time given up and Consecrated to GOD and Eternity; (4) Each hour, by the Sacrifice of Obedience, which GOD says is better than any other, in His sight, you may 'lay up Treasure in Heaven'; (8) The Monk is far above the rest of Christians, as the Sun is above the Moon in brightness and fructifying power. '*Saul* hath slain his thousands, but *David* his tens of thousands'; (9) The Monk has a most faithful spouse. 'His quiver is full of children who shall live for ever, and be as the olive branches round God's table in Heaven for ever more'; (10) In the Monastery you have the sweet interest of helping others hour by hour to become true brides of JESUS, and to grow more and more like Him; (11) You have the Monastery boys to lead in the highest steps of holiness and self-denial for JESUS' sake; and to form their souls, Christ's image—not only by precept but by practice —in look, in word, or deed. They, even the youngest, will judge of Christ's beauty and the truth of His Word, by your method of showing it forth;[13] (12) You have a beautiful and stately shrine wherein to adore GOD's Majesty, and your days and time are so regulated, that you may join the Angels in their Heavenly Business at eight stated times during the 24 hours of each day; (14) You have the magnificence of Nature, in scene and sound all about you, mountain, rocks, valleys, woods, ravines, rivers, streams and flowers—GOD everywhere; (15) You have the world shut out, with its vanities, snares, sins, follies, anxieties and cares; (16) Your Monastery is Mount Tabor where you have 'lifted up your eyes and see no *man* any more save JESUS *only* and yourselves'; (17) Your Monastery is the Home of Spiritual Multiplication by the figure 1,000: '*One day* in Thy Courts is *better* than 1,000'; (19) You are living at the Gate of Heaven—'waiting for the coming of our Lord JESUS Christ'; and (20) Your life in the Monastery is a daily, hourly, momentarily, a living Sacrifice of self, in Humility and Obedience, in silence, love and praise—a ceaseless 'laying up of Treasure in Heaven' for Love of Him who loved you and gave Himself for you, and this in a way unattainable outside the Cloister of the Monkish Life."

Many young men and women were unable to resist the allure of the *Twenty-two Teachings of Ignatius the Monk,* feeling that the only place in Britain where they could be sure of reaching Heaven was in the cloister hidden away among the Black Mountains of Wales. The Abbot was prepared to welcome anybody who, in his opinion, had "found salvation", and sought nothing more than to live for JESUS *only* in the beautiful and stately shrine. The truth was that he was easily imposed on by both men and women, who could talk to him about salvation and so forth.

The tattered vellum-bound Register, still preserved, contains the names of at least forty men, of whom six left with the Abbot's consent. Twelve ran away and never came back. Fourteen were expelled for disorderly, dishonest or violent conduct. Ignatius wrote again and again of "a very bad person"—"broken vows" —"insolent and rebellious"—"conceit and deceit", and so on. Br Cuthbert Mary of St Paul was "sent away for trying to ruin every single person in the Monastery, and he succeeded with many". Another monk was said to be "entirely under the domination of Satan thro' temper and disobedience". There is also reference to Br Dunstan of St Ignatius who "carried on his love affairs from these very walls, deceived me thoroughly, ruined all the Monastery by his Evil example *while I was away begging.* He turned Protestant and Romanist in one fortnight. Then married. He has been miserable ever since. Still writes to me." Then there was Br Bede of St Sebastian, an "almost diabolical man", who "ran away because he was tired of playing a game of deceit". Br Dunstan of the Crown of Thorns cleared off, begged to be received back again, but eventually "killed himself by poison".

So far as possible Abbot Ignatius kept quiet about the seamier side of life in his monastery, and if he did refer to it, never accepted any responsibility for scandals. He preferred to dwell on the bright side, and made sure that the *Hereford Times* printed a detailed report of Sister Ermenild of the Sacred Heart of Jesus being "walled up alive" on the Sunday within the Octave of the Assumption 1882.

We are told that this long function started with the Abbot standing on the steps of the Lady altar in the narthex of the nearly completed church, where he delivered a discourse to the congregation, and to the novice, who knelt with face veiled beside a draped bier. Then her hair was cut, after which she was clothed in a cowl, given a ring, and "the terrible black veil" was imposed. Over it was draped a crimson "sacramental veil". The Abbot placed a wreath of flowers on her bowed head. Having made her life-vows, she was given communion from the tabernacle.

"A stream of monks, nuns, sisters, acolytes, and layfolk from the congregation, one by one prostrated themselves before the newly-wedded Bride of Christ, kissing the border of her garment, while she placed her hands very lovingly on their lowered heads . . . This over, the Sisters for the last time led the new Nun into the outer church. The crowd reverently drew back as she approached. The Sisters laid her on the bier, her hands were folded on her breast, and they covered her with the heavy funeral pall. The Abbot now came with the acolytes, vested in black garments over the white underdress. A plain white linen mitre was now on his head, the Service Book and a long taper in his hands. Thus he came and stood at the head of the Bier, the chant sounding the Funeral Service. The Sisters, the little girls, the acolytes, and the black-hooded monks, stood round the Bier, holding tapers. The Bier was incensed by Fr Ignatius, who received the censer from one of the surpliced boys. 'Earth to earth, ashes to ashes', was said, and earth thrown over the dead-to-the-world Nun. There was a deep silence—the laboured breathing of the deeply affected congregation was heard in sighs. The Nuns began, with quavering voices, to chant for the Dead; the organ only whispered; the muffled toll of the great bell sounded; the Monks lifted up the Bier, and with slow steps, to the chant of the Nuns and the tolling of the bell, the acolytes raising the great candlesticks aloft at the Bier corners, Mother Ermenild was borne into her Living Tomb. I saw that the altar was now covered with a black pall also and its lights put out. When the Bier and its attendants were all inside the Monastic Choir, the gratings were closed, and a thick curtain drawn across them, so that, strain as they did, the congregation outside, representing the outer world, had to bid farewell to the newly made Nun of Llanthony."[14]

The bodies as well as the souls of the Llanthony nuns depended on the whims of their often absent, dictatorial Major Superior. Nobody but himself was allowed to give them spiritual conferences. By this time Ignatius had ceased to believe in the value of the sacrament of Penance, so it did not matter that they were unable to go to confession. The Prioress hardly dared to make suggestions on changes in the observances she might feel would be beneficial, remembering what had been the fate of Mother Hilda. The Abbot would have been horrified at the idea of appointing a Visitor to the community, or even to call in a clergyman to conduct an annual retreat. What more did the nuns need than his *Twenty-two Teachings*?

By 1883 the buildings at Llanthony were completed in the state they remained for the next quarter of a century. They were erected on the lower slopes of the more than 2,000 feet high Fwddag ridge above Capel-y-Ffin.[15] Four continuous blocks surrounded a small garth.[16] Its north side consisted of what were intended as offices. The passage above them was known as the "Crucifix Cloister". The lower floor on the opposite and south side formed one large room, called the "Bible Cloister". In the course of time it became cluttered up with a canopied lectern, statues, a Lady altar, and other *bondieuserie*. At its western end was the guests' refectory. Exterior stairs led up to the abbatial apartments, one of which was given the name of "The Prophet's Chamber". They were comfortably furnished in a Victorian manner as befitted the status of a man who firmly believed that he held the place of Christ in the monastery.

The cells (more correctly cubicles) for both monks and guests, were identical, formed by wooden partitions, about ten feet high, open at the top. Each held an iron bed, with a straw mattress and blankets. The scarlet coverlets had white crosses in the middle. There was just space for a chair and a small iron washstand. Like all the monastery windows, those in the dormitory were deeply splayed, narrow, and glazed with leaded diamond-shaped panes. As stated already, they looked over the garth, facing north. The result was a very dim religious light, especially in winter.

The planning of the whole monastery was as impractical and as inconvenient as Mr Buckeridge's imagination could have made them. Almost all the rooms opened into each other. The two narrow staircases were at opposite ends of the buildings. All the ground-floor rooms were tiled or paved, which increased the cold and damp. Most of the few chimneys smoked, and there was no other means of heating. The monks spent much time in the long gloomy "Bible Cloister", where they shivered on cold winter days for the lack of a fire-place. Neither the kitchen nor the small scullery could be described as "labour-saving".

To reach the church, more correctly only the three-bayed choir of the more than 200 feet long building which Fr Ignatius hoped would materialise in 1870, the brethren had to go down a dark, damp corrugated-iron passage with many steps (said to be haunted). The entrance was right in the middle of the choir stalls. The

118

narrow windows, very high up, were filled with stained glass, which helped to create a sense of gloom. There were brown-stained oak canopied stalls, with "misericordes" on either side of the choir, and above them galleries. The mighty organ stood in the centre of the gallery, beneath which was a screen. The door in the middle was trellised, and often had a thick curtain over it, so that seculars in the narthex could not peep at the monks. The comparatively small space was largely filled up with an altar and the shrine of Our Lady of Llanthony, before which were votive lamps, candlesticks and many flower-vases.

The nuns' means of access to the church was even more inconvenient than that of the monks. To reach their choir in the tribune above the monks' stalls, they went through a passage and up dark winding stairs. A heavy wooden grille, with iron spikes and curtains, prevented them from being seen by their brethren down below. In order to receive Communion, having donned their scarlet veils, they descended a steep flight of stairs on the Gospel side of the high altar, and knelt at a small grating.[17]

Raised on seven steps above the choir was the high altar. The stone reredos brought from Munich was said to have cost over £2,000. It rose up to not far below the vaulting of the roof, and was a mass of carved statues, crockets and pinnacles. In the centre was a large brass tabernacle, with its doors encrusted with jewels. Immediately above it, on ruby plush, was the word JESUS in gold. Then came the exposition throne, surmounted by a many-crocketted canopy reaching to the vaulting. Normally about fifty candles were lit on the gradines, with floral bouquets in brass vases mixed up with them. On the greater feasts when there was Solemn Exposition yet more tapers added to the brilliance of the *mise en scène*. The effect was quite equal to what had been visualized in *Leonard Morris*—the hundred wax tapers glittering star-like in the dimness of the sanctuary.[18] It was a pity that the *tout ensemble* was never completed by thirty or forty lamps with ruby glasses, "swinging in the air, high up before the Exalted Presence", as described in the novel.

Within the sanctuary stood two or three canopied shrines, each with candle-sticks. Two lofty brass candelabra rested on the footpace. Around the walls were banners and bannerettes. Two more candlesticks stood on pedestals beside the *prie-dieu* in the midst of the choir. The Gospel lectern was draped with a rich brocade cloth.

Even if monastic life at Llanthony continued to be eclectic and exotic, having no affinity with what could have been found in any other Benedictine community throughout the world, yet the ceremonial—supposed to be a revival of the "Use" of the Illustrious Church of Sarum—became the yard-stick by which could be measured the advance of the Catholic Movement in Church of England parishes. Few, if any, managed to reach the Llanthony level.

Yet there was always something sinister about the monastery and convent, with their mock medievalism. The dull grey-brown sandstone buildings became more and more gloomy as trees and shrubs grew up, especially on a wet day, when the mountains were shrouded in mists. Most of the outer doors, provided with grilles and turn-hatches, had painted on them in white letters *Pax, Jesus Only*, or *Jesu yn Unig*. The warning of *Solemn Silence* greeted guests on the walls of the staircases. The whole Abbey was pervaded with an atmosphere of mould and damp, some-times that of stale cooking, granted that the church seldom lacked the mixed perfumes of flowers and incense. Such then was the outward expression of the restoration of Benedictine life on medieval lines in the Black Mountains of Wales during the eighteen-eighties.

Ignatius of Mary, having reached the age of twenty, revisited his old home in

THE CLOISTER GARTH, LLANTHONY ABBEY, *c.* 1900

Note the large black wooden cross, and the cast-iron fountain, said to be "of chaste and elegant design". Not shown are the graves of the Rev. Father's "very tame and affectionate little Dove", and of Sister Ermenild of the Sacred Heart of Jesus, who died in 1882.

BENEDICTINE BIBLE-READING IN THE CLOISTER AT
LLANTHONY ABBEY, *c.* 1900

1882, after six years at sea. During this time "Baby" had written "very lovingly" to his foster-father, who on seeing him again, felt that they deserved a holiday together. A brief entry in the Register ends the story of the Infant Samuel, which started in 1864: "He robbed me of £10. Went back to Edinburgh and got married."

The general public formed the impression that everything was forging ahead at the double-monastery, when confronted by a printed statement like the following:

Adoremeus in aeternum Sanctissimum Sacramentum

The Solemn Pilgrimage of the Miraculous Sacrament of Llanthony on Ascension Day, May 22, 1884, at Llanthony Abbey.

Special Notice

Mass every half-hour from 5 a.m. until 10, according to number of priests wishing to celebrate. Application to say Mass at the Shrine should be made some time before. Roman, Greek, Anglican (Sarum), or even Prayer Book Rite may be used. Only celibate Priests at the Shrine. Married Priests say Mass at Altar in outer Church. "Low Church" Clergy permitted to celebrate in their own way. Application for lodgings. Donations towards the very heavy expenses of the Pilgrimage are earnestly solicited for food for the Pilgrims (gratuitously supplied), lights, incense, flowers, shrubs, books for the Church. For particulars apply, etc.

It is not surprising, however, that the Anglican Welsh bishops gave the monastery a wide berth when they read of these riots of Ritualism indulged in at intervals. One fears that the Baroness was not telling the whole truth when she wrote that, from the episcopal point of view, "the Reverend Father's chief defection lies in the fact that he is a Monk. His black habit and tonsure, together with the additional aggravation of his Monastery being a self-governing institution—and therefore out of reach of diocesan jurisdiction—have been sources of inflammation not to be condoned".[19]

The Abbot-General of the Anglican Order of St Benedict got plenty of free publicity in 1885, when he gave two eight-day Missions in the Westminster Town Hall. At the final service of the first Mission in May Dr Chinnery-Haldane, Bishop of Argyll and the Isles, imparted a benediction on the vast audience. In October a petition was sent to Dr Temple, who had succeeded Dr Jackson as Bishop of London, begging him to allow the Monk to preach in a church again. This was granted, and on the first Tuesday in Advent Ignatius, at the invitation of Canon Trench, occupied the pulpit of All Saints', Notting Hill—his first sermon in a London church since his inhibition sixteen years previously.

Another spectacular function at Llanthony Abbey was the pontifical obsequies of Sister Mary Etheldreda, O.S.B., which took over four-and-a-half hours. She died on February 14, 1886, in the nineteenth year of her religious profession.[20] The long newspaper account of the funeral was even more turgid than that of the solemn profession of Sister Ermenild of the Sacret Heart of Jesus in August 1882.[21] Once again there were mourning monks, weeping nuns, acolytes and little girls, twinkling tapers and clouds of incense, not forgetting black vestments. The grave was blessed, not only with holy water and incense, but also with earth from the Garden of Gethsemane. It had been a long winter and the ground was still covered with snow, which, as the reporter remarked, "seemed to speak that word of love—whiter than snow—of the redeemed soul of the departed saint of Jesus . . ." The coffin was lowered into the deep grave. As the procession left, a procession of the cloistered nuns, always invisible, came with tapers along another cloister to put flowers in the grave, then silently they turned away, and all was over. And so they left the

THE HIGH ALTAR, LLANTHONY ABBEY, *c.* 1890

"Unmistakably awful is the sacred mountain shrine. . . The monks 'relieving guard' before the Glorious Sacrament exposed in a magnificent *ostensorium*, standing in a throne over the tabernacle—carrying on the *one* work to which they have dedicated their lives."

(Fr. Ignatius in *Leonard Morris, or The Benedictine Novice*.) The nuns' stalls were in the grilled galleries on either side.

body of "Dear Sister Etheldreda" to sleep in their midst among their quiet cloisters until He shall come, at the sound of whose glad trump "the dead in Christ shall rise first, and then we who are alive and remain shall be caught up together with them to meet the Lord in the air; and so shall we ever be with the Lord".

About nine months after the death and burial of Sister Mary Etheldreda, a 431 pages volume entitled *Mission Sermons and Orations by Fr Ignatius O.S.B., Evangelist Monk of the Church of England,* was published. One oration—"Why were the Monasteries of England Destroyed?"—contained the following statement:

"I have tried, for twenty-five years, to give the Church of England a Monastery, and as far as the attempt has gone, I do not hesitate to say, it has utterly failed. You may say it is my fault. I know that there are a great many faults inherent in my peculiar character which are against the success of the work. No one knows this so well as I know them, but Almighty God put it into my heart to be the first to come out and dedicate myself to this work.

"If some of our persecutors and critics would come forward and take my place, I would very thankfully retire into my own cell, and become an ordinary monk. I know my utter incapability for the leadership of so great a work; but God has called me to begin this work, just the same as he called St Benedict, and put it in his heart, to begin the work.

"I think that in this nineteenth century, Monasticism is more needed than ever it was, as an antidote to the sham religion and restless spirit of the age. It is more than ever needed as a practical proof of the Christian religious reality.

"I repeat, brethren, that I should be happy to lay down the position I have held, by force of circumstances, for the last twenty-five years, if any of those who can sympathise with my incompetency for the work will come forward and take my place, after undergoing a year's training."[22]

The spirit of the training the future Abbot would have to undergo was found in the eleven verses of the *"Hymn of the Benedictine Monks of St Mary and St Dunstan's Abbey at Llanthony"*. Here are five of them:

"We come, we come, the children of Salvation,
　　The mystic spouses of our wondrous King;
　　For all the nations of the earth we're pleading,
　　For Holy Church our solemn praises bring.

Amid the silence of our lonely mountains,
　　Living for *'Jesus Only'* and alone;
　　We come, we come in joyous adoration,
　　And pour forth our homage at His Altar Throne.

Ah! children of a dying world! we see you
　　Straying to darkness—weeping as you go;
　　For you we pray—for you His merits plead we,
　　You *must* be saved from the dread ageless woe.

Like Moses on the mountain top—we bless you,
　　A Host we bring, O peoples, to your aid;
　　Our praise like Mary's ointment shall refresh you,
　　By Christ we are your greatest helpmates made.

For this we raise our songs and intercessions,
　　Our praises from our Rolling Planet fling;
　　They glad the ear of our Tribune JEHOVAH,
　　Are precious in the presence of the King."[23]

Shortly after the publication of *Mission Sermons and Orations delivered by Fr Ignatius O.S.B.*, a thirteen year-old boy, Benjamin Fearnley Carlyle, then living with his parents at Rosario, on the banks of the River Parana in the Argentine, heard a clear call to revive Benedictine monasticism in the Church of England, unaware that a young Anglican deacon had made the same decision a quarter of a century earlier, or that there was now a double-monastery of his Order in South Wales.[24] The inspiration came from *Monks and Monasteries* by the Rev. Samuel Fox, which he chanced to pick up in his father's library.[25] This typical Tractarian period-piece, tinged with Gothic Revival romanticism, published in 1845, filled young Ben with visions of ruined abbeys all over England waiting to be rebuilt and refilled with monks. This would be his life-work, and he began to picture himself as a mitred abbot.

To return to Mother Hilda and her nuns at Feltham. The little community, which had led a more or less hidden life since 1878, was still supported mainly by the benefactions of a few loyal friends, the chief of whom was a Miss Charlotte Boyd.

It is recorded that in 1850, during a visit to Glastonbury, she heard a voice bidding her to restore the ruins of the Abbey, as well as those of other pre-Reformation monasteries, so that they could be handed over to Church of England brotherhoods and sisterhoods. Six years later, Dr Neale encouraged her to persevere with this pious intention. It was in keeping with what he had proposed already in his romance *Ayton Priory, or the Restored Monastery* (1843). Miss Boyd might prove to be his "Colonel Amberly", who dreamed of reviving the medieval monastic system. In 1875 she formed a trust, the funds of which were to be administered by the Society of St John the Evangelist—"The Cowley Fathers". Meanwhile she had become an Associate of the Sisters of the Church.[26] So rapid was the growth of this community that by 1879 it had erected an orphanage at Kilburn, large enough to hold 250 children, Miss Boyd was one of the ladies who helped to run it during the eighteen-eighties.

Not long after the Golden Jubilee of Queen Victoria in June 1887, two young men, Reginald Camm and Henry Worth, paid their first visit to the Benedictine convent at Feltham.[27] In 1888 they found themselves fellow curates at St Agnes', Kennington Park, a South London church celebrated for its ornate worship based on Charles Walker's *Services of the Church, with rubrical directions according to the Illustrious Church of Sarum*, first published in 1866.[28] It is easy to understand why Mr Camm and Mr Worth were drawn to the Benedictine nuns, so different to other Anglican sisterhoods, with far more of a medieval flavour about them.

The community was forced to find a new home because the lease of the farmhouse fell in after twenty-one years. By this time they had a resident chaplain, the Rev. Arthur Dale, who had been licensed by Bishop Temple about 1887.[29] It was his father who offered to rent a property at Twickenham to Mother Hilda. She and her nuns moved there on October 15, 1889, the feast of St Teresa of Avila.[30]

Thanks to some "Reminiscences of Llanthony" by the late Dom Cyprian Alston, published in the Christmas 1913 issue of *Pax*, it is easy to picture what life was like in the Anglican Benedictine double-monastery between 1888 and 1894.[31] At the time of his arrival the twin-community consisted of the Abbot, two brothers, three boy-oblates, and three nuns. The numbers fluctuated continually. The high-water mark was reached in the summer of 1890, when the male section counted a dozen. Looking back on the past Dom Cyprian wrote:

"The frequent coming and going of postulants and boys certainly relieved the monotony of the life, but it was not conducive to stability or a very constant standard of observance. I have sometimes wondered since how we managed to keep the divine office and everything else going with as much regularity as we did. But we certainly managed it somehow. The rule we tried to observe was as severe as the surroundings. Perpetual abstinence from flesh meat was the ideal aimed at, though not always strictly adhered to; very little recreation or relaxation; a good deal of silence; and conditions of life that were none too healthy."

Just as in the past, Abbot Ignatius "did not live the community life; his occupations, his meals, his recreations, and even his devotions were all, for the most part, quite different from those of the rest of the community. His absences from the monastery were lengthy and frequent, and even when he was at home we sometimes saw nothing of him for days together . . . The Superior's appearances amongst us were meteoric and uncertain; if things had been going smoothly he was kindness and fatherly geniality itself when we saw him, but if there had been any trouble or slackness he could be very much the opposite. The fact that we nearly always had a few boys in the monastery, living with the community, tended, I think, to lower the strictly monastic ideal amongst the brothers, besides being sometimes a cause of friction between them and their superior."

The Divine Office was still recited mainly in English, being a translation from the *Breviarium Monasticum*. Bits, however, remained in Latin, e.g. the Antiphons of Our Lady, and the Litany of Loreto. The Benedictus, Magnificat, and the Sunday Vespers psalms were in Welsh. When a clergyman was a guest, which was not often, he was asked to consecrate a large amount of bread and wine before leaving, so that the deacon-Abbot could give communion from the tabernacle.

After sixteen years' experience of normal monastic life at Downside, the one-time Cattwg Fair of the Holy Trinity wrote about his seven years at Llanthony: "I think I can truly say that so long as we succeeded in satisfying our superior, and avoiding his displeasure, we did not really know or care very much about the principles of the religious life itself. And this is not to be wondered at, seeing that we had no regular course of spiritual instruction, no proper training in the exercises and spirit of the monastic state, and no opportunity of learning for ourselves what was necessary for the formation of the true monastic character. We had no studies, properly so-called, for Fr Ignatius used to say that the only books a monk needed to study were the Bible and the Holy Rule, and that if he knew those well he required nothing else.

"There was a library, it is true, but its contents were kept under lock and key, and only very sparingly did Fr Ignatius lend out some special book for one or other of the brothers to read. The two books already mentioned, together with Butler's *Lives of the Saints,* were practically our sole intellectual nourishment. We had daily Bible-reading together, at which Fr Ignatius sometimes attended, and if he did so he was wont to expound the chapter of the day in his own individual way. When he was not there one of the brothers would sometimes essay to explain the passages read, but I dare not imagine what a qualified professor of Sacred Scripture would have thought of the novel attempts at exegesis that were made. The careful supervision which Fr Ignatius thus exercised over our reading, whilst it kept from us the possibility of learning anything opposed to his teaching, at the same time defeated its own ends, because it prevented us from knowing anything about the monastic life beyond what we heard from his own lips.

"He dictated to us the doctrines we had to accept, and from them there was no appeal to any recognised Rule of Faith. These doctrines were a curious blend of a certain amount of Catholic dogma, with evangelical ideas about conversion and salvation almost verging on Calvinism. His ritualism was kept in the background when dealing with Low Church people and Nonconformists, but in the monastery itself it was much to the fore. His position in the Church of England was somewhat peculiar, in that he was absolutely unrecognised by the authorities of that Church; in fact, he was at different times inhibited by most of the bishops from preaching in their churches, and he was eyed with suspicion and distrust by the majority of the clergy. He was a believer in so-called national churches, each autonomous and independent, though forming part of one universal whole; hence, whilst he always spoke of the Pope with respect, and allowed him to be the 'first Bishop in Christendom', he denied his universal supremacy.

"As, in matters of doctrine, so also in the management of his monastery, he acknowledged no Superior or higher authority over himself. Though professing to follow the Rule of St Benedict, it was his own interpretation of it, coloured by his own private whims and fancies and a somewhat variable will, that became the standard of life at Llanthony. This vacillation, as it were, has been, I think, one of the causes of failure. . . . In spite of his claim to be Benedictine, the rule at Llanthony was, in fact, an eclectic one devised by the superior himself. . . . Many regulations of details were either his own invention or else adapted from various un-Benedictine sources. And yet the claim that he had restored the Benedictine Rule in the Church of England was his constant boast."

The nuns who were shut up in their convent of wood and iron were even more the slaves of the Superior. Postulants came and went at intervals, but only three nuns remained faithful between 1888 and 1890. It was their loyalty to Fr Ignatius that kept them walled up alive. Dom Cyprian recalled: "We, of course, saw nothing of them, but we heard their voices in the church, joining in the offices, their choir being in a tribune immediately above the monks' stalls. Their life must have been one of considerable hardship, for they were strictly enclosed and their convent was none too comfortable a habitation, extremes of both heat and cold being emphasised by the nature of its construction. The fewness of their numbers, too, must have made their daily life a monotonous and prosaic one. It is true that when Fr Ignatius was at home he used frequently to be with them in the convent, but during his absences they had no other chaplain or confessor to minister to their spiritual needs."

In spite of all the amateurish character of the monastic life, Dom Cyprian had to admit that the place itself had a "fascination", which so many both before and after him have felt. "It is not so much the solemn grandeur of its surroundings, lovely and inspiring as they undoubtedly are, nor is it any special beauty there may be about the buildings, because, frankly, these are disappointing; but there is about Llanthony a sort of indefinable charm which cannot be described, but which undeniably entwines itself around the heartstrings of all those who have known and loved the place. Do not think me sentimental when I say that no one who has known at all intimately either the monastery or its founder could ever again think of it with indifference, especially if one, as in my own case, has spent a number of years there. I cannot imagine such a person revisiting the abbey, after an interval of years, and catching the first glimpse of the gable of the church on coming up the valley, or hearing the sound of the monastery bells re-echoed by the solemn mountains all around, without experiencing that species of emotion prosaically described as 'a lump in the throat'. And this, mind you, in spite of, or perhaps because of, all the sad disappointments, the rudely-shattered hopes, and the pathetic failure of the whole venture. At any rate, to my mind, the history of Llanthony will always be one of touching tragedy and pathos, of fervent aspirations that have fallen short of realisation."

The Anglican Order of St Benedict was very much in the limelight after the feast of the Beheading of St John the Baptist, August 29, 1889, when the Abbot of Llanthony was solemnly initiated into the Druidic Circle of Wales during the National Eisteddfod at Brecon. The Venerable Arch-Druid Clwydfordd bestowed on Ignatius of Jesus the title of Dewi-Honddu (David of the Honddu) in the presence of 12,000 people. The Monk delivered what was described as "a vigorous and impassioned address", bursting into Welsh at intervals.[32] He proclaimed: "Your Christianity, Oh, people of Cymru, is apostolic. . . . It was brought to you and by your own people in God's providence from the mouth of the apostle, St Paul . . . The Church of the Cymry existed long before there was any Church of England. It existed long before there was any Pope of Rome. It existed when the divine lips, the divinely-inspired lips, of the apostle sent back the good news of Christianity in His salvation to your ancestors, by the mouths of your countrymen. Therefore, her history, her origin, her religion, from the Druids to the Christian Church, possess a magnificent uniqueness of antiquity that I do not think any other Church on the face of the globe can equal . . . Why, the very names of the four large dioceses of Wales show that they existed long before there was a Church of England. Llandaff, St Davids, St Asaph, and St Deiniol of Bangor; all of these are bulwarks of the Christian faith since the martyrs of the Cymry—martyrs like Tydfil—were put to death by the heathen English. These names form a witness to the reality, the power, and the truth of your grand history."[33]

From then onwards there was no more militant Welsh Nationalist than the Abbot of Llanthony.[34] On March 1, 1890, he re-dedicated his Abbey to Dewi Sant and cast out St Dunstan, having no further use for this Anglo-Saxon Archbishop of Canterbury.

Soon after this proof of loyalty to the Church of the Cymry, the *Pall Mall Gazette* and other newspapers reported the death of Fr Ignatius—one even reproducing a photograph of "the late Abbot". We are told that "the Monk's followers were heart-broken, and many of his friends sent beautiful floral offerings for his funeral . . . This untoward occurrence caused the Father no end of annoyance and expense, besides placing him in the unique position of reading, and commenting on, his own *oraison funèbre*—a two-sided privilege not granted to many. Fourteen pounds sterling were disbursed at the Abbey in stamps and telegrams alone, for the influx of correspondence provoked by this misleading rumour was in itself a source of severe labour and expense.[35] . . . All over England the tidings produced a vibration."

Next came the news that the ghost of the Abbot had appeared at a spiritist séance. He commented: "This proves more than ever that these materialisations are diabolical. Of course it was a demon that took my shape and acted a lie, but he was a very *stupid* demon too, or he would have known better what was going on in the world."[36]

Once again Ignatius of Jesus, O.S.B. had a *crise de nerves*, or what he used to call "brain fever". "Anxiety and exhaustion had made terrible havoc within and his medical adviser was obliged to tell him that unless he would consent to go right away for a definite period, a break-down for good and all was inevitable", for he "was in a very critical state of health".[37] The Abbot had no scruples about following this advice, because ever since he became a Benedictine twenty-seven years before he had taken for granted that the warning in the sixty-sixth chapter of the Holy Rule did not apply to himself—"It is not at all good for the souls of monks to go out abroad".[38] No longer could he hope that the ozone of Margate or Lowestoft, a holiday in the Scottish Highlands, or a pilgrimage to Jerusalem would effect a cure. Neither was it likely that "the magnificence of

Nature in scene and sound all about—mountains, rocks, valleys, woods, ravines, streams and flowers—GOD everywhere", as provided by his "beautiful cloister-home", would be sufficient sedative.[39] He decided to obey his doctor by undertaking a sea voyage of 7,340 miles, so that he could "benefit by the repose and breezes". An S.O.S. to his friends produced the sum of £437. "By this timely gift, the Reverend Father was able to start away with a comparatively easy mind." His entourage consisted of the faithful Sister Annie, Fr Michael, Br David, and Br Henry Fitzhardinge-Berkeley, a member of the Third Order.[40]

Sailing from Liverpool, they landed at New York on the feast of St Aloysius Gonzaga, S.J., June 21. A wealthy lady from Boston, who was another first-class passenger, offered the Benedictines a mansion by the sea-side, where they could lead the monastic life for the rest of the summer at her expense, but by this time Ignatius had given up all ideas of repose. He now visualised North America as "a magnificent field of labour" into which he would "carry the Gospel".

Br David, in his status of Public Relations Officer, got busy, and boosted the Anglican Abbot as "The Evangelist Monk of the British Church—the oldest in the world after Antioch and Jerusalem", or "The Druid of the Welsh Church". Then started a hectic soul-saving Mission, covering a large portion of the United States, as well as eastern Canada. In some towns "Services for the Upper Classes" were held, at which sittings could be hired "for the benefit of the Llanthony Abbey Church Endowment".[41] At first the Catholic party in the Protestant Episcopal Church opened their arms wide to the free-lance Benedictine from Wales, but their enthusiasm cooled down after he had denounced more than one clergyman for spreading heresy. It was difficult for the general public to place Fr Ignatius of Jesus O.S.B. The *Boston Times* summed him up as "a singular mixture of the medieval monk, the Methodist evangelist, the Modern Churchman, and the Catholic devotee".[42]

The oddly assorted quintette did not re-embark for Britain until July 11, 1891, the Solemnity of Our Holy Father St Benedict, having spent nearly thirteen months in North America. Soul-saving continued during the stormy homeward voyage, and many conversions were made. The Abbot was in no hurry to return to his monastery, and felt that it was worth while to make a leisurely tour of Ireland and North Wales after landing at Queenstown, now known as Cobh.

When at long last he reached Llanthony about the middle of August there were only two monks left to welcome him—Fr Cattwg of the Holy Trinity and Br William. The rest had cleared off, unable to endure the spiritual starvation, for no arrangements had been made for a chaplain during the Abbot's absence.[43]

The brethren appealed to Dr Jones, Bishop of St Davids, to send a clergyman to celebrate the Holy Communion, but he ignored the request. Neither were any of the neighbouring incumbents prepared to administer the sacraments at the Abbey, because it was banned by the Cymric hierarchy.[44]

The result was that the trio of nuns, in sheer desperation, walked out of their "Living Tomb", and "went over to Rome".[45]

Such was the end of the twin-community of Perpetual Adoration of the Blessed Sacrament established in 1881. All that Ignatius of Jesus could say was: "I cannot blame my poor people for what they have done. Just think of it! Isolated as they are they were denied the comforts of religion by the bigotry and narrow-mindedness of the ministers of the Established Church. . . . I can see how they were literally driven into the Church of Rome. They could scarcely do otherwise."[46]

NOTES

[1] *The Benedictines of Talacre* (2nd. ed. 1930), p. 2.

[2] His offence was wearing vestments and burning incense at St John's, Miles Platting, Manchester.

[3] ibid. The community must have led a very uneventful life, for this is the only incident concerning the ten years spent at Feltham in the brief history published by the Roman Catholic Benedictine nuns of Talacre Abbey, North Wales, who are the successors of Mother Hilda's community.

[4] *The Benedictine Calendar for 1881.* This publication was issued "for the use of the Monks and Nuns of the Order of St Benedict revived in the Church of England by our Right Rev. Father and Founder of our Congregation † Ignatius, O.S.B., serving God at Llanthony Abbey, Abergavenny; and Slapton Priory, Knightsbridge (sic), (Devon)—*cum permissu Superioris et Fundatoris Congregationis Nostrae*".

[5] Among modern ones were "The Miraculous Medal" in Paris (1830), "Notre Dame de la Salette" (1846), "Notre Dame de Lourdes" (1858), and "Notre Dame de Pontmain" (1871).

[6] The quotations are taken from the official account of these paranormal events printed in *The Benedictine Calendar* for 1881. It was signed by "the witnesses of this Mighty and Glorious Vision". So far as is known, nobody in Britain had ever claimed to have had a vision of Our Lady similar to those at Llanthony since she appeared to Richeldis de Favranches in 1061, bidding her to build a replica of the Holy House of Nazareth at Walsingham, Norfolk.

[7] The "Miraculous Monstrance", said to have been presented to Fr Ignatius by Dr Pusey, is now preserved by the Roman Catholic Benedictine monks at Pluscarden Priory, Elgin, Moray. It does not appear to have performed any more miracles since 1880.

[8] At the time of the Llanthony apparitions no less than twenty periodicals devoted to Spiritualism were on sale in England. Among the upper classes especially it was fast becoming the fashionable religion, although some of its devotees remained devout Anglicans.

[9] p. 552.

[10] p. 556. The Abbot and the Tertiary were almost inseparable from now onwards. They travelled around England together like Dr Pusey and Abbess Lydia had done at an earlier period.

[11] For details of the nuns' choir, see p. 119.

[12] On Maundy Thursday, after the altars had been washed with wine and water, the Loving Cup was "celebrated according to the use of the Church of England". On Good Friday at 10.30 the Solemn Unveiling and Creeping to the Cross was followed by Mass of the Pre-sanctified in the Tabernacle. "The Three Hours Agony" (definitely not "Sarum" but Jesuit) lasted from 12 to 3, after which another hour was devoted to the Litany and the seven penitential psalms. The 4 p.m. Vespers ended with a Procession of the Blessed Sacrament and Cross to the Sepulchre. Compline was sung at 6.30. The monks appear to have spent nearly nine hours in church without a break. The rubric for Easter Day starts: "At midnight let the Most Holy Sacrament be triumphantly carried with the Cross to the High Altar; after which let all crosses and images be uncovered, and the bells be rung as usual for Mass".

[13] After Ignatius of Mary had been apprenticed to the merchant navy, he was succeeded by many more boy-oblates, none of whom remained very long in the monastery.

[14] The ethos of this macabre profession service is reminiscent of that of the Brothers of Death, a quasi-eremitical congregation founded at Rouen in 1620. It was suppressed by the Holy See after a brief existence of thirteen years. The Brothers lived in an atmosphere evocative of a mortuary or charnel-house.

[15] A hamlet with a chapel-of-ease in the parish of Llanigon, in the county of Brecknock, where there was a small Baptist meeting-house.

[16] Later on it became overgrown with trees and shrubs, including two weeping-willows. On a mound in the centre a large black wooden cross was erected, with the inscription in white: JESUS ONLY—PAX. There was also a cast-iron fountain, said to be "of chaste and elegant desgn". At some date a nun was buried in the garth. Much later was the tombstone with the inscription: "St Luke III, 22. In memory of the Rev. Father's very tame and affectionate little Dove, for many years flying to and fro about our monastery, as a living type to us all of the Holy Ghost. It was killed by an act of violence on Sunday, August 20, 1899, just before the Holy Communion. Its companion never cooed again, and died of a broken heart ten days after. The grief of the Rev. Father was very great. The loss is quite irreparable."

[17] When Fr Ignatius told Mr Buckeridge that the church of New Llanthony Abbey must be a replica of the ruined one of the Austin Canons down the valley, he cannot have realised how unsuited its plan would be for a double-community. He ought to have insisted on a church of the Gilbertine type; divided for its entire length by a partition wall, high enough to prevent the canons and nuns from seeing each other, but not so high that the nuns could not hear the celebration of Mass at the canons' altar.

The arrangements of the Llanthony choir suggest that Ignatius may have studied or heard of the rules drawn up by St Bridget of Sweden, when she founded her double Order of the Most Holy Saviour in 1346. They stipulated that the monks' choir was to be raised

129

above the level of the secular church. The nuns' choir must be in a gallery on one side, so that they could look down on the several altars at which Mass was celebrated, but invisible behind their grilles. The monks were also cut off from the lay congregation by screens.

[18] See p. 119.

[19] p. 517. Among the prelates who at one time or other did encourage Ignatius with his efforts to revive Benedictine monastic life were Dr Forbes, Bishop of Brechin (1847-75), Dr Chinnery-Haldane, Bishop of Argyll and the Isles (1883-1907). The only recognition he ever received from an English bishop was in 1877, when Dr Selwyn, Bishop of Lichfield, wrote: "I only wish that your monastery were in my diocese, for I could then help you. I perfectly appreciate the need in the Church of England for the resurrection of the Contemplative Life" (De Bertouch, op. cit. p. 516). Other English bishops, while anxious to make use of Ignatius as a mission preacher, maintained that they could not raise him to the priesthood unless he gave up his nondescript costume, which he flatly refused to do.

[20] Born in 1829, she was the eldest daughter of Mr Stokeham Huthwaite, who belonged to an old Nottinghamshire family, owning a large property near Worksop. She joined Fr Ignatius' community of enclosed Benedictine nuns at Feltham at the same time that Mother Hilda was made Prioress, and was appointed Sub-Prioress. (See p. 87.)

[21] See p. 117.

[22] op. cit., pp. 386-7.

[23] ibid, pp. 389-90. Ignatius pointed out in another oration ("The Apparitions at Llanthony") that his monastery had received exceptional proofs of God's blessing, stating: "The wonders of mercy that have resulted from the Visions prove that they were of God; and that God's favour in the supernatural, is being restored to the Church of England, *if only there be the faith to receive it*" (ibid, p. 227).

[24] He was born at Sheffield in 1874. His father, James F. Carlyle, was a civil engineer by profession; his mother, Anna Maria Chapman, belonged to a Devonshire family claiming descent from both Sir Francis Drake and the 9th Earl of Mar. In 1885 Mr Carlyle was appointed General Superintendent of the Buenos Aires and Rosario Railway.

[25] See p. 26.

[26] Founded in 1870 by Miss Emily Ayckbown.

[27] The former was born at Sunbury Park, near Feltham, in 1864. Educated at Westminster School and Keble College, Oxford, he went to Cuddesdon College to study for holy orders. He was ordained deacon by Dr Thorold, Bishop of Rochester in 1888, and priest the following year.

[28] As stated already he had been one of the first novices at Claydon in 1863, with the name of Br Anselm.

[29] He was the son of the Rev. Thomas P. Dale who in 1876, as rector of St Vedast's in the City of London, had been sentenced to confinement in Holloway Prison for indulging in alleged illegal ritual and ceremonial.

[30] In spite of much research, the location of the convent has not been discovered, a proof that the community must have led a very hidden life during the four years they occupied it.
Neither is it certain whether Canon George Akers, rector of the Roman Catholic Church of St James, had any contact with the nuns. He had known Fr Ignatius in his younger days. As related already, he had celebrated the Holy Eucharist in the lodgings at Kingussie, where the Monk and Mrs Cameron stayed in the early autumn of 1863. (See p. 53.) He "went over to Rome" in 1868, together with two more of Fr Lowder's curates at St Peter's, London Docks.

[31] Henry G. Alston, born in 1869, came to Llanthony in 1887, and left in 1894. His religious name was Cattwg (Cadoc) Fair of the Holy Trinity. After his reception into the Roman Catholic Church, he entered the novitiate at Downside Abbey, where he was professed in 1900, and ordained priest in 1906.

[32] The text of this oration was printed in *Cofnodion a Chyfansoddiadau Buddugol Eisteddfod Aberhonddu* 1889.

[33] There is a legend that in 1874 Mar Julius, Bishop of Iona, revived the true Church of the Cymry by consecrating the Rev. Richard W. Morgan, with the title and style of Mar Pelagius I, Hierarch of Caerleon-on-Usk, giving him jurisdiction over Great Britain, Ireland, and Western Europe, as the first Patriarch of a restored Ancient British Church. Mar Pelagius had already written a book entitled *St Paul in Britain*, which he dedicated to Dr Thirwall, Bishop of St Davids.

[34] Two months after being raised to the rank of a Druid, he astonished most of those present at the Cardiff Church Congress by stating that the Catholic Faith and morals of the Ancient British Church, founded by St Paul, had been saved by the Calvinistic Methodists in later centuries.

[35] p. 559.

[36] p. 560. The perpetrator of this canard was never discovered.

[37] ibid.

[38] It is doubtful if between 1863 and 1890 he had ever spent more than a month—if that—in any of his monasteries without answering a call to take the road again.

[39] Cf. *Twenty-two Teachings of Ignatius the Monk*, p. 116.

[40] Br David (originally William Pritchard) became a boy-oblate at the age of ten. It was not long before he succeeded "Baby" as the Abbot's companion by day and by night.

Brought up in much the same way as his predecessor, he was petted and pent up, kept out of the company of women so far as possible. Known as "Boy David", he accompanied Ignatius on many of his Missions. Eventually he was legally adopted with the name of W. Leycester Lyne. Having endured monastic life for twelve years, he got married, and was presented by his foster-father with the farm of Ty Gwyn at a nominal rent. He acted as Mission Secretary and Public Relations Officer.

[41] Br David even managed to get the Abbot photographed in his full war-paint with "Black Bear" and "Hoop Hawk" at a Wild West Show at Philadelphia.

[42] In 1893 Fr. Michael got published a detailed account of this thirteen months' missionary tour, entitled *Father Ignatius in America*.

[43] Exactly the same thing had happened on several occasions in the past when breakdowns in health had forced Ignatius to take a long holiday. He seems to have felt that it would do his monks no harm to be deprived of Holy Communion in his absence, or taken for granted that they would be able to find a friendly clergyman to minister to them.

[44] Had Mar Pelagius I, Hierarch of Caerleon-on-Usk, Patriarch of the revived Ancient British Church, been alive it is probable that he would have come to the rescue of these spiritually starved monks and nuns of the Church of the Cymry, but he ended his erratic career at Pevensey, Sussex, on the Octave of the Assumption, August 22, 1889.

[45] The Prioress and Novice Mistress entered the Benedictine community at St Mary's Priory, Princethorpe, near Rugby, founded at Montargis in France in 1630. The third of the trio found a home with the Sisters of Our Lady of Charity and Refuge at Bartestree, Hereford, devoting themselves to the protection and reformation of prostitutes.

[46] During his long absence in North America, Dewi-Honddu had been converted to the belief that the British People are ultimately descended from the ten Israelite tribes which were taken captive into Assyria in 722-721 B.C., and thereafter disappeared from Hebrew history. This new "conversion" followed that of the belief that God made the world flat because there is no indication in Genesis that He created a round ball. It was due to a study of the works of a certain Professor Totton that Ignatius was granted the light of faith.

CHAPTER VIII

*Ben Carlyle clothed as a Benedictine Oblate with the name of
Br Aelred; Mother Hilda and her nuns moved to West Malling
Abbey; Abbot Ignatius revives his double-monastery at
Llanthony, and loses all his monks. (1891-1896)*

No similar débacle took place at the Twickenham Priory, where Mother Hilda
and her nuns never wavered in their loyalty to the Church of England. In
1890, however, while their Founder was roaming around North America, they
heard that Mr Camm had been received into the Church of Rome at Maredsous
Abbey in Belgium. Then came the news that he had entered the novitiate with
the religious name of Bede. Little did they guess that twenty-three years later
he would assist the community to follow in his footsteps.[1] Mr Worth remained an
Anglican until 1895, when he was received into the Roman Church. He, too, was
to resume close associations with the nuns as a Papist layman, for in 1907 they
sought his advice on liturgical matters, although they were still in communion
with Canterbury.[2]

Between 1889 and 1891 a long series of debates took place in Convocation on
brotherhoods and sisterhoods, which were "a turning point in the development of
the official attitude of the Church of England to religious communities". Convocation gradually came to terms "with the large and expanding institutions, whose
formation it had in no way encouraged". It took roughly thirty years to obtain
the first official recognition of sisterhoods by the Anglican episcopate, together
with the sanction of vows. So the Twickenham Benedictines could now feel that
they had at least the tacit approval of Dr Temple, Bishop of London. During the
final debate (February 1891) he declared: "I do not feel the slightest objection to
vows being taken by those who propose to work in this way, provided that they
are taken on the clear understanding that they are terminable at the discretion of
the Bishop on cause shown. . . . In the sisterhoods which have for some time
been established, it is felt to be a great grievance that permanent self-surrender
has not yet been permitted by the Bishops."[3]

Considerable attention had been drawn to Anglican conventual establishments
by the publication in 1891 of *Nunnery Life in the Church of England*, or *Seventeen
Years with Father Ignatius*. The author, Sister Mary Agnes, who had been the
Reverend Father's "pet" at Feltham in the eighteen-seventies, when she was a
novice, eventually became so puffed up with pride that he had to use the
amputating knife on her, finding that frequent correction—even strokes with the
rod—were to no purpose. "In retaliation for this dismissal, she penned a volume
purporting to be her experiences during the Novitiate so unhappily prolonged."
Fr Ignatius never descended to an elaborate defence of the outrageous charges,
implied rather than expressed in this cruel publication. "Those who are really my
spiritual children", he argued, "will know what to believe; and as for the rest,
what can it matter?"[4]

Once again Dewi-Honddu's health was in "an alarmingly shattered condition",
and "the year 1892 was one of sickness and shadows, for the pressure of business

132

was hopelessly prohibitive of any possibility of rest. Early in the year, a report of his secession to Rome gained currency, and this alone produced a hurricane of protest and congratulations, which had to be answered by innumerable and weary letters. . . . He became so ill that Masses were offered for his recovery, and all prospective Missions cancelled until further notice."[5]

In the meantime, Ben Carlyle had not forgotten his call to the Benedictine Order in the Church of England.[6] He returned from the Argentine in 1888, completed his education at Blundell's School, Tiverton, and Newton Abbot College, and early in 1892, entered St Bartholomew's Hospital, London, as a medical student. Lodging at Ealing, he soon became a militant Anglo-Catholic, sampling in turn most of the then Strongholds of the Full Faith in London, revelling in their sumptuous ceremonial.

He was already fairly familiar with the externals of Roman Catholic religious life. The first Mass he attended was at St Gregory's, Cheltenham (served by monks of the English Benedictine Congregation), on August 30, 1889.

The previous year he had cycled from Brighton to visit St Hugh's Charterhouse, Parkminster. The bearded Brother Porter, who showed him round this vast monastery, gave him a small crucifix, and he always maintained later on that the Carthusians were his first love among monks. When staying with relations in Devonshire he added to his superficial knowledge of Roman Catholic communities. At Teignmouth there was the choice of the chapels of Benedictine nuns and Redemptorist fathers. Not far off were the Austin Canonesses at Abbotskerswell, who carried on Perpetual Adoration of the Blessed Sacrament. Even more exciting were the strictly enclosed grey-habited Bridgettine nuns at Chudleigh, who could claim that they had been founded by King Henry V at Syon, Middlesex, in 1415. As a would-be Benedictine, young Carlyle, felt it worth while to pick up as many tips as possible at Buckfast Abbey, re-founded in 1882 by a group of exiled monks from Pierre-qui-Vire in France, belonging to the Cassinese Congregation of the Primitive Observance.[7] It was easy for him to go over from Newton Abbey, attend Mass or Vespers, and keep his eyes open on how monks behaved. Their ritual and ceremonial could be adopted when he had founded his first Anglican monastery.

Shortly after his nineteenth birthday, February 7, 1893, the feast of St Romuald, O.S.B., Carlyle was taken to Twickenham by Fr Taylor, curate of St Saviour's, Ealing, so that he could be introduced to the only Benedictine Prioress in the Church of England. It gave him a real thrill to talk to a nun behind a grille for the first time in his life. He was even more thrilled by the room used as the chapel, for its choir was all "grilled in", with a passage at the sides for seculars. What's more, the nuns wore scarlet veils at Mass and Benediction—a custom derived from Fr Ignatius, so he was told. He also heard that they recited the Benedictine office in English from MS copies made by hand. Then the would-be Benedictine medical-student met the chaplain Fr Arthur Dale, whose father was the much persecuted high churchman, Mr Pelham Dale, who had been imprisoned for using vestments and indulging in Romish ritual and ceremonial said to be contrary for the law of the Church of England.

Fr Dale explained that he was forming in connection with the nuns' community a group of Benedictine Oblates. They consisted of young Catholic-minded laymen, living in the world, but hoping later on to become real monks. At the moment there were six of them. Carlyle asked if he could join this fraternity, and the chaplain replied that he would be delighted to clothe him with the black habit and scapular. There was no doubt of the religious name he would take. Having read Fr Dalgairns' *Life of St Aelred of Rievaulx*, published in 1844, and discovered that the twelfth-century Cistercians "do not seem to have been so jealous of particular friendships in their communities as were the other orders", and that "the monastic system was an expression of the love of the domestic circle upon a large community", Ben resolved to adopt St Aelred as his patron. The quaint "olde-worlde" frontispiece of this little book—an engraving by A. W. Pugin—depicted the twelfth century abbot vested in a Gothic Revival chasuble, apparelled alb and amice, standing in a crocketted niche. Dalgairns had revealed a monastic world in which natural and spiritual relations could be fused, i.e. what the future Anglican Benedictine monk knew would suit his particular temperament.

The initiation into the Oblates of St Benedict took place in the Baroque oratory of St Austin's Priory, in the New Kent Road, Walworth, not far from the Elephant and Castle. "How well I remember that chapel", Carlyle wrote fifty years later. "Black and white marble tiling in the sanctuary; classic rood screen and altar." Provost Nugee had died in October 1892, and most of his "canons irregular" and their associates had departed by this time.[8] Shortly after this function the Oblates got hold of some of the chapel furnishings.

The Oblates were "mothered" by the nuns at Twickenham, and their habits were made by them. They met once a month, either at the convent or at St Austin's Priory, for what were called "Chapters" presided over by Fr Dale. Most of the young men seem to have been fairly typical specimens of the Anglo-Catholic underworld of the eighteen-nineties, and were nicknamed "spikes".[9]

On April 26 the revival of Benedictine monasticism in the Church of England was publicized by the appearance of the Abbot of Llanthony in the pulpit of St Edmund's, Lombard Street, following an interval of twenty-three years. Shortly after this he excommunicated Br James of his Third Order, otherwise Mr Marchant, a lecturer for the Christian Evidence Society. The deposed Tertiary then proclaimed publicly that he had severed his connections with Llanthony "on account of the scandalous life led by its monks", hinting that the Abbot was hardly ever sober. "It was high time", he maintained, "that the Government should take steps to investigate this sink of iniquity, beginning with the excavation of the enclosed Garth, and the unearthing of the bodies buried there". These scurrilous revelations, following those in Miss Povey's *Seventeen Years in an English Nunnery,* caused Fr Ignatius much distress. Finally "for the honour of monasticism he was forced to draw on the weapon of defence". Br James "had forgotten the existence of certain letters written by his own hand, at a date *later* than that of his last stay at Llanthony—letters that brimmed over with expressions of edification and gratitude, and were little else than rigmaroles of ecstatic devotion to 'the dear holy place' ".[10] The Abbot handed over this correspondence to the press, with the result that no steps were taken to send Government inspectors to the Abbey, or to dig up rotting corpses.

It was also in April 1893 that Mother Hilda and her nuns came out of enclosure after four years; travelling by train from Twickenham to West Malling, five miles west of Maidstone. Miss Charlotte Boyd, who had bought the land on which stood the partly ruined buildings of a Benedictine nunnery, first allowed them to be used as an orphanage, but then decided to install the nuns. The property had already been vested in the English Abbey Restoration Trust.[11] The conditions of tenancy were limited to stipulations of there being at least two subjects in whatever Anglican community occupied it, and of Church of England services being held in the chapel.

Malling Abbey had been founded about 1090 by Gundulf, Bishop of Rochester, formerly a monk of Bec in Normandy. Having placed his cathedral under monks, he established a nunnery, and appointed the first abbess, named Avicia. He wished there should be a strong spiritual bond between Rochester and Malling.[12] The monks were bidden to pray for the souls of deceased nuns. Gundulf also required a promise of obedience from the abbess to himself and his successors in the See. The rights and privileges of the Abbey were secured and confirmed by successive kings, archbishops of Canterbury and bishops of Rochester. The last abbess, Dame Margaret Vernon, surrendered the property to Henry VIII in 1536. Subsequently it passed through many hands until Miss Boyd bought it from the Akers-Douglas family.

The Abbey stands on the eastern outskirts of the little town. Admission to the gardens is by a Gatehouse, with a late Decorated Gothic chapel. Facing the Gatehouse is the ruined western tower of the Church, erected in Norman times. The Church was demolished at some period after the Reformation, leaving only the almost square south transept, lofty in proportion to its area. This was turned into a chapel for Mother Hilda's nuns. Parclose grilles surrounded the choir on three sides and defined the small space left for seculars. The high altar stood against the east wall beneath two windows. A second altar was placed in a recess in the south wall. The main block of conventual buildings then consisted of an eighteenth-century house, incorporating much old stonework. It faces the former south wall of the nave. On the other side lie the convent gardens, with the "Nuns' Walk", beyond which is a large medieval tithe-barn, also traces of fish-ponds.

Such was Malling Abbey in 1893, indeed "a haunt of ancient peace—Benedictine *Pax*". After living for a quarter of a century in make-shift quarters at Feltham and Twickenham, it was a wonderful experience for the nuns to find themselves in such a romantic home, saturated with memories of the far-off days when England was a Catholic nation. In keeping with the Ignatian tradition, a grille was erected in the parlour through which necessary conversation with seculars could be carried on.

Four months after Ben Carlyle's clothing ceremony, he decided to form his own group of Oblates. Having bought a vellum-bound manuscript book, he wrote inside the cover:

"PAX. *Omnia per obedientia*
The Constitutions of the Oblate Brothers of the Holy Order
of St Benedict. Founded in June 1893."

This piece of monastic legislation is so detailed that the conclusion formed is that the compiler had already managed to study the Constitutions of the Cassinese Congregation of the Primitive Observance when visiting Buckfast Abbey. The *horarium* drawn up by him is practically the same as that of the Devonshire community at that date. The combination of the active and contemplative lives, proposed by "Br Aelred", is virtually the same as that of abbé Jean-Baptiste Muard (1809-1854). On April 25, 1845, having already founded the Congregation of St Edmund to preach missions throughout the dioceses of France, he had a vision of a monastic order made up of three distinct classes of persons; the first devoted to prayer and contemplation; the second to study and preaching; and the third as lay-monks, to manual labour. Their life would be that of victims, "a continual holocaust of self, devoted to penance for their own sins as well as for the sins of the world, drawing men by their example rather than by their speech, to a life of mortification and of virtue". They would dwell "in some poor and solitary spot", keeping "an almost absolute silence", going out of their monasteries "only when it was required for the good of souls, living in the midst of this world as if they were in the desert". The members would observe the Rule of St Benedict, with all the austerities of the Trappists.[13] The monastery at Pierre-qui-Vire, in the Diocese of Sens, was founded in 1850, and Père Muard called his brethren the Congregation of Benedictine Monks-Preachers. Nine years later Pius IX decided to affiliate it with the Subiaco Congregation of the Cassinese Congregation.

The first part of Br Aelred's 1893 Constitutions of the Oblate Brothers contains rules and regulations, which would enable them "to discover and test individual vocations for the monastic state". He explained: "There is in the English Church today, as all must agree, a sad want of general discipline and individual austerity of life. Among all the manifold guilds and parochial societies there are very few, if any, which set before their members, as their primary objects, the mortification of self, the giving up of everything that is of the world, the shortness of life, and the endless happiness or woe of eternity."[14]

Benjamin Fearnley Carlyle's method of becoming a Benedictine was curiously different from that of Joseph Leycester Lyne thirty years previously. His visions of the near and distant future were far more realistic. He wrote:

"Of course these Oblates from the very beginning have only been regarded as a transitory state of things and in no wise permanent, but simply as stepping stones to the formation of regular communities, to gain experience in Rule and Order, and to find and prepare men fitted and called by God, to give up all things and follow Christ.

"Such is the very short sketch of our plan as has existed up to the present time, and as we hope to carry it out in the future. We are gradually doing this by working backwards, i.e. preparing men for the lowest step, giving them a severe trial, and thus leading them on to the full religious life. After living in the world, under a mild rule, some of us will go on into the novitiate, giving up everything, and taking nearly all the obligations of Religion. This is to continue for a year or so, and then those of us who are about to become contemplative monks will go into the country, and those who have found active vocations will remain in London, and thus the whole system will with God's blessing begin to work."

The nineteen year-old medical student pictured "a house in the country, not far from London, having land around it sufficient to provide agricultural work for the community . . . in the house, men dedicated to God in Holy Religion under the Rule of St Benedict". Then he set forth a most detailed horarium, with the convent bell ringing at 5.20 to call the Brothers for half-an-hour's meditation before Prime at 6. Compline would be sung at 7.40 p.m., after which the community would retire to rest: "the novices to the novitiate, and the professed monks to their cells which are really divisions of one room . . . At ten minutes to two the community rise to chant the night office . . . which lasts till 3.30, then those who like, and are allowed by the superior, stay in the church for meditation and prayer, the others retiring again to their beds till 5.20 when the bell rings again summoning them to the work of God."

Few details were forgotten in these Constitutions. For instance, it would be possible for a monk to pass from the active to the contemplative life, as with the Camaldolese Benedictines. The so-called "secular monks" would be a species of Third Order Regular, living in the world, although taking the vows of religion.

A hired room over a fish-shop at Ealing became the first "monastery" of Carlyle's threefold Order of St Benedict. Here the Oblates met to recite Vespers and Compline, having donned their black tunics and scapulars after their day's work in the world. Before long they found the money to rent a whole house, and this quasi-monastic life in Oxford Road lasted for two years, during which time, besides testing their vocations, they engaged in parish work. A second group of the Oblates was formed at Chatham. The oratory was furnished with "relics" from St Austin's Priory, Walworth—including one or two statuettes. On Sunday afternoons Benedictine Vespers was chanted. Occasionally one of the curates from St Cuthbert's, Philbeach Gardens, came over to say Mass.[15]

The whole atmosphere of the Ealing "monastery" in 1893 must have been quite unlike that of Claydon rectory in 1863, mainly because there was so little in common between Carlyle and Lyne. The former is thus described by the late Rev. George Chambers at the time of their first meeting in 1892: "He was just over medium height, very quick and athletic in movement, wearing white flannels, with a black and white-striped blazer. His hair was slightly curly, his features handsome, and his eyes as penetrating as his speech, which poured forth in banter keeping us all in continual laughter. To us boys Carlyle seemed utterly different from any other young men of our acquaintance. Although at that time he was fully seven years my senior—he would have been eighteen and I eleven —nevertheless we had much in common. I was a choir-boy and an altar-server. Already in the life of Ben Carlyle there were distinct indications of a leaning and yearning in the direction towards which he ultimately found his vocation; a calling in which I too would have a share later on."[16]

The future Dom George also recalled: "How impressed I was when I first heard Vespers sung in the little chapel. Rightly or wrongly, these developments did not receive the entire approval of the local clergy, so I was not allowed free access to everything represented by this new venture. But surreptitiously or otherwise, I managed to obtain rather literally a 'look in' on certain occasions."[17]

During the intermittent run at the Lyceum Theatre in 1893 of Lord Tennyson's blank-verse tragedy *Becket,* with Sir Henry Irving playing the part of the martyred archbishop, Br Aelred felt it worth while to attend the show three times. It gave him a thrill to watch and hear Miss Ellen Terry, in the part of Rosamund, invoking the Father of Western Monasticism—"O blessed saint, O glorious Benedict". During the last act monks chanted bits of Vespers back-stage. The final curtain went down amid flashes of lightning and the rumble of thunder, after Sir Henry had cried out:

"I do commend my cause to God and the Virgin,
St Denis of France and St Alphege of England,
And all the tutelar Saints of Canterbury"

This theatrical re-creation of medieval Catholicism gave young Carlyle further inspiration to forge ahead with reviving the Benedictine Order in *Ecclesia Anglicana.* Abbess Hilda also encouraged him, and he recalled: "She was a royal little figure with a great heart. . . . She did all she could for me personally with her wise advice and motherly help. I owe to her more than to any other woman, both the inspiration to work out those plans for a community of monks, and for perseverance in overcoming many obstacles . . ."[18]

From April 1893 to June 1895 Br Aelred and his Oblates often travelled on the London, Chatham and Dover Railway from either Holborn Viaduct or Victoria to West Malling. Nowhere else in Britain could they be sure of finding such full "Catholic Privileges" on the greater festivals. They had the illusion of being transported to the far-off Middle Ages, as pictured in the *Lives of the English Saints,* or in Dr. Neale's poem, starting

"Oh, the good old times of England, ere, in her evil day,
From their Holy Faith and their ancient rites her people fell away".

Strolling around the gardens in their black Benedictine tunics, hooded scapulars and sandals, or kneeling before the tabernacle in the tiny secular chapel, getting a peep of Abbess Hilda and her nuns behind the grilles, or when on some great

L

festival the "royal little figure", wielded her crozier at Solemn Vespers or at the *Missa Cantata*, the Oblates had every reason to believe that Dr Neale was a true prophet when he wrote:

"Again shall long processions sweep through Lincoln's minster pile;
Again shall banner, cross and cope gleam thro' the incensed aisle;
And the faithful dead shall claim their part in the Church's thoughtful prayer,
And the daily sacrifice to God be duly offered there . . .".[19]

Indeed there were more than enough rose-coloured omens in the early eighteen-nineties for Br Aelred and his Oblates to form the opinion that "The Good Old Times of England" would return before very long. In 1893 a young artist named Aubrey Beardsley, hitherto unknown, became famous by his drawings illustrating *La Morte d'Arthur*. Moreover, Dr Benson, the ninety-fourth successor of St Augustine as Archbishop of Canterbury, "a man of fervent piety, was also an aesthete, an artist, an antiquary, and a ritualist, delighting in Christian art and tradition, and loving to use ancient forms of devotion and hymns from Breviary and Missal"[20]

Maurice Maeterlinck had already conjured up visions of a dim twilight medieval world, even more glamorous than those of Dr Neale, in his plays *Pelléas et Mélisande* and *La Mort de Tintegelles*. Jules Massenet's opera *Thais* helped to arouse interest in the wealthy and beautiful courtesan of Alexandria, converted by St Paphnutius, and walled up for three years in a cell before she was allowed to become a nun. Rumours were afloat that Lord Halifax and the abbé Portal, in the hope of promoting reunion of the Church of England and the Holy See, were about to initiate conversations at Rome.

Miss Charlotte Boyd, who had arranged for Mother Hilda and her community to take over Malling Abbey, lacked the patience to wait for the reunion of Rome and Canterbury. She had visited Maredsous abbey and met Dom Bede Camm, now a monk in simple vows, and founded there a Mass to be said daily for the Conversion of England, after being told that it would be irregular for the intention to be the reunion of the Churches of England and Rome. Partly as the result of seeing the well organised life in this Belgian abbey, and attending its liturgical functions, she decided that there was no alternative but to enter into immediate communion with that Church to which the pre-Reformation nuns of Malling had been united. Paranormal experiences also had influence. It is recorded that on two successive nights when she was living in the Gatehouse, she believed that some of the old nuns had awakened her from sleep, urging that she must take some important step, the nature of which was not revealed; Abbess Hilda admitted that she had also met "spirit nuns" in the chapel and cloister, and used to stand aside and let them pass.[21]

Meanwhile the Abbot of Llanthony continued to spend more time outside his monastery than within it, so busy was he giving Missions, attending Church Congresses and denouncing heretics and infidels, the chief of whom at the moment was Dr Gore, Founder of the Community of the Resurrection, and editor of *Lux Mundi*, a series of studies on the religion of the Incarnation, first published in 1889. He was equally active in attacking the proposed Bill for disestablishing the Church of the Cymry as an "act of national robbery".

On September 14, 1893, a second attempt was made to establish a double-monastery, when Miss Isabella Kennedy Stewart, after a two months' postulancy, was clothed as a novice. Fr Ignatius recorded: "She has been a Novice two years in the secular Sisterhood of St Margaret of Scotland in Aberdeen, a branch of the East Grinstead Sisters". Two widows, Sisters Annie and Monica (members of the Third Order), acted as her "matrons". She was professed in 1895, but left soon afterwards owing to poor health, but also because of "self-will and impatience". Her Abbot wrote: "She tried to worry me into giving her the Black Veil". The behaviour of another nun was far worse, because "she seemed utterly unable to understand what Monastic Obedience was, after three years of patient teaching". Ignatius was more fortunate with Jessie Dow, who entered her "Living Tomb" as a novice in 1898, with the name of Sister Tudfil of the Holy Name of Jesus. She persevered for nine years.[22]

The Associate Brothers of the Benedictine Scapular were formed for men and boys who found that the Third Order did not provide all they wanted in the way of relations with the monks and nuns. It was a bitter disappointment to the Abbot when after the death of Mrs Marie Yolande Lyne-Stephens (a cousin by marriage), he found that he was not mentioned in her will, although she had promised that he should never want.[23] She left £80,000 to a stranger, and not a penny to Ignatius of Jesus O.S.B. His biographer remarked: "By this final disposition, Llanthony was deprived of a hope of many years' standing, and its Abbot of the anticipation of a twilight of rest, in the uninterrupted seclusion of his Monastery home".[24]

Among the many boys who were encouraged to join the community was a chorister named Bertie Cannell, the son of a Baptist mother and a Roman Catholic father. At the age of fourteen, his mother having died, he was handed over to the care of Fr Ignatius. The boy first met the Benedictine when the latter was attacking the sins of society during a Mission at the Kensington Town Hall. He recorded long after: "Fr Ignatius rushed in something like a hurricane. His monastic habit impressed me very much. He sat in an armchair, and got me to kneel by his side, holding me by the hand. . . . He spoke very softly and close to my face—I did but notice—he must have had some kippers for his breakfast! He gave me a very strict cross-examination about entering the Church. What were my ideas, etc.? He said: 'That is all very well, but you must be "converted" first'."[25]

Bertie arrived at Llanthony, and soon succeeded "Baby" and later "Boy David" as the Abbot's personal attendant. He remained a postulant for over a year, when he was clothed as a novice with the name of Br Gildas. The news came that his father had died, but Ignatius refused to allow him to attend the funeral, saying that it would involve breaking his vows. This roused a bitter spirit of resentment, which burst into flame in the autumn of 1894.

One morning when the handful of monks were gathered for Chapter after Prime, the Abbot bade them confess breaches of the Forty-nine Observances. To his amazement, Br Gildas replied that it would be easier if he asked what rules *had* been kept; pointing out that the Abbot himself did not observe any of them except those he fancied, so how could he expect his monks to do so? Such insubordination was too much for Ignatius of Jesus. The day passed in an atmosphere of an impending thunder storm, and when the brethren assembled for Compline, the Abbot ordered them to kneel on the steps of the high altar, and remove their scapulars, to symbolize penitence for defying his God-given authority. They did kneel, but showed no signs of starting to strip. Roused to fury, Ignatius darted out of his stall, with eyes flashing, seized hold of each monk, and hauled off his scapular. Then he conducted them to the guests' quarters and said: "Now, gentlemen, you can make your arrangements to leave as soon as possible". Early the following morning the whole male section of the twin-community made its way down the Vale of Ewyas, leaving behind the Abbot and three nuns. Before this mass-exodus, Ignatius offered to forgive Br Gildas, because he was sure that he

139

had been perverted by the others, also because of a promise made to his deceased father that he would take care of him for the rest of his life. But like his sixth-century Cymric patron, Cannell was "Wise", and cleared off while the going was good.[26]

Shortly after this repetition of the 1865 "Monks' Rebellion on Elm Hill" and "The Monastery in an Uproar", Theodore Willoughby, one of Br Aelred's Oblates, suggested that the latter should join forces with him on the Isle of Dogs. He had rented a little house on this peninsula in the Lower Thames. At that date it was mostly covered with mud-flats, docks, and mean streets—a world apart from the rest of East London. Here was an opportunity to combine the active and contemplative forms of Benedictine life. Br Aelred arranged with Abbess Hilda for the Oblates to lodge in the Gate House at Malling for the Whitsun weekend of 1895, so that they could hold a Chapter.

Their Brother Superior pointed out that the acceptance of this offer would be a further step towards the completion of their ultimate ideal, i.e. the observance of the *whole* Rule of St Benedict in its primitive form, together with all the ancient customs and traditions of the Benedictine Order, of which he himself had acquired an adequate knowledge to make a foundation. Here was the Church of England, Catholic in Constitution, the Mother of the English people, indigenous to the soil on which had lived and died so many holy monks and nuns, with valid Orders and Sacraments, Jurisdiction, and all her medieval Cathedrals intact. There were plenty of active communities of men and women, but not a single monastery of the Benedictine Rule, though so many had formed her crown three hundred years ago. Nothing left but desolate and empty ruins. No home for weary souls and loving hearts. No men to be found for the work of prayer and no room for such.[27] To continue in his own words:

"But were there really no men? Was there no room? My picture told me there were both. I saw a revival of the Spiritual Life spreading through England, with here and there men waiting and longing for the opportunity of withdrawing themselves from the hurried life of the day to seek the peace and regulated discipline of the cloister. I thought that surely if the need were felt, it would be met; that authority would once more sanction the system which had so abundantly flourished, and had been so blessed in the past. The revival of external activity in the Church, the increased effectiveness of parochial work, the growing love and appreciation of the Sacraments, the care lavished on the fabrics themselves and upon the sanctuary, all showed that a corresponding revival of the Interior Life was needed, nay demanded, as a balance to the marked increase of exterior organisation. And that as the Catholic Church in all ages has possessed her Religious Communities, so now, after a long sleep, the Church in England, roused at last to the realisation of her Catholic heritage, would awake to the fact that she alone in Catholic Christendom possessed few Religious Houses for men, and none dedicated solely to the Life of Prayer."[28]

Br Aelred then set forth in further detail how his Anglican Order of St Benedict would be organised

"(1) A Community of Benedictine Monks living in the country; devoting themselves to the strictest Religious Life, as laid down in the Holy Rule; spending their time in prayer and intercession, study, and manual work; external work, such as teaching, preaching, ministering to the sick, etc., coming *to* them, rather than being sought *by* them, the Monks being seldom allowed away from the Monastery.

"(2) A house of the same Order, under the same Rule, but in a modified form in London (such as now offered on the Isle of Dogs), or any great city filled with

140

Active Religious whose work would be among the poor, the ungodly, the outcast, and any who need their help. The chief object of their lives being to save souls, to teach, preach and hold missions, care for the sick, and fulfil the thousand obligations of the perfect Missionary. They would give up their lives to the work, and would undertake no secular avocations.

"(3) Living in the same House, under the same Rule, the same Vows of Poverty, Chastity, and Obedience, would be men who, though of the world, do not belong to it—lawyers, doctors, business men, clerks, etc., each working in his daily profession, a zealous missionary, showing by intensity of life, with purity, his unswerving and manly faith in God; drawing men to Him, gaining their trust and respect, and raising the tone of the Society by which he is surrounded, and in which he moves, a shining example of a Christ-like Christian, a living witness to the truth of his belief."[29]

The twenty-one year-old medical-student Founder had arranged the day of his future Contemplative monks thus:—"5.20, Rise; 5.30, Prayer and Meditation; 6, Prime, Chapter of Faults; 7, Clean cells, and do share of housework; 8, Pittance (¾ pint of coffee, 2½ oz. bread); 8.10, Terce; 9-11.40, Work of various kinds; 11.40, Sext, and dinner; 12.30-1.45, Rest; 1.45, Nones; 2-5.30, Classes, work, etc.; 5.30, Vespers, and Mental Prayer; 6.40, Supper; 7.15, Conference and Compline; 8, Bed; 1.50-3.30, Night office."[30]
He explained that "in both Houses there would be absolute and real simplicity, there was to be entire renunciation of *all* for the sake of Christ: only the barest necessities of life would be allowed: food of the simplest, no carpets, curtains, or other comforts; a bare table, hard bed, restricted speech; a literal forsaking of house, brethren, sisters, father, mother, wife, children, and lands (S. Matt. 19, 29; S. Mark 10, 29; S. Luke 18, 29) for Love of Christ".
The long oration ended with the *fervorino:*

"God has called each one of you, Oblate Brothers, to decide now, whether you will once and for all take up your Cross, and follow Christ, embrace the life of the Active or Contemplative Religious, that you may each in your own sphere of work do the Divine Will of your Father; or whether you will throw off the Habit of St Benedict and return to the life of the world. . . . Brethren! be up and doing! Here is work to your hand. Be careful how you trifle with it. Do you think you can put aside the decision for a time, because you have not the courage to face it? No. Decide now! 'Now is the accepted time.' . . . Let your conscience decide, and fear not to abide by that decision; for so surely as you choose, God will require an account of your choice. May He guide you and direct, may He bless and strengthen you to decide aright and for His greater glory."[31]

Not one of the Oblates had the courage to follow their leader. Each threw off his Benedictine habit, and returned to London on Whit Monday evening. For some reason or other Br Aelred doubted whether his own vocation lay on the Isle of Dogs, at any rate for the moment. He spent the greater part of the next nine months with his mother in West Kensington.[32]
By this time monastic life had been resumed at Llanthony, thanks to the arrival of a few young men and boys. Had Carlyle felt the urge to join them he would have found a very different sort of Benedictine life to what he had planned so carefully. Fr Ignatius would have assured him affectionately that he had been

"Called from this world's allurements,
Called from its noise and strife
To live for 'JESUS only'
A consecrated life.

Called from the raging tempest,
Safe from the billow's crest,
Into the Cloister's Haven,
Into a life of rest."

Indeed, life at the Abbey of Our Ladye and St David, in comparison with that of Carlyle's "Community of Benedictine Monks living in the country, devoting themselves to the strictest Religious Life, as laid down by the Holy Rule", was a *dolce fa niente* existence, if the last stanza of this long Ignatian poem were true—

"Called from a life of labour
To where all labours cease;
Called from a weary warfare
To sweet unending peace."

Nothing could go wrong, eternal salvation was certain, so long as a monk kept on repeating the slogan:

" 'JESUS' my War cry! 'JESUS' my Calm!
'JESUS' my Weapon! 'JESUS' my Palm!
'JESUS' in Battle! 'JESUS' in Rest!
Let my heart pillow, here on Thy Breast."

Writing in 1938, Carlyle explained why he never considered joining the Llanthony community: "The first time I ever saw, and then did not speak to Fr Ignatius, was at the Portman Rooms in Baker Street, London, where I watched him 'converting' a crowded congregation, separating the sheep from the goats; and spell-binding people in the masterful way he had. I remember feeling: 'Whatever he may be, this is not the man or the life for me'. And yet we became great friends—within limits. I could and did always say things to him that no one else dared to. We had a sense of humour in common; and when he laughed at himself, he always ceased to be the Prophet, and became a very lovable old man. He never forgot he was a 'gentleman'. His real and fervent love of Christ was his great attraction to me; and I think I also regarded him as a very interesting psychological study."

Carlyle's unsettled state of mind can be detected in his going over from Newton Abbey to Buckfast Abbey for the Midnight Mass of Christmas 1895. He was so moved by the ceremonial, which he watched from the tribune of the temporary church (now the library) that he asked Prior Gariador to receive him into the Roman Church. This monk, however, said he would write to Fr Garnett, a priest of the London Oratory, to arrange for a proper course of instruction.

Forty-two years later Abbot Anscar Vonier recalled: "For several years Mr Carlyle, then a medical student, visited our monastery frequently, and was given every facility to study our life. I was then a junior, and much in touch with Fr Benedict Gariador, the Prior and Novice Master. I was told that this young man was going to enter our novitiate. One day I asked Fr Benedict why there was such a delay about his admittance, and why it was continually postponed. Then, for the

142

first time, Fr Benedict gave it to me as a secret that Mr Carlyle was not even a Catholic. Now I do not know when Fr Benedict made the discovery. But there is no doubt that at least for some time he was under the impression that Mr Carlyle was a Catholic applicant for our novitiate. When Fr Benedict was told, or found out the truth, he was very kind to the man, as was his wont. He seems to have overlooked readily the first period of partial deception. Fr Benedict is dead. Like all other men, he was not anxious to advertise the fact that for some time at least he had been taken in. It seems certain however that Mr Carlyle never received Holy Communion when he was here. My summing up is that Mr Carlyle told Fr Benedict, but only after a certain time. So you have enough light and shadow on the story."[33]

The medical student, however, took no immediate steps about "going over to Rome", having told at least one of the Buckfast postulants (the future Dom Ernest Graf) that he hoped to join him in the novitiate in the early autumn. Accompanied by a fellow-oblate, Br Maurus Sutton, he spent his twenty-second birthday, February 7, in the Guest House at Mount St Bernard Abbey. This was his first and only contact with Cistercians until after he became a Roman Catholic in 1913.[34]

Having returned to London from Leicestershire, Carlyle went to call on Fr Garnett for a first interview. To quote his own words at the age of sixty-four: "When I got to the great church I went in for a few moments to pray, and noticed a funeral in progress with stole and biretta on the coffin. Going to the Oratory House, I asked at the door for Fr Garnett, and was told that he had died three days previously, and that unknown to myself, I had just been assisting at his Requiem. This was a tremendous shock, for I was all screwed up for my first interview with a Catholic priest. With the intensity of youth, and having taken so long to come to this tremendous step, I now felt that all was lost, so I turned away in great depression of spirit, and went home to tell my Anglican confessor, Mr De Bourbel, what had happened. He said very properly, according to his lights, that it was his conviction this was a clear 'sign' from God that my true vocation lay in the Church of England, and not in the Church of Rome. I was to take this as the settlement of my doubts and questionings and go bravely on with the work I had been given to do. Everyone got busy with me after that, and I was soon floated on the stream that was to carry me on until 1913 when it flowed at last into the sea."[35]

In a chronicle kept by Prior Benedict Gariador there is the brief entry during the year 1896: "Mr Carlyle stayed here from February 14 to 17". What actually happened during that weekend is not clear. Forty years later one of the older monks recalled that Carlyle assured him that he would be entering the novitiate in September. This story differs from what Carlyle recorded at the same date; that he had explained to the monks he was quite sure that God meant him to remain an Anglican, and that he could visit them no more. "This hurt terribly, because I loved and admired Prior Benedict with all my youthful heart, and I knew that I risked much understanding. . . . It must have been a disappointment to him also, after all his kindness to me, that I felt unable to make my submission to the Catholic Church; but there was not one word of reproach, nor any urging to the contrary decision."[36]

After this last visit to Buckfast, things moved quickly. Early in April Carlyle left his mother's house near the Earls Court Exhibition and took up his abode in a small two-storied terrace-cottage in Glengall Road on the Isle of Dogs. His friend Theodore Willoughby had been living there for nearly two years. So it was that Br Aelred the Oblate started to carry out his boyish determination to revive the Benedictine Order in the Church of England, combining it with what was called "rescue work among boys".

[1] See p. 265.

[2] See p. 208.

[3] A. M. Allchin, *The Silent Rebellion* (1958), p. 168.

[4] p. 568. Later on Miss Povey (ex-Sister Mary Agnes) repented of having published this book, coerced by Protestant influence, and withdrew the remaining copies, giving her reasons in a letter to a newspaper.

[5] p. 569.

[6] See p. 124.

[7] A temporary church had been built, but the community were then living for the most part in the pseudo-Gothic mansion erected in 1806.

[8] For Nugee's Order of St Augustine, see p. 107.

[9] Other more or less secret fraternities flourishing at that date were the Order of the Holy Redeemer (with an inner circle known as the Brotherhood of the Holy Cross), which was nothing if not Anglican Papalist; the Guild of St Alban the Martyr (founded in 1851 on monastic lines); the Society of St Paul (founded in 1888, working in the parish of Holy Trinity, Shoreditch); Brotherhood of St Paul (working in Maida Vale after 1891); and the Brotherhood of St Augustine, Kilburn, associated with the Sisters of the Church, whose members devoted themselves especially to the welfare of railway navvies, organising canteens and recreation centres for them. But it was only the Order of the Holy Redeemer which could claim that it was sponsored by a prelate, i.e. Dr F. G. Lee, the Order of Corporate Reunion's Bishop of Dorchester, who wore a purple-edged cassock, purple zuchhetto, black chimere and episcopal rochet. When the brethren attended services in All Saints', Lambeth, on the greater festivals, they had the thrill of seeing him in a mitre—just like the Abbot of Llanthony!

[10] p. 576.

[11] See p. 233.

[12] Dr Randall Davidson, who was appointed Bishop of Rochester in 1891, showed no interest in the foundation of a Benedictine nunnery in his diocese, and never visited Malling before he was translated to Winchester in 1895.

[13] Cf. Dom Romanus Rios, O.S.B., "The Servant of God, Fr John-Baptist Muard" in *Benedictines of Today* (Stanbrook Abbey, 1945), pp. 72-89. It is possible that Carlyle may have read *The Life of the Rev. Mary John-Baptist Muard* by the abbé Brullée, translated from the French by Dom Isidore Robot, O.S.B., Abbot and Prefect Apostolic of the Indian Territory, published at New York in 1882.

[14] He ignored the recently founded Anglican male communities of the Order of St Paul (1889), and the Community of the Resurrection (1892). When he drew up his Constitutions in 1893, both the Society of the Divine Compassion, and the Society of the Sacred Mission were in process of being established.

[15] It could be that Br Aelred, like Fr Ignatius, took the line that monastic chapels lie outside the jurisdiction of the local ordinary, for no licence was sought or obtained for this chapel in Oxford Road, Ealing.

[16] P. F. Anson, *Abbot Extraordinary* (1958), p. 27.

[17] ibid, p. 32.

[18] P. F. Anson, *The Benedictines of Caldey* (1940), p. 9.

[19] A young architect, Ninian Comper, had already recreated a real medieval altar at Cantley, near Doncaster, and was about to transform the crypt of St Mary Magdalene's, Paddington, into a gorgeous gilded and painted evocation of a late medieval dream-world. Even the newly completed Tower Bridge over the Thames harked back to the Middle Ages.

[20] G. W. E. Russell, in *Dictionary of English Church History* (2nd ed. revised, 1919), p. 53.

[21] Cf. *The Benedictines of Talacre*, p. 3.

[22] See p. 215.

[23] Formerly the famous Parisian ballet-dancer, Mlle. Duvernay, she found herself a rich widow. In the 1880s she paid for the erection of the gorgeous Roman Catholic church of Shefford, Bedfordshire. In 1890 she defrayed the cost of the great cruciform church of Our Lady and the English Martyrs at Cambridge.

[24] p. 580.

[25] The quotations are taken from B. G. A. Cannell's *From Monk to Busman*, published in 1935.

[26] In 1898, Ignatius paid Cannell's fare from London, still hoping to make him a good and obedient monk, but without success.

[27] Apparently Br Aelred did not recognise the Abbey of Our Ladye and St David at Llanthony as an Anglican monastery of the Benedictine Rule.

[28] Cf. *The Benedictines of Caldey*, p. 18.

[29] Cf. *Pax*, September, 1904, pp. 10-11.

[30] ibid, p. 11.

[31] ibid, pp. 11-12.

[32] The records of St Bartholomew's Hospital suggest that he had never taken his medical studies very seriously. All they reveal is that he passed examinations in elementary anatomy and physiology, and belonged to certain social organisations. He seems to have spent more

time with his Oblates, or helping to run clubs for boys, holding services for slum children, and even street-preaching.

[33] Written to the author. When shown this letter Carlyle, then a secular priest of the Archdiocese of Vancouver, replied that he was glad Abbot Vonier had cleared up past misunderstanding.

[34] Looking back in 1938 he got the date wrong, and stated it was his 21st birthday.

[35] Quoted in *The Benedictines of Caldey* (1940), p. 10.

[36] ibid, p. 11.

M

THE CHAPEL, WEST MALLING ABBEY

Br. Aelred Carlyle was clothed here as a novice in 1896, and solemnly professed in 1898.

146

CHAPTER IX

*Br Aelred Carlyle clothed as a Benedictine novice; the life led
by his Brotherhood on the Isle of Dogs; his solemn profession;
and the early years of the quasi-Benedictine Order of St Paul
(1896-1898)*

ON Easter Sunday 1896—roughly a month after Carlyle had assured the Buckfast
community that he would be back again in the autumn—he was clothed as
an Anglican novice by Fr Dale in the chapel of Malling Abbey, in the presence
of Mother Hilda and her nuns. He pledged himself to keep the Rule of St Benedict
for twelve months, and to renew this promise annually until his profession.[1]

Meanwhile the house on the south side of Glengall Road, Isle of Dogs, had
been re-named "The Priory". To create the impression that its inmates were
"enclosed", a high wooden fence with a door in the middle was erected in front.
Two rooms were transformed into an oratory, and two more into a club-room.
There was sleeping accommodation for five, but at first the community consisted
only of Brs Aelred and Theodore, together with a Cockney lad, named Henry
Watts. Before long they were joined by a good-looking, and well-educated youth,
Alfred Brooke-Rose, who was given the religious name of Alban.

By September 13, when Leo XIII in his encyclical *Apostolicae Curae* condemned
Anglican Orders as invalid through defect both of form and intention, Br Aelred
had settled down to a very different sort of life to that which he would have led as
a novice at Buckfast. He was his own superior and novice-master, a law unto
himself to all intents and purposes; able to make changes according to his fancy,
in much the same way that Br Ignatius of Jesus did in his rectory-monastery in
Suffolk in 1863. Indeed life beside the Lower Thames was much more lively than
it would have been on the banks of the river Dart. The Priory rule made provision
for boxing and football matches, jolly tea-parties, and rowdy "sing-songs", for
what was described as "Rescue Work among Boys" was the special apostolate
undertaken by the Benedictine Brothers. The corporal works of mercy often
included washing the feet of the dirtier lads—even giving them hot baths, for
some were verminous. A plentiful dinner was provided for them on Sundays,
although the normal diet of the community was strictly vegetarian. Open hospitality
was practised: one never knew who might drop in for tea after Vespers on Sunday
afternoon. The young Benedictines took charge of the Church Lads' Brigade.
More than one visitor was surprised to find a stock of rifles just inside the front
door. The embryo monks became more familiar with the latest music hall songs
than with the 1883 *Graduale* and the 1891 *Antiphonale* published by the
Benedictines of Solesmes. Their knowledge of plainchant was limited to the
rumbling Gregorians that were then the correct music for the psalms in almost
every Anglo-Catholic church.

The *Breviarium Monasticum* was recited in the oratory. On Sundays a few
extern oblates travelled down from Fenchurch Street to Millwall Docks station,
which was quite near the Priory, unless they preferred a horse-drawn bus from
Aldgate along the Commercial Road. This meant a full-choir to sing Vespers. The

brethren attended the daily Eucharist at St John's Church, round the corner, where the ritual and ceremonial were "high" but not "extreme". The Vicar, the Rev. D. G. Cowan, and his curate, the Rev. E. Hartley, made good use of Br Aelred and his Benedictines, who not only ran clubs for men and boys, but also visited poor families. The community had an allotment garden on the mud-flats at the back of the Priory, where they grew vegetables. On Saturday afternoons, parties of boys used to be taken on outings, frequently to Greenwich Park, which could be reached by the tunnel under the river.

Few of the neighbours bothered about the black robes worn by the Benedictine Brothers, all that mattered was that they were decent sort of chaps. The *Cubitt Town Protestant Banner*, however, did try to stir up strife, but with no success. The people didn't care whether these young men were "garbed in habit, hood and sandals", or if they had broken the Fourth Commandment by buying ice cream off a cart on "the Christian Sabbath Day". Br Aelred was never attacked by mobs as was Br Ignatius. Henry Watts was clothed as the first novice early in 1897, but none of the other young men who hung around showed signs of a monastic vocation.

Yet this handful of embryo monks had the satisfaction of knowing that they were performing "The Work of God", even if in a modest manner, as it had gone on at the only five-miles distant Westminster Abbey for nearly 600 years. They could also feel that the mantle of the Cluniac monks at Bermondsey Abbey on the opposite side of the Thames, founded about 1069, had fallen upon them. Likewise there was the knowledge that they had, in a sense, begun to build up more distant Benedictine waste places, e.g. Bury St Edmunds, Colchester, Rochester, and St Albans.[2]

During the very hot summer of 1897, while Queen Victoria was celebrating her Diamond Jubilee, a party of the Church Lads' Brigade were taken to Malling Abbey. They were entertained by Abbess Hilda and her community, who allowed the boys and the Brothers to camp in the medieval tithe-barn. The revived Order of St Benedict now consisted only of the Founder, one novice (Br Henry), and Br Alban, who was still a postulant.

None of the other five aspirants had persevered. Br Theodore's health soon broke down, and he had to return to the world. This was awkward, for he had paid the rent of the Priory, and most of the living expenses.

Protestants were growing alarmed by the increase of "Monkery" in the Established Church. In the past eight years seven more communities of men had been founded, and six new sisterhoods had been added to the list.[3] Mr John Kensit (1853-1902), who became secretary of the newly founded Protestant Truth Society in 1890, never ceased to fulminate against what he believed were romanizing tendencies. In 1896 he filled up the great part of his shop window in Paternoster Row with "Instruments of Torture", said to be used especially by Anglican monks and nuns.

The publication of the first edition of Walter Walsh's *Secret History of the Oxford Movement* in 1897, caused a sensation by its lurid revelations of alleged scandals in sisterhoods. The Church Association, founded in 1865 to maintain the Protestant ideals of faith and worship in the Church of England, was so scared by the sinister machinations of the English Church Union, Society of the Holy Cross, Confraternity of the Blessed Sacrament, Guild of All Souls, and other "monkish" brotherhoods that were "actively promoting the avowed object of 'un-Protestantising' our Church", that it sent forth into the countryside eleven horse-drawn "Travelling Vans", each with a "Colporteur Evangelist".

From the point of view of the Church Association, Protestant Truth Society,

National Protestant League, and Mr Kensit's Wycliffe Preachers, there was no more insidious spot in Britain than St Mary's Abbey, West Malling. They kept a close watch on this ritualistic nunnery, also on the Benedictine brotherhood, whose few members were trying to pervert boys on the Isle of Dogs, even if there were no "priestlings" with their "persevering blandishments" in the community. What Br Aelred did not realise was that these Protestant organiastions had already succeeded in bribing his favourite postulant to be their agent *provocateur*.

* * *

By the Diamond Jubilee of Queen Victoria a young Anglican who heard the call of the cloister, and yearned to take a hand in building up the old monastic waste places on medieval lines, could take his choice of three communities, for Fr Ignatius and Br Aelred now had to compete with Fr Michael and his quasi-Benedictine *Order of St Paul*.

Fr Michael (Charles Plomer Hopkins), son of a master-mariner, was born at Brewster, Massachusetts in 1861. He made his first long voyage before he was a year old, when his parents took him to England. Seven years later another sailing ship was his home for a hundred and forty days on a voyage round the Cape of Good Hope to Rangoon. He was sent back to England, again in a windjammer. From then onwards he was never happy except amongst seafarers. They went on drawing him for the rest of his life.

His parents, still living in the Far East, obtained for their son the post of organist and choir-master at the Anglican Pro-Cathedral at Rangoon, where he started work in 1883. But the sea called louder than music. Young Hopkins felt he must become a maritime missionary. Having been ordained deacon and priest by Bishop Strachan, he was appointed Port Chaplain at Rangoon in 1885. Before long, however, both the Bishop and the British Colony grew alarmed by the chaplain's Socialist activities. He had formed what he called "The Seamen's Friendly Society" on the lines of the Association founded at Sunderland by Havelock Wilson. In their opinion it was a dangerous species of a Trade Union. The result was that after two years Mr Hopkins was moved to Akyab, a smaller port on the west coast of Burma. Here he began to dream of founding a brother-hood whose members would identify themselves with the seafaring class.[4] To quote his own words: "There rose up before me what *might* be done amongst our sailors, if a community of the right sort could be formed. To seamen themselves I would turn for the material, for it seemed to me that only those who had gone through ship-life would ever understand what it really was, and so be able to sympathise with and work for seamen."

His health broke down at Akyab, and he was invalided to England, almost blind, and stricken with fever. Having arrived in London, he got into touch with a small brotherhood, known as the Society of St Paul, whose Superior was a certain Br John. Its members worked in the parish of Holy Trinity, Shoreditch, under the Rev. Osborne Jay. After a brief novitiate, Hopkins took the three vows of religious, and the name of Michael, on February 14, 1889. A month later Dr Johnson, Bishop of Calcutta, appointed him River Chaplain at this busy port.

A house in a large garden on the banks of the river Hugli was turned into a priory. Two young mercantile marine seamen were clothed as novices, and given the names of Br Paul and Br Stephen. Before long a few more ex-sailors were admitted. In this Calcutta monastery there was only Br James who had not been a seafarer. Fr Michael also formed a new group of his Seamen's Friendly Society, with the object of promoting the spiritual and temporal well-being of Merchant Sailors and Sailor Lads in Foreign Ports. Its objects were defined thus:

"1. To provide Religious Instruction, Worship and the Means of Grace at the Seamen's Church.
2. To provide Healthy Recreation and Intercourse for Men and Lads at its Recreation Rooms.
3. To offer the Hospitality and Advantages of 'Home' at the Priory or Mission House.
4. To shelter the Homeless and Destitute.
5. To defend the Weak from imposition and wrong.
6. To care for the Sick and Dying on board and on shore.
7. To guard and tend the Graves of the Dead."

Fr Michael's seven objects were far more in keeping with St Benedict's seventy-two "Instruments of Good Works" than with Fr Ignatius' forty-nine "Observances", which were mainly negative and repressive. The monastic life at the Priory took on a nautical character, including the method of keeping time. So the brethren were roused to "show a leg" at "four bells", and at "five bells" (6.30 a.m.) they met in the chapel for Prayer Book *mattins*. Their office book was the *Day Hours of the Church of England*. The long day ended with Compline at "five bells" of the second watch (10.30 p.m.). The entertainment of seamen, hospital and ship-visiting filled up most of the time. The windjammer crews were a tough lot eighty years ago, and steam had not superseded sails by any means. There were smoking concerts and "sing-songs" of an evening—a far cry from life in the Abbey of Our Ladye and St David in the Black Mountains of Wales! Before long Fr Michael established branch houses at Chittagong and Budge-Budge. In 1891 a general office of the Seamen's Friendly Society of St Paul was opened in London, and District Secretaries appointed. That same year the first issue of *The Messenger* appeared; advertised as "a Monthly Paper on subjects connected with the Church's Work amongst our Sailors and Sailor Boys in Foreign Ports".

Bishop Johnson grew alarmed. The Chaplain was told that he must confine himself to spiritual ministrations. It was not his business to reveal how badly mariners were paid, housed, fed and treated. This would only lead to unpleasantness with the directors of shipping companies, some of whom were good churchmen. A crisis was reached when the newspapers reported that the Superior of the Society of St Paul had succeeded in getting several government measures passed in the seamen's interests. Both the civil and ecclesiastical authorities were scandalised when they discovered that the "Monk" had formed a branch of the Seamen's and Firemen's Union at Calcutta. This proved his disloyalty to the Empress of India, far worse than if he had indulged in riots of ritualism in the Priory chapel. Subscriptions dropped, just like they had done in Wapping when Ignatius of Jesus refused to give up wearing his monastic motley. The Brothers might have starved had not some young Army officers come to their rescue and issued an appeal on their behalf.

Early in 1893 Fr Michael decided to send Br James to England, to open a Priory at Barry, near Cardiff. Dr Lewis, the broadminded, hard-working Bishop of Llandaff, said he would welcome the Brotherhood into his diocese. There was more than enough work waiting to be done at Barry, where the Taff Vale Railway had opened the first basin in 1889, with the intention of developing a big coal-exporting centre as a rival to Cardiff. A small house was rented, but Br James died on June 29 that same year. His Superior felt that he must return to England so that he could direct operations. Leaving some of the community in India, he served his passage before the mast to save money.

It is recorded that after being paid off at Southampton, he bought a donkey with panniers and set off for South Wales. On the road he heard of land for sale about four miles west of Alton in Hampshire, which he felt he ought to acquire, so that he could provide a home for destitute mariners. Having reached Barry, he rented a seven-roomed cottage, which was turned into a priory. Within three months it became too congested, so two houses were taken over. Every night as many as 300 seamen were "dossing down" in this "monastery", under the charge of Br Austin. In 1894 Fr Hopkins (as he became known rather than by his religious name of Michael) terminated his appointment at Calcutta, but a few Brothers were left in India for work among seafarers.

The spirit of the Order of St Paul—as the brotherhood was renamed—was set forth in a *Messenger* article, where it was stated: "The Order is still in process of formation. When a man becomes professed, and gives himself to work 'for God and our Sailors', he takes upon himself not to obey a perfected Rule, but to help to build up a Rule. Into the framework of the Benedictine Rule we are fitting in, not the things which we think *correct* or suitable, but just what our daily experience teaches us we want, just to develop in us the religious spirit, secondly to send us forth to our work and equipped for the work.

"We make no effort to revive old-time asceticisms, to be externally in agreement with the monastic system of earlier days—rather do we wish to acquire the *spirit* that sent the old monks out to endure hardness, to meet death in the doing of the work to which they had put their hands. . . . We are not gathered together in cloistered seclusion to win our own salvation. . . . Our life is very matter of fact sometimes, and there is not the slightest hint of the glamour that is popularly supposed to exist in the life in the cloistered cell, far from the sorrows of men, and the turmoil of the world."[5]

Early in 1895 Dr Benson, Archbishop of Canterbury, licensed Fr Hopkins for two years, and at the same time Bishop Lewis gave him permission to minister to seafarers in the Llandaff Diocese.[6] Meanwhile the Founder of the Order of St Paul—like the Abbot of Llanthony—was spending most of his time moving around Britain preaching, and trying to raise money.

During the early spring of that same year, while Br Aelred Carlyle was dreaming of establishing his first monastery in the country, not far from London, a handful of the Order of St Paul arrived at their newly acquired property in Hampshire, "footsore and weary after a long tramp from Barry. The land on which they settled was a few acres of virgin copse. Trees had first to be cut down and sufficient ground cleared to enable them to pitch their tents. In these they lived for many months whilst busily engaged in building a little wattle Church and temporary Abbey. In addition, there was the additional work of cutting down the copse-wood, planting and cultivating vegetables on the land so cleared, which vegetables were to be their main, almost their only diet for some time to come. . . . The monastic offices were, for the time being, recited beneath the trees."[7]

It was intended that the new home of the quasi-Benedictine brotherhood, situated about 700 feet above sea-level within a mile of Medstead, should serve as a novitiate. Sailors, however, soon discovered the Abbey Camp (as it was then called), even if it was right off the main road between London and Southampton, and remote from other south of England shipping centres. Some of those who turned up were too old or infirm ever to go to sea again. So Fr Hopkins felt that a temporary corrugated iron building must be erected to accommodate them, the only alternative being the workhouse.

THE ABBEY, ALTON, HANTS, *c.* 1900

Disguised as "Malford Abbey" in Sir Compton Mackenzie's novel *The Altar Steps*—
"what it most resembles is three tin tabernacles put together to form three sides
of a square . . ."

THE GOTHIC GATEHOUSE AND CHAPEL, ALTON ABBEY, HANTS

Designed by John C. Hawes (the future "Fra Jerome", Hermit of Cat Island), it was
opened in 1903.

For the first two or three years life at the Abbey Camp was as penitential as it had been at New Llanthony Abbey for its foundation in 1870.[8] The brethren toiled for many weary months in gathering and stacking the larger flints that "grew" so plentifully, but which would come in useful once permanent buildings could be erected.

The first phase in the history of the Order of St Paul ended in 1896 with the closing down of the priories at Calcutta, Bombay, Chittagong, and Budge-Budge, and the concentration of the work for seafarers in England. Dr Randall Davidson, Bishop of Winchester, gave permission for the Holy Communion to be celebrated in the Abbey chapel for residents. A regular novitiate was opened in June that year. A fair number of men came to test their vocations, but few persevered. Neither did churchpeople show much practical interest by providing the means to build even temporary quarters in which to house the Brothers. The work at Barry proved too hard for Br Austin, and he was succeeded by Br Hugh.

Two elements were already at war in this never stable community trying to follow the Rule of St Benedict—the maritime and the monastic. They never managed to fuse happily. The Founder provided an explanation for this instability: "On establishing ourselves in England, chiefly landsmen applied for admission to the Brotherhood and were accepted for training. At that time considerable interest was being manifested in the revival of the Religious Life in the Church of England, and many aspirants came to us.[9] As a natural consequence, I suppose the Community of Brothers commenced to show signs of being more concerned for 'recognition', 'orthodoxy', and the 'real thing in monasticism' than for the battles or the betterment of seamen. I had adopted the religious life myself and established my Brotherhood as a Religious Community because, and only because, I felt it would make more efficient our endeavours for the seamen. The seamen and their causes were our first concern.[10] An element in the Brotherhood after we had settled in England protested that the life—the religious life—must be our first concern, and the activities for and amongst the sailor should be spiritual and philanthropic, nothing more. I could not agree, and insisted on my freedom and the freedom of other Brothers too—of the whole Brotherhood in fact—to co-operate in any movement which had to its object the betterment of the conditions and surroundings of the seafaring class. The domestic differences resulted in some of the more spiritual and monastic-minded Brothers leaving the Community—and eventually getting married most of them! Whilst the more earthly—'worldly' minded would not convey the true significance—remained and continued to carry on along the old lines."

So it will be realised that although the Order of St Paul was striving after the monastic life, the attitude of its Founder was quite different to that of either Fr Ignatius or Br Aelred, each of whom saw Benedictinism as an end in itself, not as a means to an end.

What life was like at Alton Abbey while Br Aelred and his few companions were trying to be Benedictines on the Isle of Dogs, has been recorded by Sir Compton Mackenzie in *My Life and Times, Octave Two*. By the summer of 1897 the tents which had sheltered the brethren had given place to a fairly large corrugated iron block, awaiting a side of equal length. The little chapel built by the monks themselves of mud and flints, and thatched with reeds, was separated from the main block, the front of which was taken up by a wide corridor known as the cloister.[11] *The Day Hours of the Church of England* continued to be used for the Divine Office. Fr Hopkins was seldom at home for long. He spent part of the time at the Barry Docks Priory, or trying to raise money by preaching. The ritual and ceremonial as recalled by the then fourteen year-old Mackenzie were eclectic.

Br Cuthbert, the Prior, wore a purple *pileolus* (skull-cap), normally reserved for bishops and certain prelates who have this papal privilege. He was addressed as "Reverend Father" by the brethren, although not a priest. Brothers Paul and James were more interested in farming, working hard to bring back the land to cultivation. Certain Calcutta customs had survived, for instance, breakfast and afternoon tea were still referred to as "tiffin", which infuriated Fr Sandys Wason, an extreme Anglo-Catholic priest, who was equally shocked by these "monks" using an Anglican diurnal instead of the *Breviarium Monasticum*. Still there was Reservation in a tabernacle, presumably without permission from Dr Davidson, Bishop of Winchester, who, so far as is known, never visited Alton Abbey before he was translated to Canterbury in 1903.

It is easy to believe that Fr Hopkins grew impatient with most of the men who wanted to become "real monks". They were of a different type to the young sailors who were his first novices in India, for they knew more about the thirty-two cardinal points of the compass than of the six points of eucharistic ceremonial which were still the minimum demanded by ritualistic Anglican priests. Monks who tried to live up to their motto "For God and our Sailors" ought to know that it was more important for them to be expert in "swinging" a boom, lead, or yard than a thurible. Sir Compton recalls that in the summer of 1898, Fr Hopkins took three of the brethren to Hayling Island for a sailing holiday, where they camped in a large tent, and how he teased them as landlubbers when they were afloat.[12]

By this time a Constitution for the Order of St Paul had been drawn up, which defined its purposes as follows:

"The objects of the Society are charitable and religious works among seamen, particularly *(a)* to lead into the way of truth and righteousness of life those who go down to the sea in ships, and occupy their business in great waters (i.e. seafarers employed in the Mercantile Marine of all countries). *(b)* to administer in the private oratories for the benefit of merchant seamen, the sacraments, rites and ceremonies of the Catholic Church according to the use of the Church of England. *(c)* to extend to merchant sailors (especially such as are homeless and destitute) the hand of fellowship and friendship in the Name of Christ."

Such was the quasi-Benedictine community that offered what was perhaps a more healthy form of monastic life as an alternative to that of New Llanthony Abbey and the Isle of Dogs Priory. It appears that Fr Michael got more postulants than did either Fr Ignatius or Br Aelred, but—just as in both these places—very few persevered beyond their novitiate. This is not surprising, for they received little real religious training.

Alton Abbey and the Order of St Paul are easily recognised in Sir Compton Mackenzie's novel *The Altar Steps* (1922) as "Malford Abbey" and "The Order of St George". Fr Hopkins is very thinly disguised as "Fr Burrowes", and his little community engages in mission work among soldiers instead of seamen. "Mark Lidderdale"—the young Anglo-Catholic who visits "Malford Abbey"—writes: "What it most resembles is three tin tabernacles put together to form three sides of a square, the fourth and empty side which is by far the most beautiful, because it consists of a glorious view over a foreground of woods, a middle distance of park land, and on the horizon the Hampshire downs".[13] We are told that "the Rule of Malford is a not very austere adaptation of the Rule of St Benedict".[14] The ephemeral nature of the "Order of St George" is brought out strongly. The frequent comings and goings are just what took place in reality. Octogenarians can vouch for the truth of the period atmosphere. Even the gossip between the monks both during and outside times of recreation revive memories of the chitchat in at least one Anglican monastic community about the turn of the century.[15]

* * *

"Paint your picture in strong colours, keep it ever before you, and strive to live up to it; if you do this conscientiously, you will not find yourself very much out in the end." This had been the advice given by Fr Maturin S.S.J.E. in a sermon heard by young Ben Carlyle. He took it as a direct message from God as to the scale on which the Benedictine Order was to be revived in the Church of England —far more comprehensive, in fact, than the Confederation of all the Black Monks of St Benedict, created by Leo XIII in his Bull *Summum semper* on July 12, 1893. This was a month after Carlyle had composed the *Constitutions* of the Oblate Brothers. Maybe the medical student already visualised himself as the Anglican opposite number to Dom Hildebrand de Hemptinne, Abbot of Maredsous, whom the Pope nominated as the Confederation's first Abbot-Primate, with world-wide responsibilities. It seems that soon after taking the Isle of Dogs Church Lads' Brigade to Malling Abbey when Queen Victoria was celebrating her Diamond Jubilee, Benjamin Fearnley Carlyle also began to picture himself as a sort of Benedictine Thomas John Barnardo. This English philanthropist, who, like Carlyle, was a medical student, founded in 1870 the first of his celebrated homes for destitute children. The main apostolate of the Anglican Benedictine Order would be what was called "Rescue Work among Boys".

Three months later came an omen that this was God's will, in the shape of an invitation from the Rev. J. E. Green, Mus. Doc., Vicar of Lower Guiting with Farmcote, Gloucestershire, to take over the empty vicarage of the former parish as a reformatory for guttersnipes and raggamuffins. Br Aelred replied that this letter was a direct answer to his prayers. He was quite certain that the monastic system was "the obvious solution for many social problems",[16] Dr Green called at the Isle of Dogs Priory on the feast of the Holy Cross, September 14, and appears to have been impressed by the rescue work for boys carried on there. The following week Br Aelred and Br Maurus Sutton inspected the long-abandoned vicarage and decided that it could be transformed into a monastic-reformatory school. The two black-robed Benedictines soon realised that their host was an original, if not an eccentric, character, for he introduced them to the villagers as the "Bishop of Jerusalem" and the "Pope of Rome", which was enough to alarm these simple country folk.

Dr Green assured Br Aelred and Br Maurus that they need not bother to find a chaplain, for he knew just the right priest for the job—the Rev. Herbert Drake. For the past year he had ministered to the Society of St Margaret (East Grinstead) at its Home for the Dying on Clapham Common. This meant that he was quite accustomed to giving Benediction with a monstrance. Dr Green regretted, however, that he would not be able to pay the chaplain's salary, partly owing to the sequestration of the living of Lower Guiting for a debt owing to Queen Anne's Bounty, so the monks would have to maintain him.[17]

This did not worry Br Aelred, and after he returned to the Isle of Dogs he wrote to Dr Green requesting him to get a local joiner to make refectory tables and an enclosure grille, hoping that the Vicar would not regard them as "too extravagant".[18] At the same time he was sorry that "some rather difficult work in connection with the Boys' Club" would prevent him from directing operations for the moment.

Things began to move fast. Dr Green had already explained to Fr Drake: "Brothers Aelred and Maurus have decided to start a community at Lower Guiting, and they would very much like to have you with them, and it would be a great benefit for my parishes for you to reside there. Allow me therefore to ask whether you could go there on the following terms: (1) that I make myself responsible to pay £35 per annum to the gradual paying off of the debt you name to me; (2) that you agree to be licensed to me as Vicar, that amount £35 being stated on your licence; (3) that you live at Lower Guiting priory on the charge of the Order; (4) that when required you would take Sunday duty in other churches for your travelling expenses and hospitality. A copy of this letter is being sent to Br Aelred for his approval asking him to advise you (probably by wire) thereon." Fr Drake agreed to conform to the four proposals.

Br Aelred then informed Dr Green that his only postulant would be "a competent Brother to leave in charge" of the rescue-home-monastery; adding: "I am very satisfied with Br Alban and we can thoroughly trust him. The ground can be planted and the house properly arranged by him. He goes into the novitiate on Sunday, October 10, and will come to Guiting prepared to work hard and keep as much Rule as is possible under the circumstances." Before long there would be more monks because several clergymen had "practically signified their intention" to enter the novitiate. Mr Cowan was enthusiastic about the reformatory school for boys about to be opened. He intended to write to Dr Temple, Archbishop of Canterbury, to arrange for Br Aelred's overdue profession, hoping that the Primate of All England would give official sanction to the revival of the Benedictine Order.[19]

Alfred Northbrook Rose changed his religious name from Alban to Oswald on being clothed as a novice, and the following day, October 11, he departed for Lower Guiting with the rank of Prior. Dr Green had been apopinted "Father Procurator", and Fr Drake—now known as "Fr Anselm, O.S.B."—took on the duties of Resident Superior and Spiritual Director of the future monastic rescue home.

Meanwhile Br Aelred had been kept busy buying bedding, furniture, groceries, household utensils, etc. from the Army and Navy Stores. A good supply of printed writing paper was ordered with the red heading: *"S Bernard's Monastery, Lower Guiting, Cheltenham,"* together with the intimation: *"All letters, whether private or on business should enclose a stamp for reply—as an act of charity"*.

Throughout the month of November many letters passed between Dr Green and Br Aelred, mainly as to how he and Fr Anselm should act in their respective capacities. He requested that the following notice should be displayed in the common-room: "Owing to pressure of work and general irregularity, I wish each man to be a law unto himself, keeping his own Rule and being responsible to *me alone* for it. Offices to be said together at stated times, as nearly as possible under such difficult circumstances. Each man will tell me himself how Rule has been kept, *as far as it concerns himself only*. I trust that everyone will do his best in obedience to it."

Owing to the heavy expenses in connection with the foundation the Order was on the rocks financially. Usually the Superior-General had to borrow money for his fairly frequent train journeys between Paddington and Notgrove. Then he also needed 21s. to buy a habit "of the best serge" for Br Sylvan, still this boy-oblate would not require another "for at least two years". Fr Anselm was told that the thurible at the Isle of Dogs Priory could not be spared, and that there was no cash in hand to buy another, so he would have to postpone burning incense in the parish church.

One day Dr Green received a letter with the request: "Please let Br Oswald come to London tomorrow . . . I fail to see why he should wish to delay; he is not coming to be *judged*, but merely to have a quiet talk with me. He shall return to Guiting doubtless before the end of the week so that the secular world will not be exercised in its mind. There is no need for you to come with him; the matters I wish to discuss occurred before you knew us. I think he is needlessly frightening himself and making himself more uncomfortable by his delay." The truth was that Prior Oswald had been playing a double game for quite a long time. Not only had he stolen valuable books from Canon Cecil Deedes at Brighton, but he had accepted money from the Church Association for a report on transactions of the Society of the Holy Cross. This enabled secrets of this extreme Anglo-Catholic group of priests to be published in the ultra-Protestant *Church Intelligencer*. Yet Br Aelred still refused to believe that his favourite novice was guilty of these offences. He explained to Dr Green: "I am not telling Br Oswald much, as I deem it bad for him to dwell too much on affairs which might make further living together in the novitiate impossible, or at all events very difficult". So the Novice-Prior remained on the Isle of Dogs, having already threatened to invoke the law for the cruel way he had been treated by some of the brethren. They had searched his "cell", where the stolen books and a letter from the Church Association were discovered.

On December 1, just as Br Aelred was about to leave the Priory, a telegram was handed to him from Archbishop Temple's chaplain, postponing the interview already arranged because of sudden illness. In spite of the worries over Br Oswald, he felt able to write to Dr Green three days later: "In coming to Guiting the dearest wish of my life is realized—more than I realized, for I never thought God would send two priests who would so nobly throw in their lot with ours. I look around, and I see openings which never entered my thoughts in my most golden dreams. We must not have the nut without the kernel or the flower without the fruit, and we must water and tend our seedling, and pray and watch and wait."

Ten days later he wrote again: "Br O's game is up now, and you need not be at all alarmed at his threat of legal proceedings. I have the whole affair in my hands, and I shall get rid of him as quietly and quickly as possible". This was done, but not in the way that the Brother-Superior intended—for the Prior of St Bernard's Monastery, Lower Guiting, was arrested, and taken to Brighton, where he appeared in the police court on February 3, 1898. The Anglican Benedictine Order got nation-wide press publicity after the trial at the Sussex Assizes at Lewes on the 14th, where Br Aelred gave evidence—not in his "monkish robes" as was reported, but in a clerical suit bought for the occasion. Mr Justice Grantham sentenced the twenty-two year-old Br Oswald to three years' penal servitude. Dr Green was informed: "You will by this time know of poor Rose's severe sentence, and I suppose all the details. I need only say that we were all treated very kindly yesterday and that there was no scandal of any sort."

On February 11—three days before the trial at Lewes—Br Aelred went to Lambeth Palace for the long postponed interview with Archbishop Temple, which had been arranged by Mr Cowan, Vicar of St John's, Isle of Dogs. According to the later monastic version of this interview, Br Aelred "was received with the greatest kindness and sympathy."[20] The Archbishop had closely followed the movement from the beginning, and fully grasped the situation. He went into every detail concerning Br Aelred, catechising him as to his life, work, motives, and plans with characteristic thoroughness, sudden glances of humour lighting up his strong face, and revealing his keen interest and goodness of heart. He spoke of his own attempt to establish a Religious Community, and dwelt with much emphasis on the increasing need for restoring the Religious Life, especially for men.[21] He said he had a great veneration for the Benedictine Order, which had done so much for England in the past, and might again do much in the future; he

157

laid particular stress on the scriptural tone of the Holy Rule, with which he was quite familiar; he felt it was singularly adapted to meet the needs of the present day, and heartily prayed God to bless his present action in regard to it."[22]

Having blessed Br Aelred the Primate of All England "told him to come back again at the end of two years to receive his Official Sanction for the Foundation of the Order of St Benedict in England". Such is what "Marcellinus" recorded. Just how far it is true is not altogether certain. No matter, on the same day that the ex-Prior of St Bernard's Monastery, Lower Guiting was ordered to lead a strictly enclosed life for three years at the cost of the State, Dr Temple wrote the following letter addressed to "Aelred Carlyle, Esq."

LAMBETH PALACE
S.E.
14 February, 1898

My dear Sir,

You have my permission to ask Mr Richards the Chaplain of West Malling Abbey to receive your profession and he has hereby my sanction for receiving it.
Yours faithfully,
F. Cantuar.[23]

The reference to "Mr Richards" was due to the fact that Fr Dale, the first chaplain, had already followed Miss Boyd on the road to Rome. He was succeeded by the Rev. Morley Richards, who came to Malling after a brief chaplaincy to the Order of St Paul at Alton Abbey.[24]

On Saturday morning, February 19, a few Oblate Brothers and a handful of friends went to Malling. The following day, Quinquagesima Sunday, Br Aelred made a promise before the chaplain of stability, and of living the monastic life of obedience, so that if he ever broke that promise he would know that he would be condemned by him whom he mocked.[25] It was a historic event as the first episcopally authorized profession of a Benedictine monk in the post-Reformation Church of England.[26] Although the 1604 *Constitutions and Canons Ecclesiastical* of the Provinces of Canterbury and York contain no reference to religious vows, only certain oaths made by ministers to bishops, Br Aelred regarded this profession as "Solemn" as understood in the canon law of the Roman Church.[27] After the function the Order's only other member, Br Henry, who was still a novice, gave his Superior the monastic tonsure in the sacristy adjoining the nuns' choir, using a pair of horse-clippers and a razor. In shape it conformed to the coiffure adopted by the Buckfast Benedictines, leaving a two-inch ring of hair round the skull. From then onwards the solemnly professed Monk called himself "Father" instead of "Brother", just as Ignatius had done after his profession in 1864.[28]

NOTES

[1] Fr Dale did not think it necessary to obtain permission from either Dr Edward Talbot, Bishop of Rochester, or Dr Frederick Temple, Bishop of London, in whose diocese Carlyle was domiciled.

[2] It was in 1892 that Roman Catholic Benedictines of the English Congregation were put in charge of the mission of East Dulwich. In 1897 Cardinal Vaughan invited the Downside community to take over the parish of Ealing. Two years later a monastery was built, and the first part of a large church.

[3] (1) Society of St Paul (1889), Brotherhood of St Paul (c. 1891), Oblates of St Benedict (1892), Community of the Resurrection (1892), Society of the Divine Compassion (1894), Society of the Sacred Mission (1894), and the Order of St Benedict (1896).

(2) Sisterhood of the Holy Ghost the Comforter (1891), Community of the Holy Comforter (1891), Community of the Ascension (1894), Sisterhood of the Holy Childhood (1894), Society of the Incarnation of the Eternal Son (1894), and Community of St Michael and All Angels (1895).

[4] His ideal was that of the French "Seamen Priests" of the *Mission de la Mer* more than sixty years later, or the maritime fraternity of the Little Brothers of Jesus at Concarneau in Brittany.

[5] op. cit., 1894, p. 77. This *apologia* for the Order of St Paul was written a year after Carlyle had drawn up Constitutions for his Benedictine Oblates.

[6] This indicates that Fr Ignatius was mistaken in presuming that the Welsh bishops gave him a wide berth mainly because he persisted in going about in his bizarre Benedictine costume. Fr Hopkins at that date always wore his simple black habit in public.

[7] *For God and our Sailors* (Alton Abbey, 1930), p. 7.

[8] See p. 94ff.

[9] In 1894, Dr Gore, founder of the Community of the Resurrection, having been appointed Canon of Westminster, was living in the Little Cloisters of the Abbey with a few of the Brethren, the rest remaining at Radley Vicarage. That same year the Korean Missionary Brotherhood changed its name to the Society of the Sacred Mission, and moved its headquarters from Kennington, South London, to Mildenhall, Suffolk. In January 1894, the first members of the Society of Divine Compassion took over the mission church of St Philip's, Plaistow. Before long they became a familiar sight in their black habits and capuces, like those of the Friars Minor Conventual.

[10] This was not inconsistent with Benedictine tradition. In 1884 Dom Andrew Amrheim, a monk of Beuron, had founded the Benedictine Congregation of the Sacred Heart for foreign missions, especially in German East Africa. Its name was changed in 1897 to the Congregation of St Ottilien. In 1969 the total membership was 1,256, of whom 501 were priests.

[11] op. cit., p. 190.

[12] ibid, p. 230.

[13] p. 232.

[14] In 1893 "the liturgical worship of the day" began "with Lauds and Prime at six". It is interesting that the daily *horarium* at Alton remains practically the same today, ending with Compline at 9.15.

[15] For the latter history of the Order of St Paul, see pp. 206ff.

[16] The quotations relative to Lower Guiting are taken from a collection of letters from Br Aelred to Dr Green preserved in the archives of Nashdom Abbey.

[17] In 1704 Queen Anne handed over to the Church of England large sums of money paid by clergymen on being appointed to a living, which had been paid to the Crown since the Reformation. This substantial income became known as "Queen Anne's Bounty".

[18] This insistence on a grille is reminiscent of Fr Ignatius' monasteries at Norwich, Laleham and Llanthony. It implied that Br Aelred intended his monks to be strictly enclosed once they had started to run a rescue home for boys.

[19] It would have been more consistent with Canon Law had Mr Cowan approached Dr Creighton, Bishop of London, in whose diocese the Isle of Dogs Priory was situated, instead of the Archbishop of Canterbury.

[20] Many years later Carlyle wrote: "One of my chief means of introduction to Archbishop Temple was the fact of his being an old Blundellian. He was passionately devoted to our old school. He also knew of my Devon relatives and affiliations, who had been mixed up with his Powderham ancestors for generations."

[21] In his younger days he had fallen under the spell of J. H. Newman, when he was an undergraduate at Balliol College, Oxford, and later on dreamed of forming a religious brotherhood on Tractarian lines, which would devote itself to the education of the poor.

[22] "Notes on the History of the Community. 2—Formation" by "Marcellinus", in *Pax*, No. 2, December 1904, pp. 29-35.

[23] Archbishop Temple's action was somewhat irregular for Malling Abbey was in the Rochester Diocese, then ruled over by Dr Edward Talbot, whose sanction for the profession ought to have been obtained as well as that of the Metropolitan.

[24] Sir Compton Mackenzie recalled that Fr Richards' departure resulted from the Brother Sacristan refusing to give him the key of the tabernacle during the absence of the Superior, Fr Hopkins (Cf. *My Life and Times, Octave Two* (1963), p. 203).

[25] *Rule of St Benedict*, chap. 58.

[26] No higher authority had given permission for that of Fr Ignatius in 1864, or for that of any of his monks.

[27] A reciprocal engagement between the religious and his order, which undertakes to maintain him, and treat him as a member of the family for the rest of his life. In February 1898 the Aelredian "Order of St Benedict" consisted of himself, one novice, and a few oblates.

[28] See p. 57.

CHAPTER X

Mar Timotheos raises Ignatius of Jesus to the priesthood;
Fr Aelred's Order of St Benedict leads a gyrovic existence for
four years. (February 1898—March 1902)

THE life led by Fr Aelred's microscopic Order of St Benedict between February 20, 1898 and March 5, 1902 can be summed up in the words of the author of the Letter to the Hebrews: "They were strangers and exiles on the earth. . . . For here we have no lasting city, but we seek the city which is to come."

Having returned to the Isle of Dogs from Malling Abbey on the afternoon of Quinquagesima Sunday, Fr Aelred and Br Henry held a farewell tea-party at the Priory, said to have been "extremely lugubrious". The boys and their mothers were heart-broken at the departure of the Benedictines. That night the two monks slept on bare boards, for the house had already been dismantled. The following morning, February 21, the streets were wrapped in the raw mists of a river fog. After a long journey, the travellers arrived at Notgrove station late in the afternoon, whence they tramped through deep snow for three miles to Lower Guiting village. St Bernard's Monastery was bolted and barred, but Br Henry managed to get in through a lower window and opened the door. He recalled in after years: "What a change from London and its life and movement. Here there was dead silence, and the earth was wrapped in its white mantle of winter. The trees stood out gaunt and bare, and a solitary rook here and there broke the stillness with a dismal caw. It was like coming into a realm of death and the first impressions were anything but cheerful."[1]

Nevertheless the full observance of the Rule started on February 23, with the recitation of Matins and Lauds at 2 a.m. On Sundays Fr Anselm—still acting as Resident Superior and Spiritual Director—celebrated the Holy Communion in the parish church. Vespers were sung in the domestic oratory followed by Devotions to the Reserved Sacrament. On March 1 Fr Aelred wrote to the "Father Procurator": "We must do without milk and the bread we can bake ourselves rather than run up a big bill, and further limit our very limited resources. I have only £4 in the world at present, and only £6 coming in April to last to July." This was not enough money even to buy coal, but the Founder hoped that when he got "quite straight and the bills paid off", he could "run" to another postulant, perhaps two if they were good workers. A couple did turn up, but did not remain long. Occasionally Fr Bignold S.S.J.E. came over from Oxford to hear confessions.

In a vague sort of way the Brothers felt that they were rebuilding what had long laid desolate, repairing the ruins of past days. Not very far off were the ruins of the Cistercian abbeys of Flaxley, Hayles and Kingswood. Who could say that they were not taking the first steps towards restoring Benedictine life at Gloucester, Deerhurst, Tewkesbury and Winchcombe Abbeys? Yet it was not until June 27 that Fr Aelred was able to inform Dr Green that Dr Ellicott, Bishop of Gloucester, had granted permission for the Holy Communion to be celebrated in the monastery. The following morning Fr Anselm said Mass, using the *Missale Monasticum*. A monstrance had been procured so the monks were able to enjoy Benediction.

In the meantime the Church Association and other Protestant organisations were keeping close watch on this "monkery" in the Cotswolds. Local newspapers began to give space to "Scandals at Lower Guiting". Mr Kensit sent some of his Wycliffe Preachers in a horse-drawn caravan, dedicated to John Hooper, the Cistercian monk who in 1546 married an Antwerp lady at Basle, became Bishop of Gloucester in 1551, and who was burnt to death in 1555 by the orders of "Bloody Mary". The militant evangelists spent a week in the village denouncing the spread of "Romanism in the Reformed Church". Lurid tales of monastic immorality, the evils of the confessional, idolatry, etc. were told. The simple-minded villagers got so worked up that they attacked the vicarage, smashed windows, and forced open the front door. On July 25, the feast of St James the Greater, Apostle and Martyr, the Benedictines bade farewell to Lower Guiting after a brief stay of five months. They were "drummed" out of the village by an angry crowd of men, women and children beating pots and pans. Fr Aelred and Br Henry found a temporary home at Malling Abbey. Here they were joined by a party of lads from the Isle of Dogs. It is recorded that they had "a high old time" while camping in a disused hopkiln. Fr Anselm, the chaplain and spiritual director, showed no desire to continue monastic life, and returned to the world. No more was heard about Benedictine "Rescue Work for Boys" for nearly six years.

* * *

On the same morning that the monks were kicked out of their monastery on the Cotswolds the first of some sensational events took place at the monastery in the Black Mountains, with Fr Illtud Mary of the Epiphany receiving the five Minor Orders from Joseph René Vilatte, Archbishop-Metropolitan of the Old Catholic Church of America, Doctor Christianissimus, Grand Prior of the Order of the Crown of Thorns, otherwise known as "Mar Timotheos".[2] Fr Ignatius of Jesus had remained a deacon for thirty-eight years. Early in July 1898 a telegram arrived at Llanthony, signed "MAR TIMOTHEOS", stating that he would arrive within a few days. The Abbot, in his status of Dewi-Honddu, of the Gorsedd of the Bards of Wales, was absent at the National Eisteddfod. The following day came a letter from Dr F. G. Lee, still Vicar of All Saints', Lambeth. He hinted that it might be advantageous for the community to offer hospitality to this unknown bishop. When the Archbishop turned up on July 18, Dewi-Honddu was back at his monastery. The distinguished French prelate was welcomed with open arms, for it was the first occasion in twenty-eight years that a bishop had deigned to make an official appearance at Llanthony. Mar Timotheos said that he had heard of the marvellous harvest of souls reaped during the mission tour of North America in 1890. The least he could do to show his appreciation was to raise the Abbot to the priesthood, as well as any of the monks who cared to avail themselves of his services. He guaranteed that the orders supplied would be absolutely valid.[3]

Fr Illtud Mary of the Epiphany related in a newspaper article that after Vilatte's arrival at Llanthony "there went up to God a ceaseless stream of prayer from 5 a.m. to 5 p.m., besides the midnight services, that God's will might be done at the present crisis in our history, that our Lord Jesus might be glorified. The Archbishop daily pleaded the Eucharistic Memorial for the illumination of the Divine Paraclete. Our Superior presented three objections to the Archbishop".[4]

Ignatius objected to (1) the "excessive rancour of the Old Catholics towards the Church of Rome"; (2) insisted that as "a faithful son of the Church in Britain" he "must use the *Filioque* until the National Church permitted its erasure from the Creed", and (3) wanted assurance that "the Syrian Patriarch and his Church

161

were not Monophysite". Mar Timotheos had no difficulty in convincing the Abbot that his scruples were groundless.[5]

On July 26 the Archbishop raised Fr Illtud Mary to the diaconate. The following morning he ordained both him and Ignatius to the priesthood, using a vernacular version of the *Pontificale Romanum*.[6] The monk added: "We were too grateful to our dear Archbishop . . . to question or choose anything, for he won all our hearts by his humility and courtesy". Before leaving Llanthony, Mar Timotheos blessed veils for the nuns; confirmed a boy "lately converted by the Grace of God"; consecrated holy oils, and gave everybody his solemn benediction. Finally he blessed Ignatius as an abbot, again using the Roman Pontifical, which was odd for a bishop who claimed to belong to a Monophysite Church of the Antiochene Rite. Having told the double-community that he was bound for Moscow at the invitation of the Holy Synod, he bade them an affectionate farewell, and vanished as mysteriously as he had materialized.

The result of these highly irregular ordinations was that the Abbot incurred *ipso facto* excommunication from the Church of England, in virtue of a clause in the 1604 Constitutions and Canons Ecclesiastical. His name was removed from the next issue of *Crockford's Clerical Directory*. The *Church Times* commented: "The little monastery of Llanthony has taken a step which its best wishers must regret and deplore. . . . Having been led by his feelings into a sudden acceptance of a gift which, we are disposed to believe, has been unduly delayed, he casts about for reasons to justify his conduct, and he finds them in the anomalous condition of Celtic monasteries of many centuries ago. . . . We fail to see what precedent this affords for the act of Mar Timotheos, whatever it may mean to Fr Ignatius. . . . We cannot see that the boycott of thirty-eight years which he has been subjected to is any valid reason for so irregular a proceeding as his ordination by a Bishop fetched from the ends of the earth."

Nobody was more shocked by the Llanthony ordinations than Dr Grafton, Bishop of Fond du Lac, who had been one of the pole bearers of the canopy when the monstrance was carried through the streets of Norwich in 1864.[7] He was roused to write a very long letter, only part of which was printed in the *Church Times*. It ended with the words: "I know of no clergyman or layman in my Diocese who has any opinion of Vilatte but that his proper place is in the penitentiary. He belongs to the low class of criminal governed by inordinate ambition and an insatiate greed for money and power. He has no religious principles, as is seen from the course of his life."

Ignatius was greatly distressed, tried to defend his consecrator, and accused his old friend of telling lies, but he never bothered to check facts. He refused to believe that he had been fooled by this unscrupulous Franco-American free-lance prelate.

Less than a month before these much publicized ordinations, when life had become very difficult at St Bernard's Monastery, Lower Guiting, Fr Aelred had written to Dr Green that he had declined an invitation to stay at Llanthony, explaining: "My visit would be merely a matter of curiosity, and as no definite purpose would be served, I do not think I am justified in leaving our house. Fr Ignatius is a dear old man. I wish he were not so heretical in his opinions."

After the death of the Abbot of Llanthony ten years later, Fr Hopkins, founder of the Order of St Paul, wrote: "Some said he was no longer a minister of the Church of England. I don't think he worried much, but I do know that he was saddened by the way in which members of his few remaining friends in the ministry 'went back' on him for what he had done. I am thankful to say that I did not 'go back' on the dear old man, although I don't think I should have done as he did in a similar case.[8] And yet, I don't know. You can't be really sure what you would or would not do until you are actually pressed by the selfsame conditions and circumstances."[9]

The Anglican Order of St Benedict after July 27, 1898, consisted only of Abbess Hilda and her dozen or so nuns, together with Fr Aelred and Br Henry. The Llanthony double-monastery, ruled over by a Druid-Abbot, had cut itself off from communion with Canterbury as the result of the irregular ordinations performed by Mar Timotheos. Yet this hardly mattered, for the community could still boast of belonging to an Ancient British Church, "the oldest in the world after Antioch and Jerusalem"; if not, then to a mysterious Church of the Cymry, at the moment lacking a hierarchy.

Towards the end of August, Br Aelred wanted to rent a cottage at Kemsing, near Sevenoaks, but there was no money forthcoming. He wrote on September 9: "I am longing to get settled as much as everyone is; truly there are many compensations in all our troubles, for God has raised up to us many friends. The Archbishop is very good. He has written us four letters, and Fr Steedman is to go to London to be licensed as our Chaplain on September 20."[10] But something prevented this, so the two homeless monks gratefully accepted an invitation from Fr Page, then Superior of the Society of St John the Evangelist, to make the Mission House at Oxford their base. Here they lodged for three months.

On October 23 Fr Aelred felt he ought to avail himself of a generous offer from the Archdeacon of Zululand to pay the fares of himself and Br Henry to South Africa, together with a house and land, plus a salary of £100 a year. The work proposed "seemed exactly suited", for it included "the nucleus of a small school (five or six boys) and a tiny convalescent home". Moreover both the Archdeacon and the Bishop were "good Catholics and quite sympathetic". The former had assured Fr Aelred that he and his companion would find what they most needed at present—"time and opportunity for development". As nothing else had turned up this looked like "quite a distinct call". The Cowley Fathers and other friends felt that the two monks ought not to reject it.[11]

Although the Cowley Fathers were sure that the two Benedictines ought to go to South Africa, Fr Aelred suddenly decided not to undertake the 6,228 miles voyage, having formed the opinion that an island twenty-five miles south west of Lands End offered better opportunities for development than Zululand. Ten days later he wrote from the Royal Hotel, Par, Cornwall: "Mr Athelstan Riley and I have just been to lunch with the Bishop of Truro [Dr Gott] at the Palace.[12] His Lordship was exceedingly kind to me, and says we shall be gladly welcomed into his Diocese; he thinks that Padstow is not at all a good place for us, and says that he will see the Archbishop about giving us part or the *whole of one of the Scilly Isles!*[13] These are admirably adapted to our needs; they are, you know, called the Gardens of England, and enjoy a lovely climate, spring beginning in January. The Bishop says we shall have scope of making the fortune of the community as the Islands send to London every year more than £12,000 worth of flowers and fruit which grow from shore to shore. The Bishop has a wonderful grasp of the Religious Life. The chapel attached to the house is most Catholic and beautiful. The Bishop mentioned one of the islands containing the ruins of an ancient monastery which might do for us."[14]

In spite of the chapel at Lis Escop being furnished in a Catholic manner, Bishop Gott did not provide *maigre* food for his Benedictine guest at that Friday luncheon party, so Fr Aelred had to satisfy his appetite with vegetables, not being sure if his host had the power to dispense him from abstinence.

It is not certain why the two monks came to the conclusion that the Scilly

Islands were no better suited for leisure in which to develop than was Zululand. It could have been that it dawned on them that they had no previous experience of market gardening; if not, then they lacked the cash to rent or buy an island. So Fr Aelred returned to the Mission House in Marston Street, Oxford, for another spell of plain living and high thinking.

During the summer of 1898 Robert Hugh Benson (1871-1914), the youngest son of the former Archbishop of Canterbury, who had died two years previously, having served at the Eton mission at Hackney Wick after his ordination as deacon in 1894, was a curate at Kemsing, seven miles west of Malling. He often visited the Abbey, and his reactions to the enclosed and contemplative life led by the nuns formed the subject of one of the fifteen tales in *The Light Invisible*, entitled "In the Convent Chapel".[15] He wrote:

"The lay-sister who opened the door to me asked me to come into the parlour while she told the Reverend Mother; and after waiting for five minutes in the prim room with its bees-waxed floor and its religious engravings and objects, a wonderfully dignified little old lady, with a quiet wrinkled face, came in with my letter open in her hand. We talked a few minutes about various things, and I had a glass of cowslip wine in a thick-lipped wine-glass.

" 'Our object' said the old lady, 'is perpetual intercession for sinners. We have the great joy of the Blessed Sacrament amongst us in the chapel, and, except during the choir offices and Mass, there is always a nun kneeling before It. We look after one or two ladies incurably ill, who have come to end their days with us, and we make our living by embroidery.' "

The story ends: "It almost seems to me as I look back now as if the air in the chapel was full of murmurous sound and luminous mist as the currents of need and grace went to and fro. But I know really that the silence was deep and the air dim. Then I made a foolish remark:

" 'If you feel like that about the Contemplative Life, I wonder why you did not try to enter it yourself?'

"The priest looked at me for a moment.

" 'It would be rash, surely, for a little shopkeeper of no particular ability to compete with Rothschild'.[16]

Fr Morley Richards, the chaplain at Malling, lived in the Gate House. Before long he began to have bad dreams. Ghostly visitants urged him to give up his priesthood and submit to the Church of Rome. One night matters reached a crisis. He rose from his bed, dashed down the stairs, rushed across the gardens past the great Norman tower of the church, and bolted into the tiny sacristy. Here he felt safer, having the companionship of what he would have called "The Prisoner in the Tabernacle", with the ruby light flickering before the high altar in the darkness.[17] But the ghosts, as in the case of Miss Boyd and Fr Dale, were too powerful to be resisted. Fr Richards resigned his chaplaincy within a year. Having made his submission to the Roman Church he joined the Order of Friars Preachers. He paid a visit to Malling after his profession, and tried hard to induce Abbess Hilda to follow his example, but without success. Yet she did promise to send for him before she died. His own death, however, preceded hers. So the Dominican priest was unable to reconcile her from schism and administer the Last Sacraments.

The year 1898 was a troubled one for Anglo-Catholics all over England. On Good Friday Mr Kensit had created a disturbance at St Cuthbert's, Philbeach Gardens, during the Mass of the Presanctified. His Wycliffe Preachers were travelling around the country in their horse-drawn caravans, Lower Guiting was far from being the only village where idolatry and superstition had been denounced.

Walter Walsh's *Secret History of the Oxford Movement* had reached its sixth edition. More than 42,000 copies had been sold in two years. A new preface drew further attention to the sinister character of "private burial grounds" and much worse scandals in "Ritualistic Sisterhoods".

Mr Walsh remarked: "After all, Convents are no more 'private houses' than are the factories in which women are employed, and they ought to be as fully open to Government inspectors. Those who have read what had already taken place in Ritualistic Convents, as revealed in the *unrefuted* books of Miss Margaret Goodman, Miss Cusack, 'Maude', and 'Sister Mary Agnes', will be the first to laugh the plea of privilege to scorn. . . . The plea of privacy did not avail for Convents at the time of the Reformation, and I do not think it should avail now."[18]

Particularly revolting was the Convent of St Mary and St Scholastica at West Malling, Kent. Mr Walsh had no idea how many nuns were confined within its walls. He explained that this establishment had been "originally under the control of the Rev. J. L. Lyne, who calls himself 'Father Ignatius', after Ignatius Loyola, founder of the Jesuit Order" before "a schism took place in its ranks". Mr Walsh added: "I had an interview with 'Ignatius' himself, who told me that his Nuns 'never see the face of man'—his own face, I presume, excepted". *The Monastic Times*, published at Llanthony Abbey, had confirmed the use of the "Discipline, or cat-o'-nine-tails by these Nuns". Worse than this, was the horrible but apparently true story told by Sister Mary Agnes of the "Discipline" being inflicted by the 'Mother Superior' against the will of the unfortunate Nun". This incident had never "been publicly denied by Ignatius", and it "read like a chapter of Convent life taken from the Dark Ages. . . . What an outcry there would be raised all over England if it were discovered that the humblest woman in East London were subject to torture such as this, even though it were inflicted by herself! Is it not evident that the inherent evils of Convent life are growing rapidly in what used to be termed the *Reformed* Church of England?"[19] Indeed it was high time that steps were taken to suppress the Benedictine nunneries at Llanthony and Malling.

Abbess Hilda and her nuns began to fear that Dr Talbot, who had been Bishop of Rochester since 1895, might order the cessation of the Reservation of the Consecrated Elements in the chapel, which would involve giving up both Benediction and Exposition; also the fairly frequent processions of the Host with lighted candles, banners, lights and incense. But the Bishop took no action. From his point of view Malling Abbey was little more than a moribund backwater of his diocese. Only a few seculars, mostly lady-guests, attended the services, for the chapel was far too small to admit the general public.

Fr Aelred and Br Henry were still living at the Mission House in Marston Street, Oxford, as guests of the Cowley Fathers. Feeling sorry for the two Benedictines, Fr Page suggested that they should take charge of the domestic arrangements at the London house of the Society, as there appeared to be no hope of the foundation of a monastery on one of the Scilly Islands. The two monks moved to 29 Great Tichfield Street on January 12, 1899. They were given a room as their private oratory so that the *Breviarium Monasticum* could be recited.

"Rescue Work among Boys" still drew the former, and on Sundays he went by bus, horse-drawn tram, or steam-train to Lewisham, where he gave catechism classes at the Orphanage conducted by the All Saints' Community. This was the start of a friendship with the Superior, Sister Mary Pauline Ewart. He talked to her of the Benedictine nuns at Malling, and arranged for her first visit there on August 15, the feast of the Assumption. She took part in an outdoor procession of the Blessed Sacrament. A bull got roused by the long red veils worn by the nuns over their black cowls. He was pawing the ground, just waiting to jump over the stream flowing through the grounds. Sister Mary Pauline wondered whether she should take the aged and diminutive Abbess in her arms, and carry her to a place of safety. One of the acolytes, however, managed to drive off the enraged beast, whose behaviour would have been applauded by Mr Kensit.[20]

In June that same year, Fr Aelred, who never doubted that he was the *de jure earl of mar* (Premier Earl of Scotland), spent two months with Br Henry in the Bishop's House on Iona, which had been handed over to the Cowley Fathers by Dr Chinnery-Haldane, Bishop of Argyll and the Isles. The romantic beauty of the island appealed to him so much that he would have been happy to remain there, for it was even more glamorous than any of the Scilly Isles. There was also the thrill of discovering some bones, which he believed might be part of the long-lost relics of St Columba. After returning to London, Br Henry made his simple profession on September 14, and George Chambers was clothed as a novice.[21]

On Sunday mornings the monks often worshipped at Berkeley Chapel, Mayfair. At that date it was under the charge of Fr "Jim" Adderley, who had given up his membership in the Society of Divine Compassion, of which he was the Founder. It was he who put Fr Aelred in touch with Mr Bousfield, the vicar of Milton Abbas, a Dorset village six miles from Blandford. The Benedictines were told that there was an empty gamekeeper's cottage they could rent as a temporary refuge—most fitting because an abbey had been founded here by King Athelstan in 964.[22] Fr Aelred jumped at this chance to get away from London.

On September 30, a week before the start of the Boer War, the community, consisting of the Superior, Br Henry and Br George, made the slow train-journey to Blandford, where they were driven to their new home, up and down hill for nine miles. For the first three days they slept on bare boards, for their furniture had not arrived from Lower Guiting. Had it not been for a box of provisions sent on in advance by Sister Mary Pauline, there would have been nothing to eat. Frugal meals were cooked over an open fire.

"The Retreat"—the name given to the little cottage—was enclosed on all sides by a dense beech wood, and approached by a rough cart-track. The nearest human habitation was some two miles away. In a southerly direction the rolling hills of Dorset hid the waters of the English Channel, about sixteen miles distant, with Poole Harbour visible to the east.

At the same moment that soldiers in South Africa were being put into khaki uniforms to make them less conspicuous, Fr Aelred decided to make his monks more noticeable. A white tunic was substituted for the black garment worn hitherto, but the black scapular, cowl or cloak were retained. To differentiate the brethren from Cistercians, the leather belt was worn beneath the scapular instead of around it. Sandals were still the correct footgear. The traditional Trappist sign-language was introduced, also the singing of the *Salve Regina* after Compline throughout the year—another Cistercian custom. An English translation of the Abbot de Rancé's *Traité de la sainteté des devoirs de la vie monastique* became the ideal of the spiritual life.

Permission having been obtained from the Lord of the Manor, Sir Everard Hambro, the brethren were able to use the choir of the pre-Reformation Abbey for the nocturnal function at Christmas.[23] Br Henry recalled that "dim and ghostly looked the great church at that hour. Far away at the high altar twinkled the two altar-lights; while at the end of the vast choir a few candles shed their feeble rays throwing heavy shadow in the aisles and transepts." A *Missa Cantata* followed Matins, during which a cloud of incense filled this ancient shrine of Benedictine monks from the tenth to the sixteenth century. Lauds having been chanted the brethren made their way back to their cottage-monastery through the dark night.

THE CHAPEL, THE RETREAT, MILTON ABBAS, DORSET, 1899

The *décor*, typical of Anglo-Catholicism at the turn of the century, also found
expression in the chapel at Painsthorpe Abbey, opened in 1902.

The mist lay heavy among the trees. They lost their way, and it was well into the morning when they got home.

Although Fr Aelred and his handful of monks liked to think they were re-living up to a point, the sort of Benedictine life led at Milton Abbey for six-hundred years, plus later Reformed Cistercian accretions, they saw no reason to revert to the Middle Ages when it came to furnishing a little wooden chapel. This was erected in the garden of "The Retreat" during the 217 days that Baden Powell and his troops were forced to lead a strictly enclosed life in the town of Mafeking which was being besieged by the Boers.

There was no question of asking Mr Ninian Comper to design an "English Altar", like those at Cantley, St Mary Magdalene's, Paddington, Malvern Link, and Downside Abbey; or to find a benefactor to donate a suspended pyx for reservation. Fr Aelred preferred to fall into line with contemporary Anglo-Catholic fashions, which Percy Dearmer had just denounced in the first edition of his *Parson's Handbook*. He would have been shocked by the veiled box-like tabernacle set in a tall gradine, above which was an exposition throne, even more by the fourteen candlesticks and flower vases. The deep super-frontal was adorned by a row of bobbins. Mr Comper would have pointed out that the riddel-curtains ought not to project at an angle of 45 degrees, but at right angles to the wall, in accordance with medieval precedent. Fr Aelred, however, could have replied that this was merely copying the accessories of the high altar in the church of Mount St Bernard's Abbey. Plaster statuettes of Our Lady and St Bernard of Clairvaux, resting on brackets at either side of the tiny sanctuary, helped to create a devotional Catholic atmosphere.

Unlike Fr Ignatius, Fr Aelred did not take the line that his monastic chapel was exempt from episcopal jurisdiction. He sought and obtained permission from Dr John Wordsworth, Bishop of Salisbury, for the celebration of the Holy Communion therein. A minister, in the person of the Rev. Alban Baverstock, rector Hinton Martel, was licensed to perform such other offices and services of the Church of England as were specified in the licence. He came over to minister to the monks about once a month, otherwise they could only hear Mass on Sundays in the parish church at Milton Abbas, unless a priest happened to be staying with them.

People in Dorset were just as curious about these black and white robed Anglican Benedictines as their ancestors had been in regard to the French Trappists after they settled at Lulworth in 1794, but no Protestant opposition was aroused as had been the case at Lower Guiting. From time to time gifts of eggs, fruit and vegetables were made to the community by neighbours. Friends and associates felt it worth while to make the long journey involved in reaching the remote "Retreat". Among them was the then seventeen year-old Compton Mackenzie.[24]

The Abbot of Llanthony was still keeping very much in the public eye, denouncing Anglican bishops, deans, and other clergymen for preaching heresy, although he could now hardly claim to be in communion with them. On New Year's Day he issued an encyclical in the form of a Message to the People of Britain, which was printed verbatim in the *Hereford Times*. He warned them of "the Spirit of Unbelief in the National Church", and bade them go forth to quell it "by a determined rally round their Bible and the sacred creeds of Christendom". Shortly before this he announced that the Syrian-Jacobite Patriarch of the God-protected City of Antioch and of all the Domain of the Apostolic Throne had suggested his consecration as Archbishop and Metropolitan of a British Old Catholic Church.[25] Apparently the Abbot declined the honour, feeling that he could not sever himself altogether from his beloved National Church so long as she retained the Nicene Creed as her test of orthodoxy. Taken all round, the life he continued to lead had very little in common with that of any other abbots in England, or those of previous centuries.

The half-a-dozen black-and-white robed brethren in their tiny cottage monastery in the heart of Dorset heard no call to go round the countryside converting the masses. It was enough to feel that they had revived more or less the same observances started by the Cistercians at Bindon and Ford Abbeys in the twelfth century, and so put back the clock eight-hundred years. For the moment there was no urge to recreate the later medieval form of Benedictine life as led at Abbotsbury, Milton Abbey, and Sherborne. This must wait until vocations increased.

Having no desire to leave "The Retreat", it was a shock to Fr Aelred to be informed that new owners would require the cottage for estate purposes, shortly after he had renewed the annual lease. While the community were wondering what to do next, a letter arrived from the Rev. W. Done Bushell, the owner of Caldey Island, off the coast of South Wales, saying that he was prepared to offer them a temporary home in the dwelling house adjoining a pre-Reformation priory, if they would agree to work in the gardens and be paid wages. The strange thing was that the patron saint of Milton Abbey was Samson, who in the sixth century had been Abbot of Caldey. This in itself was enough to convince the monks of the supernatural source of this invitation from a clergyman whom they had never heard of previously. God was indeed moving in a mysterious way His wonders to perform. Fr Aelred replied that he would like to discuss matters as soon as possible, and left Dorset very early on the morning of November 8, bound for Tenby, where the steamer *Firefly* was waiting to transport him to the island.

It was a case of love at first sight. Here was indeed the ideal home for the community. Romance got the better of realism, just as had been the case with the Rev. J. L. Lyne when he first beheld the ruins of Llanthony Priory in 1861. Fr Aelred was absolutely convinced that the brethren must migrate to Inis-Pyr—the Welsh name for Caldey—so steeped was it in monastic associations. Mr Bushell's offer was accepted, although the little community was on the rocks financially, without a penny to pay for the removal. But the angels stepped in, in the form of the estate agent agreeing to hand over £100 if the cottage were vacated by March 1900.

Christmas came, but without a Midnight Mass. The monks chanted Matins and Lauds in their little chapel. Fr Aelred, although merely a layman from the point of view of Anglican canon law, felt that the end justified the means, and exposed the Blessed Sacrament in a monstrance. There would have certainly been protests from Dr John Wordsworth, Bishop of Salisbury, if he had heard of this function. Although an enthusiastic worker in the cause of Reunion with the Old Catholic and Swedish Churches, he would have pointed out that there was no precedent for a layman lifting up and carrying about the Consecrated Element of Bread in a private chapel. The episcopal reprimand would have been written in the manner of his *De succesione episcoporum in ecclesia* (1890), and *De validitate ordinum anglicanorum* (1894).

On January 10, the community, now increased to five, drove to Dorchester, fourteen miles distant, whence they travelled by train to Tenby through the night, with more than one change. The *Firefly* rolled, for there had been a storm, and one of the monks was sea-sick. The long-bearded Mr Bushell welcomed the brethren as they stepped ashore. He remained on the island until the term started at Harrow, where he was a housemaster, celebrating the Holy Eucharist in both the Old Priory and Village churches. Before leaving, he consecrated a large

169

number of hosts so that Fr Aelred could give communion to himself and his monks. This also enabled them to enjoy the service known later to Anglo-Catholics as "Devotions", for a monstrance had been brought from Milton Abbas.

The six young Benedictines felt that they had "come home" when they glanced at the east window of the chancel in the Priory Church, the centre of which had a medal of St Benedict in stained glass. Br Henry wrote in his diary: "How the very stones of the vaulted roof seemed to take their share in the praise of God, multiplying our voices and re-echoing our notes till it seemed as if the old dwellers of the long-deserted cloister had returned, and were blending their voices with ours to welcome our arrival on this hallowed spot".

Caldey was indeed a holy island—an island of saints. While the six Anglican Benedictines recited the seventeenth-century *Breviarium Monasticum* they fancied they heard the voices of the sixth-century saints Briocus, David, Gildas, Illtud, Machutus, Paul Aurelian, Samson, and many more Celtic monks—not forgetting Pirus "an excellent man and a holy priest"—mingling with theirs. To swell the invisible chorus there were also the ghostly voices of the medieval Tironian Benedictines, who had come to Caldey from the Abbey of St Dogmael, near Cardigan, in the twelfth century. For nearly a thousand years Caldey Island had been monastic. "From about 450 to 1530 it was the chosen Home of Peace—peace broken then by the storm which the sacrilegious tyrant raised against it in the sixteenth century, when the Monks were dispossessed, their Monastery seized, and their peace silenced."[26]

Mr Bushell had assured his monastic employees that he regarded them as part of "the family of St Benedict", and that he was quite satisfied with their "unique position in relation to the see of Canterbury". So Fr Aelred and his brethren had no doubt that they were the successors of the Celtic sailor-monks who "in this remote spot, in those remote times had chanted the praises of God, telling forth the glorious Gospel of the grace of God, and by their lives commended it to a wider world than theirs".[27]

The whole atmosphere was so stimulating that they could almost hear the prophet Isaiah crying out: "Ancient ruins shall be rebuilt and sites long desolate restored; they shall repair the ruined cities and restore what has long lain desolate. . . . And so, because shame in double measure and jeers and insults have been my people's lot, they shall receive in their own land a double measure of wealth, and everlasting joy shall be theirs."[28]

The first thing to do was to vest the altar in the barrel-vaulted chancel of the Priory Church with a frontal, add six candlesticks, and a large tabernacle, surmounted by an exposition throne, its white curtain draped gracefully from a brass corona.

Storms raged over Inis Pyr during January 1901. Queen Victoria died on the 22nd of that month. A national day of mourning was observed throughout Britain on the feast of the Purification of St Mary the Virgin, February 2. The monks chanted the *Officium Defunctorum* for the repose of her soul. Nearly all the layfolk resident in the village attended Vespers of the Dead, most of them garbed in black. Br Henry recorded: "Music practices have been started for the men, to teach them plainchant—if only at the same time we could teach them Personal Religion!" Lantern lectures were given in Lent, and the men told that they could come in their working clothes.

Yet strange to say Fr Aelred soon found it impossible to feed and clothe his community of six bachelors on their weekly wages of 16s each, for an eight hour day, which Mr Bushell had agreed to pay them. A rent-free house, milk, and vegetables had also been thrown in. Before very long only three monks at a time were able to devote themselves to manual labour out of doors. They soon tired of digging, hoeing and weeding, especially in stormy weather. Unpaid bills accumulated. Benefactors were few and far between.

The Bushell family took over their Victorian mansion for the Easter holidays, and the Benedictines had to move into the cramped quarters of the medieval Gate House. By this time Fr Aelred had made up his mind that Caldey must be the permanent home of his community, so he launched an appeal to build a wooden monastery, with a cloister sixty feet square. The site chosen was above Paul Jones Bay. Images of Our Lady and St Benedict were buried there in a box. He also planned to erect a statue of Our Lady Star of the Sea on the cliff above the stone quarries. The estimate given was £1,500, but the response to the appeal was disappointing. People showed little interest. On the other hand Lord Halifax wrote that he might be able to buy "an old monastic foundation" on the mainland and present it to the community.

One of the curates at Tenby came over on Maundy Thursday to celebrate the Holy Communion, after which the brethren kept watch before an Altar of Repose. On Good Friday Mr Bushell performed the Mass of the Presanctified in Latin. For some reason he was unable to carry out the long liturgical function on the morning of Easter Eve, or even to read the Ante-Communion service from the Book of Common Prayer.

The financial situation went from bad to worse. Novenas to the Holy Ghost and the Sacred Heart failed to reduce the £60 overdraft at the Bank, or to pay the ever rising pile of bills. On the feast of Corpus Christi Mr Bushell, vested in a cope, carried the monstrance during the outdoor procession. "The whole service was most devotional", one of the monks wrote, "and everybody exceedingly reverent, which is a good beginning to teach them the whole Faith of the Church". Very different, however, was the behaviour of a party of "Romans" who came over from Tenby with their parish priests. The ladies were extremely annoyed when told that it would violate enclosure for them to enter the Priory Church. The monks "hurried them out of the way with little ceremony".

The months of August and September had to be spent in three second-hand bell-tents that leaked badly. The "refectory" and "kitchen" were in the open air, unprotected by canvas. It was only Br Martin who managed to keep dry on nights when it rained, for he slept in a disused hen-house. No matter what was the weather the brethren walked from the pine woods to the Priory Church, carrying lanterns, so that they could recite Matins and Lauds at 2 a.m., followed by intercessions for seafarers. Br Samson was clothed as a novice, and Br George made his simple profession on August 30.

On September 7 Fr Aelred and Br Samson went off to stay with Lord Halifax in Yorkshire. They returned with the news that he hoped to buy Caldey with the help of the English Church Union. Its secretary, Mr H. W. Hill, visited the island shortly afterwards. His report was not encouraging, for it pointed out difficulties not suspected by the ever-optimistic Halifax. The latter then proposed to raise a loan of £15,000 on the title deeds of Caldey. Mr Bushell would be paid a sum not exceeding £10,000, leaving him the free use of the mansion adjoining the medieval Priory for his lifetime. Mr Hill raised no objections to this scheme. Meanwhile the overdraft at the Bank had soared to £400, and the unpaid bills to close on £100. Fr Aelred had not realised that leading the purely contemplative life on this small island would prove so costly, even with the help of the wages paid to his monks by Mr Bushell.[29]

During the autumn of 1901 many strange things began to happen after the monks had resumed residence at the Priory mansion, for which no natural explanation could be found. Heavy steps were heard at night in the passages. Doors opened and shut by invisible hands. Fr Aelred was not the only one who was certain that he had met a ghostly black habited Benedictine in the lane leading up to the Priory from the village, reminiscent of the spectre seen by Dr Lee at Laleham, and who followed Fr Ignatius and his community in 1870.[30]

There was no Mass at Christmas for lack of a priest, however Vespers were sung with copes. Fr Aelred exposed the Blessed Sacrament before Matins and Lauds, after which there was a solemn procession of the Bambino around the little garth. Daily Exposition throughout the Octave of Christmas helped to create a Catholic atmosphere.

On the feast of the Epiphany, 1902, the monks had to face up to the fact that their unpaid bills amounted to £140. Lord Halifax had been unable to relieve the situation. There appeared to be no possibility of building the temporary wooden monastery, far less of rebuilding even one of the dozen Cistercian abbeys in Wales, or the Benedictine monastery of St Dogmael's, which had been dreamed of twelve months before. No hope of making these dry bones live again. Fr Aelred feared he would have to "sell up" and return to London. Br Henry recorded: "The professed will have to don secular clothes and obtain employment in the city to keep the home together. The novices will thus be free for training. We are writing this with an appeal for the necessary expenses to our few friends, and asking Lord Halifax to write to the papers, asking for the lease of a suitable house within ten miles of London. This seems to be the only alternative to disbanding, which none of us will consider for a moment."

Then came a suggestion from Fr Herbert Kelly, Founder and Director of the Society of the Sacred Mission, that it might suit the Benedictines to move from South Wales to South Africa. They would be able to assist a few members of his own community to lay the foundations of missionary work in the Orange Free State. This invitation, like that of the previous one two years before to go to Zululand, tempted the ever adventurous Aelred, but it was turned down as was the invitation from Ignatius to migrate to Llanthony.

Lord Halifax wrote on February 1 that he had asked his agent how long it would take to prepare Painsthorpe Hall, situated in the parish of Kirby Underdale, Yorkshire, for the reception of the monks, if they cared to occupy it. Fr Aelred decided that under the circumstances there was nothing else to be done. The community annalist commented: "So ends all our hope of permanency on this Island. *In omnibus glorificetur* Deus!"

After this Fr Aelred told the talented Br Malachy to write in medieval script with illuminated capital letters a so-called "Charter", stating that the seven monks had elected him to be their Abbot, believing him "to be fitted for that Office by reason of his piety, zeal, and discretion". This document would be sent to Dr Temple, Archbishop of Canterbury, requesting his confirmation of the election. On February 23 it was signed by the brethren and witnessed by Mr Bushell as a Clerk in Holy Orders, and posted to Lambeth Palace.[31]

Mr Bushell preached a final sermon, in which he stated quite frankly how disappointed he was that the monks had been unable to support themselves by paid manual labour on the island, for he had done his best to help them in every way possible.

NOTES

[1] Cf. Article in *Pax*. No. 31, p. 574.

[2] Joseph Rene Vilatte (1854-1929) was born in France, where he was brought up as a Catholic. He went to Canada as a youth, and changed his religious affiliation many times, with four returns to the Church of his baptism. In 1885 he was ordained deacon and priest by Dr Herzog, Christian Catholic Bishop in Switzerland. After this he ministered to lapsed Belgian Roman Catholics in the Protestant Episcopalian Diocese of Fond du Lac. Next he indulged in a short flirtation with the Russian Orthodox Church after Bishop Grafton had refused to consecrate him as Bishop-Abbot of the American Old Catholics. After this he toyed with the idea of returning to communion with Rome. In 1892 he managed to get raised to the episcopate by Julius Alvarez, who styled himself Metropolitan of the Independent Catholic Church of Goa, Ceylon and India. Claiming that this consecration has been approved by the Syrian-Jacobite Patriarch of Antioch, Vilatte returned to the U.S.A. calling himself "Mar Timotheos". The next six years were spent mainly in trying to spread schism among expatriated Polish Catholics by providing them with priests and bishops. He also tried to set up schismatic churches in England, France, and Italy. In 1915 he launched what was known as the American Catholic Church, and sponsored more than one schismatic sect. In 1925, having returned to France, he made his final submission to the Roman Church. His last years were spent at a monastery of the Cistercians of the Common Observance near Versailles, but even there he could not resist conferring irregular orders on one of the novices. After his death he was buried as a layman. (Cf. H. R. T. Brandreth, *Episcopi Vagantes and the Anglican Church,* (2nd ed. 1961), pp. 47-69; P. F. Anson, *Bishops at Large* (1964), pp. 91-129.)

[3] A possible explanation for Vilatte taking the trouble to visit Llanthony Abbey could be that having heard that Ignatius was able to rake in money by his missions, it would be to his own advantage to get on the right side of a "goose that laid golden eggs". During his long career "Mar Timotheos" had no scruples about insinuating himself on any individual or organisation capable of assisting him financially. Unfortunately, however, he never backed a winner, and in the end had to fall back on the Church of Rome to provide him with an eventide-home.

[4] *The Recent Ordination of Fr Ignatius at Llanthony Abbey,* reported from the *Hereford Times* (1898), pp. 9-10.

[5] Vilatte had never regarded himself as subject to the Syrian-Jacobite Patriarch of Antioch since his consecration in Ceylon in 1892, and it is possible that the patriarchal bull was forged.

[6] Some years later this monk, having reverted to lay-life, was re-ordained by Dr Winnington-Ingram, Bishop of London.

[7] See p. 61.

[8] Fr Ignatius was only 61 in 1898, so it is curious that each of these writers refers to him as a "dear old man".

[9] *Hampshire Post,* October 24, 1908.

[10] Dr Temple at the age of seventy-seven seems to have had very vague ideas of his metropolitan powers of jurisdiction if he believed that he possessed the authority to license a monastic chaplain in the Rochester Diocese.

[11] Cf. *The Benedictines of Caldey,* p. 41.

[12] Athelstan Riley, Seigneur de la Trinité on the Isle of Jersey, born in 1858, was one of the chief lay-leaders of the Catholic Movement in the Church of England throughout his long life. In 1887 he published *Athos, or the Mountain of the Monks.* He took a keen interest in the revival of Anglican Benedictine life until his death. (See pp. 210, 225.)

[13] Dr John Gott had been Vicar of Leeds and later Dean of Worcester. He succeeded Dr Wilkinson as Bishop of Truro in 1891.

[14] ibid, p. 42. The island mentioned was probably St Helen's where there are ruins of a medieval church, dedicated to St Illiad; also traces of circular and rectangular cells, and the boundary wall of a sixth-century Celtic monastery.

It was hardly likely that Thomas Algernon Smith-Dorrien-Smith of Tresco Abbey would have welcomed monks on his island, or allowed them to rebuild the priory of St Nicholas, founded by the Benedictines of Tavistock Abbey about 1085.

[15] The book was published in 1903, the same year as that of his reception into the Roman Church, after five years with the Community of the Resurrection at Mirfield.

[16] op. cit., pp. 109-26.

[17] Similar apparitions were also a feature of life at Llanthony. Innumerable manifestations of evil spirits, sometimes noisy and malicious, or just mischievous and silly, were recorded.

[18] op. cit., (6th ed.), pp. xvi-xvii.

[19] ibid, pp. 184-5.

[20] Cf. *The Benedictines of Talacre,* p. 4.

[21] The latter had first met Carlyle at Ealing in 1892, and kept in touch with him while he was at St Paul's School, where he was Compton Mackenzie's great friend—the prototype in after years of "the voluble Chator" in the novel *Sinister Street.*

[22] It was suppressed by Henry VIII. Most of the conventual buildings were taken down in 1771, and replaced by a stately mansion, but the choir, transepts and tower of the abbey church were left intact.

[23] Services seldom took place in the Abbey because the parish church was more convenient for the villagers.

[24] "The Retreat" was thinly disguised as "Clere Abbey on the Berkshire Downs" in his novels *Sinister Street* (1913) and *The Altar Steps* (1922), although he had denied this. "Dom Cuthbert Manners, O.S.B." is almost prophetic of what Dom Aelred Carlyle became ten years later. We are told that the monks were "so strict that St Benedict himself, were he to abide again on earth, would seriously consider a revision of his rules as interpreted by Dom Cuthbert Manners, O.S.B., the Lord Abbot of Clere".

[25] It is more probable that this proposal was made by Mar Timotheos, and if not, then, from Mar Julius (Alvarez), head of the Independent Catholic Church of Ceylon, Goa and India.

[26] *The Benedictines of Caldey Island* (1907), p. 44.

[27] ibid.

[28] Isaiah 61 : 4, 7 (New English Bible).

[29] For some reason he had felt it a duty to settle the debts of a quasi-Old Catholic Benedictine brotherhood, founded by his friend Henry Bernard Ventham, whom he had first met at St Austin's Priory, Walworth, and who later on was a frequent guest at Malling Abbey. Having been a novice at Llanthony, he appears to have seen nothing inconsistent in combining the status of a Roman Catholic layman with that of an Anglican lay-reader in the Diocese of Bath and Wells. Having been raised to the priesthood (probably by "Mar Timotheos"), and adopted the religious name of Columba Mary, he tried to found a Benedictine community, sponsored by Fr O'Halloran, the suspended Roman Catholic priest at Ealing. The first novice was a lapsed Papist, who had been dismissed from the novitiate at Erdington Abbey, near Birmingham, known as Br Ambrose. The two monks were unable to pay for the furnishings of their oratory, so Dom Columba vanished and lay low, and Br Ambrose fled to Caldey Island, where he persuaded Fr Aelred to deal with the demands made by the creditors. After this Ambrose sailed from Caldey on a ketch bound for Bideford, with the intention of being "put right" at Buckfast Abbey. He changed his mind, however, and entered into communion with Canterbury.

[30] The ghost-monk on Caldey was said to have been seen at intervals in later years. Carlyle himself had taken a keen interest in psychic phenomena since boyhood, e.g. automatic writing, crystal-gazing, hypnotism, and poltergeists. He was certain of what Theosophites call the "astral" or "etheric" body. He used to relate how he and his sister had been present at the death of another sister, when they actually saw her "etheric body" poised above her "carnal body". These were connected by a kind of umbilical cord, which snapped as the astral body floated away.

[31] The signatures were those of Brothers Henry Watts, George Chambers, Augustine Green, Placidus Cooper, Samson Carrington, Malachy Matthews, and David Tugwell.

CHAPTER XI

Fr Aelred and his monks at Painsthorpe Abbey, Yorkshire; his blessing as abbot and ordination to the priesthood; erection of "The English Congregation of the Strict Observance of the Holy Rule of St Benedict"; the monks remain mendicants; the first solemn professions; and the failure to obtain possession of Llanthony Abbey (1902-1906)

ON the morning of March 4, 1902, Fr Aelred, six monks, two oblates, and two St Bernard puppies, boarded the *Firefly*, crossed over from Caldey to Tenby, and set off on the fifteen hours' journey to Stamford Bridge. Then followed a seven miles drive to Painsthorpe Hall, situated on the western slopes of the Yorkshire Wolds. The Rev. W. R. Shepperd, rector of Kirby Underdale, and some of his flock were waiting to welcome the monastic tenants. Fires were burning, lamps were lit, and a substantial meal all ready.

The first reactions were that it was a pity that Painsthorpe Hall did not look like a proper monastery. It was merely a plain, square-shaped, two-storied red brick house, with six bedrooms. Surrounding it were well-stocked vegetable gardens and a wooded meadow. A small farm went with the property, which stood 700 feet above sea-level, protected from the east winds by the hills rising behind it. These amenities suggested that ere long the brethren would be able to become true monks, and live by the labour of their hands, as laid down in the Holy Rule, which had proved impossible on Caldey Island. If local conditions or poverty should require them to get in the crops themselves, they need not be distressed. The fact that the community had arrived on the feast of St Aelred of Rievaulx, whose ruined monastery was about twenty miles distant, was in itself a propitious omen. Another presage was a telegram worded: "Just paid into your account £200", and signed "An Irish Protestant". Unfortunately a letter soon followed, explaining that it was only a loan. Six years passed before the Ulsterman was repaid by the brethren.

They waited nearly twelve weeks for Archbishop Temple to return the document, requesting him to confirm the election of Fr Aelred as abbot. It did not arrive until the end of May. Beside the already engrossed cross was the signature "Approved F. Cantuar". A subsequent "History of the Community" recorded: "It is difficult to describe the thankfulness with which the Abbot and his Community received the document which gave them at last an assured status. They went into their chapel, and with grateful hearts sung their *Te Deum* of thankfulness to Him who had given them their desire. Their purpose had never been in the nature of a private venture. It had been undertaken soberly, and it had sought at every stage the sanction of authority. Their endeavour had not been wanting in courage and resolution, but it had ever been loyal to Catholic order and discipline. And now, after nine years of preparation, the Primate conferred on the Superior the rank and title of Abbot, and gave the Community the right to exist as a fully authorized Community in the English Church, thus fulfilling the promise made in 1898. . . . For the Archbishop's signature meant nothing more than the sanction-

THE PRIORY, GLENGALL ROAD, ISLE OF DOGS, 1896–1898

To create the impression that its inmates were "enclosed", a high wooden fence was erected in front.

PAINSTHORPE ABBEY, YORKSHIRE, 1902–1906

Merely a plain, square-shaped, two-storied brick house. Surrounding it were a well-stocked vegetable garden and a wooded meadow.

ing with the authority of the See of Canterbury the revival of the Benedictine Order in the English Church."[1]

Whether the now eighty-one year-old Dr Temple believed that he had revived the Order of St Benedict in *Ecclesia Anglicana* by approving of "the election of Brother Aelred Carlyle, Founder of the Community of Brothers living under the Rule of St Benedict to be their Abbot"—as was stated in the schedule—is doubtful. No matter: the Abbot-elect wrote on May 28: "Your Sanction means a great deal to us, and men can now come to us for the Religious Life who might otherwise have sought it outside our own Communion".[2]

There happen to be several canonical irregularities in connection with this so-called "Charter", which probably did not strike Fr Aelred and his monks. Although his election took place within the Diocese of St David s, which was then a unit of the Canterbury Province, arrangements had already been made for the removal of the community to the Archdiocese of York within a fortnight. Such being the case, the schedule ought to have been signed by the Local Ordinary of the diocese in which the Abbot-elect would be domiciled. Mr Bushell, as a clerk in holy orders, who witnessed the signatures, must have forgotten that the Archbishop of Canterbury is without primatial jurisdiction in the Northern Province. To be valid, the "Charter" ought to have been signed by "William Ebor" instead of by "F. Cantuar". Since each Archbishop, within his own Province, has the right of confirming the election of every person to a bishopric, the same rule could apply equally well to an abbacy.

On the other hand, the Community might have pleaded that the restoration of the Benedictine Order in the post-Reformation *Ecclesia Anglicana* had been effected by reason of the provisions made in the terms of the statute of 25 Henry VIII, which gave to the Primate of All England or his commissary the authority to grant such privileges extended to such as had been accustomed to hold at the See of Rome, or by authority thereof, or of any prelate of the realm. In the sixteenth century the Archbishop of Canterbury and the reigning Sovereign were substituted for the Pope. Lambeth replaced Rome as the source of many privileges and dispensations.[3]

Another point which may not have been remembered by "The Community of Brothers living under the Rule of St Benedict" is that an Act of Parliament (1536) made provision for the reigning Sovereign to re-found religious communities as well as to suppress them. To be on the safe side the parties concerned ought to have consulted His Majesty King Edward VII, to make sure that he would confirm this new abbacy in Yorkshire. It could have been explained that Abbot Carlyle did not, for the moment, expect a seat in the House of Lords, as the sole *de facto* successor of the pre-Reformation abbots of *Ecclesia Anglicana*.[4]

As patron of the living of Kirby Underdale, Lord Halifax had chosen an old-fashioned High Churchman, in the person of the Rev. W. R. Shepperd, to minister to his tenants. Relations between him and the monks could not have been more amicable, for the latter soon began to take part in parochial activities. The Abbot's medical training helped to break down any lingering suspicion against these bachelors wearing black and white garments. On Sundays the community attended All Saints' Church, both for the "Early Service" and the Choral Eucharist, returning again for Sung Evensong.

After six months Mr Shepherd wrote to Lord Halifax: "From the time of their arrival at Painsthorpe, the Brothers have worked most cordially and loyally with me, anxious to help in every way they can, and to strengthen the influence of the Church. Their singing in the choir has greatly improved the services, both in musical character and in reverence; and the teaching of the children by the Abbot

Q

and Br Augustine has been most valuable and successful. But apart from this active parochial work, the quiet witness of their lives, the constant round of prayer and praise, their regular attendance at the Sunday services and frequent reception of Holy Communion, have been an immeasurable influence for good, not only in the parish, but over the whole district where they are now well known and appreciated."

It began to look as if this small Benedictine brotherhood would soon be accepted as an integral part of Anglican churchmanship in Yorkshire, like the Community of the Resurrection. During Holy Week 1902, Fr Hugh Benson came over from Mirfield to hear the monks' confessions, his first and only visit to Painsthorpe. Abbot Aelred felt it worth while to call at Buckfast Abbey about this time, and was surprised that Abbot Boniface Natter was almost rude to him. Some of the monks laughed at this apparition in black and white—from their point of view—pretending to be a Benedictine abbot.

One of the first visitors to the Yorkshire abbey was a young man named John C. Hawes, at that date a student of the Lincoln *Scholae Cancellarii*, who had been trained as an architect, and already dreaming of becoming an Anglican Franciscan. He turned up on a March evening, having walked seven miles through deep snow from Stamford Bridge station.

"Everything surpassed my expectations", he wrote long after. "I longed to join the community then and there for the sake of the monastic life, but felt I could not because for me the religious life meant definitely the Franciscan form of it and nothing else. . . . The Abbot saw that I was of a yielding, subjective nature, easily influenced and handled. But he did not reckon how absolutely and uncompromising I could be on a matter of real principle, so we never got down to definite conclusions."[5] Having failed to persuade Hawes to enter the novitiate, the Abbot asked him to prepare designs for a chapel. The foundation stone was laid in June 1902, and it was dedicated on November 11, the feast of St Martin of Tours.

Compared with the church at Llanthony Abbey it was a very humble affair, built of red brick, and linked up to the house by a passage which served as a cloister. The white-washed brick interior pre-dated Percy Dearmer's similar treatment of the choir and sanctuary at St Mary's, Primrose Hill, London, by two months. The furnishings, however, would have disgusted the author of *The Parson's Handbook*, a revised and enlarged edition of which appeared in February 1903. Abbot Aelred saw no reason to fall into line with the so-called "English Use", or to recreate the austerity of early Cistercian ritual and ceremonial. The altar, vested with a silk frontal and super frontal, was surmounted by a tall gradine decorated by six Gothic-shaped panels. In its centre was a large box-like curtained tabernacle, on which rested the crucifix. The tabernacle also served as the exposition throne. A silk veil was draped from a brass corona, above which was enthroned a painted plaster statuette of St Bernard of Clairvaux—a relic of the chapel at Milton Abbas. Six brass candlesticks stood on the gradine, holding dummy candles, with shields on top, into which were fixed bits of real candles. The décor was completed by a brocade dossal and riddel-curtains, projecting at an angle, as was then the fashion. A wooden grille fitted into the round archway dividing the choir from the small narthex allowed seculars a peep of the monks in the stalls, and stressed the idea of strict enclosure.[6]

Feeling that the moment had come for more publicity, Abbot Aelred published an illustrated brochure in June 1903. Entitled *The Benedictine Monastery, Painsthorpe, Kirby Underdale, York,* it conveyed the general impression that these monks were sound Anglican churchmen, without a trace of Romanism in their

THE CHAPEL, PAINSTHORPE ABBEY, YORKSHIRE
Designed by J. C. Hawes, and opened in 1902.
179

outlook and observances. Lord Halifax contributed a Foreword, stressing that the principles on which the revived Benedictine Order were based might provide "the true solution of the many social problems which perplex the present generation".

Mr Shepherd wrote enthusiastically of the marvellous work done by the monks among the children and lads of the village. The daily round of life at the monastery was "a silent witness, more eloquent than words, for the Higher Life, so easily neglected and forgotten by those who are absorbed in every day cares". He was "deeply thankful" that the brethren had come to his parish, and hoped they would be permanent residents. Church-people were assured that "the Tone of the Community" was "calm, restful and strong", with "no trace of excitement"; also that "the Life was full of verve", for there were "no sentimental idlers". An important point—"the Rule of the Community", had stood "the test of 1,378 years". There was no sign of "slackness" anywhere. The Rector could vouch that the "Sympathies of the Community" were "wide and deep". He had failed to find any "trace of Selfishness" among their good monks. They had "no intention or need to be always begging", yet they did require immediately at least £500 "to develop means of self-support".

Charles Lindley Wood, second Viscount Halifax, President of the English Church Union, an Ecclesiastical Commissioner for England, who had been Groom of the Bedchamber to King Edward VII when he was Prince of Wales, enjoyed playing the part of *grand seigneur* to the Benedictine tenants on his Garrowby estates. Normally he resided at Hickleton Hall, near Doncaster, but when he was staying in the East Riding, distinguished guests were always driven over to Painsthorpe to pay their respects to the young Abbot. As he claimed to be the *de jure* Earl of Mar, there was an even stronger reason for him to be treated as a landed gentleman, in keeping with late medieval abbatial status.[7]

Lord Halifax explained to his friends that this community had been founded by the venerable Primate of All England, ninety-sixth successor of St Augustine of Canterbury, so it held a unique position in the Establishment. Indeed he took a keen interest in his "pet monks", having already presented them with a cow and a horse to start farming. Another visitor to the monastery was Sir Tatton Sykes, fifth Baronet, who, now past the age of eighty, rode over from Sledmere to discuss both church-building and horse-breeding.

Yet strange to say, during the four-and-a-half years the community lived in Yorkshire, the only members of the world-wide Anglican hierarchy who called on them were Dr Grafton, Bishop of Fond du Lac, Wisconsin, and Dr Richardson, who had resigned the see of Zanzibar in 1901. Although the Archbishop of York's palace was only fourteen miles distant from the abbey, he never made even an unofficial visitation.

Lord Halifax wrote to Lord Stanmore on October 16, 1903: "I think that Fr Aelred and his people—so far as I can judge—are perfectly simple. The *religious life,* which after all, in its essence, does not vary very much with time and place, is their object. Such work as they do or may come to them occupies the second place. Their life is not for the sake of the work, but the work grows out of it and is possible on account of the life.[8] Five weeks later he wrote: "So many novices are applying that we must beg, borrow or steal £2,000 to provide accommodation".

One work which had grown out of the life was vestment making. Two of the monks had presided over a stall at the Art Exhibition during the Bristol Church Congress that same October. Protestant visitors were horrified. *The Record* reported: "Their 'get-up' is painfully like that of the Roman Order. Their heads are shaven, they wear beneath their cloaks a vestment of white serge, and suspended from their girdles are strings of beads. They would not be at all flattered if they heard the criticisms passed on them."[9] Even more revolting was "an extremely Babyish garment" which Dr Gott, Bishop of Truro, intended to wear in his private chapel at Lis Escop. The editor of *The English Churchman* "hoped that Dr Browne, Bishop of Bristol, would not dare to don the set of 'Low Mass vestments' made by the monks which was to be presented to him".[10]

Ever since May 1902, when Archbishop Temple had confirmed the election of Aelred Carlyle as Abbot, Lord Halifax had wondered how to get him installed and blessed in the traditional medieval manner. Had the parties concerned been content with the letter of the *Rule of St Benedict* Dom Aelred could have assumed office at once after being elected unanimously by his brethren, subject to the approval of the bishop of the diocese in which the monastery was situated. No further formalities were demanded in the sixth century. It was not until many centuries after Benedictine monasticism spread over Europe that abbots began to be blessed with ritual and ceremonial based on that of the consecration of bishops. The Anglican Abbot of Painsthorpe, however, believed that he ought to conform to the prescriptions of post-Tridentine Roman canon law. This laid down that lawfully elected regular abbots *de regimine* (i.e. those governing an independent monastery) must receive the required blessing from the bishop in whose diocese the monastery is located within three months from the date of election. After receiving it, they enjoy the power of conferring the tonsure and minor orders on their own subjects, and certain other privileges.[11]

Abbot Aelred's position was both delicate and difficult, since the formularies of the post-Reformation Church of England made no provision for minor prelates, abbots having been abolished in the sixteenth century. Archbishop Maclagan would have been unwilling to perform the blessing with medieval rites and ceremonies, if asked to do so. He might have hesitated to invite any other bishop in Britain to be his delegate, for fear of arousing Protestant antagonism.[12]

The problems were solved finally after Dr Grafton, Bishop of Fond du Lac, Wisconsin, came to stay with his old friend Lord Halifax at Garrowby.[13] Dr Maclagan, having raised no objections, an impressive function took place in the monastery chapel at Painsthorpe on October 30, 1903. The ornate ritual and ceremonial had to be curtailed, for not being a priest, the newly-blessed Abbot was unable to concelebrate with the Bishop, after he had received the insignia of his office—mitre, crozier, pectoral cross and ring. On his own authority, Dr Grafton ordained Dom Aelred subdeacon after giving him minor orders, even if the subdiaconate is not recognised in Anglican canon law.[14]

The twenty-nine year-old Lord Abbot of Painsthorpe could now feel that he was on a par, not only with the Abbot of Llanthony, but also with the Papist Abbots of Erdington, Ampleforth, Downside, Douai (Woolhampton) and Farnborough who in 1903 were still the only ruling Benedictine abbots in England, the others being titular.[15]

Yet not all was rosy in the garden. When the Archbishop of York had given informal permission to the Benedictine brotherhood to settle in his diocese, he did not think it worth while to investigate its finances. Roman canon law lays down that no religious house may be opened unless it can be prudently foreseen that, from its own income, from customary alms, or from some other source, it will be able adequately to provide for the proper housing and support of the members attached to it. Abbot Aelred had never bothered about canonical regulations affecting the foundation of monasteries, his general idea being that contemplative monks ought to be mendicants, like friars, and should exist mainly on the charity of benefactors. Shortly after the abbatial blessing, the community's bank manager threatened to stop payment of cheques. The overdraft appears to have risen to over £500. After eighteen months it had become clear that it was quite impossible for the brethren to be self-supporting, in spite of their farm, vegetable gardens, rent-free house, handicrafts and many other advantages.

The only thing to do under the circumstances was to appeal to the generous benefactor and landlord to lend them £1,000. Lord Halifax complained to Mr H. W. Hill on January 4, 1904 that the Abbot's request was "very audacious"; adding "it's always a bad sign when people want money on the stand and delivery principle".[16]

Mr Shepperd's opinion that monastic life at Painsthorpe was "calm, restful and strong", with "no trace of excitement" was not altogether true after Br Malachy, who had inscribed and illuminated the much revered "Charter", was arrested by the police on various charges of larceny, and sentenced to nine months' imprisonment. Had Dom Aelred taken the trouble to investigate his previous career, it is improbable that he would have clothed him as a novice of Caldey, for it was nothing if not shady.[17]

It was discovered that Br Malachy had been acting as an *agent provocateur* for the Church Association, and supplied it and other Protestant organisations with "secrets of the cloister" which came in useful for propaganda purposes—just like Br Alban (or Oswald) had done on the Isle of Dogs in 1898.[18]

The Record, The English Churchman, and *The Church Intelligencer*—each violently opposed to Anglo-Catholicism—published lurid revelations of life in this Yorkshire "monkery". Mr Kensit sent a group of his "Poor Preachers" to Painsthorpe Abbey, where they were entertained to tea. After this they ranted and raved against their hosts in the village of Kirby Underdale.

Next came an illustrated pamphlet entitled *Playing at Monks*. Readers got more than enough value for their money what with the hair-raising stories of the Benedictines indulging in idolatry and flagellation. Mr Kensit remarked: "We have little pity for these gentlemen, for they fully deserve the lash . . . their idolatry is appalling. Images abound within and without." The monastery was described as "the last piece of treachery to the Church of England associated with the name of the President of the English Church Union", i.e. Lord Halifax.

The year 1904 was also marked by the publication of *The Life of Father Ignatius, O.S.B., The Monk of Llanthony,* by the Baroness de Bertouch. It contained more tales of the unseen world than were found in Montague James' *Ghost Stories of an Antiquary,* which appeared about the same time. Abbess Hilda of Malling found herself in disrepute for the tale of her self-assertiveness and Ignatius' excommunication of the Feltham nuns was re-told with realistic detail.[19] The Baroness, writing at the Abbot's dictation, left no shadow of doubt that this nun had no conception of the holy obedience she owed to her Major Superior. The last chapter of this 607 pages volume was entitled "Greater Love hath No Man" with the caption:

> " 'Jesus Only' shall be
> My glad watchword here:
> 'Jesus Only' will be
> My only treasure there".

On page 595 was the statement: "According to present dispositions, Father Ignatius bequeaths Llanthony to the people of his prayers—Anglican Monks. Some years back, Lord Halifax assisted into being an Olivetan congregation of Anglo-Benedictines, and later on he gave them as a Settlement a picturesque manor house on his own estate, now known as 'Painsthorpe Abbey'. It is to these religious—so long as there are *two* members of the Order extant to keep the Rule—that Llanthony will eventually pass. Failing them, the property will revert unconditionally to the (Roman) Benedictines of Buckfast Leigh, Devonshire."

The bare fact of the existence of a second Anglican Monkery, is in itself a supplementary crown to the Reverend Father's hardly-won victory. Were the subject less solemn, he would surely be tempted to laugh outright at the "then" and "now" of Time and Bishops, with regard to their ancient and modern toleration of the "absurd dress".

But Father Ignatius is too devoted a Monk to resent this aspect of the question. He merely thanks God that the Shadow which he has given his life to resurrect in his Church is at length assuming flesh and blood development. It matters not to him, that his own hands have had to hew the rocks and dig the paths of the revival. His reward is in the knowledge that these rocks are now foundations, and the paths growing smooth with the tread of sandalled feet. Whether the Church of England is grateful for the gift or not, Father Ignatius has given her back her Monks. Llanthony the Mother House, and Painsthorpe her Benjamin, are stone and mortar monuments of the realisation of this dream.

Some of the illustrations in this monumental biography suggest that life at Llanthony in the reign of Edward VII had not changed much in the thirty years since the foundation of the double-monastery. Ignatius took care that Messrs. Elliott and Fry's photographers recorded the desired devotional effects. One camera-study depicts five monks posed picturesquely around their Abbot in the "Bible Cloister", and is entitled "A Characteristic Group".

Another photograph shows him sitting on a rustic bench in the garden, with two black-hooded monks gazing down demurely at two little boys and one baby girl, holding an umbrella. Evidently the now aged Abbot still found "pleasure and solace in the patter of tiny feet about him", as had been the case forty years previously.[20] No doubt he was still trying to "train and fashion from bud to blossom", oblates of unsullied purity, and "worthy to be numbered among such as are of the Kingdom of Heaven". The frontispiece, signed "Ignatius of Jesus, Monk O.S.B." records him against the carved wooden back of a throne-like settle, robed in a voluminous cowl. He grasps a large rosary with both hands, attached to which is a big metal crucifix. His now white tonsure is brushed up like a crown. The dedication indicates that Dewi-Honddu was still a militant Welsh Nationalist, for it is worded: "Y GWIR YN ERBYN Y BYD—JESUS ONLY PAX. *To every fellow-soul without distinction this volume is dedicated, in the hope that it may interest some, comfort many and help all.*"

In September 1904 Llanthony's "Benjamin" issued the first number of *Pax*, described as "The Quarterly Paper of the Benedictine Community, Painsthorpe", with the explanation that after ten years a magazine had become a necessity for the community to keep in touch with an ever-increasing circle of friends. Bound in stiff green paper, with "olde worlde" gold lettering designed by Br Malachy before he was forced to lead a strictly enclosed life, it was printed by the Society of the Sacred Mission at Kelham. In the Foreword readers gathered: "God may call us in time to come to more active work in His service than at present engages us; but the chief reason for our existence is now, and if we are true to our constitutions, always will be—Prayer, the Work of God, as St Benedict calls it."

Active work outside the enclosure had already started. Having heard that rescue work among boys was badly needed in the Diocese of Worcester, the Abbot had sent Br Austin to Birmingham. The Rev. C. N. Long, Vicar of St Aidan's, Small Heath, assured the monk that a Benedictine reformatory in his parish would be most welcome. This church was a real Catholic stronghold, and its clergy would be able to prepare the lads for the Sacraments. On hearing this, the Abbot came along, met people who had promised financial support for the foundation, and rented a small house five minutes' walk from the church. St Benet's Home for Boys was opened at Michaelmas. There was no lack of the very poorest type to fill it at once. Their ages ranged from ten to thirteen. Brother Austin was put in charge. His first job was to get the boys clean and tidy and then see about their education. An attic was turned into "a very nice Oratory". Here the whole family met every morning for prayers, and their day ended with the recitation of Compline.

Br Austin told readers of *Pax:* "The type of face one sees among the boys here is distinctly better, I should say, than that which is common in the same class in London. They have a bright intelligent look, full of promise of good results if taken in time." He wanted to get hold of them *"before they have been convicted".* In his "Community Letter" the "Br Aelred, O.S.B., *Abbot",* wrote: "The very fact of working this Home by members of a Community who are specially fitted for it, is in itself a departure from most existing methods. The Brothers will live among the boys, and our chief aim, which I wish to emphasise, is to try to make each household a real family. . . . Those we want are the little heathen lads of our great cities whose homes have never been homes for them; whose little lives have been almost animal in their limitations; and who have never known the love of father or mother, or the healthy affection of decent friends." Br Austin stressed that "as a Community we have nothing but ourselves to give", and begged for "furniture, strong chairs; clothes, especially boots for boys; pictures, games, gifts of food and vegetables".

In the December issue of *Pax,* the Brother in Charge of St Benet's gave a detailed account of life at the Home, which included the recitation of the *Horae Diurnae* in the Oratory, for which he wanted: "small harmonium, candle extinguisher, Holy Water stoup, faldstool, pictures, crucifixes, Bibles, Prayer Books, and Hymn Books". But his appeals met with little response, and he was soon released from his monastic obligations.[21] This Benedictine effort to undertake Rescue Work among Birmingham boys was no more successful than the previous one in Gloucestershire.

The truth was that the community lacked both men and money in the summer of 1904. At that moment it mustered only nine monks in simple vows, six novices and two oblates. An idea of the hand-to-mouth existence at Painsthorpe is conveyed by the Abbot's letters and the appeals printed in each issue of *Pax.* He stated in September that no more postulants could be received until "some good Christian" came forward "with the sum of £3,000", which would pay for adding another wing to the house. He explained: "it is hard to refuse suitable men when they ask to try their vocation with us". Still, the vestment work was "going on apace". Br Samson had "almost more orders than he and his two assistants can execute". Even more encouraging was that the St Bernard dogs had "been doing well", and that the monks had "just sold a litter of five pups for £18 10s.". Br David, who had been "looking rather sad lately at the amount of biscuits they eat", felt "well repaid for the time and trouble spent on them". The garden had also been "doing well", though "the climate and land of these North country wolds" were "both unsuitable for anything but the most elementary gardening". Crops had "a trick of staying on the land longer than they ought, and thus delay the appearance of those which should follow on".

The section entitled "Community Needs" began with the explanation: "It must be understood that . . . we have no endowment, and are entirely dependent for our existence on our own work, and what subscriptions and donations are sent to us. Only with great difficulty are we able to meet our current expenses, so that we have nothing to spend on stock and plant, hence, the following list, which may seem rather formidable, but so many friends are often anxious to give us something, and naturally, they would like their gifts to be of real service to us, so that we here indicate the things we are most in need of."

The formidable list began with £150 to pay off the debt on the new Chapel, and then followed more than twenty books for the library, with the proviso "second-hand will do admirably". The brethren were so poor that a gift of £60 was urgently needed to cover the printer's bill. There happened to be "a qualified printer in the Community, but *no press*". The monastic gardener would be most grateful for "£1 10s. to complete amount already given towards a new lawn-mower", and another £1 10s. for a new wheel-barrow. But this was far from being all. "Plants or cuttings of white and yellow marguerites" were requested, likewise "bulbs, triangular garden-reel and line". Just as urgent were "two cows, carriage-jack, and thirty-six pure-bred Orpington pullets". Then some friend might like to give "£20 for one year's coal supply", which "if bought in quantity" would come much cheaper, for the coal had to be carted seven miles from the nearest railway station. Neither could the men who called daily—described as "Wold Rangers"—for bread and cocoa be forgotten. They cost the community at least £25 a year. Winter was approaching, so warm flannel shirts for the monks were essential, because cold winds blew over the Wolds from the North Sea.

On the other hand, these Anglican Benedictines were most grateful to the "Ladies of *Quis Separabit*", who had knitted stockings for them; also the "Clifton lady" who had presented a carriage to convey them to and from Stamford Bridge station. Thanks to a priest, the library had been enriched by all the bound volumes of the *Church Review* and other useful books. "Coniston" had donated copies of the monthly Anglican magazine, *The Treasury*. "Grandmother" had sent *Amateur Gardening*, and the Vicar of East Markham *Profitable Farm and Gardener*.

The "Handicrafts" advertised included Church Embroidery and Vestments; the latter in either "Plain silk with velvet orphreys edged with Church Lace; Figured Damask Silk, velvet orphreys, silk lined"; or "Special cheap sets for Missions, made of Satin Roma". The metal Work ranged from cigarette, hat-pin, and match-boxes, to cope-morses and crucifixes—even "Art Jewellery". Pedigree St Bernard puppies were on sale from £2 5s. each. Strong sandals at 7s. 9d. post free were another side-line, as well as mounted and unmounted photographs of the Community, Monastery and Village. On the last of the twenty-eight pages of the first number of *Pax* was printed a "Form of Bequest" to encourage people to leave money to the monks, "free of duty", for this would be for the Greater Glory of God.

Nevertheless this little community, which found it almost impossible to make both ends meet, regarded itself as an early twentieth century successor of Rievaulx and Fountains. As seven Cistercian abbeys were founded in Yorkshire between 1132 and 1150, there was no reason why the same thing should not happen again if the Catholic Movement could be speeded up. Before long Carlyle's boyhood visions of reviving the medieval glories of Benedictine life in Britain might take shape, with foundations on a scale with those of Selby and Whitby Abbeys, or St Mary's, York.

From the point of view of Anglican canon law, the Abbot of Painsthorpe was still merely an ordinary layman, even if he had been given the rank of a sub-deacon at his blessing. He stood no chance of being raised to the diaconate and priesthood by any English bishop because he lacked the so-called "quality" specified in the Constitutions and Canons Ecclesiastical for such as are to be made Ministers. Unfortunately he had never been sufficiently instructed either in Holy

185

Scripture, or in the doctrine, discipline and worship of the Established Church, nor was he a graduate of any university.

Once again the difficult problems were solved by Dr Grafton, Bishop of Fond du Lac. He suggested that the Abbot should slip over to North America, more or less incognito, so that the ordinations could be carried out *sub rosa*. Rather surprisingly Dr Maclagan, Archbishop of York, raised no objections, and wrote to Bishop Grafton on September 26, 1904: "On Abbot Aelred's return I will very gladly welcome him as a clergyman in Colonial Orders, and I do not suppose that the requirements of the Colonial Clergy Act need put any impediment in his way, so long as he remains in his present position. I feel well assured, from all I can learn, that the work he is carrying on is one for which there is a very real need; and that he is endeavouring to discharge his duties in a devout spirit, and in true loyalty to the Church of England."[22]

A benefactor offered to cover the cost of the more than 4,000 miles journey from the Yorkshire Wolds to Wisconsin and back again. On October 19, the Abbot and Br Bernard Lawson sailed from Liverpool on the White Star liner *Baltic*. Garbed in their magpie-like motley they made a picturesque pair, even more conspicuous than was Fr Ignatius when he crossed the Atlantic on his soul-saving mission-tour fifteen years previously.

On landing at New York the two Benedictines were set upon by reporters. One described the Anglican Abbot as "a young man of very pleasing address, a reincarnation of the old-time religieuse (sic). Except for his garb he is modern and practical. . . . Says Americans have drug habit." Having been rushed around all the Manhattan strongholds of Episcopalian Catholicism, visited the Community of the Holy Cross at West Park, the couple moved west to Chicago, and thence to Fond du Lac.

There was no time to waste. On November 12 Bishop Grafton raised the Abbot to the diaconate in St Paul's Cathedral. Three days later he ordained him priest in St Peter's, Ripon, also giving the subdiaconate to Br Bernard.[23] The two monks certainly deserve to be called Gyrovags for within six weeks they managed to stay in no less than twenty-six places before embarking from New York, homeward bound for Liverpool.

Having got back to Painsthorpe, Dom Aelred presented himself at Bishopsthorpe, when Archbishop Maclagan gave him permission to minister in the monastery chapel, pending his consideration as to what form the licence should take.[24] The Primate required of the newly ordained monk neither a declaration of assent, nor an oath of allegiance. Nothing more was said about giving him the canonical status of a Clergyman in Colonial Orders in virtue of the 1874 Act of Parliament.

Yet the Abbot presumed that he had the right to adopt *insignia pontificalia*, when he celebrated his first High Mass at Christmas; using the 1606 *Missale Monasticum* instead of the 1662 *Book of Common Prayer*. At the same time he believed that his prelatical status involved following the *Caeremoniale Episcoporum*, which in 1600 had been made obligatory for abbots as well as bishops of the Roman Rite by Pope Clement VIII.[25]

Archbishop Maclagan was afraid of rousing the Church Association and other Protestant organisations, so he insisted that no publicity must be given to the ordinations. The "Community Letter" which appeared in the December 1904 issue of *Pax* (headed "St Peter's Rectory, Ripon, Wisconsin") implied that this trip to North America had been undertaken "to see what possibilities there were for the establishment of a Community of our Rule—the Bishop of Fond du Lac greatly desiring such a foundation".[26] He added: "In fact, there is every probability that we may have two or three Postulants from here during the next year at Painsthorpe.

From what I have seen, I feel that if a Community is to begin in America, it must be formed primarily of American citizens, and it seems to me essential that they should leave their country for a time, and come to our quiet English home for training . . . American life is so strenuous and fast; people here have no time to think, and there is a natural impatience with anything of slow growth, such as a Religious Community must have, if it is to take firm root."

The March 1905 issue of *Pax* contained the intimation that the Painsthorpe community, consisting of no more than a dozen members, had been given the official title of *"The English Congregation of the Strict Observance of the Holy Rule of St Benedict"*. But it was not stated whether this new congregation had obtained authorization from either the Archbishop of Canterbury or the Archbishop of York, or whether the Abbot had felt it worth while to have it legalized at the Royal Court of Justice as a registered company.

Since the turn of the century the Roman Church in England had acquired many more monasteries, thanks for the persecution of the religious orders in France. In 1901 the Benedictines of Solesmes found a refuge in the Isle of Wight. Two years later the English monks left Douai and settled at Woolhampton, near Reading. Breton Benedictines were forced to flee from their monastery at Kebéneat, and migrated to Caermaria in Cardiganshire. Two communities of French Cistercian monks had found homes in South Devon and Hampshire. The Observant Friars Minor made three foundations in England. Numerous congregations of women, both active and contemplative were also driven into exile.

In spite of having no licence to minister outside his own monastery, Dom Aelred had no scruples about saying Mass at both Garrowby and Hickleton Hall when Lord Halifax was in residence at either of them. He also began to accept preaching engagements, when he was usually advertised as "The Right Reverend the Lord Abbot of Painsthorpe". Protests were made to Dr Winnington-Ingram by the Church Association, but he did not feel justified from banning the Benedictine from the pulpits of churches in his diocese, or forbidding him to celebrate the Holy Communion. Most Anglo-Catholic clergymen took the Lord Abbot on his face value. As a preacher he could hardly have been more different from Fr Ignatius, yet he could grip a congregation by his personality—above all by those hypnotic eyes. When he was booked to appear in a London church, it was generally a case of "standing room only".

Moreover he played the part of a "Lord Abbot" to perfection. When away from his monastery he wore a simple but dignified uniform: the black habit and scapular hidden beneath a double-breasted *douillette*. To complete the prelatial ensemble were silver buckled shoes, and a wide-brimmed furry hat with tassels. There was nothing of the flamboyant appearance of Fr Ignatius about Abbot Aelred, for the latter aimed rather at looking like a Roman *monsignore*.

More than one sisterhood consulted him. As early as October 1903 Mother Agatha, foundress of the Community of the Holy Comforter at Edmonton, sought his advice about giving up active work, and leading a more contemplative life.[27] The Abbot went to Edmonton for the first time a month later, and by March 1904 the Community had started the recitation of the *Breviarium Monasticum*, and adopted certain Benedictine customs.[28]

In the spring of 1905 he renewed contact with Abbess Hilda and her nuns at Malling Abbey. Shortly after this readers of *Pax* were recommended to buy the sweets made by Sister Frances. He wrote that the old Abbey was "well worth a visit", and that "guests receive every courtesy from the Nuns".

The English Church Union invited "The Lord Abbot of Painsthorpe" to give a lecture at Hull on February 9, that same year, the subject being "The Revival of the Religious Life for Men". His next letter in *Pax* contained the statement: "We believe that God's blessing does rest upon us. Those who know us speak hopefully, while they are candid as to our defects. The desire for the contemplative life is only just beginning to take form again after a lapse of three hundred years; traditions have been lost, many useful practices have been laid aside; and much has to be done before the Life of Prayer once more takes its proper place in our Ecclesiastical system."[29]

Fr Page, Superior-General of the Society of St John the Evangelist, agreed with the Lord Abbot of Painsthorpe that the time was ripe for the Contemplative Life to be regularized in the Establishment. Both he and other Cowley Fathers were acting as spiritual directors to ladies who yearned to devote themselves to a life of prayer. Fr Hollings had already formed the nucleus of an enclosed community of women, sponsored by his Superior-General.[30] He found time to write a number of little devotional books recommending the study of Mysticism. Fr Congreve was also encouraging a higher form of prayer-life by his writings and in the retreats he gave to religious communities.

In the September 1905 issue of *Pax* Abbot Aelred published the first of three long articles entitled "Our Purpose and Method." They revealed a remarkable knowledge of the fundamental principles of the monastic life—solid and sensible, with little or no medieval romanticism about them. Based entirely on standard Roman Catholic authorities, they indicate that he must have done more reading than one would have suspected, considering the very active life he had led since the foundation of his brotherhood in 1896.

Mainly with the desire to increase interest in the contemplative form of the monastic life, the first Ward of the Confraternity of St Benedict was formed at St James's, Hampstead Road, London, by the Rev. George E. Barber on October 10, 1905. The obligations were simple, and the annual subscription only half-a-crown.[31]

The Painsthorpe monks were not allowed to forget their special vocation as twentieth-century rebuilders of medieval monastic waste places. During the summer of 1902 there was a pilgrimage to Rievaulx Abbey. Vespers were sung in the ruined choir by Abbot Aelred and his brethren—a mere handful in comparison with the 140 monks and 600 *conversi* who filled this Cistercian monastery in St Aelred's time. The following summer the community undertook a longer journey to Fountains Abbey, and in June 1904 they travelled north to Whitby. Here again, Vespers were chanted in St Hilda's ruined abbey on the cliffs above the North Sea. It was explained in *Pax:* "Our annual visit to one of the many ruined Monasteries built by the piety of our forefathers, not only saves us from getting 'stale', but such a pilgrimage nerves us for our work of trying in ever so small a degree to recover something of what England has lost". But these pilgrimages were expensive, and in September 1905 it was explained: "We could not compass a visit to Bolton Abbey this year, the cost being prohibitive; so we went to the Gilbertine Priory at Watton instead".[32]

Early in December that same year, while the winds were blowing keenly off the Yorkshire Wolds, the Lord Abbot wrote in *Pax:* "God is stirring men's souls to come and share our life. And we must be ready for Him to do what He wills. He is strengthening our purposes and deepening our hopes of permanency. And with this there is ever in our minds the need of a Monastery of our own. For this there is a little nest-egg of £2 11s. 1d., which we hope may be largely added to by the gifts of our well-wishers. For some time to come, by Lord Halifax's generous desire, Painsthorpe is to be our home, and we are glad that this should be the case. But during this time we ought to be laying by a store which we may draw upon when the time for action arrives, and God bids us 'Arise and build, for this place is too strait for you'. All money paid into the *Monastery Building Fund* will be banked, and the interest will thus be accruing until the time, the need and the means arrive. God grant that these may be synchronized. That we are solvent should encourage both us and you to do our best."[33]

The reason why the community needed a new home had been explained to Lord Halifax at about the same date that the Abbot wrote his "Community Letter" in *Pax: "All* negotiations are broken off between Father Ignatius and ourselves. He had proved himself most impractical and quite impossible to deal with. After all Mr Heatley's trouble in preparing the documents, at the last moment he refused to execute them unless we agreed to throw in our lot with him, adopt his methods and opinions, and surrender ourselves entirely to him as Abbot of Llanthony".[34]

Since the publication of the Baroness de Bertouch's biography in 1904, the Painsthorpe Benedictines had taken for granted that Llanthony Abbey would eventually become their property, because Fr Ignatius had stated that he now regarded them as his "Benjamin".[35] Relations between the two Abbots became so friendly that they exchanged visits.[36] Abbot Aelred's visit to Llanthony was not altogether enjoyable. Forty-seven years later when asked to confirm the alleged haunting of the Abbey, he replied: "The poltergeist business was perfectly authentic, because Br Henry and I experienced it. I had a shower of what seemed to be like small shot all over my bed and cell during one night, but nothing was seen on the floor, and the next night I was suddenly wide awake and something began pulling my bedclothes from my feet, and they were slowly and cautiously drawn from me. I lay there in a sweat, and Henry let out a yelp from the next cell, and said: 'Father, what's going on? Somebody dragged my clothes off me'. There were all sorts of other incidents too, but I never think of them now."[37]

During the Octave of the feast of the Apparitions of Our Lady and the Most Holy Sacrament, which included the Solemn Commemoration of the Reappearance of the Mother of God and her Divine Son on September 12, Abbot Ignatius unveiled a white Carrara marble statue of Our Lady of Llanthony in the meadow where she had manifested herself in 1880. A journalist reported that "after a hearty tea in the monastery, the pilgrims made their way homewards through the mists of evening, not waiting for Vespers". He added: "Fr Ignatius is an inconsistent compound of the mystic and the evangelical, and in his preaching he uses alternately the perfervid oratory of the Salvation Army and the stateliness of utterance to be envied by the staidest churchman in the orthodox fold".

By this time a Trust had been set up, consisting of Lord Halifax, Mr H. C. Richards, K.C., Br Samson Carrington (of Painsthorpe), and a trustee appointed by Fr Ignatius himself, who had expressed the wish that his own observances should be maintained by the double-community until his decease. He hoped to start raising funds for the completion and endowment of the monastery. Yet all this proved a waste of time and money. The Painsthorpe Benedictines never became the owners of about three-hundred acres of land in the Black Mountains, because they felt unable to adopt the heterodox opinions of Dewi-Honddu, and to submit themselves body and soul to his autocratic authority.

Their own observances continued to be a fairly close imitation of those of the Buckfast Benedictines, without anything exotic about them. They still rose at 2 a.m. to recite Matins and Lauds, and the long day ended with Compline at 7.30 p.m. Then followed a prayer for the repose of the soul of the Founder—*"pro famulo tuo Frederico"*, and the lively hymn, *Salve Mater misericordia*. After this the black cowled figures slipped away into darkness. The monastery was silent until

1.50 a.m. when the bell summoned them to take up again the Work of God.

The English Congregation of the Strict Observance of the Holy Rule of St Benedict never failed to remind readers of *Pax* that it had no endowment and depended entirely on their subscriptions and donations, for the profits from handicrafts were meagre. The poverty at Painsthorpe seems to have been more than Franciscan. By March 1906 it had become necessary to charge priests and laymen 25s. 6d. per week for board and lodging in the two old railway carriages that had been transformed into a Guest House.[38]

The Metal Work "in gold, silver, bronze, copper, etc." did not do much to keep the wolf from the door. Neither was the Church Embroidery and Vestment department able to support its own staff. On the other hand the "Community Thanks" pages of *Pax* prove that friends were amazingly generous in sending books, papers, magazines, and gifts in kind. At the same time they did their best to swell all the community funds—Wold Rangers, Altars, Monastery Building, General, Chapel Building, and Community-Pilgrimage.

It would be difficult to count the flannel shirts which Lady Alice Howard and other ladies presented to the monks during the year 1905, all of which were acknowledged. Stockings and handkerchiefs were also donated to the Community wardrobe. Lady Halifax, only daughter of the eleventh Earl of Devon, had the inspiration to bequeath a live peacock, pea-hen and chicks.

In March 1905 the situation must have been really desperate, judging from the pathetic hint: "Friends feeling inclined to send a little tea, or a parcel of groceries, etc., for the Monks, need not fear that their gifts will be rejected for such presents help materially to keep down our expenses".

After this S.O.S., gifts of every kind began to be showered on the mendicant monks in Yorkshire. They included an alarm-clock, altar cloths, altar kneelers and apples; blankets, brass vases and bulbs; carpenter's tools, cork lino, curtains and cuttings (for the garden); embroidery frames; yet more flannel shirts and foreign stamps; garden seeds and glass tumblers; half-a-pound of incense; a knife-cleaning machine; missal markers and mending; ornaments for the chapel; rhubarb and jam; extra stockings and handkerchiefs; vegetables and wool. There were books of all sorts, both heterodox and orthodox. Fr "Jim" Adderley did not forget the community. Before Christmas 1905 a large hamper arrived from Saltney, Birmingham, brimful of bottles of wine, cakes, puddings, etc.

It may seem irrelevant and uncharitable to drag up such trivial details, but they have a historic interest in showing how the Painsthorpe Benedictines regarded themselves as deserving objects of charity—just like Fr Ignatius' monks at Norwich in 1864, who also found it impossible to support themselves.[39] Abbot Aelred and his brethren were better off, because they had a rent-free house, a small farm, vegetable garden, and various handicrafts.[40]

Some curious types could be found among the guests. Among them was the Rt. Rev. Mgr. Herbert Ignatius Beale, rector of St Edward's, Nottingham, who had managed to obtain the rank of Protonotary-Apostolic in an irregular manner.[41] On one of his visits to Painsthorpe he presented the brethren with medals of St Anthony of Padua, and ordered several sets of vestments. James Ingall Wedgwood, a goodlooking young Anglo-Catholic, suddenly converted to Theosophy at York by Mrs Annie Besant, found a refuge at the monastery after he had been turned out of All Saints' rectory by Fr "Pat" Shaw, for he knew that Abbot Aelred shared his interest in occultism.[42] Another ecclesiastical rolling-stone associated with the community was the Rev. F. S. Willoughby, founder and first Principal of St Chad's Hostel, Hooton Pagnell from 1899 to 1906, for which prayers were asked in every issue of Pax.[43]

A closer friend of the monks was a Roman Catholic layman, James Columba McFall, who ran an antique shop in Belfast.[44] Early in 1905 he stayed at the guest house, presenting the Abbot with a wooden crozier and prayer desk carved by himself. On his return to Ireland he wrote an article, entitled "Anglican Benedictines", which appeared in *The Catholic Times* on June 6. His extravagant praise of the community roused a certain Mrs Jeffery to protest violently. In her opinion "the well-meant efforts of Mr Carlyle and his young brethren" was "nothing more than a somewhat unpleasant species of masquerade". Mr McFall tried to defend himself, but Mrs Jeffery was not convinced by his arguments. Her second attack was even more vituperative. She was certain that "this small ritualistic community, who, in playing at monasticism, have embarked upon a game which is not a pastime in which Catholics can express their sympathy, or to which they should give any encouragement."

This roused Dom Bede Camm, now a monk of Erdington Abbey, to rally to the support of the Painsthorpe Benedictines. He wrote: "If only Catholics could realise the immense harm they do by rash and unkind judgments of those outside the Fold! I know nothing of these good young men at Painsthorpe, save from hearsay. No doubt they have no real claim to be members of our Holy Order, but they do love St Benedict, they do try to keep his Rule, they do serve God to the best of their lights, living lives of self-denial, mortification and prayer. I contend that the Painsthorpe monks are at least worthy of our respectful and sympathetic interest. If we cannot honestly speak well of them, it would be far better to keep silence and to pray for them."

Another convert-monk of Erdington—Dom John Chapman—went even further in his defence of Anglican monastic life.[45] He wrote: "Had Mrs Jeffery any idea of the difficulties she is putting in the way of those whose office it is to deal with souls and help them, I am sure she would have cut off her right hand rather than have written such disastrous lines."[46]

Life at Malling Abbey went on quietly, but Abbess Hilda was growing old, and novices were few and far between. A few lady guests came to stay, for the sake of the full Catholic privileges offered.[47]

For thirty-seven years the nuns had led an enclosed life, with very few changes in the observances, or contacts with other Anglican communities. To all intents and purposes Malling had become an old fashioned Anglo-Catholic backwater. Some of the aged nuns whose knowledge of the outer world had ceased in the early eighteen-seventies, when ladies were wearing bustles, had never seen girls riding bicycles, though the extern sisters told them that this was now quite common. This mode of transport, so they felt, must tend to discourage vocations to the enclosed and contemplative life. Indeed, it must be "more difficult now than ever to anchor a girl to her home, and the bike was not a vehicle that lent itself to chaperonage. The element of restfulness imparted to life by the stay-at-home woman of the Victorian tradition was now, like many other Victorian traditions, quite out of date. It was a hustling age, and life was speeded up for Jill as well as for Jack."[48]

The Catholic Movement too had changed out of all recognition from what the older nuns remembered in the days of their youth. They would have agreed that there was now much "lamentable confusion, lawlessness and vulgarity", as the Rev. Percy Dearmer had pointed out in the Introduction to the first edition of his *Parson's Handbook*, published in 1899. When they were young, Dr Pusey and like-minded clergymen would have not encouraged the use of such a manual of devotion like *Catholic Prayers for Church of England People*, which was now popularizing ultramontane piety among Anglicans. Mother Hilda herself had

191

never seen a motor-car, though by this time she had probably grown accustomed to the loud noises made by these contraptions as they chug-chugged along the road outside the enclosure walls at a slow pace.

Life was certainly more lively and go-ahead at Painsthorpe. On January 25, 1906, the feast of the Conversion of St Paul, the Lord Abbot, without reference to any higher authority, received the Solemn Vows of Dom Henry Watts, Dom George Chambers, and Dom Samson Carrington. The abbatial action involved a reciprocal engagement between the three monks and the *"Congrega-Anglicana a Primaeva Observantia Regulae S.P.N. Benedicti"*, so designated in the Latin formula which each of them read aloud and signed. The Congregation undertook to maintain the trio and treat them as members of its household for the rest of their lives. They could only be dismissed in canonical form for incorrigible persistence in some grave public fault. But no Anglican bishop had the power to dispense them from solemn vows; granted that the Clergy Discipline Act 1892 authorized a bishop to dispense from holy orders; yet it made no reference to dispensations from monastic vows, either simple or solemn.

Having adopted the post-Tridentine system of monastic probation Abbot Aelred ignored the fact that in the Roman Church, dispensation from Solemn Vows at that date was extremely difficult to obtain. To all intents and purposes it was reserved to the Pope himself.[49] Of course he may have felt that the Primate of all England would be prepared to act as a substitute for the Pope. On the other hand, he may have been so confident of the stability of these three monks that he dismissed the thought that one or other of them might ask for a dispensation, or have to be dismissed.

The whole procedure was highly irregular, considering that the Lord Abbot of Painsthorpe was merely a free-lance young clergyman whose name did not appear in *Crockford's Clerical Directory*, and whose Licence merely allowed him to carry out services according to the *Book of Common Prayer* in the chapel of a certain "charitable institution" in Yorkshire. Had Archbishop Maclagan been consulted beforehand, it is improbable that his theological advisers would have been prepared to recognise the subtle Ultramontane distinctions of religious profession as set forth in the Sacred Canons of the Roman Church.

The Right Reverend the Lord Abbot informed readers of the March issue of *Pax* that the first three Solemn Professions were "a final step in the history and development of the Community". The trio would now take their place permanently at the head of the Order, having finally accepted its Rule and manner of life. Mr Shepherd preached a long sermon at the function, ending with the words: "Let me urge upon you this thought: God has called you to this life, you have finally embraced it frankly and unhesitatingly, you have resolved to cling to it while life shall last, and you must recognise that many eyes are fixed upon you, waiting to decide as to their attitude, whether it is to be friendly or hostile, towards this movement; and that the continued existence of the Community and extension of the movement depend upon God, upon you as consistent members of it. And therefore for the fair fame of your Community, and your own influence on the world through it, do your best to make the right impression, by the single-minded devotion to all your duties. So will come in due course your reward here, and the consummation of glory hereafter, when your solemn dedication to a life service of God will have its full fruition".[50]

"The Community Letter" also stated that three of the brethren had been working hard during the past three months, preparing for examinations which had just taken place. Dom Henry had obtained his Testamur at Durham, with a view to the degree of Mus. Bac. Two juniors were taking the central Examination. The

Abbot commented: "We are hoping that they also will pass, and so we shall at least begin to gather to ourselves a Benedictine reputation for learning". Dom George had spent little time in his monastery for the past four years, because he had been studying for the priesthood with the Society of the Sacred Mission at Kelham. Shortly after his solemn profession he was ordained deacon, and remained a curate at St Philip's, Dalston for two years, where he led a very active and far from contemplative life. Dom Samson was the only one of the trio who led a cloistered existence, keeping busy with vestment making. After Easter 1906 the Abbot took him off to Belgium for a course of face and figure embroidery.

About the same time the Abbot helped to acquire a house at Baltonsborough, a remote village about five miles south-east of Glastonbury, for the Sisters of the Holy Comforter. They left Edmonton in April, and the first Mass was celebrated in their new convent on June 6. The following day enclosure was set up. About a dozen nuns then started to lead a contemplative Benedictine life. Such was the real birthday of the present community of St Mary's Abbey, West Malling.[51]

NOTES

[1] *The Benedictines of Caldey Island* (1907), p. 33.

[2] ibid, p. 34.

[3] In 1545 Archbishop Cranmer conferred the pallium on the former Gilbertine monk, Robert Holgate, on his translation from Llandaff to York. This was in virtue of the authority given to him by 15 Henry VIII, ch. 20.

[4] Unfortunately, presuming that the Primate of All England had restored the Benedictine Order as it existed in the later Middle Ages, he was unable to bestow on it "every privilege, grant, indulgence, faculty, and other prerogative which had ever belonged to the ancient English congregation". This had been done in 1633 by Urban VIII in the Bull *"Plantata"*, which restored the federation of Benedictine monasteries in England which had been formed in 1138.

[5] P. F. Anson, *The Hermit of Cat Island* (1957), p. 20.

[6] Shortly after this John Hawes designed a gatehouse and church for the Order of St Paul at Alton Abbey, Hants. (See pp. 152, 206.)

[7] Among the nobility who visited Painsthorpe were the 15th Duke of Norfolk (with his second wife, the Hon. Gwendolen Mary Constable-Maxwell, daughter of Marmaduke, 11th Baron Herries), the 7th Duke of Northumberland, the 7th Earl Beauchamp, and the 1st Baron Stanmore (youngest son of the 4th Earl of Aberdeen).

[8] J. C. Lockhart, *Charles Lindley Viscount Halifax* (Part II, 1936), p. 205.

[9] October 16, 1903.

[10] October 22, 1903.

[11] For instance the performance in churches subject to them of pontifical functions with the throne and the baldachin, together with the other pontifical insignia. Blessed abbots are allowed to wear at all times a pectoral cross, a ring with a precious stone, and a black skullcap.

[12] At that date almost the only Anglican prelate in Britain who would have enjoyed blessing an abbot was Dr Chinnery-Haldane, Bishop of Argyll and the Isles from 1883 to 1907.

[13] See p. 62 n. 10 for reference to the Bishop's associations with Fr Ignatius at Norwich in 1864.

[14] It was felt worth while to add the following note to the "Charter": "By permission of the Lord Archbishop of York we have this day conferred the Abbatial Blessing on Brother Aelred Carlyle, and installed him as Abbot of Painsthorpe on the Feast of the Holy Relics 1903. †C. C. Fond du Lac". This codicil was witnessed by Lord Halifax.

[15] Although Ampleforth Abbey was only eighteen miles from Painsthorpe, there were no ecumenical relations between the two communities from 1902 to 1906.

[16] Lockhart, op. cit., Vol. II, p. 205.

[17] Henry Matthews, born in 1868, turned up at Llanthony in 1898. Having eventually convinced Ignatius that he had "found salvation", he was admitted to the novitiate with the name of Br Cadoc Mary of the Holy Cross. Soon after his profession the following year he ran away in his monastic habit, returned as a prodigal son, but bolted for the second time two months later with all the house money. A brief sojourn with the Y.M.C.A. in London was enough to make him realise that he might find a more congenial niche among Roman Catholics, so he moved over to Ireland and entered the novitiate at Mount Melleray Abbey. He seems to have remained with the Trappists for about a year, after which he found his way to Caldey Island, having no scruples about joining an Anglo-Catholic

193

community, in which he became known as Br Malachy. (These details are taken from Fr Ignatius' Register.)

[18] See p. 157.

[19] See p. 107.

[20] See p. 64.

[21] Br Austin died a year later, and the Abbot wrote an appreciative obituary in the March 1906 issue of *Pax*. St Benet's Boys' Home was carried on more successfully by a Miss Wright.

[22] Cf. *A Correspondence* (Caldey Island, 1913), p. 41. The Colonial Clergy Act of 1874 (37 and 37 Vic. c. 77) regulates the conditions under which those ordained for the Anglican ministry in the British colonies can receive preferment or officiate publicly in Great Britain. The written permission of the archbishop of the English province and a Declaration of Assent in terms similar to those provided for in the Clerical Subscription Act of 1865 are required.

[23] Dr Grafton in his later years combined an almost fanatical detestation of "Romanism" with a love for Roman ritual and ceremonial.

[24] This was in accordance with the provisions of the Private Chapels Act of 1871, for the monastery could be regarded as a "charitable institution" situated in the parish of Kirby Underdale. Abbot Aelred (as its minister) received permission to celebrate the Holy Communion, read the Common Prayers, preach, and at the same time perform other offices and services of the Church of England as were implied in the archiepiscopal permission to officiate.

[25] The *insignia pontificalia* assumed by the "minister" of the "charitable institution" at Painsthorpe consisted of the ring, pectoral cross, mitre, gloves, dalmatic, tunicle, buskins and crozier. In actual practice the abbatial "minister" exceeded the rights of abbots as regulated in the Decree of Alexander VII (1659), which limited permission to pontificate to three days in the year, also laying down that an abbot cannot have a permanent throne in the monastic church.

[26] op. cit., p. 48.

[27] This small sisterhood was founded in 1891 by Miss Jessie Park Moncrieff, formerly a member of the Order of Holy Charity, established at Edinburgh in 1889.

[28] See p. 269.

[29] op. cit., pp. 85-6. Painsthorpe was setting an example to Roman Catholics, who in 1905 had no contemplative communities of either men or women in Yorkshire.

[30] The embryo Sisters of the Love of God. (See p. 188.)

[31] Within a year other Wards had been established at St Nicholas's, Blackwall; St Michael's, North Kensington; and at Chester. By 1906 the membership of the Confraternity had reached 226.

[32] *Pax*, no. 5, p. 179. A "Community Pilgrimage Fund" had been launched, but it only produced the sum of £8 15s.

[33] op. cit., pp. 241-3. The "Amount required" for the "Monastery Building Fund" was £3,000, so on November 30, 1905, £2,997 8s. 6d. had still to be raised. The sum of £97 11s. 6d. was needed for the new altar in the chapel; also £17 15s. for the "Wold Rangers Relief Fund". Only £18 18s. 8d. had been donated to the "General Fund" between September 1 and November 30.

[34] Lockhart, *op. cit.*, Vol. II, pp. 206-7.

[35] See p. 183.

[36] In the autumn of 1905 Fr Ignatius contributed £1 towards the "Painsthorpe Pilgrimage Fund".

[37] Letter to the author, February 1951. Similar paranormal experiences appear to have been fairly frequent at Llanthony for nearly half-a-century—perhaps one of the reasons why so many monks ran away?

[38] This sum is what would have been charged by a good second class hotel at that date.

[39] See p. 57.

[40] In 1905 the small communities of exiled French Cistercians at Woodbarton, South Devon, and Martin, near Salisbury, were never forced to beg; because they had more experience of farming, etc., than the Anglican monks in Yorkshire.

[41] In 1910 he was raised to the episcopate by A. H. Mathew, along with Mgr. Arthur W. Howarth (formerly Roman Catholic priest at Corby, near Grantham), who at that date was Regionary Old Catholic Bishop for England and Wales.

[42] He moved on to London, became General Secretary of the Theosophical Society, and in 1916 was raised to the episcopate by Bishop F. S. Willoughby. Later on he became first Presiding-Bishop of the Liberal Catholic Church.

[43] Having seceded from the Church of England, he was consecrated by Archbishop A. H. Mathew in 1914, as titular Bishop of St Pancras in the so-called "Ancient Catholic Church of England".

[44] In 1916 he was consecrated as Old Roman Catholic Bishop for Ireland by Archbishop Mathew, but shortly after the function he was excommunicated by his consecrator.

[45] Born in 1865, he was received into the Roman Church in 1890 after serving a curacy at St Pancras's Church, London. He was professed as a monk of Maredsous in 1893, and in 1929 blessed as Abbot of Downside. He died in 1933.

[46] Neither of these two monks guessed that eight years later they would be called to assist both the Painsthorpe monks and the Malling nuns to "go over to Rome".

[47] It seems that there were only two churches in the London Diocese that had "public reservation" in 1905: St Cuthbert's, Philbeach Gardens, and St Columba's, Haggerston. Elsewhere, in accordance with episcopal regulations, reservation was permitted only in a chapel not open to the laity. In the Rochester Diocese only two churches had "probable" reservation occasionally. Many of the tabernacles elsewhere were merely empty boxes on which rested the altar-cross.

[48] Esmé Wingfield-Stratford, *The Victorian Sunset* (1932) p. 366.

[49] Tacit solemn profession was abolished by Pius IX in 1858.

[50] op. cit., p. 300. Each of the trio abandoned the monastic life eventually.

[51] See p. 269.

CHAPTER XII

"The Home Coming" of the Benedictines to Caldey Island;
death of Abbess Hilda Stewart, and the blessing of Dame
Scholastica Ewart as second Abbess of Malling; further notes on
the Order of St Paul; the death of Fr Ignatius of Jesus, and
the closing down of Llanthony Abbey (1906-1909)

FROM the practical point of view there was not much wrong with Painsthorpe
Hall as the home of a small Benedictine brotherhood. The property was rent-
free. The monks had their own farm, vegetable gardens, and many more amenities.
Nobody could have been more friendly to the community than Mr Shepperd, the
rector of Kirby Underdale. Lord Halifax raised no objections to the house being
enlarged, so long as he did not have to foot the bill. But the truth is that the Lord
Abbot had reached the point early in 1906 of feeling that his unique status
demanded complete autonomy. As a minor prelate he ought to be independent of
all higher authority. His aspirations could have been expressed in the words of the
poet William Cowper:

> "I am monarch of all I survey,
> My right there is none to dispute;
> From the centre all round to the sea
> I am lord of the fowl and the brute."[1]

Caldey Island appeared to be the best place in Britain where he could be a law
unto himself, for it was said to be both extra-diocesan and extra-parochial. If this
opinion was correct, then Dom Aelred would be able to hold the rank of an *abbas
nullius diocesis,* i.e. the highest class of abbot in the Western Patriarchate. These
prelates preside over territories separated from any diocese, with their own clergy
and people; with the same powers, the same obligations, and the same sanctions
as residential bishops in their own dioceses.[2] At the moment, however, the Painsthorpe Benedictines lacked the money to become the legal owners of Caldey.

Shortly before Christmas 1905 a young man named Edmund Bryan Burstall
stayed at the guest-house. Having fallen under the spell of monastic life, he paid
a second visit in the spring of the following year. He explained to the Abbot that
he was a bachelor of private means, with about £10,000 at his disposal, and no
commitments. Here was the omen for which Dom Aelred had been waiting and
praying—almost a star in the east (since Mr Burstall came from East Anglia),
going before him and resting over Inis Pyr. So the Abbot confided to his guest
his visions of becoming the Lord of the Manor of this glamorous little island off
the coast of South Wales, so obviously meant to be the permanent home of a
purely contemplative Benedictine community.

The result was that Mr Burstall asked if the Abbot would accept £6,000 as a
loan towards buying Caldey, if the owner would agree to selling it. The ever-
adventurous and quixotic Aelred accepted the offer without a moment's hesitation,
and got moving at once. The Rev. William Done Bushell replied that he was
willing to hand over the island for £4,000 in cash; the remaining £8,000 to be on

196

mortgage to him for a term of five years from 1906. If the monks wished to take over the farm another £2,000 would be needed, for it was already let on a fourteen years' lease.

Life was nothing if not hectic during the summer of 1906. Dom Aelred rushed off to London, and advised John Hawes to give up his curacy at the Holy Redeemer, Clerkenwell, so that he could take on the job of architect. The pair travelled to Tenby, where the purchase of Caldey Island was completed on July 20. After this the Abbot launched an appeal for £7,000 to enable really essential building to be started immediately.

Fr Hawes was told that he must first design a Guest House, perched on the edge of a precipitous cliff, with accommodation for a dozen visitors. Then would follow the Gate House of the future monastery, to accommodate thirty brethren. Eventually it would serve as a House of Retreat for laymen, or as a school for boys of Catholic parents of moderate means, who would like their sons to be educated by Benedictines. This was not all by any means: the medieval Priory Church must be restored, provided with a stone altar, wooden rood-screen and choir stalls. At the same time the ancient Village Church must be re-furnished in a Catholic manner. The round tower above the future Guest House must be transformed into a tiny oratory for the celebration of private Masses. Finally there was the great Abbey, to be designed in Romanesque style—evocative of Cluny, Vézelay, or Durham's nave. The site for this immense range of buildings for at least a hundred monks had already been chosen in 1901—level ground above Paul Jones Bay, covered with turf, bracken and gorse-bushes. The pine wood on the western side secluded the future abbey from curious eyes. The steep cliffs prevented access from the sea. Fr Hawes was overwhelmed, but felt he must do his best to give shape to the abbatial visions.

Before returning to Painsthorpe, Abbot Aelred clothed Mr Burstall and Fr Hawes as Oblates. The former became Br Illtud, and took on the duties of unpaid clerk of works. The latter was given the religious name of Jerome. They moved into a vacant cottage, with no modern conveniences, so there was no choice for them to lead anything but a very "primitive" observance of a modified form of the Benedictine Rule. As "The Homecoming" had already been fixed for October, there was much to be done in two months, and they worked from dawn to dusk.

When the next issue of *Pax* appeared—two months late—the Abbot explained why he felt it wiser to postpone publication until he could reveal to his friends and benefactors the epoch-making event of the purchase of Caldey Island. He stressed that he expected them to hand over at least £7,000 in the near future to cover the cost of building, also another £12,000 to clear off the debt incurred in buying the island. Though realising that it was indeed "a venture of faith", he felt that "under the circumstances" his recklessness was "perfectly justifiable", and he called for "the willing co-operation of all those who are interested in it". The very long letter ended with the words: "We have just a year in front of us before our new buildings, or parts of them, must be ready; but work can go on at Caldey all the year round, and if this £7,000 is subscribed now, we shall be in time. . . . If each reader of *Pax* will do his best and try to interest others, I have no fear for the result."

A letter from the architect was also published. Br Jerome assured readers that the Gate House would be "in the most simple and severe round arched style possible". No money would be "squandered on oriel windows or traceried cloisters". In the designs submitted his object had been to "gain character" by the grouping and proportion of the various parts "so as to give a general effect of solidity and repose". Letters from Lord Halifax, Mr Shepperd, and the Archbishop of York were printed, each saying in his own way that he was glad to hear that the monks had found a permanent home. Halifax did more, and sent a very long article to the *Church Times* for he was wildly enthusiastic over the return of Benedictine monks to Caldey Island after nearly three centuries. He proclaimed:

"This is indeed a building up of the waste places. It must needs silence the cry of those who, not understanding the Monastic Life and aims, exclaim thoughtlessly against the selfishness of those who shut themselves up from the world. Here is no selfishness! No disregard for the needs of others! But rather the willing acceptance of a charge laid on them by God, who led them there six years ago, and now bids them return to tend and care for the souls of the Islanders, who will once more be brought within the pale of the Catholic Church.[3] . . . And now the time has come when we who profess our loyalty to the Catholic Faith, and proclaim our unfaltering conviction in the Catholicity of the Church of England, must rally round Abbot Aelred, who, in the sphere of the Religious Life, has been enabled by the Grace of God to win a position for the Benedictine Order in the English Church, which at one time seemed to be impossible." English Catholics must realise that it was "not a mere question of another community having come into being", rather was it "the recovery of a great principle, for the lack of which the Catholic Revival has been incomplete". Readers of the *Church Times* were reminded that the Order had obtained "the active co-operation and practical interest of the late Archbishop of Canterbury" . . . that it had "official sanction and internal worth". The "great Catholic Revival had gone on", the "heritage of the Church had been recovered step by step", so that now there were not only many active religious communities of men and women, but also one of "Benedictine monks". By the Grace of God it had "won through the early and tentative stages of a task of singular difficulty", and it had claims upon English Catholics which they ought "to recognise in a definite and practical way". It was for them to insure for these monks "the monastery that they are now fairly entitled to build upon the island which their worth has won from those who know them well". The long article ended with a passionate appeal for the faithful to unite together and assist in the building up of Benedictine waste places, so that the Isle of Caldey could become once again, not only a sanctuary of the Contemplative Life, but a proof to all the world that *Ecclesia Anglicana* was still Catholic. No time must be wasted in contributing generously to the £7,000 urgently needed by Abbot Aelred.

On September 29 a legal document was signed and "The Reverend Benjamin Fearnley Carlyle" became Lord of the Manor of Caldey in the County of Pembroke, thus succeeding the Rev. William Done Bushell. Mr Carlyle could also feel that he was in the direct line of succession from John Bradshaw of Presteigne to whom Henry VIII had alienated not only St Dogmael's Abbey, near Cardigan, but also its cell on Caldey, and other church lands in Pembrokeshire. This also meant that he had inherited the temporal and spiritual privileges granted by Henry I to the Tironian Benedictines of St Dogmael's Abbey, founded about 1115, who established a "cell" on Caldey and a priory at Pille. As Lord of the Manor of an alleged extra-parochial and extra-diocesan island, he felt it was unnecessary to apply to Dr Owen, Bishop of St Davids, for a licence to minister within the diocese.[4] Holding this insular property very remotely from a medieval sovereign Carlyle liked to think that he had now acquired the rank of a nobleman. None of his tenants would be free to leave the estates, nor could any be evicted. He would be able to hold courts, and keep a manorial record of the services due from each of his subjects. On the other hand, he seems to have forgotten that as a Benedictine monk in solemn vows he was incapable of holding or disposing of property without the permission of the Holy See.[5]

The Lord of the Manor of Caldey Island had more than enough irons in the fire between July and October 1906. One day he received a letter, dictated by the now totally blind Abbess Hilda, asking him to come to Malling so that she could discuss important business with him. He recalled how his former spiritual mother "groped her way into the room, and on to the terrace in the garden", and greeted him "with her gentle smile and brave counsel". She explained that she had decided to resign office, and wanted his advice about a successor. On September 15, having come to the conclusion that none of the nuns had the requisite qualifications, he wrote to Sister Mary Pauline Ewart, asking if she would be prepared to become second Abbess of Malling, were the nuns to elect her. For the past year or two she had been leading a retired life at All Saints' Hospital, Eastbourne, run by her own community.

News of the migration of the Anglican Congregation of the Primitive Observance of the Holy Rule of St Benedict from Yorkshire to South Wales had reached South Africa. Canon Wirgman of Grahamstown wrote to Abbot Aelred: "Your establishment on Caldey Island affords a unique opportunity to Catholics in communion with the See of Canterbury. There are thousands of us in full sympathy with your noble aims and efforts, and I earnestly hope and pray that you will promptly receive the support necessary to enable your Community to be firmly established on an Island hallowed by the Benedictine Rule, and now, under the Providence of God, once more restored to the Benedictine Order. Your Community is faced by a grave responsibility. In your hands lies the vindication of our Communion from the reproach that her atmosphere is too chill to allow the fair flowers of the Contemplative Life to bud and blossom. I know nothing more likely to further the great cause of the reunion of Christendom than the fact of the revival of the Rule of St Benedict within the Church of England under the sanction of her Primates."[6]

The monastic exodus was almost as dramatic as that of the removal of Fr Ignatius of Jesus and "Baby", together with a handful of monks from Laleham to Llanthony in 1870, even if "the Divine Mysteries" were not transported in a "Most Sacred Tabernacle".[7] On the afternoon of October 17, Lord and Lady Halifax with their son the Hon. Edward Wood, bade farewell to the brethren, presenting Abbot Aelred with the sum of £500 towards the expenses of the so-called "Home Coming". The *Itinerarium* was recited in the parish church of Kirby Underdale, after which the Rector imparted his blessing. The monks were packed into two large horse-drawn brakes, and driven to Stamford Bridge station, most of their worldly possessions having preceded them in the morning. There was much bustle as the Lord Abbot, twenty-five young men, six turkeys, a brood of hens, and several St Bernard dogs were stowed away in a crimson-painted double-saloon carriage supplied by the Midland Railway, which served as chapel, dormitory and refectory for the next fifteen hours. Vespers were chanted above the noise and rumble of the wheels. Fr Ommanney and members of the St Matthew's Ward of the Confraternity of St Benedict were waiting on the platform of Sheffield station to bid the monks god-speed. As the train moved on southwards, Compline, Matins and Lauds were said. At Gloucester Br Martin put his head through a window of the double-saloon, and so cost his brethren 7s. 6d. in damages.

Tenby was reached at 6.35 a.m. Three Oblate Brothers were waiting to welcome the party. Every bath at the Cobourg Hotel was requisitioned, after which the monks enjoyed a substantial breakfast. Two hours later a group of twenty-five Benedictines processed down to the harbour, where they found the steamer *Firefly* gaily decked from stem to stern in many-coloured bunting. In spite of the swell after a heavy storm during the night, nobody was seasick. Nearing the land-place they beheld a long, orderly crowd of people wending its way down to meet them; all the island folk, headed by a priest and acolytes.

Owing to the choppy sea, the steamer would not tie up at the slip, so the monks had to be rowed ashore in a dinghy. A procession was formed on the cliff-edge, headed by the thurifer, cross-bearer and taperers, which soon began to wend its way up the winding path amid bracken, gorse and bramble-bushes. The Cantors intoned the antiphon *Deprecamur Te Domine,* said to have been sung by St Augustine and his companions as they approached Canterbury in 597. After this the *Litaniae Sanctorum* were chanted. The laity followed the monks into the Village Church, where Martin Luther's hymn "Now thank we all our God" was sung, and the Abbot imparted a blessing on his manorial tenants. Then in the same order, accompanied by the chanting of the *Psalmi Graduales,* they reached the old Priory. A *Te Deum* having been sung, there followed a solemn *Missa Cantata* of St Luke celebrated *coram abbatem.* In the evening everybody on the Island—monks and layfolk—sat down together for a hearty supper, served by the novices. The next few days were busily spent by the brethren in putting their house in order, Mr Bushell having allowed them to occupy the Victorian mansion as a temporary monastery.

"Welsh Island bought by English Monks" and similar captions had already appeared in most newspapers in Britain. *The Illustrated London News* devoted a whole page to Caldey, with a photograph of "The Abbot of the English Benedictine Brothers, a community connected with the Church of England". The *Catholic Times* was sympathetic, unlike *The Universe* which quoted (from the *Liverpool Post* and *Mercury*) some "strong, but not too strong remarks apropos of the handful of men, owing allegiance to the Protestant Establishment, who have gone to Caldey Island to establish a monastery, and who call themselves Benedictines". The editor dismissed the whole thing as "childish nonsense, absurdity, and religious play-acting". The *English Churchman* insisted that it was high time for "Protestants of every denomination, in self-defence, to demand the suppression of these communities which are fast becoming a menace to our civil and religious freedom".

The Abbot wrote in the December issue of *Pax:* "Our life began at Caldey, where our life at Painsthorpe ceased: and all goes on here as it did there, and as it does in every Benedictine house the world over. The bells on Caldey ring for Mass and Office, never again, we hope, to be silenced; hour succeeds hour, and the quiet round of monastic duty occupies each day, bringing us ever nearer to that moment when day and night shall have an end, and time shall pass into eternity."[8]

An article entitled "My Lady Poverty" indicated the vast number of gifts which would be welcomed by the Lord of the Manor and his monks, who wanted so many things, but had no money to purchase them. For instance, there were "neither Bibles, Prayer Books, nor Ornaments" in the Village Church. A copy of "Mr Percy Dearmer's Altar Book—*The English Liturgy,* £2 2s.", at least fifty copies of *The English Hymnal,* likewise Mr Jervois' *Christian's Manual* were demanded, besides other objects of piety. The children of the Island had no school, where they "would be taught to 'Fear God, and Honour the King' ". They would love to be given a Christmas Crib. It was hoped that "the Children of England" would send 50s. for "My Lady's Children (big and little) in Wales". The future Guest House needed crockery, knives, sheets, blankets, chairs, tables, pots, and pans for twelve to fifteen people, but the monks could not afford to pay for them, even if the Abbot had made £15 8s. 7d., by preaching at All Saints', Clifton; All Saints', Clevedon; and St Cuthebert's, Philbeach Gardens, London. It was explained that "the Abbot will rarely leave the Island to preach; but an occasional visit to centres of Church work will enable him to bring the Active and Contemplative Life into touch with each other, and so demonstrate the unity underlying both".

Having found after four years that farming was an unprofitable monastic handicraft, the Benedictines decided to try their luck with sea-fishing. It was explained in *Pax:* "Caldey waters abound in fish, so arrangements have been made for Dredging, Seining and Line fishing, which will afford both recreation and work". The revival of the contemplative life could go hand in hand with a revival of the once famous oyster-beds off the island, which had been most remunerative in the Middle Ages, and later on. Seine-netting was not incompatible with the singing of Solesmes plainchant, or line-fishing with the daily manual labour prescribed by the Holy Rule, so long as it was "done with due moderation, for the sake of the faint-hearted".[9] Unfortunately nothing had been landed before Christmas but "twenty Dog-fish, a Whiting, and a Whitebait, or something akin thereto". Still it was hoped that better results would "reward the casting of the net soon, as the herring season is drawing close".[10] Twelve months later it was reported: "The fishing has been poor this year. But, now that we have a better supply of nets, the Brothers are becoming experts, and the 'Gentle Art' goes on apace in our bays. Many a prawn also is induced to leave his or her seaside resort", and so one day was a young shark. But as time went on the Benedictines decided it was better to concentrate on poultry farming under Mr Longhurst's direction. The fishing industry faded out.

In the late autumn of 1906, however, the monks were virtually marooned on their little island. The response to the abbatial appeal had fallen far short of expectations. After four months only £1,800 of the £7,000 had been received. Dom Aelred informed his friends that unless the balance of £2,200 materialized at once all building would have to stop.

The money was required not only for buildings. Lord Halifax had already drawn attention to the fact of the Caldeyans being "almost as cut off from spiritual care" before the arrival of the Benedictines "as were the survivors of the *Bounty* on their lonely island in the broad Pacific". So there was an apostolic reason for English Catholics to shower their money on Abbot Aelred. His mission field deserved their support as much as Bishop Hine's on the islands of Zanzibar and Pemba; or Bishop Hornby's on the many islands of the Bahamas, as well as the Turks and Caicos Isles. For the first time since the sixteenth century the poor neglected Caldeyans were being taught the elements of the Full Faith.

During that first autumn the monks could hardly make both ends meet, so desperate was their poverty, as was stressed in every issue of *Pax.* Just as at Painsthorpe, however, benefactors and benefactresses did their best to keep the wolf from the door, what with gifts of altar-lace and amethysts; books, boots, bulbs, and boxes of tea; cakes, carving-tools, and a copper kettle; an Empire typewriter and ikons; flannel shirts and fruits; magazines and a machine for bread-making; a plush curtain and Christmas puddings; sandals and stockings; vegetables and woollen helmets—not forgetting an old rain-coat.

Every night the brethren arose to recite Matins and Lauds at 2 a.m. in the Old Priory Church. Strict silence was broken only by an hour's recreation—daily for the novices, and three times weekly for the seniors. Simple *maigre* meals were prepared by amateur cooks. Br Jerome himself learned to wash clothes and to bake bread in an old-fashioned oven. "The even course of life was sometimes agitated", especially when two of the monks left the Island without warning to be received into the Roman Church. The would-be Franciscan novice kept busy in odd moments drawing plans, sections and elevations. It annoyed him when the Abbot

201

T

THE PRIORY CHURCH, CALDEY ISLAND
Refurnished at the "Home Coming" in 1906.

202

scrapped the drawings, and insisted on something much more ambitious, for Dom Aelred's imagination ran riot. Costs were never considered. "The basically more practical-minded novice could not work up any real enthusiasm for a dream-abbey planned on a scale greater than that of any medieval Cluniac monastery." By the summer of 1907 the Abbot realised that there was no hope of ever turning him into a Benedictine. Br Jerome was allowed to grow a beard, and to retire to Nanna's Cave on the eastern side of the island. Eventually he departed to begin his brief experiment as an Anglican Franciscan on the Isle of Man.[11]

Abbess Hilda of Malling died on December 28, 1906. After her funeral things got moving. On Shrove Tuesday the following year, Sister Mary Pauline Ewart was elected her successor by the eleven professed nuns who formed the community. The Mother Superior of the Society of All Saints agreed to release her of the obligations towards it, which she had fulfilled for twenty-four years. On April 21, on his own authority, Abbot Aelred received her Benedictine solemn vows in the chapel of the Baltonsborough nuns. Permission having been obtained from Dr Harmer, Bishop of Rochester, the Abbot installed the new Abbess on April 24. The *Church Times* reported that everything "was in full accordance with ancient precedent", and that "the Ceremony itself was marked by great simplicity and dignity. . . . The promise of obedience made by the Abbess-elect, in terms which reminded, doubtless, some of those who were present of the similar promise made to Bishop Gundulph by Avicia, the first Abbess of Malling, eight centuries before." It was worded: "I, Mary Scholastica, Abbess of this congregation, do promise in the presence of God and of this congregation, fidelity to my duties; obedience and reverence to my mother the Church of England; and to the Bishop of the Diocese and his Successors; and to the lawful superiors of my Order".

The Editor (Dr Hermitage Day) ended his article by hoping that the revival of Benedictine life in England would progress and be consolidated now that Malling had been linked up with Caldey and Baltonsborough as the first units of a national Congregation. A few weeks later there were rumours that the Abbot of Caldey was seeking recognition of his Congregation from the Abbot-Primate of the Confederated Roman Catholic Benedictines. He felt obliged to issue a printed statement to the effect that he would not dream of doing anything of the kind. He was firmly convinced that Almighty God had called his monks and nuns to live Benedictine life in communion with Canterbury not in communion with Rome and that their first duty was to be "absolutely loyal and true" to their own "Spiritual Mother", the Church of England.[12]

Within five months of "The Home Coming" payment for an ever-rising pile of bills was being pressed. None of the Celtic saints—Brieuc, David, Dyfrig, Gildas, Illtud, Maglorius, Paul Aurelian, Samson, and others whose names were forgotten, appeared to be taking a celestial interest in the revival of monastic life on Inis Pyr. Abbot Aelred was forced to admit in March 1907: "The Gate House is not even begun, because we have not sufficient money. I am not going to grumble; we did our best, and told our friends the need; and it is doubtless for some wise purpose that people have not come forward to help in sufficient numbers."

Feeling that world-wide publicity was now demanded for the strictly enclosed and purely contemplative life, the ever optimistic Lord Abbot got busy. By the month of June 3,000 copies of a 112 pages brochure entitled *The Benedictines of Caldey Island* had been printed. Bound in thick deckle-edged green paper, with old-world Gothic lettering, it could be described as an interesting Edwardian period-piece, contemporary with the Ritz and Piccadilly Hotels in London, the Lady Chapel of the Anglican Cathedral at Liverpool, and Hampstead Garden City. A bird's eye view of the island, drawn by Br Jerome, depicted both the existing and the projected buildings.[13]

The dreamed of Abbey Church would rival the already started Anglican cathedral at Liverpool, and consisted of a long nave, two western towers, transepts and apsidal choir surrounded by five chapels. To complete the external majesty there would be another tower over the south transept, with a lofty broach spire, serving as a mark for mariners. To emphasize his unique status as the only Abbot-nullius in the Anglican communion, Dom Aelred felt it was essential for him to occupy a separate mansion in the late medieval manner, with its own private chapel.

The spirit of the community was conveyed in a quotation from A. W. Robinson's *Personal Life of the Clergy*, printed before the Contents:

> "If you can pray, if you have in any degree acquired the holy art, then for God's sake and for man's sake do not do anything else. Give yourself to it; continue on the mount with hands upraised—there will be no lack of fighters down below, who will triumph by the help of your prayers."

Lord Tennyson had expressed the same conviction when he wrote in *The Passing of Arthur*:

> "Pray for my soul. More things are wrought by prayer
> Than this world dreams of. Wherefore, let thy voice
> Rise like a fountain for me night and day."

Readers of this publicity publication were reminded: "The Community has no endowment or private means, and is entirely in the hands of those who desire to see once more in the English Church a Community of Benedictine Monks, living on their own Island, and occupying a Monastery built by the gifts of those who believe in the power of Prayer". In fact, it was the duty of every member of the world-wide Anglican Communion to provide the élite of prayer-specialists on Caldey Island with a monastery bigger than almost any other in Europe. These young men who had acquired the holy art of prayer could not be expected to support themselves, even if they were trying to earn a little money by the sale of their "Handicrafts", e.g. Church Embroidery, Woodwork, Incense, Honey, and Hens.[14]

Br Jerome's drawing of the Guest House depicted a quaint stone building, with a battlemented tower and pantiled roof. Priests and laymen who desired to make retreats, or who were in need of recuperation, were told that "the climate of Caldey is both mild and bracing. . . . Here those who seek rest, guidance and comfort may come and find health, both for body and soul." They were warned, however, that there would be no intercourse with the cloistered monks, although the Abbot himself called at the Guest House daily. A fairly strict Rule was imposed. Smoking was forbidden except in the Common Room. Visitors had to rise at 6.15 a.m. and be in bed not later than 10 p.m. Owing to the dire poverty of the Community, the tariff imposed was 15s. 6d. per week (4s. a day) for full board. Should it be impossible to cross to the Island, the Cobourg Hotel at Tenby offered dinner, bed and breakfast for 5s. inclusive.

Inis Pyr was described in what became known as "The Pamphlet" as "An Island of Monks surrounded by the blue waters of the Severn Sea, and fragrant with the scent of flowers and the memory of holy lives. It is an Island of many aspects, full of charm of many kinds, rich in historical and natural interests, which carry the mind back to the past and onward into the unknown future. The thought of what Islands have already been to the Christian world leads on to the hope that even Caldey, by the grace of God, may be in the years to come. It may never have been a Patmos, an Iona, a Lindisfarne; but storms are gathering round the Church of God, and in troublous time it may be a Home of Peace, and a Stronghold of the Faith.[15] No better place would be found wherein to lead the Contemplative Life. Far away it lies for those who live on it to see the houses of the busy world, but not to hear its sounds; yet near enough for its shores to be reached by those who seek the seclusion of the Cloister, or the aid of those who dwell therein. . . . Think, then of Caldey Island as a Home of Devotion, for a thousand years dedicated to God, then desolated, and now recovered for His service, where some at least are trying to realize their Lord's Will declared in His Divine Commands."[16]

An indication that Carlyle's conception of the "Contemplative Life" was virtually the same at the age of thirty-three as it had been at thirteen, was ending this brochure with a reprint of Dr Neale's poem *The Good Old Times of England"*, first published in 1843. It was still a business of building up waste monastic places in the late medieval manner.

It is curious that nowhere in the detailed "History of the Community" was there any indication that the first attempt to found a monastery in the post-Reformation Church of England had been made forty-three years before Abbot Aelred and his monks moved to Caldey Island. Readers gathered that "an apparently accidental visit to the Benedictine nuns at Twickenham (now of Malling Abbey, near Maidstone) made him realize that as Benedictine Life had already been revived for women, so it might be for men".[17] It was not considered necessary to mention that Benedictine life for men had been revived in *Ecclesia Anglicana* by Joseph L. Lyne eleven years before Benjamin F. Carlyle was born. There was no reference to the double-monastery said to be observing the Benedictine Rule not more than eighty miles from Caldey Island.

Even in the summer of 1907 young men and women were still hearing a call to the cloister in the Vale of Ewyas. A few parents still felt it would benefit their sons to be brought up as Boy Oblates at Llanthony. Ignatius of Mary ("Baby") was seldom without at least one successor. Just as in the past, aspirants of both sexes, who sought information about the life led by the monks and nuns in their double-monastery in the Black Mountains, usually received copies of leaflets such as *Llanthony Abbey—a Picturesque Sketch, The Monastery and What I saw There, How I would like to be a Nun, Daily Life at Llanthony Abbey, Lent at the Monastery, The Twenty-two Teachings of Ignatius the Monk,* or *The Abbot and Abbey of Llanthony: their Authority.*

The Caldey community was not nearly so well supplied with publicity matter as Llanthony. It was still possible to buy *Mission Sermons and Orations,* and *Llanthony Teachings,* both published in 1890. Nothing could have been more uplifting than *The Monk's Ascension Book,* and *The Monk's Christmas Song.* Just as stimulating were *The Monk in the Church of England,* and *Why were the Monasteries of England destroyed?* That the Abbey was a real stronghold of the Faith was made clear in such leaflets as *The Glorious Church, Her Altar and Host, Her Crucifix and Candles, Her Sanctuary Lamp,* and *Her Incense and Vestments.* If these publications were not enough, there were still left a few copies of both *Brother Placidus and Why he became a Monk,* and *Leonard Morris or the Benedictine Novice.*[18]

All this Llanthony literature was far more fascinating than the green and gold-covered pamphlet published at Caldey Abbey. So it is easy to understand why men, women and boys felt that monastic life as led in the Black Mountains must be much more soul-satisfying than that on the Island of Monks. There was a considerable difference in the *mystique* of the two South Wales monasteries.

* * *

The quasi-Benedictine Order of St Paul had more or less faded out of the picture as a rival to the Aelredian and Ignatian Congregations. To go back eight years, the O.S.P. had been legally incorporated in 1899, the Founder having transferred the Supreme Authority to the Community under a Rule and Constitution. The Alton Abbey property was made over to Trustees. That same year a Priory was founded at Greenwich. It was intended as a temporary refuge for out of work, destitute merchant seamen, seeking ships in the Port of London, or attending hospitals as out-patients. The Priory at Barry Dock continued to be patronised by mariners of many nations.

At the same time Fr Hopkins did not neglect the monastic side of his Order. On September 29, 1901, the north transept of the Abbey Church was ready for use. A year later the foundation stone was laid of a flint-built Gothic Gate House, designed by the Rev. John Hawes. Intended as a novitiate, it was opened at Michaelmas 1903.[19] A start was made on the nave of the Abbey Church on Maundy Thursday 1905, the Gate House having been completed on September 29 the previous year.

A photograph of the interior of the chapel proves that the Order of St Paul provided Full Catholic Privileges, and had reached the same level as the Painsthorpe Benedictines in ritual and ceremonial, even if its corporate worship was conducted in the vulgar tongue instead of Latin. Six tall candlesticks and a crucifix stand on a very lofty gradine. There is a large veiled tabernacle, more candlesticks and flower vases, also a lace-trimmed super-frontal. Two plaster statuettes rest on pedestals on either side of the altar. A pair of massive standard candlesticks, with dummy candles, help to clutter up the foot-pace. This interesting collection of *bondieuserie,* evocative of a typical Edwardian "Catholic Repository" is set off by a rich dossal. The *tout ensemble* is in tune with the sanctuary at Llanthony Abbey at the same date.

Fr Hopkins wrote a month before the Caldey "Home Coming": "Our backs have ached, and our fingers have bled, but, well, there it stands, the nave of our Abbey Church. And we have not finished yet; wait until you see the monastic buildings and the choir." The nave of five bays, built mainly by the Founder and a few of his monks, was used for the first time at Easter 1907. The cream-coloured Dorset bricks of the pillars and arches matched happily with the flint walls.[20] The original chapel was demolished, and the building of the tower and nave started, with hardly any outside labour. Whatever may have been lacking at Alton, there is no doubt that the Order of St Paul were true monks from the point of view of St Benedict because they lived by the labour of their hands, as did their fathers and the apostles.[21]

An indication that the little community was still hoping to develop on traditional monastic lines is found in a statement published in *The Messenger:* "We men of the Order of St Paul are endeavouring in our own humble way, but please God, a thoroughly real way—to build up the old wastes, to raise the former desolations— the desolations of many generations—and it is a very substantial kind of comfort to see thick strong walls rising up about us as a still living faith in the power of the Religious Life and Brotherhood, and of our determination to bring forth both

THE GATEHOUSE CHAPEL, ALTON ABBEY, HANTS, *c.* 1906

Cluttered up with *"bondieuserie"*, it was typical of the most *avant garde* Anglo-Catholic fashions in church furnishings at the turn of the century. Compare with the drawings of the Benedictine chapels at Milton Abbas and Painsthorpe.

to bear upon the religious and social problems and difficulties of the generation in which our lot is cast."

* * *

This is where Fr Hopkins differed from Abbot Carlyle. The latter now took little practical interest in religious and social problems—not even rescue work for boys. Neither did he encourage his monks to do so, for this might have distracted them from contemplative prayer, and been a temptation to abandon their strictly enclosed way of life.[22]

By the autumn of 1907 it was perfectly clear that "The Home Coming" had been a fiasco from the financial point of view. What with creditors pressing for payment of outstanding debts, it almost looked as if the monks would find themselves bankrupt, and be forced to sell the island. Abbot Aelred wrote to one of his benefactresses three years later: "One night I particularly remember between waking and sleeping, I had a most vivid dream, in which I saw a great demon of bankruptcy scaling the cliffs of the Island to take possession, and at the same instant there flashed into my mind the idea of forming an Association of people who would promise to contribute a small sum for a fixed period. This organisation was to be called 'The Caldey Helpers', and when I got up the next morning, I was able to write out the scheme almost as if someone had dictated it to me, so easily and clearly did it come."[23]

Abbess Scholastica, unlike Abbot Aelred, did not suffer from periodical nightmares. Granted that the Malling community was poor, it was not in debt. The new Abbess was an astute business-woman. During her long career as a member of the Society of All Saints, she had taken her share in reviving some of its many houses scattered over England. We are told that "her powers of organisation and magnetic influence" immediately gave success to her efforts, for on entering the community, she had been described by Canon Knox-Little, her spiritual director, as "the cleverest woman with the strongest will I have ever known."[24]

She did not know whether she would achieve anything at Malling. The community was more or less moribund. There had been no novices for a long time. The first thing to be done was to win the confidence of the mostly elderly nuns. After six months the Abbess decided to re-open the novitiate for postulants. Then she asked Mr Henry Worth to advise on changes in liturgical worship.[25] Hitherto most of the Divine Office had been in English, with Mass and Benediction in Latin. On the feast of the Assumption, August 15, 1907, the *Breviarium Monasticum* was used for the first time in its entirety. The *Solesmes Antiphonale* and *Graduale* soon superseded the Anglican manuals of plainchant for the choir offices and Mass. Few of the nuns had any knowledge of Latin, so at first the Abbess had no choice but to act as Chantress and Hebdomadary. She also read the Martyrology at Prime as well as the Lessons at Matins. Not until she had trained one of the nuns did she give up the duties of Novice-Mistress. The text-books used were Dom Cuthbert Doyle's *Principles of the Religious Life,* and Fr Augustine Baker's *Holy Wisdom.* The more intellectual nuns were bidden to study Thomist philosophy, which no Caldey monks ever attempted. Those who strove after contemplation were advised to stick to the sanctified common sense of St Teresa of Avila and the English mystics.

* * *

No longer could Malling and Baltonsborough claim to be the only contemplative communities for women in the Church of England. By 1907 the Servants of Christ, founded by Mother Elizabeth ten years before to train foreign missionaries, were waiting to move from the busy East London suburb of Upton Park to the House of Prayer at Pleshey in Essex so that they could lead an enclosed and contemplative life. The result of a visit to Malling Abbey had been to divert Mother Millicent, the foundress of the Society of the Precious Blood from active work in the slums of Birmingham to a life of prayer in the country.[26]

In 1906 Fr Hollings, S.S.J.E. had formed a small community, giving it the name of Sisters of the Love of God. He began to train these ladies to lead an enclosed and contemplative life. Their first tentative efforts were made in conditions of great simplicity and poverty, in a small artisan's house. Dr Francis Paget, Bishop of Oxford from 1901 until his death in 1911, was most sympathetic, being sure that so long as these ladies were under the direction of the Cowley Fathers there would be no danger of their wanting to recite the offices in Latin, or to demand Romish devotions, like Benediction, Exposition, and the Rosary, which were indulged in by the Benedictine nuns at Baltonsborough and Malling.[27] By this time most of the Cowley Fathers were a little suspicious of Aelred Carlyle, whom they had befriended in his younger days.[28] Although they appreciated his efforts to revive the purely contemplative life for men and women, they deprecated his methods, which, in their opinion, were not in keeping with the best traditions of Tractarianism as set forth by their founder Fr Benson.

The arrival of more postulants in 1908 made it necessary for Fr Hollings to find a new home for the Sisters of the Love of God. A house on the Cowley Road was rented, but it was hardly suited to leading an enclosed life. The Sisters soon found that they got in each other's way when recreating in the small back garden. Bishop Paget approved the simple Rule drawn up in 1909. The following year he made his first official Visitation, and blessed the tiny chapel which had been erected in the garden. Fr Hollings wrote: "How much this recognition of the aims of the Congregation by the Bishop of the Diocese means; what encouragement it gives us and what strength. It is the confirmation of the desire that I have had throughout, that this Congregation should be really for the Church—the Church of England—and that in a humble way it should strengthen that side of her life which is hidden prayer."

There was nothing in the original Rule that was incompatible with the Report of the Committee presented to the Lambeth Conference in 1908 on the relations between Religious Communities and the Episcopate. It stated emphatically that the Rules of each community must contain a clause affirming distinct recognition of the Doctrine and Discipline of the Church of England as supreme, and another promising that no rites or ceremonies would be used in the chapel other than those contained in the Book of Common Prayer. In this respect the enclosed and contemplative community of women founded by Fr Hollings was really part of the Church of England as by Law established. The same could not be said of the Benedictine nuns at Baltonsborough and Malling, who preferred to think of themselves as belonging to the Catholic Church, not merely the Anglican branch of it.[29]

*   *   *

Abbess Scholastica did not confine her activities to developing the liturgical and spiritual life of her now growing community. She was a "woman of the world" in the best sense, determined that any talents possessed by her nuns should be put to practical use. The December 1907 issue of *Pax* featured the first advertisement for sweets made at Malling Abbey—"of the very best quality". Orders "for Dessert, Bazaars, Bon-bons, etc." were welcomed. Samples could "be sent at 6d. a box". Knitting and "all kinds of needlework" provided remunerative employment for the elderly nuns. So many ladies wanted to stay at the Abbey that it was decided to borrow money and rebuild the ancient guest-house, which had been used as a store and stables.

U

Meanwhile Caldey Island was being boosted as a holiday resort, not only for priests and laymen, but also for families. Church people "in search of the best air, combined with full Catholic privileges, could hardly find a better holiday than to stay in the Abbey Guest House", where the terms were moderate considering what was provided.[30]

After Easter 1908 Abbot Aelred and Dom George, who had just ended his two years as a curate at St Philip's, Dalston, where he began to take a keen interest in left-wing politics, went off together for a long continental holiday. They managed to find the money to enable them to visit several pilgrimage famous shrines and tourist resorts in France, Italy, Switzerland and Belgium, including Chartres and Einsiedeln, despite the never ending appeal for the support of the community.

In July the Abbot gave permission to Abbess Scholastica to leave her enclosure in order that she could study the observances of his monks, and decide what could be adopted at Malling. He also arranged for Lord Halifax, Sir Samuel Hoare Bt., Mr W. J. Birkbeck, and Mr Athelstan Riley—a quartette of leading Anglo-Catholic laymen—to stay on Caldey Island at the same time.

Halifax was enchanted with Caldey, which he described as "a paradise". He wrote of the "very comfortable arrangements, delightful room, very good food and wine". The Conventual Mass, preceded by Terce and followed by Sext, was "very well done and most moving"; but he got a shock of finding that the Lady Abbess of Malling was shut up in a curtained box "enclosed for all the world, like an old hen in a coop".[31] Never had he expected to find such beauty —"oh, what cliffs, what caves, what sandy bays: *quite, quite* ideal". After breakfast the Lord Abbot and the then sixty-nine year-old Viscount scrambled down the steep cliffs of Drinkim Bay, and had "the most delicious bathe that ever was". The latter admitted that he had never enjoyed anything more in his long life. At 6.30 p.m. he attended Evensong in the Village Church, followed by Exposition of the Blessed Sacrament with intercessions. The finale of this glorious day was Compline in the cottage-monastery chapel. The letter to his daughter Agnes (Mrs George Lane-Fox) ended with the words: "It really was the chief dream of my life realized. If Caldey did not belong to the Monks I would give anything to have it myself."[32]

That carefully staged visit of the President of the English Church Union to the Island of Monks had just the result hoped for by Abbot Aelred. Shortly afterwards Halifax confided to Athelstan Riley: "Caldey and the Abbot appeal to all the things I care for most". He was seeing "enormous visions"; determined to raise the money needed to erect the great Abbey, so obviously required by the only enclosed and contemplative Benedictine community of men in the Anglican Communion. By January 1909 he had got so far as to make preliminary arrangements to pay off the £8,000 mortgage on the Island, and hand over another £2,000 for building purposes. His solicitor, however, managed to prevent such reckless generosity, much to Dom Aelred's disappointment, for he still had to pay back the £4,000 borrowed from Mr Burstall, which had enabled him to become Lord of the Manor of Caldey, in addition to the £8,000 still owing to Mr Bushell.

The Lord Abbot, usually accompanied by his private secretary, was very much in the public eye during the summer and autumn of 1908. The first of his many engagements was a talk on the monastic life to undergraduates at Keble College, Oxford. In October he preached at St Benedict's, Ardwick, Manchester, and gave a lantern lecture at St Stephen's Mission Room, Bristol. Sermons at St Saviour's, Roath, Cardiff; All Saints', Margaret Street; St Clement's, City Road, and St Mary's, Graham Street—all in London—kept him on the go for the first half of November.

Meanwhile things were going on prosperously at Malling Abbey. On September 26, 1908 Dom Aelred blessed the new Guest House and clothed another novice. Thirty ladies attended the first Retreat. One wrote that there was "a pleasant Bohemian flavour of 'camping out' for the visitors, who, no doubt, would have cheerfully slept on the back-door steps if necessary, while the rooms were being adorned for their comfort". Before long every room had "pretty blue curtains at each window, and well-arranged pictures on the walls". Abbess Scholastica hoped that the Guest House would "fill a need in the Church of England from the fact of its being entirely separate from the Abbey itself, which makes possible more of freedom and less of rule than is perhaps desirable in the Guest Houses of other English Communities. In this respect our Guests still find it more like what is customary in foreign Religious Houses. Of course we shall ask them to remember that they are within the precincts of a House dedicated to prayer, and that the main object of their visits must be to deepen their own sense of the Presence of God."[33]

The nuns themselves, when they were not praying, kept busy with a knitting machine and two looms. They were hoping "to produce some really lovely material", also "knitted stockings for customers". Then "Mr Palmer of Plainchant fame" was trying to make the music "a little more worthy of being The Work of God". A studio had been built for one who was well known as "the All Saints' Sister who paints". With permission from her Superiors, Sister Catherine Weekes had joined the Malling community. "Lace prints" designed by her were now on sale, and she was also hard at work on tempera paintings. The first commission had come from North America. Business at Malling went on booming. Orders poured in for sweets, marmalade, hand-woven materials, and knitted stockings. On April 24, 1909, Abbot Aelred gave the habit to seven more postulants.

The Caldey Handicrafts, except sea-fishing which had been given up, were not doing too badly. In addition to Church Embroidery and Vestments, incense was now on sale—strongly recommended because "the combination of the choicest gums burns without any disagreeable fumes". Just as in the Painsthorpe days, "Strong sandals" (now priced at 8s. 6d. post free) were a profitable side-line. A new handicraft was the carving of Celtic Crosses "of very beautiful, hard and durable Marble of refined and quiet colours, eminently suitable for both outside and inside work". Sun-dials and Garden Seats, carved from the grey Caldey limestone, could be supplied, polished or unpolished. The half-dozen varieties of Wood Work— still "designed and carved after Ancient Models"—proved the versatility of these monks whose speciality was contemplative prayer. They also offered a nice line in Welsh Dressers, and almost any kind of "Household and Garden Furniture from Mr Carter's designs". Finally the Monastery Poultry Farm appeared to be doing big business with at least seven breeds of "Hens, Stock Birds, Reliable Sittings of Eggs, Prize-Bred Mammoth Bronze Turkeys, and High-Class Table Birds (fattened on the Sussex principle)".

Since the late summer of 1907, the Rev. William C. G. Prideaux had been living on the Island as the result of a breakdown in health while serving as an honorary curate at St Cuthbert's, Philbeach Gardens, London.[34] The following year, having been clothed as an Oblate, with the name of Denys, he was appointed Warden of the Guest House, in succession to Br John Blaker, who was made Parish Priest.

From that date Br Denys in his quiet, almost secretive way, became the virtual "power behind the throne" on Caldey Island, with an influence which almost exceeded that of the Lord Abbot. During the summer months the Guest House was usually filled with young men, many of whom were Oxford undergraduates. They sat at the feet of the erudite Oblate whose brain was as difficult to fathom as the *corpus* of theological writings attributed to the sixth-century Dionysius the Pseudo-Areopagite. Most mornings he retired to the round tower oratory above the Guest House, where he celebrated a private Mass in Latin. For the rest of the day, with his round bald head covered by a black zucchetto, he was buried in books, periodicals and pamphlets in many languages. Very long reviews, signed "B.D." became a regular feature of *Pax*, conveying the idea that the Caldey Benedictines must be as learned as the seventeenth and eighteenth-century French Maurist monks. Many years later Monsignor Ronald Knox wrote: "How well some of us remember Br Denys, afterwards Abbot of Nashdom, shrugging his shoulders and pointing to the motto PAX on the Guest House wall, when you tried to find out what he really thought of Father Abbot and his enterprises".[35]

Br Denys' review of Dr F. H. Dudden's *Gregory the Great, his place in history* (1905), consisted of three articles entitled "Cassiodorus, St Benedict and St Gregory the Great", which ran to over 25,000 words. It gave him the chance to express his opinions of Christian monasticism in general and particular, with diversions on many more subjects, for it was never easy for him to stick to the point. He could seldom resist the temptation to wander off into countless sidetracks. Neither Fr Ignatius nor Abbot Aelred had ever tried to produce solid historical reasons for their respective Benedictine foundations in Provinces of the Western Patriarchate no longer in communion with it, hence the importance of this learned *apologia*. Both rebuilders of monastic waste places had been too busy to bother about the subtle differences between "Orders" and "Corporations", or even the nature of the Catholic Church. Neither of them was a theologian or a historian.

*   *   *

Ignatius of Jesus, O.S.B. in his late sixties was almost evocative of a broken-down actor, obviously due to retire from the stage, but unable to resist the lure of footlights and greasepaint, feeling that "The Show Must Go On". Still garbed in his sombre monastic motley, white cord, rosary and sandals, the tonsured Benedictine "busker" went on tour as in the good old days, but his audiences were not as they used to be when he played at popular seaside resorts during the season. The bill-posting and bookings of halls were done by the Abbot's adopted son, Br David (W. Leycester Lyne), who was always ready to leave his family and farm in the Vale of Ewyas when the call came to take the road again.[36] But he had to be careful with the now greatly reduced box-office receipts and collections during the Missions. The Monk and his devoted companion usually had to stay in lodgings unless old friends were prepared to offer hospitality. Ignatius was always prostrated after preaching, and Br David often had to spend hours at night massaging his hands before he got to sleep. As he lay in bed, the aged Benedictine would murmer: "Let me do all I can *while* I can. All I pray is that I may be allowed to work for Jesus to the last, and die glorifying His Holy Name."

After one of his brief interludes of monastic life the Abbot of Llanthony had a slight stroke, just before starting for a soul-saving expedition in Lent 1908. Once again he heard angelic voices, also the song of a miraculous cuckoo. On the doctor's advice he was moved to a cottage near Evesham for change of air. When the summer came Br David took him to Sheringham, where the Abbot spent much of the time in a deck-chair on the beach, enjoying sea-breezes and sunshine, just as he had done at Margate in 1865, with "Baby" to amuse him.[37] One day he whispered affectionately: "Child David, I want you to promise me something. Never leave me." His adopted son made the promise, but was unable to keep it, for business recalled him from Norfolk to the Black Mountains.

The Abbot's condition grew steadily worse. His last months were passed at "Darjeeling", his sister's house at Camberley, Surrey. He died there on October 16, 1908 after a third stroke. "Praise be to Jesus" were his last words.[38]

It was in keeping with his nearly forty years as a roving recluse that the death of Ignatius of Jesus took place some two hundred miles off his monastery, for he had always been a Gyrovag kind of monk. The Great Western Railway provided a special train to transport the mortal remains of the Druid-Abbot from Reading to Llanfihangel-Crucorney. It would be hard to say how many times he had made this same journey via Worcester during his life-time. That night a watch was kept over the coffin as it rested before the high altar of the Abbey Church. The following morning there were two celebrations of the Holy Communion, one in English and the other in Welsh. A solemn Requiem High Mass followed at 11 o'clock, carried out according to the Llanthony version of the Use of the Illustrious Church of Sarum. Only a small congregation assisted at the obsequies.[39]

Neither the Church of England nor the Church of the Cymry felt it worth while to be represented.[40]

The *Church Times* published an obituary, entitled "The Lessons of Llanthony". The anonymous writer stated: "For the personal piety of Fr Ignatius, and for his devotion to what he conceived to be his duty, we feel nothing but respect. For his attempt to found a Benedictine house we can have little but criticism. . . . For the cowl does not make the monk, nor the building of a monastery, a community. And the result of the attempt and the failure has perhaps been to delay the real restoration, to create a certain prejudice, to hinder the generosity of Churchmen towards more strict and loyal efforts to restore the Contemplative Life. It is not easy to see what part Fr Ignatius may have been intended to serve in the whole movement. To us it seems but the total failure of work which at the first was rich in promise."[41]

Fr Hopkins, founder of the Order of St Paul, wrote a far more understanding obituary in *The Hampshire Post*, with personal memories of this often ludicrous yet always loveable monk-evangelist who defied archbishops and bishops, shouting clergy and pursuing policemen at many a Church Congress. He had steered Ignatius "safely through a crowd of many, umbrella-shaking, shouting females", and he got for his pains "only a reprimand from the dear old soul for being much too 'modern', and a bit 'worldly' for even a dear friar! . . . He always insisted that I was really a friar, not a monk! And I used to tell him I didn't mind which it was so long as he blessed me and didn't curse. 'I never curse anybody', he replied. 'But you've just been cursing poor Gore and Freemantle', I said. 'Not *cursing*', he retorted, 'only *anathematizing*'. 'Then you think there is really a chance of salvation for even them?' The old thing was literally trembling with anger and indignation; and I bowed my head, not I am afraid to say Amen, but to hide a smile, as he said, 'Yes, but they will both get it very hot first'."

In the opinion of Fr Hopkins, "Fr Ignatius believed himself to be called to revive the monastic life in the Church of England. He saw visions and dreamed dreams. Visions of modern Saint Gregories and Augustines re-converting England. Dreams of 'building up of the old wastes, the raising up of the former desolations, the desolations of many generations'. In other words he dreamed of old abbeys like Netley and Glastonbury and Tintern and Llanthony being restored and repeopled by really holy men separated and consecrated to the work of the salvation of souls. True to what he believed to be his own 'call' in this respect he shaved his crown, took the tonsure—this was nearly fifty years ago—he donned the Benedictine habit, he put on sandals—he made a start.

"The people tried to howl him down, and once very nearly succeeded in lynching him. The bishops first called him to 'order', then threatened, then inhibited him. But the dreamer, the fanatic, the what-ever-you-like-to-call-him, held on his course; crunched through the ice, and opened out the way—making it easy for the likes of us who came after to follow in his wake with our later attempts at reviving various forms of religious life in the Church of England. Don't let us forget it, we Kellies and Carlisles, and Freres and Hopkinses."[42]

Having stressed that Ignatius was "ever a trusting, as well as a loving old soul—far too trusting"—Fr Hopkins recalled "the numbers of wretched fellows who joined themselves to him, calling him 'Father', and afterwards either deserting him or having to be expelled". The long obituary ended with a reference to the "visions". He was absolutely convinced that Ignatius of Jesus O.S.B. "honestly thought he saw what he said he did; he honestly thought he performed the miracles to which he laid claim. I'm not made of the human stuff that even thinks he could possibly see such visions, or thinks he could possibly work any such miracles, but I am quite sure that Fr Ignatius believed himself to be a medium of that kind of thing on the Christian or right side, just as he honestly believed the spiritualists to provide mediums on the devilish or wrong side. He lived in an atmosphere peopled with angels or devils—possibly created out of his own imaginings; but nevertheless to him very real."[43]

In view of subsequent events it is worth quoting from "the last Will and Testament of Joseph Leycester Lyne, in Religion Ignatius of Jesus". It reads:—

"I leave the Monastery of Llanthony, the convent and monastery church thereof, and the garden and other lands (if any) now held and enjoyed therewith, including the farms of Trecas and Ty-Gwynne, and all that they contain (save those few things hereinafter mentioned and specifically bequeathed) unto Alfred Harris (Father Asaph) and Jessie Dow (in religion Mother Tudfil) of the Convent of Llanthony, absolutely, as joint tenants, subject to the right of my adopted son, William Leycester Lyne, for life, to continue farming the lands of the said monastery as he is now farming, at a nominal rental of one shilling, in return for the services which he renders and shall render to the monastery as heretofore".

At the time of Ignatius' death, the twin-community—said to have been founded "according to the precedent of the Old Saxon Abbeys"—consisted of Fr Asaph of the Blessed Virgin, Mother Tudfil of the Holy Name of Jesus, four monks, two nuns, and three extern sisters, making a total of eleven. After the funeral a Chapter was held at which the Rev. Richard Courtier-Foster was elected as second Abbot of Llanthony. For the past year he had been a curate at St Giles', Cambridge.[44] This young clergyman, who had no knowledge of monastic life other than what he had acquired during a few visits to Llanthony as a guest, on being told of his election, replied that he could not accept the honour without the approval of Dr Owen, Bishop of St Davids. Apparently His Lordship raised no objections, and Mr Courtier-Foster resigned his curacy. Early in May 1909 Abbot Aelred went to Cambridge, where he and Abbot-elect Richard discussed the future relationship of their respective communities.

Not long after this, Fr Asaph of the Blessed Virgin and Fr Gildas Mary of the Resurrection, without the approval of their Abbot-elect or that of the Bishop of St Davids, cleared off to Canada. They were raised to the diaconate and priesthood, probably at Winnepeg, by Archbishop Joseph René Villate, otherwise "Mar Timotheos".[45] It is not known how the two monks managed to find the money for the transatlantic return journey. On their return home they were surprised and distressed when Bishop Owen refused to recognise their possibly valid though highly irregular orders. Their Abbot-elect decided that, under the circumstances, he had better give up the idea of adopting *insignia pontificalia*.[46]

Before long the twin-community found itself penniless, and almost starving, for Llanthony, like Caldey, had no endowment.[47] Matters reached a crisis in the autumn of 1909. Fr Asaph asked Abbot Aelred to preside over a Chapter, held after a brief Retreat. The upshot was that Mother Tudfil, the senior of the two remaining nuns, agreed to make over her share of the property and to leave the convent. To quote from what the Abbot wrote in the December issue of *Pax:* "This wise and generous action on her part has considerably simplified the situation; and it was decided that those of the Brethren who wished should be given every opportunity of testing their Vocation with us at Caldey. Fr Asaph and three of the Brethren have now definitely joined our Community as simple laymen, and Llanthony Abbey itself is being made over to us."

Regarding the Ignatian vows as invalid, Abbot Aelred insisted that the already professed monks must start off again as novices, after a brief postulancy. Neither were Fr Asaph and Fr Gildas allowed to celebrate Mass. The former was the only one of the quartette who persevered. The other three soon departed, realising that life in the *Congregatio Anglicana a Primaeva Observantia* was not their cup of tea.[48]

Abbot Aelred informed his friends in December 1909: "The passing of Llanthony into our care will of course mean an additional responsibility, but with the arrangements in contemplation, this responsibility will, I think, be reduced to a minimum, and I am sure that all lovers of the Benedictine life will rejoice that now the whole of the Benedictine work in the Church of England will be concentrated under one form of government. In the present state of things, this concentration of effort—because of its unity of purpose—will help to make for stability and permanence. Isolated attempts in the revival of the Religious Life have been, in many cases, doomed to failure for want of support and help at the critical moment, but with a Congregation such as ours, we hope to avoid many difficulties, and mutual help will be forthcoming when it is needed."

Apparently the Lord Abbot of Caldey forgot that "Benedictine work" was being carried on by other communities besides Caldey, Malling, and Baltonsborough, which formed his "Congregation" at that moment. The Sisters of Our Lady of Nazareth had been observing the Rule of St Benedict, and reciting the Day Hours of the *Breviarium Monasticum* since their foundation in 1865. The Community of the Holy Cross was already on its way to becoming enclosed and contemplative, with monastic observances based on the Benedictine Rule. Fr Hopkins could have pointed out that the Order of St Paul had been trying to observe the Holy Rule since 1889 and that its work for aged and infirm mercantile marine seamen was in keeping with the Benedictine spirit and tradition.

It is difficult to understand why Dom Aelred should have taken for granted that all Anglican "lovers of the Benedictine life" would "rejoice" at the news that he had placed himself in supreme control of "the whole of the Benedictine work" in *Ecclesia Anglicana* without reference to any higher authority. He seems to have forgotten that Benedictine monasticism grew up by a series of "isolated attempts" to keep the whole or part of the Rule for nearly three hundred years, and that it was not until 817 that the first attempt was made to federate a certain number of monasteries, and only those of a single kingdom. The first veritable Benedictine "Order" to be formed was the Congregation of Cluny in 910.[49] It was the fourth Lateran Council of 1215 which changed materially the whole trend of Benedictine polity by its decree that all monasteries of each ecclesiastical province were to be united into a congregation and cease to be independent. Br Denys must have shrugged his shoulders and grunted when he read the Abbot's letter in *Pax*, for he had already made clear the basic difference between *true* Benedictine monasticism and the *"Papal monopolies"* which resulted from the 1215 Lateran Council in one of his learned articles.

For some reason or other the Llanthony property was never made over legally to the Benedictines of Caldey Island, and remained in the possession of Alfred Harris (Fr Asaph). Had he left the community he could have sold the estates, without Abbot Aelred being able to stop him.[50]

NOTES

[1] *Verses Supposed to be Written by Alexander Selkirk.*

[2] Present-day Benedictine *abbates nullius diocesis* are those of Monte Cassino, Subiaco, S. Paolo ab Urbe (Rome), Cava di Terrwni, Monte Oliveto (all in Italy); Einsiedeln (Switzerland); Pannonhelma (Hungary); Belmont (North Carolina); Muenster (Sask., Canada); Rio de Janeiro (Brazil); New Norcia (Western Australia); Pietersberg (South Africa); Tokwon (Korea); and Peramiho (Tanzania).

[3] Considering that the "Islanders" had been reckoned as parishioners of Penally since the Reformation, and that in recent years they had benefitted from the spiritual ministrations of Mr Bushell when he was in residence, it is curious that Halifax should have believed that they had been in a state of schism for over three centuries.

[4] Carlyle explained to Dr Gore, Bishop of Oxford, in 1912: "On coming to Caldey, we decided to wait till it was seen whether the Community could remain permanently on the Island, before approaching the Archbishop of Canterbury about my Licence". (Cf. *A Correspondence*, p. 42.)

[5] On October 19, 1906, he formed a Trust composed of eight professed monks to ensure that the island would remain in the hands of the community after his death.

[6] "A Message from South Africa", in *Pax*, Christmas 1906, p. 67.

[7] See p. 96.

[8] op. cit., p. 66.

[9] Ch. 48.

[10] *Pax*, Christmas 1906, p. 104.

[11] Cf. P. F. Anson, *The Hermit of Cat Island* (New York, 1957) pp. 28-30.

[12] *Pax*, September 1907, p. 281.

[13] The latter now consisted of the Gate House Monastery, the great Abbey, Hermitage and Chapel of St Bernard, Calvary School, and two rows of cottages.

[14] So-called "Handicrafts" were all the rage in the Edwardian era. They went hand-in-hand with the "Simple Life" movement, and "Higher Thought".

[15] The chief storm affecting the Anglican branch of the Catholic Church in 1907 resulted from the *Report of the Royal Commission on Ecclesiastical Discipline* published the previous year. The times were indeed troublous for Strongholds of the Faith.

[16] op. cit., pp. 47-8.

[17] ibid, p. 13.

[18] See pp. 101, 102.

[19] This was shortly after the completion of the chapel at Painsthorpe Abbey which he designed. (See p. 178.)

[20] At Easter 1907 no monastic building had begun on Caldey Island, and the monks carried out the Holy Week functions in the old Priory Church. Their brethren at Alton had got well ahead of them.

[21] *Rule of St Benedict*, Ch. 48.

[22] Had the O.S.P. been the owners of Caldey Island in 1907, it is probable that a small priory would have been opened at Tenby for the benefit of the crews of the Brixham fleet of brown-sailed smacks that used the harbour throughout the summer.

[23] Printed by John Kensit in *The Churchman's Magazine*, September 1925.

[24] *The Benedictines of Talacre*, p. 5.

[25] The one-time curate at St Agnes', Kennington, who had been received into the Roman Church in 1895, was now a lay-oblate of Erdington Abbey, and a member of the Vatican Commission on Plainchant, set up by Pius X. (See pp. 132.)

[26] Cf. Sister Felicity Mary, S.P.B., *Mother Millicent* (1969) p. 41.

[27] The Bishop was what might be called a "Modernist Tractarian". In 1889 he had contributed an essay on the Sacraments to *Lux Mundi*. Two years later the chapter on "Accidie" in his *Spirit of Discipline* showed that he understood the spiritual desolation that affected so many medieval monks and hermits.

[28] See pp. 160, 163.

[29] See p. 269 for the latest history of the Sisters of the Love of God.

[30] Among the better-known visitors after the Guest House had been opened were the Duke of Newcastle, Lord Wolmer, Sir Hubert Miller Bt., the Hon. Niall Campbell (future Duke of Argyll), Ronald Knox, Samuel Gurney, Vernon Johnson, Dr W. B. Randolph, Fr Paul Bull, C.R., Br Andrew S.D.C., Rev. Hermitage Day (editor of the *Church Times*), and Rev.

Percy Dearmer, who brought his first wife and their two sons. But no members of the hierarchies of the Provinces of Canterbury and York ever compromised themselves by spending even one night on the Island during the six years it was owned by Abbot Carlyle as an Anglican monk. On the other hand, the overseas Bishops of Carpentaria, Nyasaland, Salina and Zanzibar found their way to Caldey.

[31] By this time the community was living in a row of cottages originally planned for workmen. The chapel consisted of two small rooms thrown into one, with hardly any space for more than two or three seculars.

[32] Cf. Lockhart, op. cit., Vol. II, p. 207.

[33] *Pax*, September 1908, p. 41.

[34] Born in 1864, he was admitted at Clare College, Cambridge, in 1885, where he took the degree of B.A. in 1889. Three years later he entered Cuddesdon College, and was ordained priest at Peterborough in 1893. He served curacies at Syston, Leics. (1892-5); St Mary's, Wolverton, Bucks. (1895-6); and St Margaret's, Liverpool (1896-1904). It was during his honorary curacy at St Cuthbert's, Philbeach Gardens that he first met Abbot Aelred. In January 1907 a Ward of the Caldey Confraternity of St Benedict was formed at this then famous (or notorious) church by the Vicar, Fr St Leger Westall.

[35] "Dom Aelred Carlyle, a Memoir", in *Pax*, Spring 1956, p. 30.

[36] See p. 128.

[37] See p. 72.

[38] Apparently he died without receiving the Last Sacraments or formal reconciliation with the Church of England, from which he had incurred *ipso facto* excommunication in 1898 after his irregular ordination to the priesthood.

[39] On August 5, 1972, Solemn Evensong was sung in the ruined and roofless choir of Llanthony Abbey by a clergyman of the Hereford Diocese to mark the centenary of its foundation; following a procession to the statue of Our Lady of the Apparitions, with the hymns accompanied by the Abergavenny Town Band. None of the six bishops of the Church in Wales was present, neither did they send delegates. Their absence, however, was made up for by Mgr F. E. Glenn, founder of what is now called "The Old Catholic Church of England", who was given precedence over the Anglican Abbot of Nashdom. During the course of his sermon Fr Brocard Sewell, O. Carm, informally canonized the Rev. J. L. Lyne. On October 8 the "world première" on a play for one man in two acts, entitled "The New Saint Ignatius" took place at St Philip's, Earls Court, London, starring Richard Carey. So this "true Anglican exotic" (as the *Church Times* styled Fr Ignatius of Jesus, O.S.B. in an article on July 28) is not forgotten in these days, even if only by an elite.

[40] The Abbot of Caldey sent Br Illtud Burstall. Also among the mourners was the young Baron de Bertouch, son of Ignatius' official biographer, who happened to be staying in the Black Mountains for the autumn shooting season.

[41] October 23, 1908.

[42] Fr Herbert Kelly, founder of the Society of the Sacred Mission; and Fr Walter Frere, co-founder of the Community of the Resurrection, Bishop of Truro from 1916 to 1932.

[43] op. cit., October 24, 1908.

[44] The Abbot-elect had been educated at University College, Durham. Ordained priest in 1904, he had served curacies at Carlisle and Windermere before going to Cambridge. He was a fairly recent friend of the community, and had given Communion to Fr Ignatius after his first stroke at Llanthony early in 1908.

[45] By this time he had broken off all relations with the Independent Catholic Church of Goa, Ceylon, and India; the Syro-Jacobite Patriarchate of Antioch; and the Old Catholic Churches in Europe. He was moving around North America, ready to ordain or consecrate almost anybody who paid for his services, thus sponsoring more than one schismatic sect. Since raising Fr Ignatius to the priesthood in 1898 he had consecrated Gulotti, Marsh-Edwards, Ventham, and probably other men, as free-lance bishops for Europe.

[46] In 1910 Mr Courtier-Foster became Acting Chaplain at St Paul's Cathedral, Valetta, and until 1919 held a roving commission as Chaplain at Odessa and the Russian ports on the Black Sea. Having returned to England, and served a London curacy, the once would-be Benedictine was appointed vicar of St Giles', Norwich, in 1927, where he ended his clerical career instead of at Llanthony Abbey.

[47] Fr Ignatius had left stocks of a nominal value of £1,200 to cover his funeral expenses and debts, with the residue to his monks and nuns, who could rely no longer on the profits made from his Missions to cover the cost of living.

[48] Dom Asaph Harris died at Pluscarden Priory, Moray, in 1967. Gildas Taylor worked for some years as a priest in one of the so-called "Old Catholic" sects in Mexico. Having returned to England, he was reconciled with the Roman Church, joined the Caldey community, and died on the island as a simply-professed monk in 1918. Br Illtud Jackson also found his way back again later on, but, conforming to Llanthony tradition, eventually ran away after stealing a considerable amount of money and some of the abbatial pontifical regalia. Ernest Odell Cope, returned to the mainland after a fortnight, got married, and, having gone through a secret consecration in 1939, decided in 1945 to revive monastic life at Llanthony. In 1948 he issued a prospectus for "The Order of Llanthony Brothers". He himself was the "Presiding Bishop" with the style of "The Rt. Rev. E. O. Cope (known as Ignatius, O.S.B.)". Other dignitaries were The Assistant-Bishop, the Rt. Rev. J. Y. Batley; the Bishop-

Abbot, the Rt. Rev. William Corke, O.S.B.; and the Prior, the Very Rev. Charles Hastler, O.S.B. This little community lived in a bungalow lent them by two nieces of Fr Ignatius, but remained there only three months, for the Bishop-Abbot found himself confined in gaol for two years. Such was also the end of Bishop Cope's so-called "Free Anglo-Catholic Church". He died in 1957.

[49] Others followed: e.g. Camaldoli (1009); Vallombrosa (1039); Grammont (1076), Citeaux (1098); Fontrevault (1099); Savigny (1105); Thiron (1117); Monte Vergine (1119); Val-des-Choux (c. 1190); Sylvestrines (1231); Velestines (1254); and Monte Oliveto (1310).

[50] In the late 1920s, Dom Wilfrid Upson, then Prior of Caldey, managed to persuade Dom Asaph to sign the documents that enabled Eric Gill to buy the property. The eventual result was that the former legal owner had a severe mental breakdown, haunted by the belief that he had been guilty of sacrilege by allowing a sacred shrine to pass into secular hands.

THE FUTURE CALDEY ABBEY AS DREAMED OF IN 1906

Designed in the Romanesque style of architecture, this immense range of buildings would be erected on the cliffs above Paul Jones's Bay. Such is how J. C. Hawes did his best to give shape to the abbatial visions of a 20th century evocation of the medieval abbeys of Cluny, Vézelay, or Durham.

CALDEY ABBEY, 1910–1913

To be used eventually as a Preparatory School for the sons of Anglo-Catholic parents.

CHAPTER XIII

The Cottage-Monastery on Caldey given a new Chapel; Abbess Scholastica decides to move her nuns from Malling to Milford Haven; Abbot Aelred dreams of making five foundations; the daily life of the Caldey Benedictines (1909-1910)

In December 1908 Abbot Aelred realised that, for lack of money, there was no immediate chance of starting to build the magnificent Gate House monastery. The plans, drawn by Mr Coates Carter, had been exhibited at the Royal Academy. As to the gargantuan Abbey, it must wait until the vast sums needed for its erection began to roll in. Still he told readers of *Pax* that he was confident that the permanent monastery would be ready for occupation within two or three years, even if only £25 8s. had been contributed to the Building Fund in the past quarter. In the meantime he intended to add a fifty-five feet-long Chapel to the row of cottages in which the community was still living. The existing chapel was far too small for pontifical functions, and there was no space for more than half a dozen seculars. Yet even then he was optimistic that the dream-Abbey would arise sooner or later, so he planted some young trees around its site, certain that they would be shooting up by the time that the walls arose, and protect them from the winds. The Cottage-Monastery, so he explained, could serve the needs of the growing community until the Gate House was completed, when it would be turned into a Preparatory School for Boys. Many parents were wanting the sons to benefit from the spiritual care of the Benedictines "before going on to the larger life of Public Schools". During the holidays Retreatants could be accommodated. He pointed out: "The Cottage-Monastery and the Chapel will give us just the necessary pause for some time to come while experience and funds accumulate".

Although heavily overdrawn at the bank, and still faced by the repayment of £12,000 on the purchase of the Island, the Lord Abbot signed a contract with the builders. An illustrated leaflet was printed and distributed far and wide. It stressed how important it was for the only enclosed and contemplative Benedictine community of men in the Anglican Communion to have a really dignified House of Prayer. Not only did Dom Aelred ask for many thousands of pounds, he also begged people to send stones from "the old ruined Monasteries which were once the glory of England", so that the altar of the new chapel could be built from them. This appeal caught on, and before long stones of every shape and size were arriving. Each stone, according to the instructions given, was incised with the name of the monastery in bold letters.

Next followed a strenuous preaching tour to arouse greater interest in the purely contemplative life; with sermons at Birmingham, Brighton, Chester, Hull, Liverpool, and London, where he occupied the pulpits of half-a-dozen churches—even a trip to the Isle of Man. The abbatial ambitions grew bigger. In honour of the Holy Trinity the new chapel must have three bells. He suggested that the Confraternity of St Benedict should pay for them. By June 1909 he had decided that Mr Coates Carter's interior furnishings were not rich enough, and too Cistercian. Something more Cluniac in magnificence was demanded. He wrote: "We want to put all we can into this new Chapel of ours, and make it as perfect as possible".

To ensure that the services would be carried out as correctly as possible by the *Congregatio Anglicana a Primaeva Observantia Regulae S.P.N. Benedicti,* it was essential to publish an *Ordo Operis Dei persolvendi sacrique peragendi juxta Ritum Monasticum.* This brochure was printed in red and black. To stress that the monks and nuns of the Congregation were absolutely loyal and true to their Spiritual Mother the Church of England, the Abbot restored one of the three State Holy Days which had been a feature of the calendar of the Book of Common Prayer from 1662 to 1859, when Queen Victoria abolished them without consent of the Church as represented in Convocation. This was the commemoration of the murder of King Charles I on January 30—*"Dies Martyrii S. Caroli Regis"*[1] The "Black Letter" feast-day of the Conception of the Blessed Virgin Mary became a "Red Letter" and was raised to the rank of a Double of the First Class, but the Office and Mass used were those for the Immaculate Conception, as printed in the Latin Breviary and Missal. Dom Aelred, as a one-time medical student, did not approve of the cultus of the Sacred Heart of Jesus for physiological reasons, so this post-Tridentine feast was omitted from the *Ordo.* Otherwise it differed hardly at all from the one published by the Roman Catholic English Benedictine Congregation.

But it was not enough for the *Congregatio Anglicana a Primaeva Observantia* to have its own *Ordo.* Abbot Aelred asked Mr Samuel Gurney, the Secretary of the Medici Society, if it would be prepared to print a complete set of Latin liturgical books. The most urgent was an *Horae Diurnae Monasticae* for the use of "some Sisterhoods who are thinking of joining our Benedictine Federation". After this the Society could get on with specially edited versions of the *Breviarium Monasticum* and *Missale Monasticum.* Considering that the "Federation" did not exceed more than sixty members, monks and nuns included, this might seem a reckless extravagance, but the ever-optimistic Abbot-General had no doubt that before long his Primitive Observance Congregation would reach the numbers of those of the Cistercian Order in the twelfth century. So the books had better be ready for the many hundreds of monks and nuns when they materialized. Mr Gurney pointed out that it would be necessary to obtain an *imprimatur* from the Primate of All England, but in August 1909, the Abbot wrote: "With regard to the Archbishop's approval, I fear we shall have to wait for the happy decease of the present Primate, for I feel quite sure he would never approve of anything presented to him with a concrete example of the practice of the Communion of Saints". This was the last said about the publication of Latin liturgical books. The Anglican Congregation continued to use those issued with the *nihil obstat* and *imprimatur* of Papist prelates.

Readers of *Pax* were reminded from time to time of the vast influence which the Congregation was having on the speeding up of the Catholic Movement. A recent guest had expressed the feelings of many people when he wrote: "Caldey was to me a great deal: a reunion with the Church I have loved—and almost lost—for I was slipping into the ways of Rome fast. My visit to your Abbey rekindled the old fires, and made me feel that the Church of my Baptism *would* be the Church of my Death. . . . The Compline Hour at Caldey was a great joy to me—I have said Compline every night since. God bless you and your work."[2]

The Island had become the most advanced Catholic stronghold in Britain. The great festivals were observed with all possible external solemnity. Outdoor processions during Rogationtide and on the feast of Corpus Christi were inspiring spectacles. The monks, followed by most of the island inhabitants, wended their way across the fields chanting the Latin Litanies of Our Lady and of All Saints, or singing English hymns. But visitors were informed that the all-Latin services in the monastery chapel were not intended for layfolk. Only by special invitation were they allowed to participate in this esoteric worship in a hieratic language. As a matter of fact, there was no accommodation for more than half-a-dozen seculars. During Holy Week the monks chanted Tenebrae in the Village Church, and on the morning of Holy Saturday the elaborate ceremonies were carried out in strict conformity with the rubrics of the Roman Rite. A "Chapel of the Sepulchre", with an Altar of Repose, was fitted up in the hut used as a schoolroom for the island children. Even if the Bishops of England and Wales tolerated nothing more than private reservation for communicating the sick, the Benedictines made reparation for this by chanting before and after every choir office the antiphon *Adoremus in aeternum Sanctissimum Sacramentum* accompanied by profound genuflections. They also enjoyed frequent Exposition of the Host in a monstrance.

In the Village Church the simple but reverent services conformed more or less to the so-called "English Use". The missal used was Percy Dearmer's *The English Liturgy*, published in 1903. The abbatial Lord of the Manor felt that his island tenants could do without the Reservation of the Consecrated Elements. So there was no tabernacle on the altar, furnished with four riddel-posts and a dossal.

On St Samson's Day, July 28, observed as the "Island Festival", there was a flower-show during the afternoon, and a concert in the evening, which the monks were allowed to attend, in spite of being otherwise strictly enclosed. St Luke's Day (October 18)—the anniversary of "The Home Coming" in 1906—was marked by Pontifical High Mass in the old Priory Church, as well as by a variety show and supper party in the evening. Taken all round, the life of the community was not quite so contemplative as stated in print.

On the financial side, however, the state of affairs went from bad to worse. The December 1909 issue of *Pax* revealed that only £10 14s. 2d. had been donated during the past four months towards the support of "the only Contemplative Community of Men in the Church of England". At least £3,600 was needed to complete the new Chapel, and only about £700 had been received since the appeal was launched. It distressed and surprised the Lord Abbot that money was not rolling in to build "a little Church devoted to the careful and continual rendering of the Divine Praises in the Work of God according to the Rule of St Benedict". Postulants were clamouring to be admitted. More accommodation was an obvious necessity. He explained:

"Here I should like to make it quite clear that, owing to the lack of funds, we have completely abandoned the idea of building the Gate House; and we have determined to build what is necessary for the growing needs of the Community by adding on to the Cottage-Monastery in which we are now living. This will serve our purpose for a good many—perhaps twenty years; and by the end of that time, the Community may be large enough to make the permanent Abbey an accomplished fact, and the present buildings will then be ready for the Preparatory School for Boys. Thus waste will be avoided. Next year we shall want a Refectory, Kitchen, Outhouses, and more cells; it will probably be (with the new Chapel) a matter of five or six thousand pounds altogether. . . . Perhaps this Christmas time will help to commend our need to the hearts of the rich, and that the new year will rejoice us by bringing enough to do what is required, so that there will be no further necessity for more subscription lists in *Pax*. With the proposed new buildings, and the assistance of our Caldey Helpers, we shall be quite set up; and it will be a great comfort for me to feel that when I sit down to write my Community Letter in future, I shall not be obliged to consider how I can ask effectively for what is wanted, without, at the same time, giving offence to our friends, and the impression that we are always begging."[3]

Yet friends had been generous with gifts in kind during the past half-year, for they included lots of Altar lace; books and magazines galore; Ivy Geraniums and roses for the altar; brass flower-vases; black stockings and sleeping suits; a valuable collection of minerals; socks and pinnies for the villagers; seeds for the Maze and the Trenches; a 16th-century sanctuary lamp; celeriac and other roots for the garden; a beautiful illuminated missal and an aquarium, together with a white silk embroidered burse and veil; plants and provisions, tapestry and a telescope; bulbs and an Arundel picture of St Benedict preaching. Honey in bottles, as well as incense in tins, and Caldey fuchsias in pots, were now on sale; likewise six breeds of hens, incubators, and Indian Runner Ducks.

Abbot Aelred got a shock on the feast of the Purification of Our Lady, February 2, 1910, when Abbess Scholastica confided that she had no intention of letting the Church of her Baptism be the Church of her death. She was convinced of a clear call to submit to the Church of Rome; not immediately, however, but after she had prepared most if not all her nuns to follow her.

The Abbot's next Community Letter was written nearly a thousand miles away from Caldey Island. He and his private secretary, Br Aidan, were the guests of Mr Harold Brocklebank, of Grizedale Hall, Lancs, and his wife, at their villa outside Florence. On his doctor's advice and the urgent wish of the community, Dom Aelred had decided to spend the whole of Lent in Italy. A sharp attack of influenza had followed six hectic weeks of preaching at London, Brighton and elsewhere. He had not taken a holiday for two years and felt he badly needed one. There was a private oratory in the villa, so, presuming that he had the privilege of a portable altar, he was able to celebrate a daily Latin Mass, and to perform the *Opus Dei* with his *socius*. He wrote: "Here at a distance, I can take a more complete view of our Island Life—as a man on the mountain-top can see many things going on below which are hidden from the inhabitants themselves". At the same time he fully realised that his long absence from the cloister would arouse comment; in fact he had already received "a postcard to say that a friend had said to a friend of ours: 'What a funny sort of Community Caldey must be if the Abbot could leave it and run about on the Continent during Lent and Holy Week'. This sort of thing causes one to smile; but at the same time we ought to realize that it has its serious side."[4]

The two Benedictines were able to visit several monasteries in Tuscany, including the Certosa di Farneta, where the community of the Grande Chartreuse were then living in exile. The Abbot got useful ideas for his new monastery, deciding that it must convey the impression that it was in sunny Italy with red pan-tiled roofs, and gleaming white walls—nothing Gothic about the exterior. Having inspected more than one *prelatura*, he realised that to stress his unique status of an Anglican *abbas-nullius*, a mansion on the same scale must be erected as his private residence. The sight of the *Volto Santo* in Lucca Cathedral made him feel that a copy of this figure of Christ the King must be made in silver for the altar crucifix in the new Chapel.

The travellers got back to Caldey for Holy Week and after many delays, the new Chapel was solemnly dedicated on May 15, the feast of Pentecost. To ensure the greatest possible correctness in functions according to the Roman Rite, the Abbot had sent his *caermonarius*, Br Bernard, to London, so that he could pick up ideas at Westminster Cathedral and the Oratory. The choirmaster, Br Wilfrid, had spent a long weekend in lodgings near Quarr Abbey, in the Isle of Wight, for the sake of listening to the Solesmes plainchant.

The exterior of the building was plain and severe, with white roughcast walls and red-tiled roof; the length eighty feet and the width twenty. Small round-headed windows, high up in the walls on the north sides, with a rose window at the east end, above the main door, provided light. The words of the Psalmist: "The king's daughter, is all glorious within, her clothing is of wrought gold. She shall be brought unto the king in raiment of needlework"[5] could have been applied to what, after all, was intended to be ultimately the chapel of a Preparatory School for the Sons of Anglo-Catholic parents. An oak screen divided the small narthex from the choir. The centre part was left open, but filled by a wrought-iron grille, which reminded layfolk that the community was strictly enclosed. Each of the two altars in the narthex had a specially designed, hand-wrought copper crucifix and candlesticks. The robed figure on St Benedict's altar had a crown inset with seed pearls. The carved and painted wooden statue had been presented by Ralph Adams Cram, the well-known American architect and bore his coat of arms. Above the narthex rested a gallery, with a small organ, designed for the correct accompaniment of plainchant. Here a limited number of seculars got a good view of the high altar.

The highly polished black Delabole slates with which the choir was paved shone like marble. The carved oak stalls with canopies were fourteenth-century Perpendicular Gothic in style, and could hardly have been more intricate in detail. Blocking up the centre of the choir was a massive carved-oak revolving lectern, surmounted by the figure of an angel. Projecting from either side were hand-wrought copper candlesticks. On the lower step of this pyramidical structure stood two high stools for the cantors. The wagon-shaped oak ceiling had the portion over the sanctuary intersected with ribbed beading, and carved gilded bosses at the points of intersection.

On the north side of the sanctuary were oak sedilia for the sacred ministers, also a grey limestone piscina. As a virtual *abbas-nullius*, Dom Aelred had provided himself with a richly carved oak throne, surmounted by a canopy displaying his ensigns-armorial.[6] This put him on a par with Dr Owen, Bishop of St Davids, who sat in a throne of great height when pontificating, part of it dating from the fourteenth century. A small aumbry contained the holy oils, and a collection of relics which were exposed on festivals.[7]

As stated already, the high altar was built of stones taken from sixty-one medieval monasteries in Britain.[8] The oldest bore the inscription "Glaston A.D. 64", suggesting that the monks accepted the legend that this monastery had been founded by either St Joseph of Arimathea or St Aristobulus. The stones were usually hidden by embroidered frontals.

The reredos, designed by Mr F. C. Eden, gorgeous in gold and colour, reached to the roof, where it came forward in a tester, below which hung the pyx, veiled in white, under its canopy of silver-gilt triple crowns. It was the work of Mr J. N. Comper, and had been donated by Mr Athelstan Riley. Below the pyx was an image of Our Lady Star of the Sea, standing on a crescent moon. There were also statuettes of St Bernard of Clairvaux and St Aelred of Rievaulx, each in a white Cistercian cowl, and enshrined in a crocketted niche. The central panel contained a tempera painting of the Transitus of St Benedict by Sister Catherine Weekes of Malling Abbey. Most of the figures were life-like portraits of Abbot Aelred and some of his monks. This magnificent reredos, with its carved, gilded and painted niches, crockets and framework, had riddel curtains on each side, made of crimson brocade shot with cloth of gold. The six candlesticks, which stood on the mensa, were made of ebony and filigreed silver. The silver figure on the cross, a replica of the *Volto Santo* in Lucca Cathedral, stood out against a background of blue lapis lazuli. Considering that the Chapel was intended to be used sooner or later as the place of worship in a Preparatory School for Boys, the furnishings might have been designed to fit in with its ultimate purpose, and on a less costly scale.

The adjacent sacristy, with its oak presses and cupboards, contained many sets of Low and High Mass vestments, valuable chalices, also a silver and enamel monstrance, designed by Harry Wilson in the then fashionable *art-nouveau* style, used for Exposition on the greater festivals. Otherwise the "Miraculous Monstrance" from Llanthony, or another which the community had inherited from the Isle of Dogs days, were used for "Devotions".[9] The squat tower on the south side of the Chapel had been planned to hold three bells, which had already been solemnly blessed by Bishop Richardson (who had resigned the see of Zanzibar in 1901) according to the complicated *Benedictio Campanae*, approved by the Sacred Congregation of Rites. But Abbot Aelred was not satisfied, and decided that it would be inspiring to have the Chard Chimes giving out their tuneful melody every quarter of an hour, so five more bells were ordered.[10] He blessed them himself with showers of holy water and clouds of incense in October 1910.

Such was the temporary place of worship built for the monks of the Anglican Congregation of the Primitive Observance of the Rule of St Benedict. What was its total cost is uncertain, but in June 1910 it was stated that £3,537 3s. 1d. had been donated by friends. Yet even then the community demanded more money. The paragraph "How to help Caldey" in *Pax* was worded:

"1. By reading and circulating the Pamphlet, *The Benedictines of Caldey Island*.
2. By subscribing to *Pax*, and inducing others to do so.
3. By prayer.
4. By contributing to the Caldey Abbey Building Fund—
   a. By a yearly subscription.
   b. By a donation.
   c. By taking a collecting card.
   d. By preaching and collections.
5. By becoming 'A Caldey Helper'."

The Abbot's old friend, Mr Athelstan Riley, Seigneur de la Trinité on the Isle of Jersey, contributed a long article, entitled "Dedication of the Monastery Church" to the next issue of *Pax*. Having described the gorgeous pontifical function, and mentioned the "nightly commemoration of the Founder, Archbishop Temple", among the prayers after Compline, he continued:

"Pro famulo tuo Frederico—Who that lived in the days of Dr Temple's nomination to the See of Exeter could have expected *this*? I well remember a conversation I had with him when he was Archbishop of Canterbury, and his strong belief in 'Brother Aelred', 'though whether he is going to succeed in re-founding the Benedictine Order in the Church of England of course I can't say'. This was, I think, in 1898, just twelve years ago; and those who go to Caldey will see the marvel which has been brought to pass. I can claim to know a little about Monasticism and the Monastic Life—as much, that is, as a secular can know—in both East and West, and enough at any rate to appreciate the stupendous task of reviving Benedictine Life within the Church of England after a complete break of nearly four hundred years. The task has been accomplished, and Caldey is to me the greatest phenomenon in the Anglican Communion at the present day."[11]

This was not all by any means: Mr Riley reminded his readers that "founded by one of the strongest of the successors of St Augustine [the Benedictines] have the kindly recognition of many Prelates of the Anglican Communion, they are

225

gaining a circle of influence too wide to be disregarded, a power too considerable to be ignored, and a body of friends resolved to help in the work. The present is full of confidence, the future full of hope. The Church of England needs, among her many needs, that which she had, and lost, and has now had restored to her—the Contemplative Life of pure Monasticism."[12]

Nevertheless the Benedictines were still so poor that they were forced to appeal to their benefactors to provide albs and rochets, even "a weekly or monthly paper on Bee-keeping". Gifts of a pair of Indian Brass Standard Candlesticks, some silver spoons, a microscope, and black stockings were gratefully acknowledged.

About four months after the dedication of the Monastery Church Dom Aelred's conception of what a Lord Abbot ought to be was expressed by the rising walls of the *prelatura*. This mansion, erected at the western end of the Cottage-Monastery, certainly helped to confirm Mr Riley's belief that Caldey was the greatest phenomenon in the Anglican Communion at that date. As a *de facto abbas-nullius* of an extra-diocesan island, he felt justified in ignoring the legislation of the Western Church that the whole house inhabited by a community of male religious (especially those under solemn vows) must be within the material *clausura*.[13]

The centrally-heated abbatial quarters consisted of an immense oak-panelled, parquet-floored reception room, and a private secretary's office on the ground floor. A stately oak staircase led up to the abbatial bedroom (of the same size as the reception room beneath it), a spacious bed-sitter for distinguished guests, and a luxurious bathroom. The most remarkable feature of the *prelatura* was a lofty Moslem-like minaret at its south west corner. It collapsed after completion, like the 278 feet-high central tower of Beckford's Fonthill Abbey in 1807, but Dom Aelred ordered it to be rebuilt ten feet higher. The red-tiled flèche ended off with a weather-vane in the shape of a fully-rigged ship.

The private oratory surpassed most continental post-Tridentine ones in magnificence. The walls were oak-panelled. The floor was paved in black and white marble. Light was provided by six round-headed windows, filled with stained glass, depicting saints who had striven after the Contemplative Life of Pure Monasticism. The Italian Renaissance altar—standing away from the apsidal "east" end—was built of pink alabaster, gifted by the Earl of Plymouth, Viscount Windsor of St Fagans, Lord Lieutenant and Custos Rotulorum of County Glamorgan, Knight of Grace of the Order of St John of Jerusalem. Six tall hand-wrought silver candlesticks stood on the low gradine, matching the crucifix. The tabernacle door was of embossed silver. The *art-nouveau* sanctuary lamp, designed by Harry Wilson, was suspended from the barrel-vaulted ceiling by a realistic galleon in full sail. The only furniture was a massive carved-oak *prie-dieu*, and a stately oak and leather fitted arm-chair.[14]

The small sacristy contained costly sets of Low Mass vestments, most of them in Italian or Spanish Baroque styles. Also kept here were the abbatial buskins, sandals, thin silk dalmatic and tunicles for pontifical functions, lace-trimmed rochets, moiré-silk mozzettas, birettas, gloves of all the liturgical colours, rings and pectoral crosses. The collection of *pontificalia* included simple, precious and gold mitres, like-wise croziers. In course of time Abbot Aelred possessed three croziers, one of ivory and silver, another of ebony and silver, and the third of carved oak.

After he had moved into the *prelatura* his permanent entourage consisted of a private secretary and a valet, known as "The Abbot's Novice". Other monks were called in to clean the abbatial apartments, or to polish its floors and stairs. Once the new refectory was in use the youthful valet had to wait on the Lord Abbot as he sat alone at the high-table. He also had to prepare his morning

THE ABBOT'S CHAPEL, CALDEY ABBEY, 1911

In 1928 all the furnishings were taken to Prinknash Abbey. Today the Chapel is inter-denominational. The alabaster altar has been superseded by a wooden communion-table.

"pittance" and carry it to the *prelatura* on a silver tray, making a genuflection after depositing it on a small table, and going off with a blessing. The same ceremonial went with afternoon tea. Another duty was to keep polished the abbatial black leather, silver-buckled shoes. There was certainly no lack of what the French Catholic novelist Joris Karl Huysmans called *"le luxe pour Dieu"* in the life led by the Right Rev. Dom Aelred Carlyle, O.S.B., Abbot of Caldey, sixty years ago.

Yet this did not apply to the strictly enclosed and purely contemplative form of Benedictine life led by his monks; at least, not until they moved into part of the new monastery in the autumn of 1912. The row of workmen's cottages was both inconvenient and congested. The downstairs rooms were linked up by a passage at the back. The small refectory also served as the library. The long dormitory, with sloping roofs, was divided into "cells" by white curtains. The outer cubicles, with access to the windows, were reserved for the senior monks; the juniors had to put up with living in a passage, with no privacy. Sacks filled with straw, resting on planks, were the bedding. A daily cold bath was compulsory. The common-dormitory was stuffy in summer; draughty in winter. Reading and study had to be done in these fo'c'sle-like quarters, where there was no heating. The brethren lived in such close contact with each other both by night and by day, that it is not surprising that some yearned for greater solitude, wishing that there was an Anglican Carthusian monastery.

The *horarium* remained just the same as at Painsthorpe, i.e. what the Abbot had taken over from Buckfast lock, stock and barrel, when he founded his brotherhood on the Isle of Dogs in 1896. Except in Lent, there was very little in the way of austerity. The meals were more than ample, and well cooked. Breakfast—known as "Pittance"—was taken standing, and consisted of bread and butter and coffee. There was a three-course dinner at midday. Meat was eaten only at Christmas. Fish arrived from Grimsby once a week—unless it was held up at Tenby by stormy weather. The mostly vegetarian menus were given variety by certain so-called "Health Foods" supplied by Eustace Miles' restaurant in London. During the afternoon, before recreation, a mug of tea and a slice of fruit-cake were allowed. Supper took the form of a "high" tea. During Lent dinner was postponed until after Vespers at 5 p.m. At midday a light collation was taken standing—often sweetened porridge or "Grapenuts" pudding. There was no afternoon tea, except for those who were dispensed.

The long narrow refectory-cum-library was quite Franciscan in its simplicity. The floor boards were covered with coco-nut matting. The wooden tables were left bare, and scrubbed frequently. In front of each place stood a water-jug, a wooden platter, and a napkin, folded round a wooden fork and spoon. A shallow two-handled bowl rested on top of the folded napkin. Aluminium plates were regarded as in keeping with the Primitive Observance of the Benedictine Rule. Butter, measured out by a wooden mould, was served on little china platters. When partaking of "pittance" or afternoon tea, the standing monk had to throw the front of his scapular over the left and not the right shoulder.

There was nothing of the melodramatic character of the monastic life at Llanthony in the Caldey observances, adapted almost entirely from those of the Cassinese Congregation of the Primitive Observance, as set forth in the 1880 Declarations. Yet there were innumerable medieval rules of behaviour that a novice had to learn—never to cross the knees—always when seated, the hands under the scapular or in the sleeves of the cowl. When making a profound inclination, the arms had to touch the knees with the hands. The novices, who wore black cloaks, had to be very careful to keep their hands wrapped in its folds, even when holding a book. Heads had to be covered by the hoods when

228

THE REFECTORY-LIBRARY IN THE COTTAGE-MONASTERY,
CALDEY ISLAND, 1908

CALDEY BENEDICTINES POSE BESIDE A ROSE-PERGOLA

walking from one part of the monastery to the other, but never drawn down over the face. A profound bow had to be made when passing the Lord Abbot, and a genuflection when going to talk to him in his room.

For some men it was a great effort trying to acquire all the minutiae that went with the strictly enclosed and purely contemplative life. To start with, there were subtleties about the rules of silence. Before speaking, permission had to be asked from another by the ejaculation *"Benedicite"*, to which the reply was also *"Benedicite"*. Little pocket-books, with shiny covers (known as "Silence Books") were used for writing down messages. Not infrequently they served for idle gossip. Each monk also had his "Chapter of Faults Book", so that he could jot down breaches of the rule for which self-accusation had to be made weekly after Prime. It was the custom to hold up in the Chapter House any article which had been broken or damaged. Very often this exhibition led to suppressed or even audible giggles. Abbot Aelred imposed penances, but they were very mild when compared with those inflicted by Abbot Ignatius.[15]

There was certainly no lack of variety when it came to manual labour. A novice was never sure whether he would be put on to work in the gardens, poultry-farm, kitchen, scullery, sacristy or laundry. He had to be prepared to unload coal from a barge on the beach of Priory Bay from time to time. During the summer months there was the chance of hay-making or helping to gather in the harvest. Before Christmas he was fairly sure to be ordered to pluck turkeys or fowls under Mr Longhurst's direction.

Postulants and novices were carefully instructed in the mysteries of plainchant. They were expected to master the subtle differences between the porrectus, scandicus, clivis, torculus, climacus, epiphonus, distropha, tristropha, oriscus, and other Solesmes rhythmic signs. Just as important was to learn the duties of *capellani* at pontifical functions as laid down in the *Caeremoniale Episcoporum* of Pope Clement VIII. In order of rank they were the mitre-bearer, crozier-bearer, book-bearer, and hand-candle-bearer. Only after much practice could one acquire the trick of adjusting the scarves *(vimpae)* with which the mitre and crozier were grasped. Conferences were given on the psalms, but never on Christian doctrine. It was taken for granted that aspirants to the Purely Contemplative Life had been well grounded in the Book of Common Prayer Catechism before they had been confirmed by a Bishop. Bible reading was not encouraged by Abbot Aelred, unlike Abbot Ignatius.

Most of the young men who came to test their vocations on Caldey belonged to what in those far off times were known as either the "Upper" or "Lower" Middle Classes. Only one in 1910 had enjoyed the doubtful advantage of a Public School education. None has studied at a university. Several had been brought up as Nonconformists. Not all were practising Anglo-Catholics before they entered the novitiate, and were puzzled and even shocked by the ritual and ceremonial, also the "Mariolatry".

The Contemplative Life of Pure Monasticism was far from being all work and no play. Except in Lent there was an hour's daily recreation. On Sunday afternoons, the whole community took tea together, and met specially invited guests. During the summer months there were Saturday afternoon picnics, usually at Bullums or Drinkim Bays. The brethren collected wood, lit a fire, and boiled water for tea. Unless special permission had been obtained from the Abbot, monks were expected to bathe in the nude, which was certainly "primitive observance"! Future historians may claim that Dom Aelred was one of the pioneers of the Naturist movement in Britain.

The more maritime-minded monks could enjoy sea-fishing as a pastime, either in the steamer *Firefly*, one of the rowing-boats, or on the *Stella Maris*. Acquired in 1910, this fast motor-launch served as the abbatial private yacht. She was lovingly cared for by Br Bede, formerly a bluejacket in the Royal Navy. He made sure that the white paint was spotless, the decks scrubbed, the brass-work gleaming, the ropes coiled away, and the fenders adjusted to prevent the least scratch on her varnished hull.

Taken all round the strictly enclosed and purely contemplative form of Benedictine life was far from penitential. There was absolutely no doubt that in whatever other way he had failed, Benjamin Fearnley Carlyle had fulfilled the task laid down by St Benedict in the Prologue of his Rule for monasteries—"to establish a school of the Lord's service, without rules that are harsh or burdensome". Always optimistic, he made men loyal to him by his usually irresistible personality. He infected his disciples by his own enthusiasm. If he erred it was on the side of charity. His geese were always swans.

As the above-mentioned Br Bede wrote many years later after he had reverted to secular life and got married. He said in one of his letters "The Caldey set-up was necessarily a one-man show by force of circumstances, I think, rather than by design or intention. The intellectual status of accepted postulants was, generally speaking, not of a very high order. We literally sat at Abbot Aelred's feet, looking up to him with veneration, as an infallible authority and guide on questions of faith, morals, monasticism, philosophy, theology, and most other matters. How many of his disciples, one wonders, would have persevered, or even been accepted as choir monks in any Catholic Benedictine monastery? The eventual realization that *my* call to the cloister, and that of many other good souls in the community, came to me in the form that it was not based on the rock of a true religious vocation, but on the unstable sands of sentiment, and a personal affection for the Abbot."[16]

As the majority of the community had received no more than an average Board School education, they were hardly in a position to query the opinions of their Superior. They took for granted, for instance, that monastic worship had to be conducted in a dead language which was an unknown tongue to them before they came to Caldey. Even when making their corporate thanksgiving for Holy Communion the brethren had to recite aloud the *Gratiarum actio post Missam* printed in the *Missale Romanum*, believed to have originated in the Middle Ages, and said by the Pope in his private chapel in the Lateran Palace. Each monk had his own black leather-bound copy of these long prayers. One of the community recalled thirty years later: "With regard to our pronunciation of Latin we were trained towards ideal *'lingua Toscana in bocca Romana'*, although I fear that some of us found it hard to arrive at this high standard. In fact, when hearing the stately Latin tongue voiced by Italian priests I have felt that had we ventured to so murder it in Rome as we did at Caldey, we should have been worthy to be laid under interdict!"[17]

When Abbot Aelred formed a group of so-called "Solitaries" in the autumn of 1910, their extra devotions included the daily recitation of the medieval *Officium parvum beatae Mariae Virginis*, according to the later version printed in the *Breviarium Romanum* issued by St Pius V in 1568. These three monks were regarded as true "Mystics", with a special vocation to the higher states of prayer. Visitors were told that they were the "Maries" of the community, their companions merely "Marthas". The Solitaries were released so far as possible from distracting occupations, with a time-table arranged to enable them to spend the greater part of the day in manual labour and spiritual exercises. It was only during the Octave of Christmas that they took part in recreation, for they were bound by a rigid rule of silence. A daily visit to the cemetery was obligatory, also the weekly recitation of the entire *Officium Defunctorum* as printed in the Breviary. The Abbot had been drawn to the eremitical life since he visited St Hugh's Charterhouse, Parkminster, at the age of sixteen.[18]

The uniform worn by the various grades in the community did not lack variety. All donned black cowls or cloaks in choir. Novices and the simply professed wore white tunics and black scapulars, with the belt underneath the latter garment. The few monks in solemn vows were distinguished by white scapulars. Some of the brethren suspended large rosaries from their belts to stress their Catholicity. The more mortified dispensed with boots and shoes, and wore sandals, with or without white stockings. Postulants and novices suggested convicts with their closely cropped heads. The professed shaved their heads weekly, leaving a picturesque deep fringe of hair above their ears. The Oblates were clothed all in black. Medieval-shaped hooded smocks of butcher's blue linen were donned for manual labour. When away from the Island monks of all grades wore black, which made them less conspicuous, though the elastic-sided shoes looked sloppy. The undergarments consisted of a flannel shirt and "shorts".

"I date my letter this Quarter from Glastonbury, whether I have come from Baltonsborough four miles away", Abbot Aelred stated in September 1910. "Here in this old town one's thoughts fly back to the old days, when the light of Faith shone so brightly, and Glaston Abbey stood witness in all its glory to the love men had in their hearts for our Lord. Nearly four centuries of desolation and ruin have passed, and standing in the holy places that once rang with the praises of God, one can only thank Him with uplifted heart that He is giving us back the Life of the Cloister; and pray that the sons of St Benedict today may become worthy successors of their Fathers in the Holy Rule. There is growing, I think, quite a general feeling that the Benedictines should come back to their own . . ."[19]

What Dom Aelred did not tell his readers was that on September 22, while staying with the Baltonsborough nuns he had accepted from Mr F. Bligh Bond, who was in charge of the excavations at Glastonbury, what he was convinced were the bones of Richard Whytinge, the last Abbot, condemned to death by Henry VIII in 1539, who was hanged on the summit of Tor Hill, overlooking the Abbey. Mr Bond had shown him the roughly scribbled communications in dog-Latin and medieval English made on an ouija-board during several séances, alleged to have been written by a long-dead monk named "Joannes". The messages encouraged the psychic archaeologist to dig deeper, which resulted in finding some bones just where "Joannes" said they would be.[20] The Abbot took these revelations on their face value, and felt that it would bring immense spiritual benefit to his community to possess these holy relics.

A fortnight later they were solemnly translated to Caldey Island. A lofty catafalque was erected between the choir stalls. On it was laid a casket containing the bones, draped with a red silk veil. Around it many tall tapers flickered. Pontifical High Mass was celebrated according to the special Proper issued by the Sacred Congregation of Rites after the beatification by Leo XIII in 1895 of the martyred last Abbots of Glastonbury, Reading, and Bury St Edmunds. The Anglican monks of Caldey saw nothing inconsistent as they chanted the Introit *"Vineam de Aegypto transtulisti"*. For they accepted their Abbot's opinion that no further authentification was necessary beyond the automatic writing by still earth-bound spirits "as yet unready for the Great Return, and in that condition that death overtook them".[21]

Thanks to his own psychic gifts, Abbot Aelred was already in great demand as a spiritual healer. Clergymen and doctors were sending their most difficult "cases" to Caldey to be treated by him. Dom George Chambers recalled long after "how people were literally crowding round and seeking help in personal difficulties. . . . Being regarded as a psychologist of the first order at a time when psychoanalytical methods were only in their initial stages, he had problems to solve which would have tried the courage as well as the knowledge of a modern trained psychiatrist. This external influence seemed to aggravate his tendency to extravagance and dominating self-assurance."[22]

The late Mgr Vernon Johnson remembered how "from the first it was the flotsam and jetsam of human life, its tragedies and failures that were drawn to Abbot Aelred, and found in him the inspiration to start their lives again. . . . With his winning smile, infectious good humour and inveterate leg-pulling, he had a great gift of cheering the despondent. For those times he had an unusual knowledge of psychology, in some ways he was definitely psychic himself, and could read the minds and hearts of men and analyse their motives to a remarkable degree. . . . A direct gift from Almighty God, so it seemed."[23]

In December 1910 Dom Aelred wrote in *Pax:* "All our friends will rejoice in the steady growth of the Community. The last year or two has been a time of sifting, and, I believe, of real advance in the Spiritual Life." The Island had become a live centre of Spiritual Healing.[24] There was no reason why the relics of Blessed Richard Whytinge should not start performing miracles.

Dr T. C. Fisher had made a retreat on Caldey before his consecration as fifth Bishop of Nyasaland, and he had written: "I knew I should find [the island] a place of great devotion and spirituality. What struck me about it as more than I expected was a something I find it difficult to describe, something of a sense of strength—of quiet underlying force. I don't mean that I expected to find you all emotional or hysterical, but there is generally a restlessness about anything new— something of a rush. When I was with you I felt that the Community might have been in existence for a century, it all seemed so natural and easy." The Abbot commented: "These words are all too kind, and I know quite undeserved, but I cannot refrain from quoting them with a deep sense of gratitude to God that He is helping us to realize our Vocation in such a way that those who come here may feel the reality of it."[25]

Meanwhile Abbess Scholastica had her own problems to solve. She realised that the sooner she found a new home for her nuns, so much the better. Were the Trustees, most of whom were Cowley Fathers, to get wind of her intention to "go over to Rome", they would not hesitate to evict the community, by informing her that the Malling property was needed for other purposes. At first she toyed with the idea of moving to Llanthony, and even sent Mr Coates Carter to examine the buildings, and report on whether they could be adapted to the needs of her nuns.[26]

Abbot Aelred, however, had other ideas. On April 28, 1910 he wrote to Miss Mary Steward, whom he had first met when conducting a retreat at Malling two years before, and who had already given him £5,000: "Owing to the arrangement of the Malling Trust, our nuns cannot build there, neither is it desirable for other reasons that they should make their home permanently at Malling. Llanthony is out of the question for them, owing to the great cost of making the existing buildings habitable.[27] It has been suggested that the Malling nuns should be given Drinkim Bay and the land adjacent to it on Caldey. This arrangement would be greatly appreciated by Mother Abbess, I know, and in many ways it would simplify matters all round. In addition to these considerations, there is the fact that in July next year our mortgage of £8,000 with Mr Bushell falls in, and if the nuns were to come here, it would be necessary to give our farm tenant notice in order to have the land at our disposal. All these things mean a good deal of money, but

X

they mean the permanent establishment of our Benedictine Congregation on land of their own where they could serve God without let or hindrance."[28]

Shortly after this Miss Steward handed over to the Abbot a second sum of £5,000 without imposing any conditions. A month or two later he told his benefactress that he needed at least £30,000 so that both the nuns and monks could be immediately under his direction on the Island. She explained that she was legally prevented from presenting him with the equivalent of something more like £300,000 in present value, so the nunnery on the cliffs above Drinkim Bay remained another Aelredian vision that never took shape.

The Abbess referred to the probable move in almost every issue of *Pax*, stating that it was essential for her nuns to be "within reasonable distance of Caldey". She wrote in June 1910: "Owing to the great distance between the two Houses, it is impossible for the Abbot of Caldey to visit us more than very occasionally; so that he cannot really know the young religious as he should; and, in consequence, the difficult matter of selection of Novices has largely to rest with the Abbess, which is quite contrary to all precedent in Monastic government. It is very important in all strictly spiritual matters, as well as those which concern the Congregation, that our Nuns should be in a subordinate position; and we are most anxious that the modern tendency for women to become independent should not find any countenance among us."[29]

It is curious that this masterful lady was prepared to put her community directly under the jurisdiction of Abbot Aelred in the same way that Fr Ignatius had believed that Mother Hilda ought to accept his selection of novices for profession, and allow him to govern her community according to his whims at the moment.[30] Abbess Scholastica also felt that her nuns ought to have a Benedictine chaplain, but this would have been impossible, for only one monk had been raised to the priesthood so far. No postulant who had already achieved ordination ever got further than the novitiate in the seventeen years since Carlyle founded his brotherhood, though many had come and gone.

Life continued at Malling with retreats for ladies, the building up of the confectionery business, together with the manufacture of hand-woven fabrics, marmalade, preserves and chutney. The great feasts were celebrated with much external solemnity. The Corpus Christi procession that summer was more than enough to make the Trustees feel that the community were already far on the road to Rome, what with the Host borne by the celebrant, "sheltered by a silken canopy", the Lady Abbess wielding her crozier, followed by the nuns holding tapers. "Flowers were strewn on the way as the Saving Victim went forth to the chant of those melodies which for ages have been used on these occasions", so a visitor wrote. "From the Garth, under the trees, along the grass-grown paths of the old-world garden, we passed where standards and pennons marked the way, to an Altar of Repose, where a 'Station' was made, and so to the Chapel again for the final prayers."[31]

It was not until December that the Abbess was able to state that a temporary home had been found in South Wales—Castle Hall, Milford Haven. She wrote: "It is a large house on the top of a hill, overlooking Pill Creek, with grounds that are largely wooded, running right down to the water. The house was built about 120 years ago, and is extraordinarily ugly—what one might call very debased Italian architecture of that period but that does not so much matter to us in a temporary home."[32]

Were it still standing, this mansion would now be raved over by the Georgian Society, but it was demolished after the nuns vacated it. It had been erected by Sir William Hamilton, whose wife, Emma, became Nelson's mistress. They had

ST MARY'S ABBEY, WEST MALLING, KENT

Founded about 1090 by Gundulf, Bishop of Rochester, suppressed in 1536 by Henry VIII, and re-occupied by Anglican Benedictine nuns in 1893.

ST BRIDE'S ABBEY, MILFORD HAVEN, 1911

"The large house was built about 120 years ago, and it is extraordinarily ugly—what one might call very debased Italian architecture of that period."

(Abbess Scholastica Ewart.)

235

entertained him there after the Battle of the Nile in 1798. In more recent times Castle Hall had been used as a Military Academy. By 1910 the buildings looked shabby and neglected. Tall Doric columns enriched the facade. Three lofty campanile in a mixture of classic styles rose above the peeling stucco walls. There were ruined terraces with broken urns, immense stables, overgrown gardens, and weeds everywhere. It would have been hard to find a greater contrast with the twelfth-century Norman and late medieval architecture of Malling. The property was within fairly easy access of Caldey, so there would not be the same danger of the nuns forgetting that Dom Aelred was their canonical Major Superior as would have been the case had they remained more than 300 miles away in Kent. Since the Abbess had explained that Castle Hall would be only a "temporary home", it is possible that the Abbot still hoped to get his nuns established on the Island, where he could keep a close watch on them, just like Ignatius of Jesus did on his spiritual daughters in their "Living Tomb".

It is doubtful if at any period of his eighty-one years on earth did Benjamin Fearnley Carlyle obey more faithfully what he believed was the direct message from God, given him by Fr Maturin S.S.J.E., to paint his picture in strong colours, keep it ever before him, and strive to live up to it, than during the autumn and winter of 1910-11. The then thirty-six year-old Abbot General of the *Congregatio Anglicana a Primaeva Observantia* had no less than five foundations in view, besides moving his nuns from Malling to Milford Haven. Unfortunately, like the Children of Israel, he lacked the straw with which to make bricks. The Caldey community numbered twenty-five young men, four of whom were in solemn vows. The only priest—Dom George—having spent two years in a North London parish, twelve months as a missionary in South Africa, was now curate of Thaxted in Essex, already wondering if he ought to get secularized, having been told by his Abbot that he had no vocation for the contemplative life. Dom Henry was studying music at King's College, London, and virtually exclaustrated. Br David had just been made deacon, and was acting as a curate at Kirkcaldy in Scotland. So far nothing had been done to get other members of the brotherhood raised to the ministry of the Church of England.

First on the abbatial list of foundations was a priory on the Isle of Man, which had been talked of since 1906, when Mr John Goldie-Taubman, an old Etonian, also a member of both the Legislative Council and the House of Keys, had invited Dom Aelred to stay with him. This wealthy bachelor Anglo-Catholic squire lived in a Gothic Revival mansion outside Douglas, known as "The Nunnery", because of the ruins of a convent on the estates. According to a Manx legend, it had been founded in the sixth-century by "The Mother of the Gael", i.e. St Brigid of Kildare. Mr Goldie-Taubman's private oratory, dedicated to this Irish virgin, was a restored medieval building at the far end of the park, and furnished in an ultra-Catholic manner. Indeed it was the only Stronghold of the Full Faith on the Island, because Dr Drury, the thirtieth Bishop of Sodor and Man, was a rigid Evangelical.

On November 21, 1907, a Ward of the Confraternity of St Benedict was erected here by the Lord Abbot of Caldey, who gave an address to the dozen members after reciting the prescribed Office. Each *confrater* was invested with one of the specially designed neo-Celtic bronze crosses, which were the insignia of the Confraternity, then with a total membership of about 500. A social meeting took place in the old refectory of the Benedictine nunnery, so that Dom Aelred could meet this brave little band of Catholic Crusaders.

Unable to provide Mr Goldie-Taubman with a Benedictine chaplain, the Lord Abbot suggested his ex-novice, Br Jerome Hawes as suitable for the post. The complete seclusion of the large park would be ideal for testing his vocation to the

Franciscan life. The chaplain's house, if stripped of most of its furniture, could be turned into a friary. Br Jerome, having been a curate of the Holy Redeemer, Clerkenwell, before he gained further experience of ritual and ceremonial on Caldey, should be quite up to Mr Goldie-Taubman's level of Catholicity. The latter agreed to sponsor the Franciscan foundation. On his return to the mainland of Britain, the Abbot met Br Jerome and Br Cuthbert—another ex-Caldey novice —at Liverpool, where he instructed them on their future status, apparently regarding himself as the Minister-General of this still nebulous fraternity. The two former Benedictines, now garbed in brown habits and sandals, remained only four months on the Isle of Man. They soon found that their patron wanted to act as Father Guardian as well as *caeremonarius*. Matters reached a crisis soon after Easter 1908, when Br Jerome and Br Cuthbert cast the Manx dust off their feet, took ship for England in search of fresh fields and pastures new.

Yet both Abbot Aelred and Mr Goldie-Taubman went on hoping that a monastic foundation would materialize ere long. The project was kept alive by Ward VII of the Confraternity of St Benedict, which continued to hold its monthly meetings. Perhaps sooner or later a priory would be established that would revive the glories of the Manx abbey of Rushen, founded from Furness in Lancashire. Of course it would be extra diocesan and outside the unsympathetic jurisdiction of Bishop Drury.

More urgent, however, was the establishment of a "cell" in Italy, otherwise an Anglo-Catholic Pilgrim's Hostel at Assisi. The Abbot of Caldey had already chosen one of his Oblates, Br Maurus Sutton, as its first Warden. He informed readers of *Pax* that the Hostel would have a private oratory in which "English priests might say Mass". This would render real service, because at the moment they could only celebrate the Divine Mysteries in hotel bedrooms, because the Province of Perugia had not been in communion with the Provinces of Canterbury and York since the sixteenth-century. The French Calvinist pastor, Paul Sabatier, whose *Vie de Saint François* had been put on the Index in 1894, the same year that its English translation appeared, was "very much interested in the scheme", and had "himself suggested the house which could be purchased" for the modest sum of £250. Should the foundation in the *città serafica* take shape, then the oratory could be licensed by the Anglican Bishop of Gibraltar, whose spiritual supervision of Anglican congregation extended from the Canary Islands to the Black and Caspian Seas. There was no reason to seek permission from the Bishop of Assisi for the establishment of this Pilgrims' Hostel, or to find out if the Benedictine monks of the Cassinese Congregation, who had founded the Badia di S. Pietro in 1613, would resent having members of the English Congregation of the Primitive Observance as their near neighbours. Dom Aelred's S.O.S. ended with the words: "If any one would like to help us to carry out this suggestion, and will write to me, I will send further particulars".[33] This was the last heard of the Caldey foundation in *Umbria mystica*. It remained of the stuff that dreams are made of.

In September 1910 the Abbot had told readers of *Pax* that a "very tangible instance" of "a general feeling that the Benedictines should come back to their own", had been "the recent gift to us of Pershore Abbey in Worcestershire". Early in July he had received a letter from Mr Henry Wise, who had been interested in the community for some time "saying that Pershore Abbey, having come into the market, he had purchased it for the Abbot and Monks of Caldey; and wished to offer it as a free gift in the hope that one day it might be possible to send a Community of Monks there to re-establish the Benedictine Life on the old ground".[34] Actually it was not Pershore Abbey which had been bought, but a somewhat inconvenient early nineteenth-century mansion, known as "The Abbot's Lodging". It was located close to the west end of the nave of the Benedictine Abbey Church, demolished after the suppression of the monastery by Henry VIII. Only the choir, one transept and the tower had been left, and were used for parochial worship.[35] If the shrine of St Eadburga could be restored, the profits from pilgrimages might help to support the community, as was the case in the Middle Ages, and even lead to miracles. Abbot Aelred himself could hear the Work of God resounding once more in this setting, as it had gone on for five hundred years from the days of St Dunstan.

But he explained to readers of *Pax:* "Although we have gratefully accepted this generous gift, it is a responsibility that has come to us unsought. For some years to come we shall have all and more than we can do in concentrating and establishing our work at Caldey, and we do not seek to hold property elsewhere. There is plenty of room on the Island, and it must be years before we can be ready to send Brethren elsewhere. We need at present adequate assistance to clear the mortgage on the Island and to develop it properly; and I hope that those who wish to do something for the Community may help us to meet our responsibilities there, rather than give us additional property and increase our responsibilities elsewhere."[36]

During the Octave of the feast of St Luke, Mr Wise paid a visit to Caldey, when there was "a very touching little ceremony". He formally handed over to the Abbot the Deeds of the Pershore property, after which he was solemnly admitted into the company of benefactors, and given a Letter of Confraternity.[37]

At the same time Dom Aelred was dreaming of yet another foundation in the distant future. Mr Thomas Dyer-Edwardes had invited him to stay at Prinknash Park near Gloucester in August that same year. During the course of the visit his host explained that he had no son to inherit the property. His only daughter, Noëlle, had married the nineteenth Earl of Rothes in 1900. He saw no reason to leave the Gloucestershire estates to their son, the Hon. Malcolm George Dyer-Edwardes Leslie. Far better to bequeath them to Anglican Benedictines because this picturesque Cotswold manor house had been the summer residence of the later Abbots of Gloucester. Like Caldey Island, Prinknash enjoyed an extra-parochial status, which might prove advantageous to future monastic owners. Another attraction was the small apsidal private chapel, all ready for a small community of Benedictines to resume the Work of God which had ceased at Gloucester in 1540, when the Prior and twelve monks, having surrendered the Abbey to the Crown, were pensioned off. Having already failed to found a monastery at Lower Guiting in Gloucestershire, Abbot Aelred was eager to make a second attempt at Prinknash, but for the moment he had no monks to spare.[38]

Last on the list of foundations was Llanthony Abbey, which had been un-occupied for the past twelve months, although two Extern Sisters were still living in the convent. The never-completed monastery and the abbey church, with its towering reredos, were a reminder of never-realised dreams. Ghosts of monks who had come and gone during the past half-century seemed to haunt the dark, damp, so-called "cloisters", with their narrow lancet windows through which the sun never shone, because they looked into the small overgrown garth. The living rooms evoked memories of the eighteen-seventies and eighties. They were cluttered up with shabby Victorian furniture, useless "ornaments", pious pictures, bric-a-brac, and what-nots of all sorts. The few bookshelves contained a miscellaneous choice of reading matter, ranging from sermons by mostly-forgotten Non-conformist divines and Biblical commentaries of a sound "Fundamentalist" character, to sentimental Roman Catholic devotional manuals, and sensational novels. More than one cupboard was filled with dusty, unsold copies of Fr Ignatius' hymns, orations, sermons, stories and tracts. The atmosphere could be summed up in the words of the well-known hymn:

"Earth's joys grow dim, its glories pass away;
Change and decay in all around I see".

Yet the two aged Sisters still tended the mountain-girt shrine. They filled the flower vases with fresh blossoms, and made sure all the lamps were kept burning before the many statues. No longer, however, was the gloomy church fragrant with the bitter-sweet perfume of incense. The almost countless candles on and around the high altar were never lit. The great brass and jewel-encrusted tabernacle was empty. The "Miraculous Monstrance" had no chance to perform further miracles. Between the choir-stalls in the midst of the pavement lay the body of the man whose devotion and enthusiasm had created this double-monastery in the Black Mountains. Around his tomb were the words: *"Here lies Ignatius of Jesus O.S.B., Founder and First Abbot of This House. R.I.P. He died on October 16, 1908"*.

Taken all round, Llanthony was better suited for leading the strictly enclosed and purely contemplative form of Benedictine life than was Caldey. Abbot Aelred could not make up his mind what to do with the abandoned monastery now that Abbess Scholastica had decided that it would not suit her nuns. So he asked readers of *Pax*, especially "those who loved Fr Ignatius", to help him to keep the place in repair. He explained: "For the time being we shall keep an Oblate Brother living in the House, and next year we shall hope to send some of our Monks to take up the life again there; and we think that a small Community might help to form a House of Studies and arrange to receive those who wish to find a quiet place where they would be able to make a Retreat and spend a time of preparation for Holy Orders. But this cannot be done unless help is forthcoming from those who love the place, and would not wish it to become ruinous and useless."[39] But the friends of Fr Ignatius failed to come forward with the £300 needed for urgent repairs. Only £124 1s. 9d. had been received three months after the Abbot had issued his appeal.[40]

In August 1911 the Caldey novices spent a three weeks' holiday at Llanthony, under the charge of Br Wilfrid, so the monastic life was resumed there again. Some of them lost their hearts to the romantic surroundings. One, however, wrote to his Abbot: "The whole place is so unlike Caldey that it gives one a complete change of surroundings and a sufficient of homesickness to get back at the end of the time. We have a constant feeling that we should like to blow out windows, to let in some light and air, and break down doors to let ourselves through. But a few dozen workmen and tons of whitewash would really work wonders and what fine bonfires there would be."[41]

The Abbot-General of the *Congregatio Anglicana a Primaeva Observantia* certainly had more than enough to do what with running his own community on Caldey Island, directing his nuns, and trying to build up Benedictine waste places, not only in Britain, but also on the continent of Europe.

LLANTHONY ABBEY, 1911

After forty years the buildings had become even more gloomy than when they were erected by the dense growth of trees.

[1] To be consistent the other two State Holy Days ought to have been inserted in the monastic *Ordo*: "The Papists' Conspiracy or Gunpowder Plot" (November 5), and "The Birth and Restoration of King Charles II" (May 29).

[2] op. cit., December 1908, p. 101.

[3] op. cit., p. 121.

[4] *Pax*, March 1910, pp. 197-8.

[5] Psalm XLV, 13-14 (Authorized Version).

[6] According to a decree of the Sacred Congregation of Rites (1659) abbots may not have a fixed throne at the side of the sanctuary unless they are *abbates-nullius*. Ordinary abbots must use a chair, to be removed afterwards, though it may have a canopy over the chair, provided that it is of simpler material than the *antependium* of the high altar.

[7] Most of these relics had been bought by the Abbot on his continental tours, but after the autumn of 1910 the alleged bones of Bl. Richard Whytinge, the last Abbot of Glastonbury, were added. (See p. 232.)

[8] It was claimed that these stones "cry out with the long-silenced voices of the many Religious Houses, desolate ruins, *Veterum monumenta virorum*. They are witnesses to a revival of faith, a resurrection of spiritual life, a restoration of holy paths, a rekindling of lamps long quenched, unlighted, forsaken but not destroyed. . . . The piecing together of the scattered stones at Caldey looks forward to the reunion of a triumphant Christendom, a gathering together of scattered flocks into one by the healing virtues of the Catholic Faith." (*Pax*, March 1911, p. 184.) This vision never took shape, because thirty years later the altar was gutted by fire. Its charred bits and pieces were thrown away.

[9] In spite of the rules of the Sacred Congregation of Rites that Mass must not be said on an altar on which the *Sanctissimum* is exposed, without necessity, grave cause, or special indult, Abbot Aelred permitted it occasionally. This late medieval "Nordic" eucharistic cultus was much enjoyed by most of the monks, if only because at least a dozen candles had to be lit, if possible.

[10] They were presented by Mr Samuel Gurney. In 1928 all but two of the eight bells were transported to Prinknash Abbey, Gloucester.

[11] op. cit., p. 318.

[12] In 1940 the Cottage-Monastery and the interior of its Chapel was burnt out by fire, and all its costly furnishings went up in flames. The chapel was restored in 1951, with new fittings of a much more simple character in keeping with the Cistercian tradition. More recently the massive stone high altar has given place to a small holy table for the daily concelebration. The side altars are redundant, for private masses are rarely celebrated. All the monastic worship is now carried on in the vulgar tongue, and plainchant is but a memory of the "good old days".

[13] At the same time he forbade women to enter the choir and sacristy of the Abbey Church, which are normally regarded as neutral territory.

[14] The altar was demolished a few years ago, and replaced by a small wooden communion table. The lamp, *prie-dieu*, and armchair were taken to Prinknash Abbey in 1928. The chapel is now used as a more or less interdenominational place of worship.

[15] See pp. 88, 89.

[16] Letter to the author.

[17] P. F. Anson, *A Roving Recluse* (Cork, 1946), p. 50.

[18] See p.133 At the age of fifty-nine he became a postulant at the Cartuja de Miraflores near Burgos, but this long dreamed of "Castle in Spain" proved to be a mirage, and he remained there only two months.

[19] *Pax*, September 1910, p. 18.

[20] Cf. F. Bligh Bond, *The Gate of Remembrance* (Oxford, 1921); and W. W. Kenewell, *The Quest at Glastonbury* (New York, 1965).

[21] *The Gate of Remembrance*, p. 97.

[22] Letter to the author. Sigmund Freud's *Psycho-pathologie des Altagslebens* appeared in 1901, and *Drei Abhandlungen zur Sexueltheorie* in 1905, but it was not until some years later that English translations were published. In 1909 Abbot Aelred had advised readers of *Pax* to study Percy Dearmer's *Body and Soul*, recently published. This treatise was but one indication of increasing Anglican interest in faith-healing, which resulted in the foundation of the Guild of Health.

[23] *Pax*, Spring 1956, p. 24.

[24] Not only were people being encouraged to read Dr Percy Dearmer's *Body and Soul*, but two "Caldey Papers" on Spiritual Healing and its Travesties were on sale. A third was entitled *In the Higher Way*.

[25] op. cit., pp. 100-101.

[26] Cf. *Pax*, March 1910, pp. 221-2.

[27] Mr Coates Carter estimated that the cost would be at least £10,000—a large sum in 1910.

[28] Cf. *The Churchman's Magazine*, Vol. 79, 1925. This letter was among those which Miss Steward handed over to John Kensit after she had failed to recover another £5,000 lent to

Dom Aelred on November 1, 1913, which had to be refunded on June 29, 1916. This loan was made eight months after he has seceded to the Roman Church.

[29] The so-called "New Woman" made her first appearance in the 1890s. After 1903 Mrs Emmeline Pankhurst and the more militant members of the Women's Social and Political Union began to make themselves a public nuisance, culminating with riots in Whitehall in 1911.

[30] See pp. 107-109.

[31] *Pax*, June 1910, pp. 313-14.

[32] op. cit. p. 113.

[33] *Pax*, June 1910, p. 287.

[34] Mr Wise, like Mr Goldie-Taubman, was a bachelor Anglo-Catholic squire, resident at Shrubland Hall, Warwickshire. He could claim descent from the Ranger of Hyde Park in the reign of Queen Anne.

[35] Pershore Abbey was founded in 972, and dedicated to St Eadburga, daughter of King Edward the Elder, and grand-daughter of King Alfred the Great.

[36] op. cit., September, 1910, pp. 18-19. Mr Wise also presented Caldey Abbey with a synchronome "Westminster" electric clock. Chiming apparatus for the eight bells had been donated by another benefactor.

[37] The community never made use of the Abbot's Lodging at Pershore. After most of them submitted to the Roman Church in March 1913, it was handed back to Mr Wise. The following year it passed into the ownership of the new Benedictine community, which moved to Nashdom, Bucks in 1926. (See p. 268.)

[38] It was not until 1924 that Mr Dyer-Edwardes formally made over Prinknash Park to the Caldey Benedictines, who were now members of the Church of Rome. The Order of Reformed Cistercians having bought the Island for a sum that enabled them to clear off their liabilities, the Benedictines were able to move to Gloucestershire in December 1928, but not until they had relieved the 20th Earl of Rothes of his grandfather's death duties.

[39] *Pax*, September 1911, p. 387.

[40] After five years on Caldey he also required £7,000 to finish the new Monastery buildings; £150 for an Infirmary; £150 to enlarge the Village School; and £500 for general purposes.

[41] ibid, p. 286.

CHAPTER XIV

St Bernard's Abbey, Caldey Island, and St Bride's Abbey, Milford Haven (1911-1912)

EARLY in 1911 Abbot Aelred was tempted to hand over the Isle of Caldey to an organisation known as "The Fidelity Trust". For a small remuneration it accepted trusteeships (joint or sole) of properties for Church purposes. He was assured that were the community prepared to give up its economic independence, enough money would be available to complete the new monastery. There would also be a sufficient income to make the brethren independent of outside help. In the end he decided that the risk would be too great. On March 3 new Trustees were appointed to ensure that the Island would remain in the ownership of the Community in the event of his death.

Anglo-Catholics, taken as a whole, were already critical of what they regarded as the extravagance of monastic life on Caldey Island. This was proved by the steady drop in subscriptions to the Building and General Funds after the opening of the new Chapel on Whit Sunday, 1910. Realising that a "cold war" had begun to be waged against his community, the Abbot felt it worth while to explain that it was "perhaps difficult for the average Churchman to understand the Religious Life without starch". The sooner that Anglo-Catholics began "to learn something of the Benedictine Spirit and the idea of Benedictine Mortification", so much the better. What most attracted visitors to Caldey and Malling was a happy mixture of "joyousness and cheerful simplicity that must disarm criticism". The abbatial use of a motor car and a private motor-boat to speed up the journeys between Caldey and Milford Haven was not contrary to the Benedictine conception of Holy Poverty. It was not in keeping with the status of an Abbot-nullius to live like the Superiors of the Cowley, Kelham and Mirfield communities.

Towards the end of Lent the Lord Abbot of Caldey and his private secretary set off for Italy. The former had been invited to take the Holy Week services in the Anglican church of St Mark's, Florence, because Fr Figgis, C.R., was detained in North America. The sight of an *"abbate Protestante"* parading about the streets, preaching and pontificating at the *"Chiesa Inglese"* created no small stir.

In the meantime the Mother Abbess of Malling had been getting ready for the move to Milford Haven. Workmen were busy with new buildings at Castle Hall, including a large wooden chapel and refectory. "My Lady" was pleased to hear that the future St Bride's Abbey stood on land owned by the Tironian Benedictines in medieval times. Early in the thirteenth century a foundation had been made about two miles north of Milford, known as Pill Priory. This gave the Abbot-General sufficient reason to believe that his nuns as well as his monks would be both extra-parochial and extra-diocesan. Even if he lacked a licence to minister in the Diocese of St Davids, he could claim full jurisdiction over the convent in virtue of being the successor of the Abbots of St Dogmael.

The exodus from Kent to Pembrokeshire took place on April 25, the feast of St Mark; a journey of thirteen hours. The following morning, Abbot Aelred, who had hurried back from Florence after Easter, sung a pontifical Votive Mass of the

Holy Spirit, served by some of his monks. During the next six weeks the nuns remained out of enclosure. One sunny morning in May Abbess Scholastica and her community left St Brides's at 6 o'clock, arriving on Caldey Island in time to assist at the Conventual Mass. The nuns were shown the rising walls of the *prelatura* and its chapel. It was explained to them that the new monastery (to accommodate sixty monks), adjoining the mansion in which their Major Superior intended to live in solitary splendour, was merely temporary. In God's good time a great abbey would materialize beyond the pine woods behind the village; a proof that at least one monastic waste place in Britain had been rebuilt in more than medieval glory. A picnic lunch was taken under the trees at the Poultry Farm. The monks and the nuns sung Nones together—on either side of the choir. Before the ladies departed for the mainland there was a lively mixed tea party in the Quarry Garden.

The Abbot wrote in his next *Pax* letter: "The coming of our Nuns to this neighbourhood has been a very great convenience to me personally, and I shall have no more to take long railway journeys to West Malling several times a year. Incidentally also it has relieved me from trying to 'work in' preaching engagements on my way to and from Malling."[1]

Nearly all the Caldey community went over to Milford Haven for the Blessing of St Bride's Abbey on June 17, and took part in the gorgeous pontifical High Mass. Nones was sung jointly by the monks and nuns. After pontifical Vespers and Exposition, there was a procession round the premises. The day's festivities ended with the Abbot locking the nuns up behind the grille in the parlour, and handing the keys to the Abbess.

Llanthony Abbey suddenly came into the picture again. It got plenty of publicity in June when Dom Ansgar Vonier, Abbot of Buckfast, made himself the plaintiff in an action tried by Mr Justice Joyce in the Chancery Division. The defendants were Alfred Harris (Dom Asaph) and Jessie Dow (Mother Tudfil). The Abbot maintained that a document, executed the same day as the Will, signed by Fr Ignatius on November 21, 1906, made clear that in the event of no community being left at Llanthony, they were to convey "the devised premises to the Abbot for the time being of the monastery of Buckfastleigh, Devon, for his absolute personal use and benefit."[2] The document ended with the words: "The wish is expressed simply to guard our beloved monastery from the Higher Criticism supported as it is by the treacherous bishops of our beloved and cruelly wronged Church of England". The judgment given was that the plaintiff had entirely failed to establish any case against the defendants, and it was dismissed with costs.

A week later the Baroness de Bertouch had a letter printed in *The Tablet*. She stated that no matter what might be the legal aspects of the case, she herself was sure that the "moral claim" of the Abbot of Buckfast was still indisputable. For "Fr Ignatius had a special affection for the monks of Buckfast. 'They keep the old original rule there', he would often tell me, and that is why I would love to have them here." Moreover he had said that "he had failed either to find or arouse the true spirit of monasticism in the English Church, and that it was 'to the Romans' that he looked for the future of the Abbey".

After February 1911 Abbot Aelred could not altogether forget a schismatic Old Catholic Benedictine monastery about sixty miles distant at Barry Dock. It had been founded by A. H. Mathew who had assumed the title of Old Catholic Archbishop of London, when he cast himself adrift from the Utrecht Union of Old Catholic Churches. One of the novices, James C. T. A. Williams, known as Br Bernard Mary, had already tested his vocation with the Caldey community. This

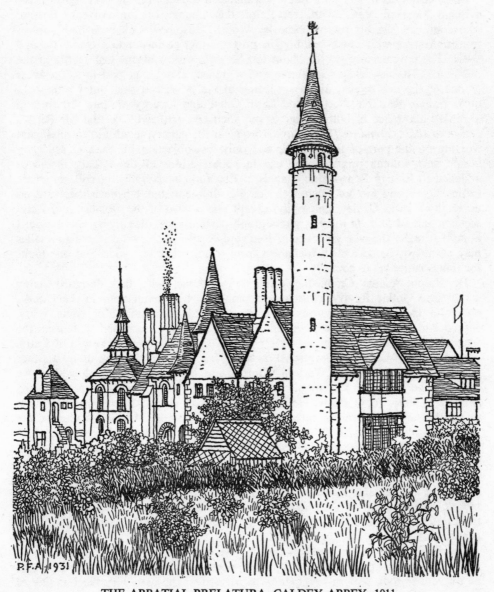

THE ABBATIAL PRELATURA, CALDEY ABBEY, 1911

The lofty Moslem-like minaret, which served no practical purpose, symbolised the unique status of Dom Aelred Carlyle as the only Abbot in the Anglican Communion. Behind his mansion are St Martin's Tower, the octagonal-shaped kitchen, and part of the refectory.

rival monastic foundation faded out before the end of the year, partly because the money promised for its endowment failed to materialise.[3]

More criticisms of life on Caldey was made in the summer of 1911 by the Rev. William Harman Van Allen, rector of the Church of the Advent, Boston, Massachusetts. On his return home he wrote: "Just now Caldey is in a sort of transition stage with much building in progress and corresponding confusion and upset. There were more people about too, as sightseers, and one lost a little of the old peace. The new chapel is simple and dignified, and I was glad to say a Mass at one of the two secular altars according to the American rite. But I must own quite frankly that the effect of the Latin Office and Liturgy (despite Archbishop Temple's allowance of both) seems to me alien and artificial.[4] To find Mr Riley's *Guide to those attending High Mass Abroad* in the gallery, as an aid to intelligent worship on the part of the visitors, was only less objectionable than to see lying beside it a volume prepared for use in congregations of the Papal Obedience attached to Roman Benedictine chapels in England *Cui bono?* In a college, where Latin is a second mother tongue, the case is different; but I believe there are no university men at Caldey, unhappily, except one or two of the Oblates, and Latin seems a sort of *tour de force*, a phonograph performance, disedifying and exotic. I hope that under the wise guidance of some episcopal visitor, two or three anomalies may eventually be corrected; for, apart from them, it is all so good that one looks for things better yet to come."[5]

Dr Ralph Adams Cram, the celebrated architect who had designed many magnificent Gothic Revival churches for non-Papist denominations in the U.S.A., and who had been a generous benefactor to the community for some years, rushed into print like a twentieth-century Don Quixote, determined to redress the wrongs done to the Benedictines by Dr Van Allen. He defended the use of Latin, not only an aesthetic and devotional grounds, but because "It links us by another chain with the rest of the Western Church, and if we abandon it altogether, we do so at the peril of irredeemable loss". Abbot Aelred himself kept quiet, feeling it wiser to suffer fools gladly. He had no shadow of doubt that monastic worship in the Western Patriarchate must be conducted in Latin. A priest-leader of the Catholic Movement in the Protestant Episcopal Church ought to be aware of it.

Yet Dr van Allen was not far wrong when he wrote of the confusion and upset on Caldey Island. This was due to the Lord Abbot having heard a clarion cry to "build up, build up the highway, clear up the stones, lift up an ensign over the peoples".[6] During the summer of 1911 the words of the prophet Isaiah were indeed being fulfilled: "They shall build up the ancient ruins, they shall raise up the former desolations; they shall repair the ruined cities, the devastations of many generations".[7]

Building went on all over the island. It gave employment to close on a hundred masons, bricklayers, carpenters, plumbers, electricians, and other labourers. None of the monks took part in this manual work as was the case with the building of Buckfast Abbey. The Cottage-Monastery was provided with a Chapter House and Statio. Then followed a Village-Shop and Club—a quaint building with high-pitched red-tiled roofs, and a deep veranda. After this arose a three-storied clock tower, dedicated to St Martin, at the corner of a rocky cliff. A picturesque pump —more correctly a gabled "Tap House"—helped to create an "olde worlde" ethos to the Village green. Up-to-date machinery was bought for the quarries. A wooden jetty was built, so that the crushed limestone could be shipped to the mainland by the monastic ketches *Elizabeth* and *Cornish Lass*. The farm was re-stocked and the extensive vegetable gardens enlarged. A spacious villa was erected for the Island Steward and his wife. Lastly came the Village Hall, with a well-equipped stage, dressing rooms, and sufficient accommodation for layfolk at concerts, plays, dances, and whist-drives which soon became a regular and popular feature of social life on this Island of Monks.

By this time the Lord Abbot had joined the Country Gentlemen's Association. He was here, there and everywhere, keeping an eye on what was going on. A striking figure with his white habit kilted up in his belt, revealing bare knees, white stockings and scarlet garters; sometimes brandishing a shooting-stick, and accompanied by a brown-haired setter. On wet days he donned a white mackintosh, sou'wester and gum-boots. He was indeed the monarch of all he surveyed, never satisfied with what had been begun, and always dreaming of some new project on an even bigger scale.

Yet he was absolutely convinced that all this miscellaneous building was essential for between twenty and thirty young men to devote themselves to the strictly enclosed and purely contemplative life. What worried him was that his never ceasing appeals for more and more money met with such little response. It suggested that churchpeople did not realise that "this work of the Revival of the Contemplative Life is really needed today". He explained to readers of *Pax* that it was making slow progress "amidst much difficulty and contradiction, and the unconscious opposition of those who have not grasped the Principles of the Life". Most Anglo-Catholics, however, inclined to doubt whether the Contemplative Life could be led only in a setting of *grande luxe*, and wondered why the Lord Abbot was not satisfied with the austerity and simplicity of the primitive Benedictines and early Cistercians.

One of the "Caldey Customs" was for the Abbot to give a conference on the fifteenth Sunday after Trinity, which was known as *"Quaerite primum"* Sunday, because of the words in its Gospel: "Seek ye first the kingdom of God and his righteousness; and all these things shall be added unto you". Having compared his monks to the fowls of the air and the lilies of the field, the abbatial *fervorino* ended with repeating in his most persuasive voice: "Take no thought for the morrow: for the morrow shall take thought for the things of itself. Sufficient unto the day is the evil thereof."[8] There was no need to worry about money, provided that the monks really did seek the kingdom of God as pure contemplatives. Benefactors and benefactresses would answer their prayers, because the heavenly Father had bidden the brethren take no thought for their life, what they should eat, or what they should drink, or what they should wear—"Ye cannot serve God and mammon" in the Contemplative Life of pure Monasticism.

Although the Benedictines were taught that the Divine Office was their supreme work and highest form of prayer, yet mental prayer held an important place. The daily 'Quiet Hour' between Vespers and Supper found the whole community kneeling or sitting in the choir-stalls, presumed to be rapt in contemplation.

Every novice was given a copy of Abbot Sweeney's 1876 edition of Father Augustine Baker's *Holy Wisdom*, so that he could digest its 667 pages, and master "Certain Patterns of Devout Exercises of Immediate Acts and Affections of the Will". It would be true enough to say that Baker took priority over the Bible, which some of the monks inclined to dismiss as "Protestant". Their knowledge of God's Word was often limited to what they heard read in Latin during the *Opus Dei* and at Mass.[9] Other spiritual authors recommended to novices were Abbot Blosius, Brother Lawrence, St Teresa, also the two French Jesuits, Jean Pierre de Caussade, and Jean Nicolas Grou.

Monks who were supposed to have reached the higher stages of prayer were encouraged to read *The Cloud of Unknowing*, as well as the mystical writings of St John of the Cross, Henry Suso, Julian of Norwich, Jan Van Ruysbroeck, Miguel de Molinos, and Madame Guyon. By 1911 the monastic library included a miscellaneous selection of books and pamphlets dealing with Theosophy, Reincarnation, Rosicrucianism, and other manifestations of non-Christian mysticism, even Bahaism, first explained in Persia by Bahau'llah (1817-92).

The year 1911 was an exciting one for all Catholics in communion with Canterbury and York, not only the Caldey community. On February 24 a group of young men, some of whom had stayed at the monastic guest house, and sat at the feet of Br Denys, including Sam Gurney, Ronnie Knox, N. P. Williams, and Niall Campbell (the future tenth Duke of Argyll), held a meeting at the offices of the Medici Society in London. In their opinion the Catholic movement needed more momentum, not by reviving out-dated ritual and ceremonial of the pre-Reformation period, but by imitating as closely as possible the contemporary worship of the Church of Rome. This was what the Caldey Benedictines were doing in their new chapel. So was founded the Society of SS Peter and Paul. Everything must be done to encourage such extra-liturgical rites as Exposition and Benediction, and to draw up a new Anglican rite, in closer conformity with that of the Western Patriarchate. Such was the obvious way to prevent *Ecclesia Anglicana* from being wrecked on the rocks of Protestantism, and the quicksands of heresy.

The now seventy-two year old Lord Halifax—still a boy at heart—encouraged these *"enfants terribles"*. He decided to invite a representative body of English Catholic clergy and laymen to take part in a Conference at Hickleton Hall, Yorkshire, on July 7. There would be "opportunities for an exchange of ideas on matters, the importance of which can hardly be exaggerated" and to see "what steps can be taken to meet dangers which seriously threaten the progress of the Catholic Revival". As President of the English Church Union, Halifax had been scandalized by an interdenominational Mass, recently held in Hereford Cathedral by Dr John Percival, who since 1895 had been the ninety-fifth successor of the seventh-century Bishop Putta.[10]

In his invitation to Dom Aelred, Halifax stated: "The action of the Bishop of Hereford and much else in the same direction, convinces me, for what my opinion is worth, that a vigorous and concerted movement on the part of the Catholic party is necessary at the present moment, both for the defence, and in the general interests of the Church".

The Abbot's detailed notes on the Hickleton Conference read like the secret deliberations of generals planning a campaign. There are several references to more than one "heated argument" on what constituted true "Catholicity". Halifax himself maintained that it could not be admitted that there were three "Schools of Thought" rightfully in the Church of England. Catholics must insist with increasing force that the Low and Broad schools had no legitimate place and did not represent the true spirit of *Ecclesia Anglicana*. He urged his guests to adopt "a position of *Revolution*". Their clear duty was "to press on" for all they could get—"waiting, working, and praying till it is unmistakably and clearly possible to return to the Communion of the Holy See". There must be "united action" against most of the hierarchy of England and Wales.

Don Aelred mentioned "saying Mass according to the Benedictine Rite". He also described a "Solemn High Mass according to the Rite of Edward VI's First Prayer Book", which was celebrated in Hickleton parish church on the feast of the Assumption of Our Lady.

Having returned home he jotted down: "My contribution to the Foreword Movement—to get two monks ordained, and to put on Benediction, which I gave up three years ago in deference to Stuckey Coles—also to bring the Village Church into line with the proposed changes in the Mass, etc."[11]

There had been gossip at the Conference about the "Romeward leanings" of the Caldey monks and the Milford Haven nuns. Apparently more than one delegate told the Abbot that were his communities to secede from the Church of their Baptism, it would be "disastrous for the Catholic Movement". It was their clear duty to go on "waiting for a time in faithful adherence to the Catholic Faith in the Church of England". By adopting this line of self-mortification "much good might ultimately accrue to the cause of Reunion with the Holy See".[12]

Abbess Scholastica had ceased to take any interest in the Catholic Movement. She had no intention of waiting much longer in faithful adherence to the Established Church, and was watching for the signal to go ahead on the road to Rome. Her health was far from good. Much of her time was spent reclining on a couch.[13]

On the feast of St Lucy of Syracuse, December 13, 1911, the Abbot-General of the English Congregation of the Primitive Observance of the Holy Rule of St Benedict decided that the moment had come to ask the Primate of All England to send him "the Permission to Minister that is usually granted to Priests in Colonial Orders"; explaining that it would give him "the necessary relation to the Episcopate that will help to ensure the stability of work which has been slowly built up during the last thirteen years".

The Lord Abbot explained, however, that from the point of view of the canon law of the Western Church this was hardly necessary, because Caldey Island was "by its ancient Charter and present general recognition extra-diocesan and extra-parochial. The Island became extra-diocesan by Papal privilege granted before the Reformation to the Benedictines who then owned it. This privilege of exemption was extended by Henry VIII at the Dissolution in his grant of the Island property to John Bradshaw from whom it has passed by sale through nine different families until it came into our possession. Caldey is subject to no parochial or country taxation, and its ecclesiastical position as a Peculiar is recognized by the nearest Diocesan—the Bishop of Saint Davids. The Island is very self-contained and belongs entirely to our Community; and all the people who work here in the little village are employed by us and under my care."[14]

Dr Randall Davidson, who had been the confidential adviser of Queen Victoria in matters both spiritual and temporal, must have been surprised to hear that an unlicensed clergyman, who described himself as "Abbot of a Community of Men living under the Benedictine Rule on the Isle of Caldey near Tenby in South Wales", believed that a bull issued by an unspecified Pope to the Tironian Benedictines of St Dogmael's Abbey near Cardigan early in the twelfth century permitted him to minister to the inhabitants of this little island as well as his own brotherhood. The whole business must have struck the legal-minded Archbishop as more peculiar than that of the alleged ecclesiastical status of Caldey as a "Peculiar".

Having given him a brief history of the community, and details of his own ordination in the United States of America, the Abbot stated: "When I returned to the Archbishop of York after my Ordination, he was failing very rapidly in health, and when I asked him for a Licence said that under the circumstances he did not think it necessary for me to apply to the Archbishop of Canterbury in the usual way; and when we came to Caldey (soon afterwards), I felt it rather premature to write to you for any permission till I knew more exactly what was needed.

"The Bishop of Saint Davids will tell you, I think, that he is able to answer for my general trustworthiness. He knows something of our work, and has been very kind to us since we came to Caldey; and twice he and his Suffragan, the Bishop of Swansea, have held Confirmation on the Island at my invitation.

"From time to time the exclusion of my name from *Crockford's Clerical Directory* has been brought to my notice, and although the Editor has on several occasions had the various particulars sent him, he refuses to include my name until I have your Grace's 'permission' to minister as a Priest in Colonial Orders."[15]

The truth was that the Lord Abbot, by getting himself ordained in the State of Wisconsin, even with the approval of the Archbishop of York, was now in the position of being "neither fish, flesh, fowl, nor good red herring" so far as *Ecclesia Anglicana* was concerned. He assured the Primate of All England that his community undertook "no outside work in the way of Missions and Retreats", because its "Ideals" were "entirely Contemplative". On the other hand, the Abbot himself did "give an occasional Retreat, generally to a Religious Community", and preached "an occasional sermon when specially invited to do so". He explained: "My engagements on the mainland are even fewer than when we first came to Caldey; for we found it necessary at that time to make known something of what we were doing. Now that we are sufficiently well known, and my work at Caldey has so largely increased, I preach but seldom away from home."

After five years on the Island the abbatial Lord of the Manor realised that it was necessary for his "own ecclesiastical standing to be duly authorized". He was "frequently asked about our present relation to Authority, especially as our extra-diocesan position leaves us, I suppose, subject to no Bishop but the Archbishop of the Province". Dom Aelred had to admit, however: "The nature of our work does not appeal to a very large number of Churchmen". On the other hand, he could state truthfully: "but we have many friends, and there are nearly a thousand members of our Confraternity, while our magazine *Pax* has a circulation of more than two thousand copies. A number of Priests and Laymen from all over the kingdom spend their holidays at our Guest House, and many come to us for days of retreat and spiritual refreshment."

The long letter ended with the words: "If your Grace will send me the Permission to Minister that is usually granted to Priests in Colonial Orders, it will give me the necessary relation to the Episcopate that will help to ensure the stability of a work which has been slowly built up during the last thirteen years. I should have asked you for this permission when we first came to Caldey, but I was strongly advised to wait until our work had passed the experimental stage and it was seen that our Community would settle permanently on the Island."[16]

On December 18 the Archbishop's Private Secretary replied that His Grace would "certainly give full consideration to the request", but many details would have to be gone into carefully. The Archbishop doubted if the Island was really "extra-diocesan and exempt", being under the impression that "during the seventeenth century it was regarded as a parish in the Diocese of Saint Davids. His Grace would like to be in possession of the facts." Dom Aelred evaded answering this query by stating that he would "put together the various facts of the case", and send them to Lambeth Palace "later on". No doubt he foresaw difficulties in obtaining a copy of the medieval document that gave him authority to minister to the community and the inhabitants of Inis Pyr.

After a delay of nearly three months, an interview between the Lord Abbot of Caldey and the Primate of All England took place at Lambeth Palace on the feast of St Colette, March 6, 1912. The affairs of the Community were discussed, but to no purpose. On the whole, the interview appears to have been as unfruitful as those between Fr Ignatius and Dr Davidson's father-in-law, Dr Tait, with regard to the former's ordination to the priesthood.[17] According to the Abbot's notes, the

Archbishop said: "I understand that you wish me to give you at the present time a Licence under the Colonial Clergy Act for officiating in the Province of Canterbury, though you neither hold nor ask for Diocesan accrediting, or Licence, or Office". The Abbot agreed that this was correct, "and went on to speak of the need of Ordination for some of the Brethren without putting them under the necessity of serving two years in secular parish work". The Primate "then read from notes he had been making that he understood the Abbot to ask under what conditions he could obtain Ordination for members of the Order who showed vocations to the Priesthood and who wished to own allegiance to the Order only and not to a Diocesan Bishop, and who would wish to exercise no outside ministration, their work lying wholly within the Community and on the Island, or in one of the affiliated houses at Milford Haven and Llanthony in the Diocese of St Davids, and Pershore in the Diocese of Worcester".

The Archbishop was told that "the use of the Benedictine Breviary and Missal in Latin, and the use of these books was confined to the Chapels of the Order". The Abbot "contended that this practice was justified on the ground that the Prayer Book was for the use of the people, and that it was unsuitable for members of a Religious Order"; yet His Grace need not be alarmed, because "visiting Priests celebrating at Caldey were asked to use the Prayer Book and nothing else".

The interview ended with Dr Davidson telling Dom Aelred that he "would go carefully into all the circumstances of the case, and send his decision in due course". The Abbot recorded: "The Archbishop was careful during the interview to avoid expressing any sort of personal opinion, but many times showed himself kindly and well disposed, bearing out in fact, during the whole interview, what he had said to the Abbot in his letters, namely 'that he was anxious to do what he could for all who were engaged in doing good work within the large and reasonable limits of the Church of England'."[18]

The immediate reaction to this "Lambeth Conference" was to make the Abbot of Caldey doubt the Catholicity of *Ecclesia Anglicana*. On his return to the Island he ordered that the rest of Lent should be spent by the brethren in studying the Papal Claims. The Librarian was bidden to arrange shelves with controversial literature, both anti- and pro-Roman. Three clergymen agreed to give lectures to the monks. First came Fr Puller, S.S.J.E. who, as the author of *The Primitive Saints and the See of Rome*, found no difficulty in debunking every papal pretension with the force of a bulldozer. He was followed by Dr R. L. Langford-James, then Vicar of St Mark's, Bush Hill Park, Middlesex.[19] This Anglican Papalist, witty and plausible, managed to produce countless reasons against immediate submission to the Holy See, yet at the same time being absolutely loyal to Pope Pius X.

To wind off the Lenten lectures there was Br Denys Prideaux, Warden of the Caldey Guest House, whose erudition was so profound that most of the monks failed to understand what he was driving at, unable to see the wood for the trees. He hinted at mysterious conversations going on between Roman and Eastern Orthodox theologians in the Balkans; of secret meetings under the shadow of the Vatican. He backed up his arguments by quotations from French, German and Russian theologians whose names meant nothing to the majority of the community.

Easter came at last, and after the Lord Abbot had pontificated as usual (still without a Licence under the Colonial Clergy Act), he composed a statement, printed in red and black inks. It was posted to friends and benefactors far and wide. The gist of this leaflet was that he and his monks were now absolutely sure that it would be wrong for them to doubt their present position in the Established Church as true members of the Catholic Church of Christ. "The privilege of the

PONTIFICAL HIGH MASS AT CALDEY ABBEY, 1912

Celebrated by a clergyman who after eight years had not yet received a Licence under the Colonial Clergy Act to officiate in the Province of Canterbury, and whose name did not appear in Crockford's *Clerical Directory*, although he had been blessed as abbot by a bishop of the Protestant Episcopal Church in the U.S.A.

Caldey Vocation" was "to pray, to labour, and to suffer that the sin of the Schism between England and the Holy See may be forgiven and the separation ended". From now onwards there would be more "care and strictness of our Regular Observance", and greater "devotion to Catholic Faith and Practice".

The monks were told that they would be transformed into a species of Trappists. This would involve not returning to bed after Matins and Lauds, also spending nearly three hours daily in mental prayer, and much harder manual labour. The spirit indeed was willing but the flesh was weak. Within little more than a month these austerities proved to be the last straw that breaks the camel's back. By Pentecost life had returned to normal, yet the abbatial attitude was summed up as follows: "I do feel that as a community we all need to go out into the wilderness, driven by the spirit of God to learn faithfulness, and to enkindle our fervour and to deepen our love and devotion". These eremitical yearnings were stressed in the June 1912 issue of *Pax*, suggesting that before long there would be more Solitaries on Inis Pyr.

The Abbot had written in March: "We have from various causes been far too much in the public eye during the past few years". For instance there had been criticisms by "Viator" in the *Church Times*—quite justified. His "caustic pen" had served the abbatial purpose well. He had put into words that the Abbot would gladly make his own—"But these good men . . . who are trying to learn to be Monks . . . are certainly no more than beginners; and yet you will not let them learn in quietness and obscurity. You make them conspicuous, when you ought to help them hide themselves. You are so anxious to have monks among you that you make it impossible for them to become good Monks. What are Monks worth if they are not good Monks? If we have the faults of the world, we are worse than men of the world, and who may be saved in spite of their faults. It is not easy for a Monk to be saved. It is a very dangerous calling unless one is kept strictly to the Rule and to the Cloister."[20]

Yet the Lord Abbot could not afford to let his monks live in quietness and obscurity. Money was still desperately needed. Only £5 4s. 5d. had been contributed to the Building Fund and £19 1s. 1d. to the General Fund during the past four months. These meagre sums would not cover the cost of the great refectory, seventy feet long and thirty wide, with an open timber roof. The vast open fireplace of limestone and brick, surmounted by a carved, painted and gilded statue of St Michael, had little more than aesthetic value. The up-to-date central heating should be sufficient for the brethren to enjoy their *maigre* meals in comfort. A more economical form of reading desk would have been devised than the quaint *pulpitum* contained in a turret, and approached by a staircase in the centre of the west wall. No matter: it evoked memories of similar medieval ones at Beaulieu, Chester, Fountains and Tintern.[21] Nothing but immense mahogany tables with carved supports were considered suitable for monks who tried to follow the Primitive Observance of the Rule of St Benedict. The lower part of the walls of the refectory were oak-panelled, and it had a red-tiled floor. A dais raised on two steps gave dignity to the smaller mahogany table at which the Lord Abbot would be able to keep an eye on his monks and guests.

That £5 4s. 5d. would not go far towards completing the ultra-modern bakehouse and laundry in the basement, or for the library, guest-house for retreatants, workshops for arts and crafts. Neither had the old-world postern gate with a crenellated high wall—creating the illusion of enclosure—been paid for so far. Then there was also the romantic artificial pond in the quarry-garden in which gold-fish swam and water-lilies grew. It was here that the brethren took afternoon tea on Sundays, weather permitting, while chatting with invited guests.

253

By the summer of 1912, 12,000 copies of a revised edition of *The Benedictines of Caldey Island* were on sale. The immediate object of this profusely illustrated paper-back was to assure the public that the community had recovered from the bad bout of "Roman Fever". The monks could now be regarded as Anglican Loyalists, well deserving of financial support. The Abbot had already stressed: "We are simply Benedictines living in the Communion of the English Church, fully persuaded that she is an integral part of the Catholic Church, with all its privileges and responsibilities, and are fully content with our heritage. Thankfully and heartily we are resolved to do our best to discharge the Commission bestowed upon us by the ninety-third successor of St Augustine, and to regain for our dear Mother the endowment of the Cloistered Life under the Rule of St Benedict of which she has been despoiled for 350 years."[22]

The new abbatial Preface ended: "We hope this account of a Contemplative Community may help to draw some souls to serve God in the hidden life of the cloister, and clear away the false mystery of prejudice and of ignorance that surrounds a manner of living in itself quite simple and easily understood by all who can accept those sayings of Our Lord which have inspired so many monks and solitaries in their dedication, and peopled heaven with countless Saints".[23]

The many illustrations, especially Mr Coates Carter's clever pen-and-ink drawings, helped souls to picture the background against which the simple life inspired by the sayings of Our Lord could be led on Caldey Island. The cloister garth would be ideal for recreations on hot summer afternoons, what with the solid oak benches, well-clipped box-hedges, and a water-lily pond in the centre. The round brick arches, white rough-cast walls, and pan-tiled roofs were evocative of the houses being built at Hollywood for some of the stars of the early silent films. Another drawing made quite clear that the hidden life of the cloister in 1912 had cast off the yoke of the Gothic Revival. The Caldey Benedictines were out for a brave new world, with the octagonal-shaped kitchen, rising in three tiers to a conical peak, even if it was said to have been inspired by the Abbot's Kitchen at Glastonbury. The pepper-box-shaped dove-cot, capped by a red-tiled flèche, and the three-storied clock-tower, were among other adjuncts to the primitive observance of the Benedictine Rule.

The late Mgr Ronald Knox recalled that the Caldey buildings "did not look altogether real", yet these unsubstantial cloud-capped towers, turrets, spires, unfunctional gables, and picturesque projections really did express the mentality of their creator, just as did the rose pergolas, crazy-pavements, bird-baths, and the sun-dial, which were among the minor accessories.

The photograph of "Dom Aelred Carlyle, O.S.B., Abbot of Caldey" which was reproduced—taken at the age of thirty-seven—helps one to understand why people were either repelled or captivated by him. There is a look of grim determination in those hypnotic eyes. His prelatical status is stressed by the large gold pectoral cross suspended beneath the capuce by a thin chain, kept in place by one of the many mother-of-pearl buttons on the white cashmere mozetta.

Br Denys contributed an erudite dissertation on the nature of Benedictine monasticism, ancient and modern.[24] Dom Henry explained that the community now regarded themselves as the *de facto* successors of the Benedictine Congregation of Tiron. He wrote: "The thread of the Religious life on Caldey was broken in 1534, but it was knitted together again in 1907, and the same life renewed as though no break had occurred. The Benedictines who were thrust out in 1534 were in communion with the See of Canterbury; the Benedictines of the restoration of 1907 are also in communion with the See of Canterbury, and in their Rule, their worship and the habit they are at one with their Brethren of an earlier age, sons of the same *Ecclesia Anglicana*."[25] Dom Henry's flight of fancy looked impressive on paper, but unfortunately the Tironians never wore white tunics and scapulars. Originally they were garbed in rough undyed woollen costumes, but before long black was adopted in keeping with the almost universal Benedictine tradition. Their worship was not identical with that of their Anglican successors, for they never used the seventeenth-century *Breviarium Monasticum* and *Missale Monasticum*.[26]

The community was still desperately poor, so the charges at the Guest House had been raised to £2 2s. a week instead of the 15s. 6d. in 1907. The brethren were still advertising numerous Handicrafts of great variety.

Lord Halifax was far from happy about the Community. Early in 1912 he had written to Mr H. W. Hill, Secretary of the English Church Union, about the much talked of abbatial extravagance. Mr Hill replied: "I do sincerely pray that Caldey is not going to become a seed-plot of foolishness, mischief and disaffection. It is a remarkable thing that Religious never seem able to learn from the mistakes of the past. If they had minded their own business in the Middle Ages, how different the course of things would have been . . . He [the Abbot] ought to stay on his Island looking after his monks and not go running about all over England doing work which others can do quite as well if not better than himself."[27]

NOTES

[1] *Pax*, June 1911. For the past five years the Abbot had been more and more in demand as a preacher in several Anglo-Catholic strongholds. He also had to pay regular visits to the Wards of the Confraternity of St Benedict, located in London (three Wards), Birmingham, Bristol, Cheadle, Chester, Douglas (Isle of Man), and Sheffield. By 1911 the total membership of the Confraternity was 937. From time to time he conducted retreats up and down England, so his own life was far from "enclosed".

[2] See p. 183.

[3] In 1916 Archbishop Mathew consecrated Bernard Mary Williams as his personal co-adjutor with right of succession. After Mathew's death in 1919 Williams took the title of Archbishop of Caer-Glow, as Metropolitan of the Old Roman Catholic Church (Pro-Uniate Rite). So the Caldey community could claim to have fostered a bishop.

[4] Dr Temple had never given permission for either the *Breviarium Monasticum* or the *Missale Monasticum*. This was merely assumed by the community.

[5] *The Living Church*, October 14, 1911

[6] Isaiah 62: 10 (R.S.V.).

[7] ibid, 61: 4.

[8] Matthew 6: 34 (Authorized version).

[9] This was in keeping with the decrees of the Councils of Toulouse (1229) and Tarragona (1234) which forbade layfolk to read vernacular translations of the Bible. Pius IV, who was Pope from 1559 to 1565, required the bishops to refuse lay persons leave to read even Catholic versions of the Scriptures, unless their confessors or parish priests judged that such reading was likely to prove beneficial.

[10] Fr Ignatius had often denounced Bishop Percival, because he and his party were "taking away Christ, the Bible, and the Creeds from the people of England—the sole foundations of our Christian Moral Code".

[11] The Rev. S. S. S. Coles was then Librarian of Pusey House, Oxford. He felt that there was pre-Reformation precedent for Exposition, but not for Benediction.

[12] Although Benediction was "put on" in the Monastery Church, yet even a year later it was stated in *Pax*: "In ministering to the people of the Island the Book of Common Prayer only is used in the public offices, and that it is the practice that the Mass should not be a composite rite; but that the whole Prayer Book as it stands, without any audible additions or interpolations". (*Pax*, July, 1912.)

[13] An indication of her state of mind is that after Christmas 1911, all her quarterly letters in *Pax* were devoted to explaining the different grades of Benedictine probation, with no reference to community affairs.

[14] *A Correspondence* (Caldey Island, 1913), p. 1.

[15] ibid, p. 3.

[16] ibid, pp. 3-4.

[17] See p. 84.

[18] ibid, pp. 11-13.

[19] In July 1913 he was elected Superior-General of the newly-founded Catholic League, which was placed under the patronage of Blessed Mary Our Lady of Victory, St Joseph (Patron of the Universal Church), and St Nicholas of Myra the wonder-worker. Its objects were to further the cause of the Catholic Revival in the Church in communion with the See of Canterbury, and the conversion of England to the True Faith.

[20] op. cit., March 8, 1912.

[21] The architect had been told to provide a medieval *lavarium*, and for this purpose a picturesque alcove had been fitted into the north-west corner of the cloister-garth. At the last moment, however, the Abbot decided to turn it into a chapel dedicated to St David, so it was given an altar instead of a basin with taps.

[22] *Pax*, June 1912, p. 110. Dr Temple is usually regarded as the 96th, not the 93rd successor of St Augustine. The "Commission" he was said to have bestowed on the Community was largely a matter of wishful thinking.

[23] p. x.

[24] Thanks to Br Denys, *Pax* now took its place as a serious theological quarterly. There were few publishers which did not send books for review. Outside scholars were quite ready to contribute articles or reviews without payment, even to return books to the monastery library. Thus the community acquired a reputation for learning that was quite unjustified, for the initials of only two monks are found: "D.H.W.", and "B.R.W.".

[25] op. cit., p. 128.

[26] In 1912 the statue of St Illtud above the rose window of the Monastery Church suddenly became St Bernard of Tiron. In 1919 he was renamed St Samson, after a relic of this 6th century Abbot of Caldey had been obtained from Dol in Brittany.

[27] Lockhart, op. cit., Vol. II, pp. 208-9.

CHAPTER XV

"Over to Rome" (1913)

AFTER the publication of the second edition of *The Benedictines of Caldey Island* in the summer of 1912, the history of the community became a more or less unconscious journey with the Church of Rome as the end of the road. Over at St Bride's Abbey, Milford Haven, the situation was quite different. Abbess Scholastica had definitely made up her mind to carry her community with her into the Roman Church when she felt the opportune moment had arrived. She had no idea what line Abbot Aelred and his monks would take.

Having waited more than seven months, and having had no luck with the Archbishop of Canterbury, the Abbot of Caldey suddenly decided to appeal to the Bishop of Fond du Lac. After all, this now aged prelate of the Protestant Episcopal Church in the United States of America (known for short as *"Pecusa"*) had solved the problems of his abbatial blessing as well as ordination to the diaconate and priesthood.

On July 24, 1912, having heard that Bishop Grafton had recovered from a serious illness, he wrote him a long letter giving a general idea of the history of the Caldey community in the past six years. Among other things was mentioned the decision made at Easter to remain in the Church of England, having formed the opinion that God did not want the monks to "go over to Rome", and that it would be wrong for them to surrender their present position. The Abbot then asked the Bishop if he would be willing to raise two monks to the priesthood at Fond du Lac. It was explained:

"*Dom Samson* has been in the Community for ten years. He stands next in order to myself. He is forty-four years old, and firmly grounded in the Religious Life. With so many Brethren in the House he naturally holds a very responsible position; and both his duties and his age prevent him from undertaking a course of studies that would come naturally to a Junior Monk.[1]

"*Brother Wilfrid* is the second candidate, and as the Novice-Master who has the training of all the Juniors, it is very desirable that he should receive Holy Orders. He is thirty-one years old, and makes his Solemn Profession, D.V., next Michaelmas."[2] The Abbot assured the Bishop that both these men were "excellent and devout Religious", and that there was "no question about their stability and personal fitness". So it would be quite safe to send them across the Atlantic to be ordained in Wisconsin. No legal question would arise. They would be ordained "solely for Community purposes, and would need to hold no formal licence". Dr Grafton was reminded that because Caldey Island was "in fact a Monastic Peculiar, very much like that of Westminster Abbey", there would be no question of the monks "intruding into any Bishop's diocese".[3] He doubted if the Archbishop of Canterbury had the canonical authority to interfere with an extra-diocesan ordination such as was proposed.

Another point: the two monks could be ordained in the chapel of the exempt Abbey of St Dunstan at Fond du Lac, of which Bishop Grafton had appointed himself non-resident Abbot, with Dom Francis Brothers as Prior.[4] The handful of Benedictines lived in a ramshackle house, with the impressive name of "St Dunstan's Abbey".

Bishop Grafton replied on August 5, stating that his heart had been gladdened by the news that the Caldey community had resisted the temptation to "go over to Rome"; for "If the Church of England is to regain her full Catholic heritage, it must be by men so firmly grounded in the Catholic Faith that Romanism has no attractions for them".[5] He described St Dunstan's as "the baby Monastery of Christendom". The brotherhood began with five members and some aspirants, but had dwindled to two. No matter, there was "a beautiful chapel", and the tiny community had "been blessed financially". Although consisting of only two monks, the fraternity has been incorporated as "The American Congregation of the Order of St Benedict". The Bishop had "no fear for it". He hoped and prayed that "in time to come the Abbey may be known as 'The Holy Abbey of St Dunstan' ". The letter ended: "I am glad to meet your invitation to ordain two of your members, with an affirmative response. It is in humble thankfulness to God that I have been so able to help the Religious Life in the Anglican Communion, as to aid in the foundation of Cowley, to assist in giving the Priesthood to yourself, and now two others, and to found St Dunstan, and the Sisterhood of the Holy Nativity.[6] . . . With the permission of the Archbishop of Canterbury I will be only too glad to give to the two Monks the Holy Order of the Priesthood."[7]

Believing that the problem of the ordinations had now been solved, Abbot Aelred composed a letter of about 1,200 words to the Primate of All England. Having informed him that the completion of the Statutes and Constitution was in hand, he related that the Caldey community had "come through one of the most difficult of religious experiences" before reaching "a most happy and unanimous decision" in regard to its position in the Church of England, not only without suffering any loss, but with the great gain of a clearer realisation of the facts of the case, and a unanimity of opinion that would have been impossible had we not been rightly guided to settle the question as we did". Then, having gone into the history of the community with considerable detail, he reminded the Archbishop once again that Caldey Island was "extra-diocesan", for which reason he had not hesitated to ask his "kind old friend the Bishop of Fond du Lac" to ordain two of the monks "for work in the Monastery". Dr Grafton had gladly consented to perform the ordinations, so the Abbot proposed to send this pair of "excellent and devout Religious" to Fond du Lac, where they would be raised to the diaconate and priesthood in the chapel of St Dunstan's Abbey "solely for Community purposes", without the need of a "formal Licence". The very long letter ended: "I am anxious to take advantage of what seems to be such a God-sent opportunity, and it is one which may never occur again. The circumstances are exceptional, and I have told the Bishop that I will gladly avail myself of his kind offer, provided that your Grace does not forbid my doing so."[8]

The Abbot felt that the Archbishop had no right or reason to appoint an Archdeacon and other Ministers to find out if Dom Samson and Br Wilfrid possessed "a sufficient knowledge of Holy Scripture; of the doctrine, discipline, and worship of the Church of England as set forth in the Thirty-nine Articles of Religion, the Book of Common Prayer, and the Ordinal; of the Latin tongue; and of the New Testament in the original Greek". Such were the minimum requirements for admitting any person into Holy Orders at that date.[9]

The sudden death of the Bishop of Fond du Lac saved the Primate of All England from expressing an opinion on the proposed ordination of the two Benedictines in a schismatic Old Catholic monastic chapel in the state of Wisconsin. Dr Davidson wrote on September 5: "The matter must in any case be postponed for the present. You should not I think follow out your purpose of putting yourself into communication with the Bishop of Oxford in order to ascertain directly from himself how he views the proposal which you contemplate. I am very sure that in the whole matter we must act quietly, deliberately, and with a due regard to the importance of precedents which we may be establishing; and I need hardly assure you that I am prepared, God helping me, to give the whole subject the calm and unbiassed consideration to which it is entitled. Further questions may doubtless arise, and they must be dealt with regularly and in proper course."[10]

Abbot Aelred, however, did not feel in the mood to act quietly, deliberately, and with a due regard to the precedents which would be established by the ordination of his two monks more than 4,000 miles away across the Atlantic. On September 6 he wrote to Dr Weller, who had succeeded Dr Grafton as Bishop of Fond du Lac, asking if he would be prepared to perform the ordinations, explaining: "Things are so tied up in England with red tape and distrust of anything definitely Catholic or, in the least, out of the usual course of procedure, that Bishop Grafton's consent to act in this matter was most welcome, and it seemed to offer us a happy solution of the difficulty. . . . Of course, in any case, the Brothers must put off their proposed visit to Fond du Lac in October; and if they are to come at all, it might be arranged after I have seen the Archbishop, which I hope to do early in November. . . . If you are good enough to give us what we so greatly desire, it will be a fresh evidence of God's favour, and of the greatest possible assistance to our Community at the present time."[11]

Bishop Weller replied on September 16, that on receiving archiepiscopal permission, he would "mostly gladly ordain the two monks at Fond du Lac" at the abbatial convenience.

So there was nothing to be done but for Dom Samson to get on with his vestment making, and Br Wilfrid to continue his duties as novice-master and choirmaster. The Abbot himself grew more and more impatient with the slow motion of the "Lambeth Walk", now further delayed by side-stepping towards Cuddesdon, otherwise Dr Davidson's "passing on the buck" to Dr Gore, who wrote on October 7 that, although he agreed that he ought to "come and visit the Community", he was afraid that he could not manage it until next year, suggesting that the first stages of the negotiations had better be "conducted in writing". He asked the Abbot to send him the "constitution, rules, and rites, other than those contained in the Prayer Book", so that he could have them under his eye, and "take the opportunity of studying them". He expected that this would "involve some difficulty, but it is a difficulty which must be faced to start with"; assuring the Abbot that he had had "very little difficulty with the eight or nine Communities" of which he was then the Visitor.[12]

Had the Bishop been aware that the Abbot, in spite of holding no licence to officiate in the Church of England, was about to bind four of his monks by Solemn Vows, and that they were already in retreat before this function, it is probable that he would have realised the insuperable difficulties involved. In none of the communities of which he was the Visitor had there ever been such disregard of both the Constitutions and Canons Ecclesiastical of *Ecclesia Anglicana* and the Canon Law of the Western Church.

On October 15, the feast of St Teresa of Avila, the minister without a licence received the Solemn Vows of Brothers Wilfrid, Asaph, Laurence and Dominic during an imposing pontifical High Mass. Yet there was no authority in the Established Church which could dispense them from such vows. From the Roman Catholic point of view they were invalid, not having been accepted as "solemn" by the Province of Canterbury.

AA★

A week later, in the course of a long letter to the Bishop of Oxford, he stated that he would send him "shortly the Rites of Clothing Novices and Professing Monks". The Rule and Constitution would follow "towards the end of the month", and the Declarations "as they come in proof from the printer". The Abbot reminded the Bishop that six months had elapsed since his interview with the Archbishop of Canterbury, and that he was still waiting for a Licence under the Colonial Clergy Act to officiate in the Southern Province, without Diocesan accrediting, or Licence or Office. He regretted Dr Gore's inability to come to Caldey before next year, being sure that a personal visit would give him "a much better and truer idea of what is going on than to read an account of Rule and Observance without seeing it in actual working". Such being the case, "it might be well if two or three responsible priests were asked to spend a few days at Caldey and to prepare from their own observations on the spot, a report of the Doctrine and Practice of the Community". The Abbot suggested the Rev. W. B. Trevelyan (Warden of Liddon House, London), the Rev. H. F. B. Mackay (Vicar of All Saints', Margaret Street), and Dr Darwell Stone (Principal of Pusey House, Oxford). Should these three priests be willing to draw up such a statement the Abbot would do all in his power "to make their report as full and complete as possible".[13]

Dom Aelred, O.S.B., Abbot, could stand archiepiscopal procrastination and vacillation no longer. On October 21 he delivered an ultimatum to the Primate of All England, stating that although the matter of the Visitorship was not yet settled, he must have His Grace's permission for the ordination of Dom Samson and Dom Wilfrid by Bishop Weller of Fond du Lac, assuring him again that the Community "would in no sense look upon such permission, if granted, as forming any precedent", because "the present need" was "really an exceptional one". The Archbishop replied three days later: "The question of the Ordination of the two men to whom you refer is a very grave one, and I am quite sure that nothing in connexion therewith ought to be decided until the election of your Episcopal Visitor has taken place, and he is able as Visitor to co-operate in whatever is done. The Bishop of Oxford, to whom I have spoken on the subject, agrees with me that this will be the better course."[14]

On the receipt of this letter from Lambeth Palace, the Abbot assured the Archbishop that he "did not wish to press the question of the Ordinations unduly"; and having laid his "need, and the opportunity of meeting it" before the Archbishop, he would submit to his decision.

The same day (October 15) he wrote to the Bishop of Fond du Lac: "The time has fully come for us to have the recognition of Episcopal Authority behind us. Whatever we might be willing to endure in the way of Episcopal neglect as private individuals is quite impossible for a rapidly growing Community. Without Episcopal authorisation we should be in danger of drifting into a positon like that of Father Ignatius at Llanthony; and at my death there would be no security whatever for the continuance of the work. What I have seen of Community Life among us has convinced me that most of the failures to keep men together are due to a want of clear understanding of the necessary conditions and of a straightforward appeal to the Bishops. If Community Life is to be stable and permanent, and the Vows of members valid and binding, there must be obedience to a properly constituted authority. . . . I have been continually told by well-meaning people that if only we will be wise and leave the Bishops alone, they will leave us alone. But that is the very last thing to be desired; for our corporate existence depends entirely upon our Rulers. As Catholics we cannot allow ourselves to be looked upon as a sort of private society; and personally I never had the least desire to be a free-lance with no dependence upon Superiors. You will understand, therfore, that much as we are feeling the need of Priests at the present time, I willingly obey the decision of the Primate, and must wait until he allows me to accept your kind help."[15]

Fr Hopkins, founder of the Order of St Paul, would have been one of the well-meaning people who would have advised Abbot Aelred to have nothing to do with bishops, for he had long since adopted this policy in regard to his own Benedictine brotherhood. While the Abbot had been trying to get two of his monks ordained, Hopkins had been acting as one of the leaders in the great strike of seamen in British ports. This free-lance Anglican monk—garbed as a typical sailor of that date—obtained much publicity, even outside England. Largely due to his efforts, peace was restored to the maritime world, but Dr Talbot, Bishop of Winchester, washed his hands of Alton Abbey. Most church people ceased to regard the O.S.P. as little more than a philanthropic institution closely bound up with the more revolutionary aspects of the Trade Union movement.

The correspondence between Caldey and Cuddesdon dragged on throughout the autumn of 1912. Bishop Gore asked many awkward questions which were difficult to answer. The Abbot had to admit that his own canonical status was as peculiar as that of the "Monastic Peculiar" of which he regarded himself the Local Ordinary, for since his ordination he had gone on ministering without any formal licence. He also had to disclose that he had given permission to priests living on Caldey Island to exercise their ministry, without reference to the Bishop of St Davids.

Dr Gore, who was studying *The Constitution of the Anglican Congregation of the Primitive Observance of the Rule of St Benedict,* as well as *The Ceremonial of Caldey,* found much in them to alarm him, even if the final clause of the former stated: "All the members of our Congregation profess under God a loyal obedience to the Archbishop of Canterbury and to the English Episcopate in all matters touching the government and extension of our Congregation as laid down in the Holy Rule of St Benedict, our Declarations thereon, and this Constitution".[16]

As to the *Ceremonial,* it bristled with statements that must have worried the legal-minded Bishop of Oxford. It ignored the Book of Common Prayer entirely. All the services mentioned, as well as devotional practices, were one-hundred per cent Roman Catholic. As the Bishop had already banned *The English Hymnal,* because it contained direct invocation of saints, it was undiplomatic to mention that selections from it were sung at Benediction on Sundays.

On November 16 he requested the Abbot to forward a copy of the Constitution to the Rev. W. B. Trevelyan and Dr Darwell Stone. All this time Lord Halifax had been keeping in the background, but on December 10 he wrote to Mr W. J. Birkbeck: "I am never happy about that Abbot".[17]

The December number of *Pax* had 60 of its 101 pages devoted to book reviews, and 18 to what the Abbot described as "Br Deny's excellent introductory article on Neo-Mysticism and Christian Mysticism, demanding all the space it can get". His own "Community Letter" was brief, and concentrated on the Will of God. Prayers were asked that "all may be rightly ordered according to God's Will", for Caldey was "in the midst of the preliminaries connected with the election by the Community of an Episcopal Visitor". References to "strong winds, rainy weather and stormy seas" in the "Fasciculi" notes, symbolized the outlook of most of the brethren.[18] Dom Aelred recommended the now 1,005 members of the Confraternity of St Benedict to read for the ensuing Quarter Miss Jean Roberts' *The Emancipation of Women: seen in Musings on the Magnificat.*

Shortly before Christmas the south-west block of the new monastery was finished, including the refectory. The feast was celebrated with all the usual pontifical functions, burning of the Yule Log, talking at meals, festive recreations and concerts, and much carol-singing.[19] The Octave ended with a Recollection Day and Exposition of the *Sanctissimum*.

Across the water at Milford Haven, the nuns were waiting for their Mother Abbess, now much improved in health, to give the "all clear" signal on the road to Rome. The community had taken little or no interest in the negotiations between Abbot Aelred and Bishop Gore.

Dr Darwell Stone and Mr Trevelyan managed to cross over to Caldey on the afternoon of January 2, 1913, in spite of stormy weather. They spent two nights on the island, most of the time being devoted to private talks with the Abbot. Before their departure they said they would prepare a joint report and submit it to the Bishop of Oxford.

On January 28, Dr Gore, fired a bombshell from his palace at Cuddesdon aimed at Caldey Island. This letter began with the intimation that he could not consider becoming Visitor to the Benedictines unless they would agree to four "preliminaries" which, in his opinion, were "obvious and outside all possibilities of bargaining and concession". They were:

(1) An assurance that the property of the institution, buildings, etc., was legally secured to the Church of England; "not private property such as might be given or left by any individual or group of individuals or Community without reference to Communion with Canterbury".

(2) That "the Liturgy, i.e., the Communion Office of the Prayer Book, would become exclusively the rite in use in the Chapel or Chapels of the Community, and that the Priests, whatever else they said, would be bound to the recitation of the Morning and Evening Prayer". Dr Gore also insisted that all the priests would have to "take the usual Oath, and make the usual declaration before they were allowed to minister".[20]

(3) That the doctrine of the Immaculate Conception of the Blessed Virgin and that of her Corporal Assumption must be eliminated from the Breviary and Missal. The Bishop explained: "I feel that the public observance of these festivals and the public profession of these doctrines, i.e. as part of the common faith, cannot be justified on any other than a strictly Papal basis of authority". He remarked: "You seem to me that you cannot reasonably assume this authority for the purposes of devotion and then appeal behind it to justify your position as a Benedictine Community. I cannot help thinking that on reflection you will see the truth of this."

(4) That Exposition of the Blessed Sacrament and Benediction given with it must be abandoned; probably also the Exposition and Benediction with relics.

The episcopal letter ended as follows: "I cannot promise that this list is exclusive. I should have very carefully to attend to a number of details, and bear in mind on the one hand the general principle of policy, and on the other hand the exceptional position of your Community. I have really not begun at this work, and therefore I make no promises about it. . . . I do not think it worth while going on until these preliminary points are taken for granted. By all means consult Trevelyan and Stone, and let me hear at your convenience. I do earnestly pray that you and I may be guided right."[21]

It never seems to have struck Aelred Carlyle that an Episcopal Visitor would expect the Anglican Congregation of the Primitive Observance of the Rule of St Benedict to conform to the Constitutions and Canons Ecclesiastical of the Church of England. He took for granted that Bishop Gore would accept ritual and ceremonial taken over from the Roman Church, lock, stock and barrel, with observances based more or less on those of the Papist Benedictines of Buckfast.

His reply, dated February 11, the feast of Our Lady of Lourdes, began with the statement: "I am bound to say that I think your letter may offer considerable difficulty to some of the Brethren. It seems to me hardly fair to the Community to put before them at once what is merely a series of negations that 'lie outside all possibilities of bargaining and concession'; and I do not see that we can reasonably expect them immediately (and without any sort of idea as to what you may further demand of them) to surrender such practices as the use of the Benedictine Liturgy and the devotions to the Blessed Sacrament to which they have so long been accustomed."[22]

Then he informed the Bishop that the monks had been "looking with great hope for wise and sympathetic guidance". They presumed that because of his "own connection with the Religious Life", they would be able to "accept with confidence" his "opinion as to the Doctrine and Practice of the Church". At the same time, however, they had been "prepared for a good deal of self-sacrifice in order to submit loyally to his ruling". It was "a great pity to prejudice their minds before they had any opportunity of knowing [his] more fully".[23]

Alarmed by the prospect of having to give up ritual and ceremonial that most of the Benedictine monks believed to be essential to "Catholicity", their Abbot went on to ask the Bishop a series of questions, pointing out that the "Faith and Practice of the Community" were "identical with those of hundreds of Church of England people". The Bishop could have replied that this species of so-called "Catholicism" was not in tune with the best traditions of post-Reformation Anglicanism or, indeed, of the Roman Church. Would the monks be allowed to go on chanting before and after every choir office *Adoremus in aeter num Sanctissimum Sacramentum?* Would it be permissible to reserve the Blessed Sacrament in one kind on the high altar for the purpose of communicating the sick, and others when necessary outside the time of Mass? He hoped that the Bishop would not demand that "the teaching of our Lord's Presence in the Holy Sacrament" must be "suppressed or made a matter of apology". The monks would fight to the last ditch were they ordered to surrender the use of the Rosary, the Litany of Our Lady, the Litany of the Saints, and the anthems of the Blessed Virgin, as printed in the Benedictine breviary. Last but not least, how could the Bishop expect the Benedictines to give up the Tridentine form of the Roman Mass, which St Pius V had insisted must be used for all eternity? They would cease to be Catholics if they reverted to the 1662 *Book of Common Prayer* Administration of the Lord's Supper or Holy Communion, even in the Latin version, first printed in 1560 for use in college chapels in the Universities. The monks really did "need some assurance on these points". The very long letter ended: "I can assure you that all the Brethren heartily desire to submit loyally to Catholic Authority; and I shall be most grateful if you can help me to give them some sort of idea of what you expect of them, in addition to the restrictions you have already laid down as beyond doubt or question".[24]

Dr Gore's answer, dated February 14, was not exactly helpful, even if he assured the Abbot that "no question would be raised about the teaching of our Lord's Objective Presence in the Holy Sacrament, or of the worship to Him in the Holy Sacrament". On the other hand he did not think there was "any possibility of obtaining sanction for the use of the Latin Liturgy". After all, the twenty-fourth Article of Religion stated quite clearly: "It is a thing plainly repugnant to the Word of God, and the custom of the Primitive Church, to have publick Prayer in the Church, or to minister the Sacraments in a tongue not understood of the people". Had Bishop Gore been able to visit Caldey, he would have discovered that hardly any of the monks understood the Latin they recited or chanted.

On the morning of February 18, Abbess Scholastica, having waited more than three years, told her community that the moment had come at last to seek admission into the Roman Church. There had been no communications between her and any Anglican bishops. Her decision had no direct relation to the correspondence in which Abbot Aelred had been engaged since December 13, 1911, when he first approached the Archbishop of Canterbury. She was not interested in details of ritual and ceremonial as were the Abbot and his monks. Since February 2, 1910 she had been drawn nearer towards the Roman Catholic Church, not by discipline but by dogma. For the past twelve months she had made sure that her nuns understood the official teaching of that Church on faith and morals. All but four of the nuns agreed to follow her.[25]

During the past two months Lord Halifax had been worried by reports of what was going on. On February 1 he wrote to Athelstan Riley: "I have had a very unsatisfactory letter from that Abbot. I am doing what I can, but have no real hope of success." On the 22nd he informed Bishop Gore: "I have just seen a correspondence between the Abbot of Caldey and yourself which makes me very unhappy. I can have but one result and will supply the Abbot with the excuse he has *perhaps* been looking for—a step we shall all regret."[26]

Abbot Aelred had often solved problems when he was asleep; waking up absolutely certain that his subconscious mind had been given paranormal guidance during the silent watches of the night. This happened between dusk and dawn before he rushed through the conventual Mass on the morning of February 18. Later on a typed notice was pinned up bidding the Brethren to assemble in his oak-panelled reception room at 3.30 p.m. It is possible that a telegram from St Bride's Abbey may have affected the result of that historic meeting, when the Abbot informed his monks that God's will had been made absolutely clear to him. He had ceased to regard himself as a validly ordained priest, and would make his own submission to the Roman Church as a layman as soon as possible. The brethren were bidden to walk over the slippery parquet floor if they were prepared to follow him on the Romeward road. All but half a dozen did so immediately. Three said that although they felt Bishop Gore's demands could not be accepted, yet they did not see that this necessitated becoming Papists. A few more protested that they could not make up their minds on the spur of the moment, so the somewhat stormy meeting was adjourned.

The following morning a letter was posted to Bishop Gore, signed by the Abbot and twenty-seven members of the brethren who stated[27] "We have as a Community carefully considered your last two letters, and we are agreed that we cannot conscientiously submit to the demands you make of us. In view of your Lordship's request for the immediate surrender of Property, Liturgy, and Devotions, together with your definite refusal to give any sort of assurance of what you might further require of us, did we accede to your present wishes, we are sure that our Life as a Contemplative Community under the Benedictine Rule would be quite impossible.

"The preliminaries that seem to your Lordship so obvious as to 'lie outside all possibilities of bargaining and concession', concern matters which are vital to our conception of the Catholic Faith; and your requirements are so decisive that we are forced to act upon what we believe to be God's Will for us."

It is almost beyond comprehension how Abbot Aelred ever supposed that Bishop Gore would be prepared to act as Visitor of his community, for the Caldeyan conception of Catholicity was virtually a different religion to that preached and practised by the founder of the Community of the Resurrection. Granted that the monks were engaged in good works, it would have been difficult to find a niche for them within the large and reasonable limits of the Establishment, unless they were prepared to surrender, not only their property, but also most of their Roman ritual and ceremonial.

From the material point of view, the Abbot could not have made a better decision. Had the Benedictines remained much longer in communion with Canterbury, they would have probably ended up in the bankruptcy courts. Their debts amounted to about £17,000, and for some time past they had been living mainly on the generosity of a few friends, two of whom had donated £43,500 and £12,000 respectively. In the past six years, so it was disclosed later, £68,014 17s. 10d. had been spent on the purchase of the island, the erection of buildings, and the maintenance of the community, although this looks like an understatement. An indication of how Church people had lost confidence in the Caldey community after the summer of 1910, is shown by the steady drop in contributions to the "General Fund" published in each quarterly issue of *Pax*. Between March 1 and May 31 1912, only £19 1s. 2d. was acknowledged.

None of the brethren, not even the seniors, were ever consulted about monastic finances, so it is improbable that they realised, humanly speaking, the only way to save the Caldey community from extinction was to cast themselves into the arms of the Roman Catholic Church. There was a lot more buried below the surface than the belief that the strictly enclosed and purely contemplative form of Benedictine life would be impossible without the Latin liturgy and Benediction with the monstrance.

A few more letters were exchanged between the Bishop and the Abbot, the former begging that the whole matter needed careful consideration, but they were merely a waste of typewriter ribbons, paper and postage. The long drawn out correspondence ended with the Bishop being thanked for having made God's Will known to the Abbot, who assured him that there was now "a real feeling of happiness and security in the conviction" that the community had "been led to do what is right".[28]

The rest of the story can be told briefly. Dom Bede Camm arrived on the island on February 25. Three days later he celebrated the first Roman Catholic Mass.[29] On the afternoon of March 4 Mgr Mostyn, Bishop of Menevia, Dom Cuthbert Butler, Abbot of Downside, and Dom Columba Marmion, Abbot of Maredsous, crossed over from Tenby in the *Firefly*. The following morning, the feast of St Aelred of Rievaulx, took place what became known as "The Caldey Conversions", i.e. the reconciliation of Abbot Aelred and twenty out of the thirty-three members of his community with the Roman Church. They were given no sort of instruction for it was taken for granted that they were firmly grounded in the Christian religion.[30]

Abbess Scholastica and twenty-five of her nuns made their submission at the hands of Bishop Mostyn, assisted by Dom Bede Camm, on March 7. Both the monks and the nuns were enrolled as Benedictine Oblates living in community to preserve the continuity of the religious life until permission had been obtained from Rome for them to start a regular novitiate.

Such was the end of the two chief attempts to build up monastic waste places on medieval lines in the post-Reformation Church of England. Both communities are still prospering in communion with Rome, but their subsequent history lies outside the scope of this book.

The Caldey Benedictines migrated to Prinknash, near Gloucester, in 1928, and were affiliated to the Cassinese Congregation of the Primitive Observance, now the Subiacan Congregation. Prinknash became an abbey in 1937. A foundation was made at St Michael's Abbey, Farnborough, Hants (previously belonging to the

Solesmes Congregation) in 1947. The following year another foundation was made at the medieval Priory of Pluscarden in Moray. The total number of the present-day successors of the "Caldey Converts" of 1913 is 72. Abbot Aelred Carlyle became a secular priest of the Vancouver Archdiocese in 1935, but renewed his monastic vows at Prinknash shortly before his death in 1955.

Abbess Scholastica moved her community from Milford Haven to Talacre, North Wales in 1920, and died seven years later. The rebel daughters of Fr Ignatius today muster 25, and have belonged to the English Benedictine Congregation since 1921.

NOTES

[1] Having seniority over Dom Samson were Doms Henry and George, but by this time they were virtually "exclaustrated", seldom staying on the island. Dom Samson happened to be a lapsed Papist.

[2] He was a convert to Anglo-Catholicism from the Calvinistic Methodist sect known as the Countess of Huntingdon's Connexion, and the son of the proprietor of a coffee-tavern in Whitechapel, London.

[3] Abbot Aelred was under a false impression. The collegiate church of St Peter in Westminster, usually called Westminster Abbey, is a *Royal* Chapel and a *Royal* (not a Monastic) Peculiar, directly under the personal jurisdiction of the reigning Sovereign, who is the Visitor.

[4] This small Benedictine community had been founded in 1906 by the Rev. Herbert Parrish. Three years later it was amalgamated with another brotherhood at Waukegan, Illinois, formed by William H. Francis, who had assumed his mother's name of Brothers, and sponsored by Dom Augustine de Angelis. This one-time monk of the Cassinese Congregation of the Primitive Observance had thrown off the yoke of Rome. It appears that both he and Brothers became associated with a mysterious Mgr Tichy, who in 1904 was acting as Vicar-General to Bishop Kozlowski, who styled himself Metropolitan of the Polish Old Catholic Church in North America. The Bishop died in 1907, when most of his followers joined the Polish National Catholic Church, leaving Tichy with a small remnant. Bishop Grafton then took him on as an un-official assistant bishop.

On October 3, 1911 the Fond du Lac Benedictine brotherhood was formally received into communion with Mgr Tichy's microscopic group of schismatic Polish Old Catholics. This did not worry Bishop Grafton, who saw nothing illogical in holding the rank of Titular Abbot of a monastery not recognised by *Pecusa*. Two years earlier it had been removed from *The Living Church's* official list of religious communities.

[5] In his old age Bishop Grafton became a militant anti-Romanist, though prepared to indulge in the most ornate Roman ritual and ceremonial.

[6] The Bishop had founded this sisterhood at Boston, Mass. in 1882. In 1905 he moved its mother-house from Providence, Rhode Island, to Fond du Lac.

[7] ibid, pp. 19-20.

[8] ibid, pp. 21-5.

[9] Neither of the two monks had ever done any theological studies. Since 1900 Dom Samson had spent most of his time making vestments. Br Wilfrid had been appointed novice master after his simple profession in 1909.

[10] ibid, p. 26.

[11] ibid, pp. 27-8.

[12] ibid, p. 31.

[13] ibid, pp. 32-4.

[14] ibid, pp. 35-6.

[15] ibid, pp. 37-8. By this time Prior Francis Brothers had moved the quasi-Old Catholic "American Congregation of the Order of St Benedict" from Fond du Lac to Waukegan, Illenois, where he rented a house renamed "St Dunstan's Abbey", having assumed the status of abbot. He managed to get Archbishop Vilatte ("Mar Timotheos") to raise him to the priesthood, and on October 3, 1916, he was consecrated in the abbey-chapel by Prince-Bishop de Landas Berghos et de Rache, of the A. H. Mathew line of succession. Soon after this he claimed to have been elected Archbishop-Metropolitan of the Old Catholic Church in America.

[16] It is curious that "the *English* Episcopate" should have been specified, because the two communities forming the Congregation were within the territorial boundaries of the *Welsh* diocese of St Davids.

[17] Lockhart, *op. cit.*, Vol. II, p. 210.

[18] For the first time in eight years there was no appeal for money. Neither were there "Community Thanks" for financial help to the Building and General Funds, or "Gifts in kind".

[19] It was then the custom for a silent Low Mass to be celebrated by the Abbot after

Prime on Christmas Day, with the *Bambino* exposed on the high altar, and carols sung almost non-stop.

[20] This would have involved assenting to the Thirty Nine Articles of Religion, and promising to use only the Book of Common Prayer for the administration of the sacraments, "and none other, except so far as shall be ordered by lawful authority."

[21] ibid, pp. 57-9.

[22] "The Benedictine Liturgy" meant the 1604 *Missale Monasticum,* published with the authority of Clement VIII. "Devotions to the Blessed Sacrament", according to Roman Canon Law, cannot be performed whenever an abbot fancies. The normal *rule* is that public Exposition and Benediction are allowed only on the feast of Corpus Christi and on every day within the octave. At other times, however, Exposition and Benediction with the monstrance rests on permission from the bishop of the diocese, even though the church belongs to an exempt religious order. Acting on the belief that Caldey Island was a "Monastic Peculiar", outside the jurisdiction of any bishop, Dom Aelred took for granted that he could put on Exposition and Benediction whenever he felt that these extra-liturgical devotions would be beneficial. A similar line had been adopted by Fr Ignatius since 1864. It is curious that neither of these Anglican abbots ever availed themselves of the Roman rule that permits simple Benediction with the ciborium at any time in churches where the Blessed Sacrament is reserved.

[23] Had Fr Ignatius been alive, he would have warned Abbot Aelred that Dr Gore was a heretic, and that ever since the publication of *Lux Mundi* in 1889 he had never ceased to denounce its editor. Moreover Ignatius had moved heaven and earth to prevent Gore's consecration as Bishop of Worcester in 1902. (See p. 168.)

[24] ibid, pp. 59-61.

[25] Two remained Anglicans, and joined the Society of the Most Holy Trinity at Ascot Priory.

[26] Lockhart, *op. cit.,* Vol. II, pp. 210-11.

[27] *A Correspondence,* p. 63. There were seven monks in Solemn Vows, twelve in Simple Vows, four novices and three Oblates.

[28] ibid, pp. 75-6.

[29] His server was Dom Samson, who as a lapsed Papist, had merely to be "put right".

[30] The "loyal remnant" consisted of one solemnly professed monk and two oblates, who joined the Benedictine community at Pershore when it was founded in 1914 (see p. 268). The other professed monks, novices and oblates reverted to secular life as Anglicans.

EPILOGUE

THE débacle in 1913 was by no means the end of Benedictine life in *Ecclesia Anglicana* as most people expected. They tended to forget that there were three communities of women and one for men following the Rule of St Benedict in varying degrees. All have survived and others have been founded. Even more remarkable is the fact that these communities should now have recognition, not only in the *Church of England Year Book*, but also in the Roman Catholic *Benedictine Year Book*. The latter reflects the changed attitude of the Roman Church since the Second Vatican Council.

The Benedictine community now at Nashdom Abbey, Burnham, Bucks, was founded in 1914, the year after the majority of the Caldey monks had taken the road to Rome. The Founder and first Abbot, Dom Denys Prideaux, formerly an Oblate Brother, and Warden of the Guest House on Caldey, died in 1934, eight years after he had moved the community from its original home at Pershore, Worcestershire.[1] At Nashdom the three elements of the common life so strongly insisted upon by St Benedict—prayer, study, and manual labour—still maintain their original order of priority. There the work of monastic renewal, urged upon Anglican communities by the Lambeth Conference of 1968 following the lead of Vatican II, is making steady progress.

Ewell Monastery, West Malling, Kent, was established in 1966 as a Cistercian community for men, and is yet in the process of formation. The few monks lead an entirely enclosed life within their monastic confines. The Roman Catholic Abbot of Mount St Bernard acts as Visitor.

The Order of St Paul, whose early history has been recorded in this book, observes the Rule of St Benedict, more strictly than in the past, and its members seldom go beyond their enclosure, except to do occasional parish work. An eventide home for aged mariners is a reminder of the original purpose of the community.[2] Fr Hopkins, the founder, died in 1922.

The oldest Anglican sisterhood following the Benedictine Rule is the Community of the Holy Cross. It was founded in 1857 by Mother Elizabeth Neale, sister of John Mason Neale (1818-66). Its first convent was in the slums of Wapping, then the heart of London's sailor-town.[3] For the first fifty years the Sisters concentrated on active works of mercy and charity in parishes up and down England. After 1887, when the motherhouse was moved to Haywards Heath, Sussex, the life became more enclosed and contemplative. Today this community, which observes the full Benedictine Rule, spends most of its time on the celebration of the Divine Office in choir. Until recently the *Breviarium Monasticum* was recited or sung, but it has been replaced by vernacular offices. The nuns engage in ecumenical activities within their enclosure. Private retreats are given for priests and layfolk. There is a Guest House for permanent or temporary lady-guests.

Next in seniority is the Benedictine community of St Mary at the Cross, Hale Lane, Edgware, Middlesex, founded in the parish of St Michael's, Shoreditch, London in 1866.[4] Right from the start the Sisters recited in Latin the Day Hours of the *Breviarium Monasticum*. Recently this has been replaced by an experimental English use, although Vespers is still sung in Latin. Sick and incurable girls are cared for. The community, like that of the Holy Cross, is under the spiritual direction of the Benedictine monks of Nashdom Abbey.

The community of St Mary's Abbey, West Malling, Kent, started off in 1891 as the Sisterhood of the Holy Comforter, working in the parish of St Mary, Edmonton, a northern suburb of London.[5] As stated already, in 1903 they sought advice from Dom Aelred Carlyle, recently blessed as Abbot of Painsthorpe, about giving up their active work. The following year they began to recite the *Breviarium Monasticum*. In April 1906 the community moved to Baltonsborough, Somerset, where their life became more enclosed and contemplative. The nuns were never admitted to the so-called "English Congregation of the Strict Observance of the Holy Rule of St Benedict", erected by Abbot Aelred on his own authority in 1905, as were the community then living at West Malling Abbey, who moved to Milford Haven in 1911.[6] The Baltonsborough nuns remained loyal to the Church of England two years later. In 1916 they took over the then vacant buildings of West Malling.

Following the blessing of Dame Osyth Lucie-Smith as second Abbess in 1951, many changes began to be made in the liturgical life. By degrees English superseded Latin in the Divine Office. In 1964 permission was obtained for the use of an experimental rite based on the early liturgies. Grilles have been abolished and the enclosure extended to any part of the grounds. A new church in an ultra-modern style was consecrated in 1966. St Mary's Abbey, with a community of nearly fifty nuns, has now become an ecumenical stronghold where Christians of many denominations gather. Dr Michael Ramsey, Archbishop of Canterbury, acts as Visitor.

The Benedictine nuns of the Salutation of the Blessed Virgin Mary have evolved out of an effort to form an Anglican counterpart to the Visitation Order. Sponsored by the community of St Mary the Virgin, Wantage, a few ladies began to lead this form of life in 1941. After an experimental period the Rule of St Benedict was formally adopted in 1952. Today the life at Burford Priory, near Oxford, is enclosed and contemplative, with the Nashdom monks acting as spiritual directors. Private retreats are given. Church needlework, printing, and other handicrafts are undertaken.

There are other Anglican communities of women which in recent times have adopted the Benedictine Rule in so far as it is compatible with their active works.[7] The Servants of Christ (House of Prayer, Burnham, Bucks) founded in 1897, lead an enclosed life of prayer and silence, with a Cistercian ethos. Another community of women which has developed on Cistercian lines since its foundation in 1914 is the Society of the Sacred Cross. In 1923 it moved from Chichester to Tymawr Convent, Lydart, near Monmouth.

Founded in 1907, the Community of the Sisters of the Love of God, evolved an enclosed and contemplative quasi-Carmelite life on its own lines. Today, with the Convent of the Incarnation, Fairacres, Oxford, as their mother-house, the Sisters have foundations at Hemel Hempstead, Herts; Burwash, Sussex; and Staplehurst, Kent (with a *lavra* for solitaries). These three convents provide opportunities for private retreats, ecumenical dialogue and small conferences for instruction on spirituality and matters relevant to Christian life at the moment.

The Society of the Precious Blood, based on the Rule of the Augustinian Canonesses, was founded in 1905. At Burnham Abbey, Maidenhead, Bucks, the nuns lead a contemplative life for the purpose of perpetual intercession for the Church and for all men. A few years ago a daughter house was established at the Masite Mission, Maseru, in the South African kingdom of Lesotho (formerly Basutoland).

Most if not all Anglican religious communities today have given up dreaming of rebuilding waste places on either medieval or post-Tridentine lines as was the urge of the pioneers dealt with in this book. The current Anglican attitude towards monasticism is more or less identical with that of the Vatican II *Decree on the Appropriate Renewal of the Religious Life*—realistic instead of romantic. It has been summed up by a member of the men's community of the Servants of the Will of God in a pamphlet entitled *Monasticism in Our Age.*[8]

"The renewal of monasticism, as with the renewal of the church as a whole, must grow out of a recovery of fundamentals which we find in the New Testament and the writings of the Fathers. Conservatism, then, as a looking back to past tradition, is a necessary element of monasticism, otherwise it could not remain true to itself. But there is always a danger that the customs and ways of thinking which rightly gave expression to some particular period of history, will be carried forward into the present and become an element of unreality in the life, forming a barrier between contemporary monks and God. The danger is greater in our own day than ever before because the secular world is changing rapidly. The work of clearing away useless traditions, so as to bring into prominence what is essential, should be a continuous process if the authentic ascesis is to remain an effective instrument in the hands of God."

Such opinions would have been regarded as almost heretical by Joseph L. Lyne and Benjamin F. Carlyle when as young men they began to dream of reviving the Benedictine Order in *Ecclesia Anglicana* during the reign of Queen Victoria. What each hoped to do was to renew a way of Christian living which was believed to have been led in the Middle Ages. Each was quite sure that a piece of unshrunk cloth *could* be put on an old garment, forgetting that the patch would tear away from it, and that a worse tear would be made. They ignored the reminder in the ninth chapter of Matthew's Gospel: "Neither is new wine put into old wineskins; if it is, the skins burst, and the wine is spilled, and the skins are destroyed". This is what happened with the old waste places that these two pioneers tried to rebuild. Such being the case, some readers may well feel that the author has wasted his time in writing this book, for it has no obvious relationship with present day enclosed and contemplative religious communities in communion with Canterbury. No matter. Here is the opinion of Professor F. M. Powicke in a book of essays entitled *Modern Historians and the Study of History:*

"The function of history is not to trace back the institutions and ways of thought which have survived as though we were at the end and climax of history. It is at least important to retrieve the treasures that have been dropped on the way and lost, which if restored would enrich our civilization."

It is for the reader to decide how many of the Ignatian and Aelredian "treasures" which "have been dropped on the way and lost" would "enrich" contemporary Anglican monasticism if put back. At the moment, however, it looks as if the whole story could be summed up in the words of Shakespeare:

> "Our revels now are ended; These our actors,
> As I foretold you, were all spirits and
> Are melted into air, into thin air;
> And, like the baseless fabric of this vision,
> The cloud capp'd towers, the gorgeous palaces,
> The solemn temples, the great globe itself,
> Yea, all which it inherits, shall dissolve
> And, like this insubstantial pageant faded,
> Leave not a rack behind. We are such stuff
> As dreams are made on, and our little life
> Is rounded with a sleep."[9]

NOTES

[1] See pp. 211-212 for references to Br Denys at Caldey.

[2] See pp. 149-153.

[3] See p. 46.

[4] See p. 82.

[5] See p. 187.

[6] See p. 243.

[7] Among them are Community of St Peter, Horbury, Yorks (1858); Community of St Peter of Westminster, Laleham Abbey, Staines, Middlesex (1858); Community of St Wilfrid, Duryward Grange, Exeter (1866); Society of the Good Shepherd, Hare Hatch, Twyford, Berks (1909); and Order of the Holy Paraclete, St Hilda's, Whitby, Yorks (1915).

[8] This small community, founded in 1938 for men (clerical and lay), is purely contemplative. It has one house: The Monastery, Crawley Down, Crawley, Sussex.

[9] *The Tempest.*

INDEX

272